Mathematics
—— LEVELS 9 & 10 ——

JEAN HOLDERNESS

CAUSEWAY PRESS

Published by Causeway Press Ltd
PO Box 13, Ormskirk, Lancs L39 5HP

First published 1993
Reprinted 1993

British Library Cataloguing in Publication Data
Holderness, Jean
    Mathematics: Levels 9 & 10
    1. Mathematics
    I. Title
    510

    ISBN 0-946183-88-0

Other books in this series:
Mathematics: Levels 3 & 4 by David Alcorn
Mathematics: Level 5 by Jean Holderness
Mathematics: Level 6 by Jean Holderness
Mathematics: Level 7 by Jean Holderness
Mathematics: Level 8 by Jean Holderness

Other titles by Jean Holderness published by
Causeway Press:
GCSE Maths: Level A
GCSE Maths: Higher Level
GCSE Maths: Intermediate Level
GCSE Maths: Foundation Level
Pure Maths in Practice

Typesetting by Alden Multimedia Ltd., Northampton
Printed by Alden Press, Oxford

Preface

Mathematics: Levels 9 and 10 is the final book in a series written for pupils in secondary schools and it follows on from the work covered in the book *Mathematics: Level 8*. It is based mainly on the programme of study for levels 9 and 10 of the National Curriculum, but it also provides consolidation for some work of earlier levels. Many topics form a useful introduction to work needed for further studies in Mathematics or other subjects. The book could be used as a basis for a year's work for the more able pupils. Others could work at a slower pace and cover the programme for level 9 only. They would need to do all the work from Chapters 1 to 5, and some topics from Chapters 6 to 10. There are some notes for teachers on page *xi*.

I would like to thank all my family and friends who have given me support and encouragement while I have been writing these books. I should also like to thank all those teachers, and others, who have provided useful comments on the series.

My thanks also go to those who have helped with the production of the books, Sue and Andrew, my brother Jim and the staff at Alden Multimedia and Alden Press. For this book, Sue has my special thanks for working so hard with all the numerous drawings, which had to be done in less time than usual.

From Causeway Press I have had continuous support from everyone, especially Mike and David. I thank them for all their constant encouragement and practical help.

Jean Holderness

Acknowledgements

Artwork, page design and cover Susan and Andrew Allen

Photography © Jim Holderness and Andrew Allen

Copyright photographs

Associated Press/Topham pp. 61 (top), 149
Kate Haralambos p. 276
Popperfoto pp. 1 (top right), 21, 60 (bottom right), 168 (left), 182, 243 (top left), 243 (top right), 297 (bottom left), 297 (bottom right)
Sally and Richard Greenhill pp. 60 (bottom left), 169 (bottom right)
The Telegraph Colour Library — cover
Topham Picture Source pp. 48 (top right), 48 (bottom right), 73 (top), 120, 168 (right), 185 (bottom right), 243 (bottom left)
UNICEF/Marcus Halevi p. 59

The data on page 59 was obtained from *The State of the World's Children*, published for UNICEF by Oxford University Press.

Contents

(COPY)

*Topics not needed for Level 9

*Topics not needed for Level 9**

*Topics not needed for Level 9

Chapter 15 *Graphs and other diagrams

Miscellaneous Section C

*Topics not needed for Level 9

Topics for Activities (included in the miscellaneous sections)

To the teacher

Mathematics: Levels 9 and 10 has been planned for use at Key Stage 4 in secondary schools. It follows on from the work in the book *Mathematics: Level 8* and the other four books in the series.

It is based on the revised (1991) National Curriculum at levels 9 and 10. It contains all the topics needed for the Programmes of Study and the Attainment Targets, as well as linking the work to that of earlier levels where appropriate.

Work at levels 9 and 10 is aimed at the more able pupils. The mathematical content in some topics is quite demanding, and cannot be linked with suitable and genuine real-life applications. Some topics form a useful introduction to further studies in Mathematics, and could also be useful for pupils going on to study Science subjects, or subjects needing a knowledge of Statistics.

The book follows the same pattern as the earlier books in the series. There are 15 chapters, roughly 5 for each term if the book is to be used for a year. However, it has also been arranged in three sections as follows:
Chapters 1 to 5 are based on level 9 work.
Chapters 6 to 10 are based on work needed for level 9 or level 10.
Chapters 11 to 15 are based on level 10 work.
Therefore, if you want to concentrate on pupils achieving level 9 and not reaching level 10, it is possible to work at a slower pace over the first 10 chapters, leaving out the topics from Chapters 6 to 10 which are for level 10 only. These are marked * in the list of contents.

The teacher should be ready to link mathematics with any topics or activities which apply directly to the interests of the class, such as studies in other subjects, or current local or national issues.

In many cases, it is difficult to tell from the wording of the National Curriculum just how much depth is wanted in some of the topics. In a year or two, we should have a much clearer idea of what is expected. Meanwhile, I have tried to keep the main chapters as simple as possible, putting some extra work in the activities of the miscellaneous chapters, so that the teacher can decide whether or not to include it in the course.

Be aware of what is needed for AT1 at level 10. Some of the work in the later parts of the book is suitable for the pupils to explore independently, but they will need to be encouraged to do this before the work is taught in class, or it will not be independent work.

Here are some notes about particular points:

Calculators. Probably all pupils will have scientific calculators by this stage, and answers have been worked out using them. Also, graphics calculators can be useful in two main ways, (1) for plotting graphs of functions, and noticing the relationship between pairs of graphs, and (2) for generating iterative sequences, especially for solving quadratic equations by iteration. If not all pupils have these calculators, perhaps there could be some available in the classroom. Alternatively, suitable computer programs could be used.

Graph paper. 2 mm graph paper with a grid 16 cm by 20 cm will be suitable for most graphs. For vectors and transformations, squared paper is a useful alternative.

Chapters 1 to 5 are based on the Programme of Study for level 9.
Chapter 3 begins with sampling. The rest of the chapter gives a reminder of statistical techniques, so that pupils can use them in carrying out their own investigations.
Chapter 5. The definitions of trig. functions for angles of any size have been included in Exercise A4, question 5. The graphs of related trig. functions would be more suitable in Chapter 15 with the other related functions, but they seem to be needed at level 9 so I have put them here. You may like to revise this work when doing Chapter 15.

Chapters 6 to 10 include topics from level 9 or level 10.
Chapter 6. The work on conditional probability is needed for level 9, and the probability for any two events (level 10) forms a general revision of all that has already been learnt.

Chapter 7. This chapter is rather long, so you may like to leave parts of it to return to later. Some of the work has been done before, so it has not been covered in full detail. Factorising is included here to give pupils a chance to absorb the ideas before using them in Chapter 11 to solve quadratic equations.

Chapter 8. In quoting the amended formula for standard deviation I have used notation which applies whether or not an assumed mean is involved, and I have found using this to be satisfactory. Other textbooks may have different notation for such formulae. Pupils get very confused if different formulae are used, so whichever version you prefer, stick to it, and make the pupils learn it, in case it is quoted in a form they do not recognise on an examination paper.
It is not clear how far to go with standard deviations and normal distributions. The method for finding the standard deviation of a frequency distribution is given in Exercise B4, question 4. Maybe some of the work on normal distributions will not be needed, but it is interesting and fairly easy to understand, and shows a link between Statistics and Probability. In Exercise C6, question 8, there is an activity which links sampling with the distribution of sample means.

Chapter 9. The ideas in this chapter will have to be explained carefully, especially the upper bound. An answer 4.7, to 1 decimal place, has an upper bound of 4.75. This is because it can include any numbers right up to just below 4.75, such as 4.749. The cut-off value is 4.75, not 4.749, as we can have numbers larger than 4.749, such as 4.74999, and even numbers larger than that. The limit of all such numbers is 4.75. The other confusing thing about this chapter is that all calculations, throughout the school course, are done as if the numbers are exact, and answers are often wanted to great precision. (This is partly so that the marker can check the accuracy of the calculation.) For all the other chapters in this book, this method still applies. We do not want pupils to analyse every question and give a range of possible answers. Only if they are specifically told to, should they use the lower and upper bounds of a number in a calculation.

Chapter 10. There are further investigations leading from this chapter in Exercise B4, question 3 and Exercise C6, question 3. Pupils may discover the rules for differentiation and integration, and if so, they can use these rules to calculate gradients and areas, and thus check approximate answers.

The first 10 chapters complete the topics needed for level 9. Chapters 11 to 15 are only needed for level 10.

Chapter 14. For the last exercise, a knowledge of matrices is needed. The work necessary for this is introduced in Exercise B4, question 5.

Chapter 15. For linear programming, I have concentrated on the method of drawing parallel lines. For many questions the x and y values needed are positive integers and the answers can be obtained more easily by trial, using coordinates of points on or near to the boundary lines of the region. If pupils find linear programming too difficult, you may like to explain this easier method to them.

I hope that you and your pupils enjoy the challenge of Maths at levels 9 and 10, and that this book is useful to you.

Jean Holderness

Tables

Time

60 seconds = 1 minute
60 minutes = 1 hour
24 hours = 1 day
7 days = 1 week

52 weeks = 1 year
365 days = 1 year
366 days = 1 leap year
12 months = 1 year

The Metric System

British Units

Length

1000 mm = 1 m
100 cm = 1 m
1000 m = 1 km

12 inches = 1 foot
3 feet = 1 yard
1760 yards = 1 mile

Area

$100 \text{ mm}^2 = 1 \text{ cm}^2$
$10\,000 \text{ cm}^2 = 1 \text{ m}^2$
$1\,000\,000 \text{ m}^2 = 1 \text{ km}^2$

144 sq. inches = 1 sq. foot
9 sq. feet = 1 sq. yard

$1 \text{ hectare} = 10\,000 \text{ m}^2$
$100 \text{ hectares} = 1 \text{ km}^2$

1 acre = 4840 sq. yards
640 acres = 1 sq. mile

Volume

$1000 \text{ mm}^3 = 1 \text{ cm}^3$
$1\,000\,000 \text{ cm}^3 = 1 \text{ m}^3$

1728 cu. inches = 1 cu. foot
27 cu. feet = 1 cu. yard

| **The Metric System** | **British Units** |

Weight

1000 mg = 1 g	16 ounces = 1 pound
100 cg = 1 g	14 pounds = 1 stone
1000 g = 1 kg	112 pounds = 1 hundredweight
1000 kg = 1 tonne	8 stones = 1 hundredweight
	2240 pounds = 1 ton
	20 hundredweights = 1 ton

Capacity

1000 ml = 1 ℓ
100 cl = 1 ℓ
1000 ℓ = 1 kl

1 litre = 1000 cm³

1 litre of water weighs 1 kg
1 cm³ of water weighs 1 g

8 pints = 1 gallon

1 pint of water weighs $1\frac{1}{4}$ lb
1 gallon of water weighs 10 lb

To change to the metric system

Length

1 inch = 2.54 cm
1 foot = 30.48 cm
1 yard = 91.44 cm = 0.9144 m
1 mile = 1.609 km

Weight

1 oz   = 28.35 g
1 lb   = 453.6 g
1 ton = 1016 kg = 1.016 tonne

Capacity

1 pint   = 0.568 litre
1 gallon = 4.546 litre

To change from the metric system

Length

1 cm = 0.394 in
1 m = 39.37 in = 1.094 yd
1 km = 1094 yd = 0.621 mile

Weight

1 kg   = 2.205 lb
1 tonne = 0.984 ton

Capacity

1 litre = 1.76 pints = 0.220 gallons

Areas and volumes

What is the best shape for tins of food ?

The manufacturers have to fit a certain volume of food or drink in each tin. To keep down costs, they want the surface area of the metal to be as small as possible.

Why are metal tins often of cylindrical shape, and cardboard packages often of cuboid shape ? Why are spherical containers not often used ?

Scene at a canning factory

An arc of a circle

and volumes

How Eratosthenes found the size of the Earth

On a day when he knew that the sun would be directly overhead at Syene (as its image could be seen on the water surface of a deep well at noon), he found the angle between the sun's rays and a vertical line, at noon at Alexandria. This angle was $7\frac{1}{2}°$. Alexandria was due north of Syene.

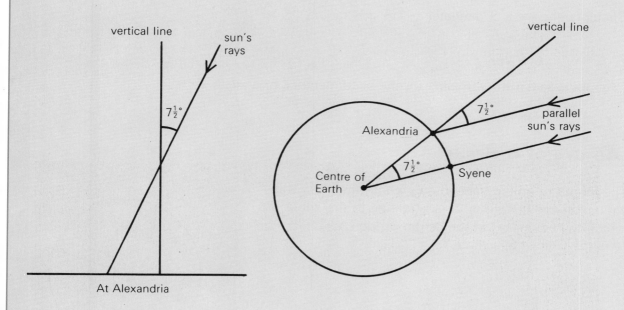

The arc between Syene and Alexandria, which was 520 miles (in modern measurements) was $\dfrac{7\frac{1}{2}}{360} = \dfrac{1}{48}$ of the circumference of the Earth.

So the circumference of the Earth was 25 000 miles.

Considering that Eratosthenes did this calculation in around 250 BC, his work was remarkably accurate. Nowadays, the accepted figure is 24 860 miles.

1 Perimeters, areas and volumes

Perimeters

The perimeter of a plane figure is the total length of the edges.

The perimeter of a rectangle = 2 × (length + breadth)

$$= 2(l + b)$$

The perimeter of a circle is called the circumference.

Circumference = π × diameter = 2 × π × radius

$$C = \pi d$$

$$C = 2\pi r$$

(You must **learn** the formulae for the circumference of a circle.)

An arc of a circle

The length of an arc depends on what fraction of the
circumference the arc is. This is related to the angle, $\theta°$,
which the arc makes at the centre of the circle.
(θ is the Greek letter theta.)

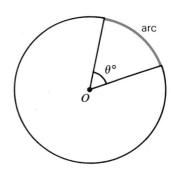

If θ is 180, the arc is a semicircle and its length is $\frac{1}{2}$ of the circumference.

If θ is 90, the arc is a quarter of the circumference,
since 90° is $\frac{1}{4}$ of 360°.

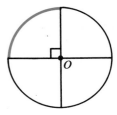

If θ is 60, the arc is $\frac{1}{6}$ of the circumference, since 60° is $\frac{1}{6}$ of 360°.

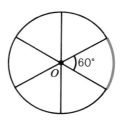

If θ is 1, the arc is $\frac{1}{360}$ of the circumference, since 1° is $\frac{1}{360}$ of 360°.

The length of an arc where the angle is θ° is $\dfrac{\theta}{360}$ of the circumference.

$$\text{length of arc} = \frac{\theta}{360} \times 2\pi r$$

Example

Find the length of the arc AB if the radius is 5.3 cm and $\angle AOB = 150°$.

$\begin{aligned}
\text{arc } AB &= \frac{\theta}{360} \times 2\pi r \\
&= \frac{150}{360} \times 2 \times \pi \times 5.3 \quad \text{cm} \\
&= 13.87 \ldots \text{cm} \qquad \text{(using your calculator)} \\
&= 13.9 \text{ cm, to the nearest mm.}
\end{aligned}$

(Does this answer seem reasonable ?)

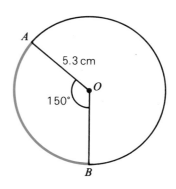

Exercise 1.1

In this exercise, where necessary, take π as 3.142 or use the π key on your calculator.

1. Find the perimeters of these figures.
    1 A rectangle with length 9.2 cm and breadth 6.8 cm.
    2 A triangle with sides 5.5 cm, 7.2 cm and 8.6 cm.
    3 A square with side 11.7 cm.

2. Find the circumferences of these circles, giving answers to the nearest mm.
    1 Radius 4.8 cm
    2 Diameter 3.5 cm
    3 Radius 7.2 cm

3. In the diagram, O is the centre of the circle.
    What fraction of the circumference of
    the circle is the length of the arc AB, if
    1 $\angle AOB = 30°$,
    2 $\angle AOB = 45°$,
    3 $\angle AOB = 144°$?
    What is the size of $\angle AOB$ if
    4 arc $AB = \frac{3}{8}$ of the circumference,
    5 arc $AB = \frac{2}{3}$ of the circumference ?

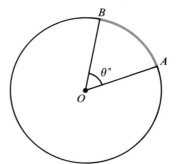

4. If AB is an arc of a circle centre O and $\angle AOB = \theta°$, find the length of the arc AB,
    giving the answers to 3 significant figures, if
    1 $\theta = 20$, radius = 5.1 cm,
    2 $\theta = 140$, radius = 9.3 cm,
    3 $\theta = 45$, radius = 4.8 cm,
    4 $\theta = 120$, radius = 6.0 cm,
    5 $\theta = 25$, radius = 10 cm.

5. Find the perimeters of these figures, giving the answers to the nearest mm.

1

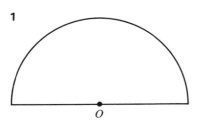

semicircle, diameter 7 cm

2

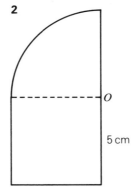

5 cm

square with
side 5 cm,
quadrant, centre O

3

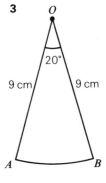

9 cm   9 cm

arc AB has
centre O

Areas

Area of a rectangle = length × breadth = lb
Area of a square = (length)^2 = l^2
Area of a triangle = $\frac{1}{2}$ × base × perpendicular height = $\frac{1}{2}bh$
Area of a parallelogram = base × perpendicular height = bh
Area of a trapezium = $\frac{1}{2}$ × sum of the parallel sides × the perpendicular distance
between them
= $\frac{1}{2}(a + b)h$
Area of a circle = π × (radius)^2 $A = \pi r^2$

(You must **learn** the formula for the area of a circle.)

Notice that in all these formulae the area units are obtained from
length units × length units.

A sector of a circle

The area depends on what fraction of the whole
circle the sector is.
This is related to the angle, $\theta°$, which the sector
makes at the centre of the circle.

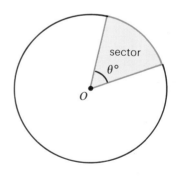

If θ = 180, the sector is a semicircle and its area
is $\frac{1}{2}$ of the area of the circle.

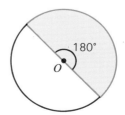

If θ = 90, the sector is a quadrant and its area
is $\frac{1}{4}$ of the area of the circle.

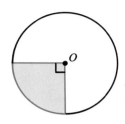

If θ = 60, the area is $\frac{1}{6}$ of the area of the circle.

If θ = 1, the area is $\frac{1}{360}$ of the area of the circle.

The area of a sector = $\dfrac{\theta}{360}$ of the area of the circle.

$$\text{area of sector} = \dfrac{\theta}{360} \times \pi r^2$$

Example

Find the area of the sector AOB if the radius is 5.3 cm and $\angle AOB$ = 150°.

$$\text{area of sector} = \dfrac{\theta}{360} \times \pi r^2$$

$$= \dfrac{150}{360} \times \pi \times 5.3^2 \quad \text{cm}^2$$

$$= 36.76\ldots \quad \text{cm}^2$$

$$= 36.8 \text{ cm}^2, \text{ to 3 sig. fig.}$$

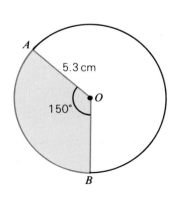

Exercise 1.2

In this exercise, where necessary, take π as 3.142 or use the π key on your calculator, and give approximate answers correct to 3 significant figures.

1. Find the areas of these figures, which are drawn full-size. Make any measurements you need, to the nearest mm.

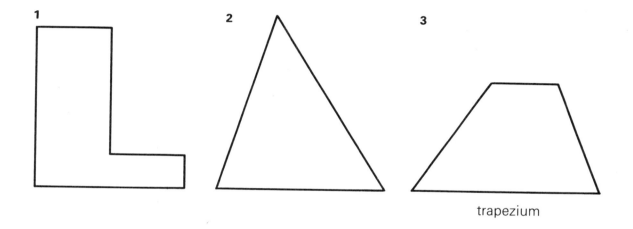

1   **2**   **3**

trapezium

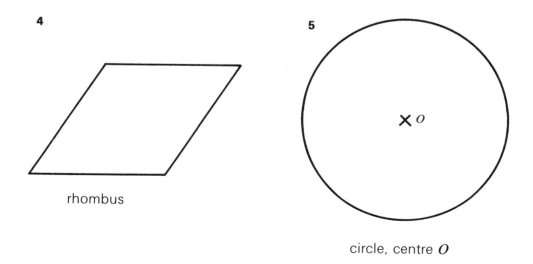

4   **5**

rhombus

circle, centre *O*

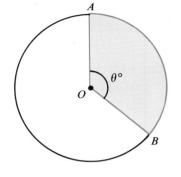

2. In the diagram, **O** is the centre of the circle.
    What fraction of the area of the circle
    is the area of the shaded sector, if
    1   $\angle AOB = 135°$,
    2   $\angle AOB = 72°$,
    3   $\angle AOB = 210°$?

    What is the size of $\angle AOB$, if
    4   area of sector = $\frac{4}{9}$ of the area of the circle,
    5   area of sector = $\frac{5}{6}$ of the area of the circle,
    6   area of sector = $\frac{3}{10}$ of the area of the circle ?

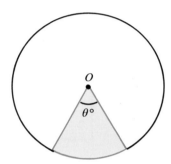

3. Find the areas of the shaded sectors in these circles.
    $\theta°$ is the angle in the sector
    at the centre of the circle.
    1   $\theta = 38$, radius = 7.7 cm,
    2   $\theta = 120$, radius = 9 cm,
    3   $\theta = 53$, radius = 4.5 cm,
    4   $\theta = 100$, radius = 2.5 cm,
    5   $\theta = 36$, radius = 10 cm.

Surface areas

The area of the curved surface of a cylinder
$\quad$ = 2 × π × radius × height
$S = 2\pi r h$

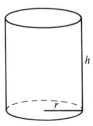

The total surface area of a **closed** cylinder includes
two circular ends.
Total surface area of a closed cylinder = $2\pi r^2 + 2\pi r h$
$$= 2\pi r(r + h)$$

If it is an **open** cylinder, e.g. a cylinder with a base but without a lid, then there is only
one circular end.
Total outside surface area of an open cylinder = $\pi r^2 + 2\pi r h$
$$= \pi r(r + 2h)$$

Example

A closed cylinder has radius 6.3 cm and height 7.7 cm. Find the area of its curved surface.

Also find the total surface area, including its two ends.

$S = 2\pi rh$

$\quad = 2 \times \pi \times 6.3 \times 7.7 \quad cm^2$

$\quad = 304.79 \ldots \quad cm^2$

$\quad = 305 \, cm^2$, to 3 sig. fig.

Total surface area $= 2\pi r(r + h)$

$\quad\quad\quad\quad\quad = 2 \times \pi \times 6.3 \times (6.3 + 7.7) \quad cm^2$

$\quad\quad\quad\quad\quad = 554.17 \ldots \quad cm^2$

$\quad\quad\quad\quad\quad = 554 \, cm^2$, to 3 sig. fig.

Exercise 1.3

1. Find the surface areas of these solid figures.

1

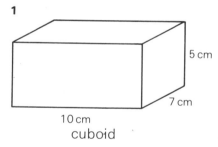

cuboid

2

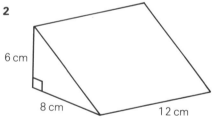

prism with a right-angled triangular cross-section

3

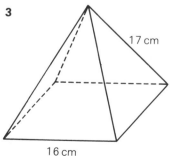

pyramid, with slant sides of edge 17 cm and square base of edge 16 cm

4

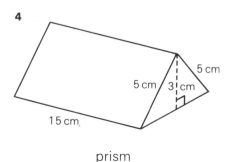

prism

2.   In this question, take π as 3.142 or use the π key on your calculator, and give answers correct to 3 significant figures.

   1   Find the area of the curved surface of a cylinder, radius 6.5 cm and height 7 cm.
   2   Find the area of the curved surface of a cylindrical rod, radius 0.4 cm and length 30 cm.
   3   Find the area of the curved surface of a disc, radius 11 cm and thickness 1.5 cm.
   4   Find the total surface area of a closed cylinder with radius 12.9 cm and height 17.1 cm.
   5   Find the total outside surface area of a cylindrical tin with a base but no lid, with radius 5.4 cm and height 7.3 cm.

Volumes

Volume of a cuboid = length × breadth × height = lbh
Volume of a cube = (length)^3 = l^3
Volume of solid of uniform cross-section = area of cross-section × height
Volume of a cylinder. $V = \pi r^2 h$
Volume of a cone. $V = \frac{1}{3}\pi r^2 h$
Volume of a sphere. $V = \frac{4}{3}\pi r^3$

Notice that in all these formulae the volume units are obtained from
length units × length units × length units, or area units × length units.

Cones

In the formula for the volume of a cone, $V = \frac{1}{3}\pi r^2 h$,
h is the perpendicular height.
The slant height is denoted by l.
If you are given r and l, you must first calculate h using
Pythagoras' theorem.

e.g. If $r = 5$ cm and $l = 13$ cm,

$$l^2 = r^2 + h^2$$
$$13^2 = 5^2 + h^2 \qquad (h \text{ in cm})$$
$$h^2 = 13^2 - 5^2$$
$$h = 12 \text{ cm}$$

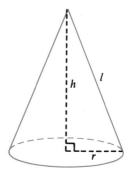

Examples

1 Find the volume of a cone with base radius 4 cm and perpendicular height 6 cm.

$V = \frac{1}{3}\pi r^2 h$

$\quad = \frac{1}{3} \times \pi \times 4^2 \times 6 \quad$ cm^3

$\quad = 100.53 \ldots \quad$ cm^3

$\quad = 101$ cm^3, to 3 sig. fig.

2 Find the volume of a sphere with radius 8.3 cm.

$V = \frac{4}{3}\pi r^3$

$\quad = \frac{4}{3} \times \pi \times 8.3^3 \quad$ cm^3

$\quad = 2395.09 \ldots \quad$ cm^3

$\quad = 2400$ cm^3, to 3 sig. fig.

Exercise 1.4

1. Find the volumes of these solid figures.

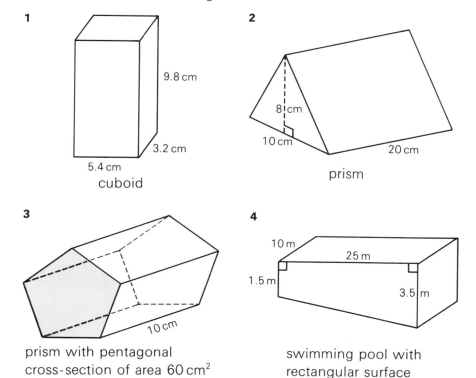

1

9.8 cm

3.2 cm

5.4 cm

cuboid

2

8 cm

10 cm

20 cm

prism

3

10 cm

prism with pentagonal
cross-section of area 60 cm^2

4

10 m

25 m

1.5 m

3.5 m

swimming pool with
rectangular surface

2.   Find the volumes of these figures. Take π as 3.142 or use the π key on your
      calculator, and give answers correct to 3 significant figures.

      1   Cylinder, radius 5.1 cm, height 6.6 cm.
      2   Cone, base radius 10.4 cm, perpendicular height 12 cm.
      3   Sphere, radius 9 cm.
      4   Cone, base radius 12 cm, slant height 20 cm.
      5   Sphere, diameter 2 cm.

3.   This solid figure consists of a cylinder,
      radius 4 cm, height 11 cm, with a
      hemisphere on the top end.
      Find the total volume.

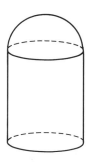

Similar figures

Similar figures have the same shape.
All corresponding angles are equal.
All corresponding lengths are in proportion, i.e. they are in the same ratio as all other
corresponding lengths.

The **areas** of similar plane figures are proportional to the **squares** of corresponding
lengths.

The **surface areas** of similar solid figures are proportional to the **squares** of
corresponding lengths.

The **volumes** of similar solid figures are proportional to the **cubes** of corresponding
lengths.

Lengths	$l : L$
Areas	$l^2 : L^2$
Volumes	$l^3 : L^3$

The results for areas follow from the fact that area units are
length units × length units = (length units)^2.
The result for volumes follows from the fact that volume units are
length units × length units × length units = (length units)^3.

Examples

1 The sides of these similar triangles are in the ratio $3:5$.
The ratio of the areas is $3^2:5^2$, i.e. $9:25$.
This means that the area of the smaller triangle is
$\frac{9}{25}$ of the area of the larger triangle.
The area of the larger triangle is $\frac{25}{9}$ (or $2\frac{7}{9}$) times
the area of the smaller triangle.

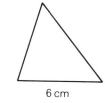

If the area of the smaller triangle is $18.9\,\text{cm}^2$,
what is the area of the larger one ?

Ratio of areas is $9:25$
Area of larger triangle $= \frac{25}{9}$ of $18.9\,\text{cm}^2 = 52.5\,\text{cm}^2$

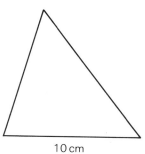

2 Two similar cylinders have heights of $9\,\text{cm}$ and $12\,\text{cm}$.

Ratio of heights $= 9:12 = 3:4$
Ratio of radii $= 3:4$
Ratio of areas of curved surfaces $= 3^2:4^2 = 9:16$
Ratio of areas of circular ends $= 9:16$
Ratio of total surface areas $= 9:16$
Ratio of volumes $= 3^3:4^3 = 27:64$

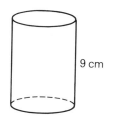

If the volume of the larger cylinder is $960\,\text{cm}^3$,
what is the volume of the smaller one ?

Ratio of volumes is $27:64$
Volume of smaller cylinder $= \frac{27}{64}$ of $960\,\text{cm}^3 = 405\,\text{cm}^3$

3 Two containers are similar in shape. The larger one is $20\,\text{cm}$ high and holds $10\,\ell$ of liquid. How high is the smaller one, which holds $3.43\,\ell$ of liquid ?

Ratio of volumes $= 10\,000\,\text{cm}^3 : 3430\,\text{cm}^3$
$= 1\,000:343$
$= 10^3:7^3$
Ratio of heights $= 10:7$
Height of smaller container $= \frac{7}{10}$ of $20\,\text{cm} = 14\,\text{cm}$

Exercise 1.5

1. These pairs of figures are similar. State the ratios of their areas. Give the answers as *m* : *n*, where *m* and *n* are positive integers (whole numbers) in their simplest form.

1

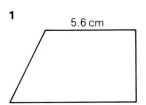
5.6 cm
3.5 cm

2

12 cm   21 cm
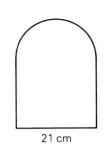

3

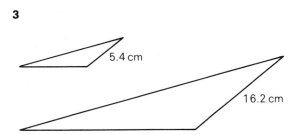
5.4 cm
16.2 cm

4

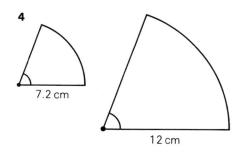
7.2 cm
12 cm

5

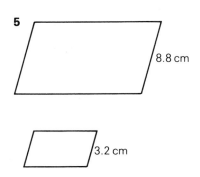
8.8 cm
3.2 cm

6

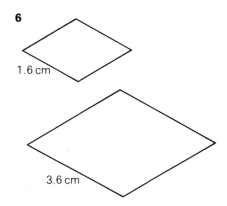
1.6 cm
3.6 cm

2. These pairs of solid figures are similar. State the ratios of their surface areas, and the ratios of their volumes. Give the answers as *m* : *n*, where *m* and *n* are positive integers in their simplest form.

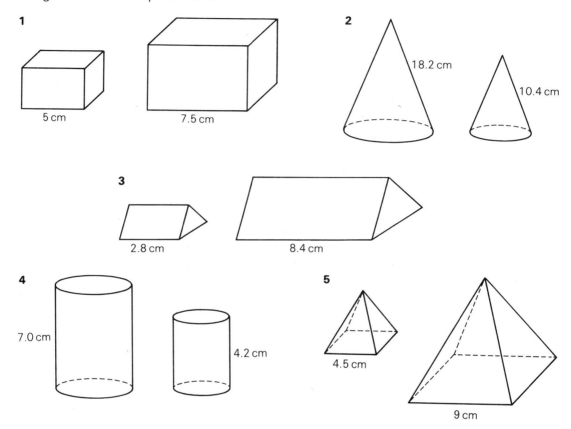

3. **1** The bases of two similar triangles are in the ratio 3 : 4. The area of the smaller triangle is 12.6 cm². What is the area of the larger one ?

    2 The heights of two cylinders are 6 cm and 10 cm. If the larger cylinder has a curved surface area of 900 cm², what is the area of the curved surface of the smaller one ?

    3 The base radii of two cones are 6 cm and 9 cm. If the volume of the smaller cone is 400 cm³, what is the volume of the larger one ?

    4 Two similar parallelograms have areas of 36 cm² and 49 cm². If the larger one has a base of 14 cm, what is the length of the corresponding base of the smaller one ?

    5 Two similar pyramids have volumes of 54 cm³ and 250 cm³. If the smaller one has a height of 9 cm, what is the height of the larger one ?

Exercise 1.6   Applications and Activities

1.   A solid figure has a uniform cross-section which
      is a semicircle of radius 6 cm, and its length is 25 cm.
      Find
      1   the total surface area of the solid figure,
      2   the volume of the solid figure.

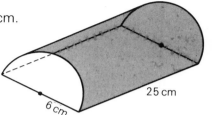

2.   Show that the radius, r cm, of the base of a cone of volume V cm^3 and

      height h cm is given by the formula $r = \sqrt{\dfrac{3V}{\pi h}}$

      A metal cube of edge 8 cm is melted down and formed into a solid cone of
      height 10 cm.
      Find the radius of the base of the cone, to the nearest mm.

3.   A projectile consists of a conical nose cap, length 1.2 m, diameter 48 cm; a
      cylindrical body, length 3 m, diameter 48 cm and a hemispherical tail, diameter
      48 cm.
      Find the volumes of the nose, the body and the tail, and hence find the total
      volume of the projectile.

4. ADB is the edge of an arch, and is an arc of the
      circle centre O. C is the mid-point of AB
      and OC is perpendicular to AB.
      The height of the arch, CD, is
      2 m and the radius of the arc is 26 m.
      Find
      1   the length of OC,
      2   the length of AC,
      3   the size of $\angle AOC$, in degrees, to 1 decimal place,
      4   the size of $\angle AOB$, to the nearest degree,
      5   the length of the arch (ADB).

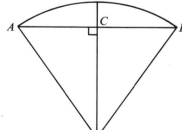

5. *AB* and *CD* are arcs of circles, centre *O*, and
    ∠*DOC*, is 80°. Radius *OA* = 10 cm, *OC* = 12 cm.
    Find the area of the shaded region *ABDC*.

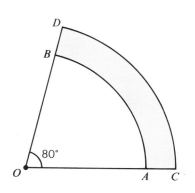

6. *ABCD* is a trapezium in which *AB* is
    parallel to *DC*. The diagonals *AC* and *BD*
    intersect at *X*.   *XB* = 4 cm, *XC* = 7.5 cm
    and *XD* = 6 cm.
    1   Name 2 triangles which are similar to
          each other.
    2   Find the length of *AX*.
    3   Find the ratio of areas of Δ*XAB* : Δ*XCD*.

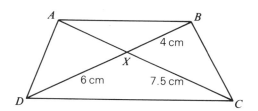

7. Two spheres have volumes of 4.8 cm³ and 16.2 cm³.
    1   Find the ratio of the volumes in the simplest form.
    2   Find the ratio of their diameters.
    3   Find the ratio of their surface areas.

8. A cone has height 12 cm and base radius 4.5 cm.
    A smaller cone is made by cutting off the top, along a plane
    4 cm from the base.
    Find
    1   the base radius of the smaller cone,
    2   the ratio of the volumes of the smaller cone
          and the complete cone,
    3   the ratio of the volumes of the smaller cone
          and the frustum (remainder) of
          the complete cone.

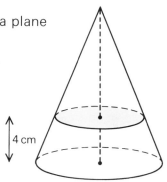

9. The scale of a map is 1 : 500 000. What is the actual distance, in km, between
    two towns which on the map are 4.5 cm apart ?
    A lake on the map has an area of 2 cm². What is the actual area of the lake,
    in km² ?

10.   A model is made of a house, to a scale of 1 : 25. The height of the actual house is 10 m, its floor area is 120 m² and its volume is 960 m³.
Find the height, floor area and volume of the model, in cm, cm² and cm³ respectively.

11.   Solid models, to different scales, are made of a statue. If these similar models are all made of the same material, find
      1   the weight of a model 8 cm high, if a model 16 cm high weighs 5.6 kg,
      2   the height of a model weighing 18.9 kg.

12.   A solid metal cylinder, radius 3 cm and height 7.2 cm was melted down and the metal was used to make small spheres, radius 6 mm.
How many spheres could be made ?
(Do not substitute for π.)

13.   **Pie charts**

      In a pie chart the area of each sector is proportional to the amount it represents. Since the areas are proportional to the angles at the centre of the circle, the amounts are also proportional to these angles.

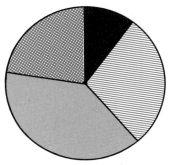

      1   If amounts £2400, £1800, £1500 and £3300 have to be represented on a pie chart, what are the angles at the centre for the sectors ?
      2   If a pie chart has 5 sectors with angles 25°, 30°, 55°, 85° and 165° and the total amount the pie chart represents is £12 600, what amount does each sector represent ?

      If two pie charts are showing different total amounts, then their areas should be proportional to those amounts. If their radii are r_1 and r_2, then

$$\frac{\text{amount represented by (1)}}{\text{amount represented by (2)}} = \frac{\pi r_1^{\,2}}{\pi r_2^{\,2}} = \frac{r_1^{\,2}}{r_2^{\,2}}$$

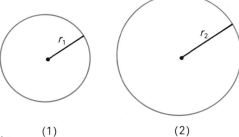

(1)   (2)

      So the squares of the radii are proportional to the total amounts.

      3   If 2 pie charts represent total amounts of £15 000 and £24 000, and the radius of the smaller circle is 5 cm, what should be the radius of the larger circle, to the nearest mm?

14. **Surface area of a sphere**

Archimedes, about 200 BC, stated that the surface area of a sphere is equal to the curved surface area of the circumscribing cylinder. This is a cylinder with the same diameter as the sphere and a height equal to the diameter of the sphere.

Use this fact to find a formula for the surface area of a sphere of radius r cm.

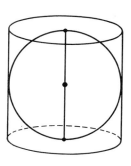

15. **Curved surface area of a cone**

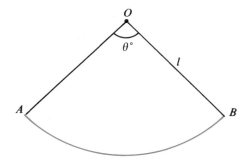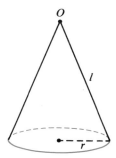

A sector AOB of a circle of radius l cm and angle at the centre of $\theta°$ is bent round to form the curved surface of a cone, by joining OA to OB. This cone has base radius r cm.

Find expressions for the length of the arc AB and the circumference of the base of the cone, and hence find an expression for θ in terms of l and r.

Find an expression for the area of the sector AOB, and by substituting for θ, obtain a formula for the curved surface area of the cone, in terms of l and r.

If a cone has base radius 5 cm and slant height 8 cm, find the area of its curved surface.

16. **Radians**

In the diagram, O is the centre of the circle, radius r cm.

The arc AB has length equal to the radius.

Find the size of $\angle AOB$, correct to 1 decimal place.

This size of angle is called **1 radian**.

In more advanced work, angles are usually measured in radians, rather than in degrees.

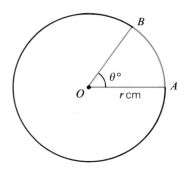

2 Thinking about congruent triangles

Congruent triangles are the same shape and the same size.

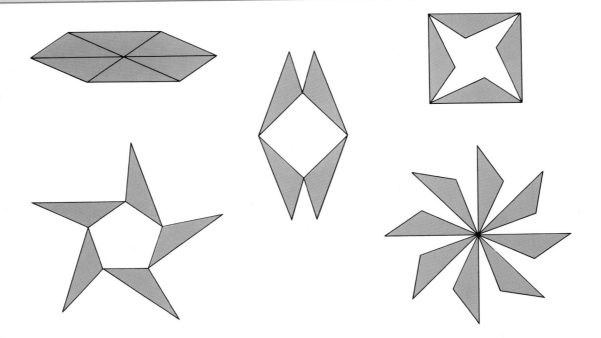

Using congruent triangles to prove Pythagoras' theorem

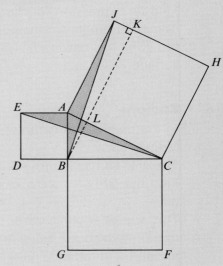

1 Prove that the shaded triangles are congruent.

2 Prove that area $\triangle AEC = \frac{1}{2}$ area square $ABDE$
   Prove that area $\triangle ABJ = \frac{1}{2}$ area rectangle $AJKL$
   This proves that area square $ABDE =$ area
   rectangle $AJKL$

3 Prove in a similar way that
   area square $BCFG =$ area rectangle $CHKL$

4 Complete the proof that
   area square $ABDE +$ area square $BCFG =$ area
   square $ACHJ$
   i.e. $AB^2 + BC^2 = AC^2$

and vectors

Vectors
A vector quantity has a size and a direction.
Forces are vector quantities.

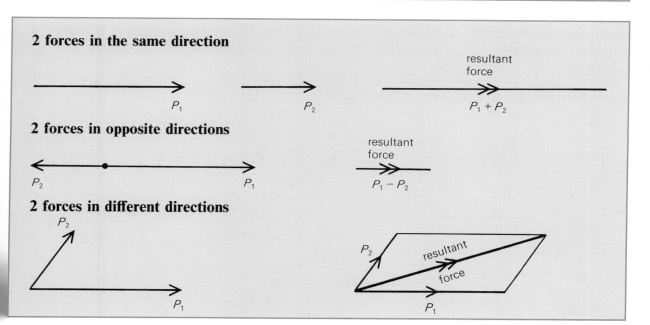

2 forces in the same direction

resultant force $P_1 + P_2$

2 forces in opposite directions

resultant force $P_1 - P_2$

2 forces in different directions

resultant force

The forces acting on a sailing ship sailing close to the wind

For good windward sailing the ratio of side forces to drag forces must be as great as possible.

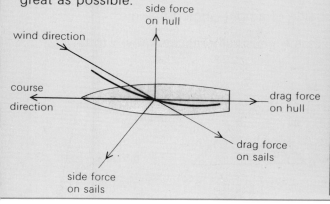

2 Congruent triangles: Vectors

Congruent triangles

Congruent figures are the same shape and the same size. If one figure was cut out and moved, it would fit exactly over another, although it may have to be turned round or turned over.

These triangles are all congruent to each other.

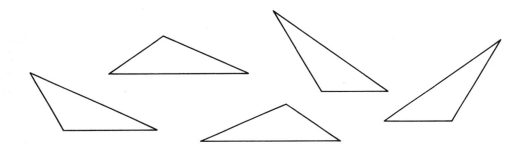

To copy a triangle it is not necessary to know the sizes of all the sides and all the angles. In fact, it is sufficient to know only 3 of these measurements.
These 3 measurements can be
(a) 2 sides and the angle included between those 2 sides,
(b) 2 angles and 1 side,
(c) 3 sides,
(d) 1 right angle, the hypotenuse and 1 other side of a right-angled triangle.

If we have 2 triangles and one of the above sets of measurements are known to be equal, then the triangles are congruent.

(a) These 2 triangles are congruent as we know that 2 pairs of sides are equal and the angles between these sides are equal. (These angles between the two known pairs of sides are called the **included angles**.)

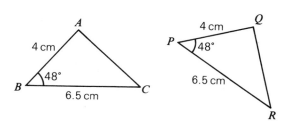

We can write

$\triangle ABC \equiv \triangle QPR$ (SAS)

$\equiv$ means 'is congruent to'.
SAS is the reason. It means 2 sides (SS) with A written in the centre of them for the included angle.

We have given the letters *ABC*, *QPR* in corresponding order, i.e. if the triangles were fitted together, *Q* would fit on *A*, *P* on *B* and *R* on *C*. It is not essential to write them like this but it is helpful.

(b) These 2 triangles are congruent as we know that 2 pairs of angles are equal and one pair of sides, which are in a corresponding position in relation to the angles, are also equal.

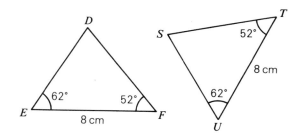

We can write

$\triangle DEF \equiv \triangle SUT$ (AAS)

If we know that 2 pairs of angles are equal the 3rd pair of angles are also equal (why ?), so it does not matter which 2 pairs of angles are known. They need not both be next to the known sides, but the sides must be in a corresponding position.

e.g. sides next to equal angles *A* and *D*,
    and opposite to equal angles *C* and *E*.

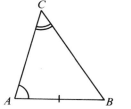 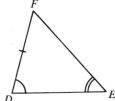

(c) These triangles are congruent
   as we know that all 3 pairs of
   sides are equal.

   $\Delta GHJ \equiv \Delta WVX$ (SSS)

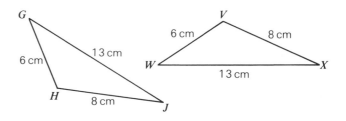

(d) Here we know 2 pairs of sides
   and a non-included pair of
   angles are equal, but those angles
   are right angles.

   $\Delta KLM \equiv \Delta YZN$ (RHS)

   RHS here stands for right angle,
   hypotenuse and one other side.

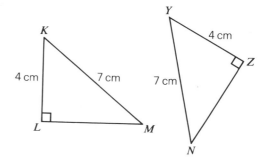

Summary

If we know these facts about two triangles, then **the triangles are congruent**.

(a) Two pairs of sides are
   equal, and the included
   angles are equal.
   (SAS)

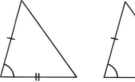

(b) Two pairs of angles are
   equal, and a pair of sides in
   a corresponding position are
   equal.
   (AAS)

 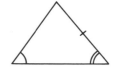

(c) Three pairs of sides
are equal.
(SSS)

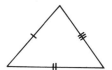

(d) Both triangles have
right angles, the hypotenuses
are equal and one other pair
of sides are equal.
(RHS)

These triangles are not congruent

(e) When you know 3 angles.
These triangles are equiangular and therefore similar but you need to know that
1 pair of sides are equal before you can say that they are congruent.
AAA is not a condition for congruent triangles.

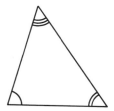

(f) When you know 2 pairs of sides and a non-included angle.

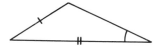

In some cases the triangles could be congruent, for instance when the angles are
right angles (and that is the condition RHS). In general, however, without knowing
more details of the lengths of sides or the sizes of the angles, we cannot say that
the triangles are congruent.
ASS, where A is a non-included angle, is not a condition for congruent triangles.

Examples

Are these pairs of triangles congruent ? If so, give the vertices in corresponding order and give the reasons for congruence.
(Cover up the answers while you try these for yourself.)

1 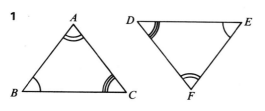   **2**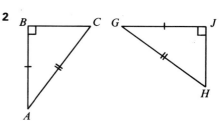

3 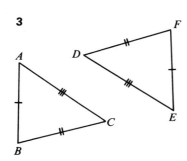   **4**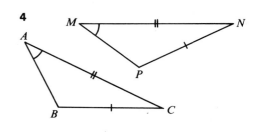

5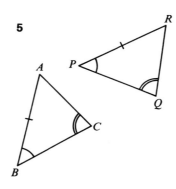

1   No (AAA)
2   Yes. $\triangle ABC \equiv \triangle GJH$ (RHS)
3   Yes. $\triangle ABC \equiv \triangle EFD$ (SSS)
4   No (ASS)
5   Yes. $\triangle ABC \equiv \triangle RPQ$ (AAS)

When the triangles are congruent, we know that the remaining pairs of sides and angles are equal.
In **2**, $BC = JH$, $\angle A = \angle G$, $\angle C = \angle H$
In **3**, $\angle A = \angle E$, $\angle B = \angle F$, $\angle C = \angle D$
In **5**, $BC = PQ$, $AC = RQ$, $\angle A = \angle R$

6 An isosceles triangle

△ABC is isosceles, with $AB = AC$.
Prove that the angles opposite the
equal sides are equal, i.e. $\angle B = \angle C$.

Join A to D, the mid-point of BC.

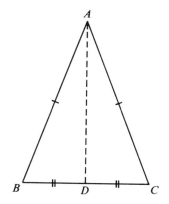

In △ABD and △ACD,

$$AB = AC \qquad\qquad \text{given}$$
$$BD = DC \qquad\qquad \text{given}$$
$$AD = AD \qquad\qquad \text{same line}$$
$$\therefore △ABD \equiv △ACD \qquad \text{(SSS)}$$
$$\therefore \quad \angle B = \angle C$$

(Also $\angle BAD = \angle CAD$, and $\angle BDA = \angle CDA = 90°$.)

$\therefore$ is a symbol meaning 'therefore'.

7 In the diagram, $ABCD$ and $DEFG$ are
squares.
Prove that $AE = CG$.

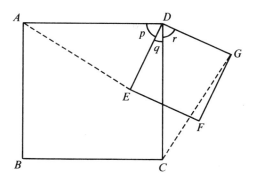

In △ADE and △CDG,

$$AD = DC \qquad \text{sides of square } ABCD$$
$$DE = DG \qquad \text{sides of square } DEFG$$
$$p = r \qquad p + q = 90° \qquad \text{angle of square } ABCD$$
$$\qquad\qquad\quad q + r = 90° \qquad \text{angle of square } DEFG$$
$$\qquad\qquad\quad \therefore \; p = r$$
$$\therefore △ADE \equiv △CDG \qquad \text{(SAS)}$$
$$\therefore \quad AE = CG$$

Exercise 2.1

1. Are these pairs of triangles congruent ? If so, give the vertices in corresponding order and give the reasons for congruence, and name the other pairs of equal sides or angles.

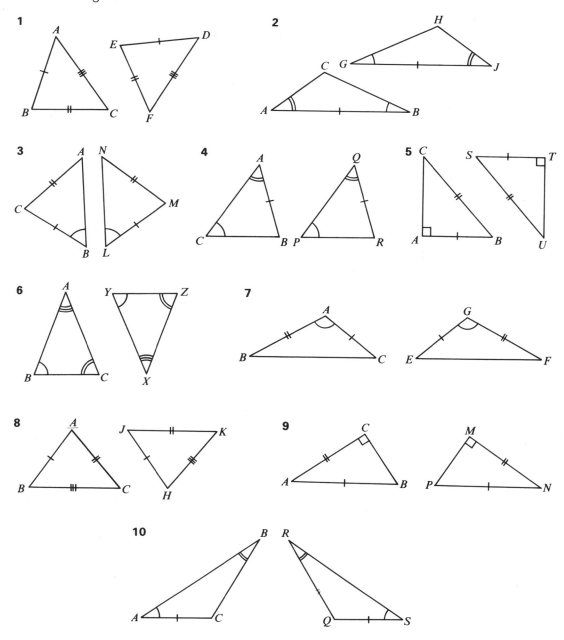

2.   In the diagram, *ABCD* is a parallelogram and *BP*, *DQ* are lines perpendicular to *AC*.
     Assuming that opposite sides of a parallelogram are equal (as well as parallel), prove that triangles *APB* and *CQD* are congruent, giving the reason for congruence.
     Hence prove that *AP* = *CQ*.

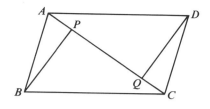

3.   In the diagram, ∠*BAD* = ∠*CAE*, *AB* = *AD*, *AC* = *AE* and *CDE* is a straight line.
     1   Prove that triangles *ABC*, *ADE* are congruent.
     2   Hence prove that ∠*ABC* + ∠*ADC* = 180°.

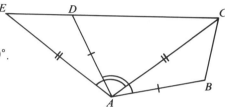

4.   In the diagram, *OA* = *OC* and *OB* = *OD*.
     1   Prove that triangles *OAD*, *OCB* are congruent.
     2   Name an angle equal to ∠*OBC*.
     3   Prove that triangles *AXB*, *CXD* are congruent.
     4   Name a length equal to *AX*.

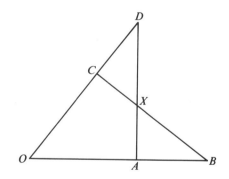

5.   *ABCD* is a square. A circle centre *A* cuts *BC* at *P* and *CD* at *Q*.
     1   Prove that triangles *ABP*, *ADQ* are congruent. Hence prove that *BP* = *DQ*.
     2   Prove that triangles *BCQ*, *DCP* are congruent and hence prove that *BQ* = *DP*.

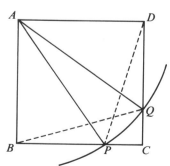

6.   *ABCD* is a quadrilateral in which *AB* = *BC* and ∠*BAD* = ∠*BCD* = 90°.
     Prove that *AD* = *CD*.

7. In the diagram, *ABCD* is a trapezium with $\angle DAB = \angle CBA = 90°$. Also $\angle BCD = \angle BDC$.
    Prove that triangles *ABC* and *BAD* have two sides and one angle equal. Explain why the triangles are not congruent.

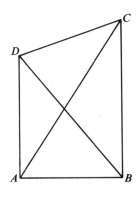

8. In the diagram, circles with centres *A* and *B* intersect at *P* and *Q*.
    Prove that triangles *APB*, *AQB* are congruent, and name the equal angles.

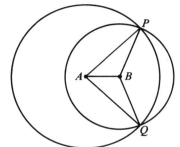

9. *ABC* is an isosceles triangle in which *AB* = *AC*.
    The perpendicular to *AB* at *A* meets the perpendicular bisector of *AC* at *D*, and the perpendicular to *AC* at *A* meets the perpendicular bisector of *AB* at *E*.
    Prove that *AD* = *AE*.

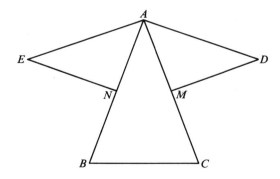

10. *ABC* and *BPQ* are equilateral triangles.
    Prove that *AP* = *CQ*.

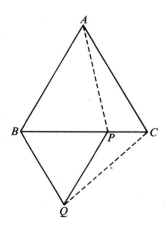

Vectors

A vector quantity has a size and a direction.

We can represent vectors by lines drawn on squared paper or graph paper.

Example

The line **AB** can represent the
vector of a displacement from
A to **B**.
This displacement is 3 units in
the x-direction and 2 units in
the y-direction.
The vector can be represented

by $\begin{pmatrix} 3 \\ 2 \end{pmatrix}$ or (3, 2).

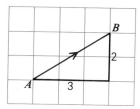

If a vector is represented by a line **AB** this vector is written as $\overrightarrow{AB}$, $\overline{AB}$ or **AB**.

$\overrightarrow{AB}$ means the line in the direction from A to B.

$\overrightarrow{AB} = \begin{pmatrix} 3 \\ 2 \end{pmatrix}$

Any other line parallel to **AB**
and with the same length also

represents the vector $\begin{pmatrix} 3 \\ 2 \end{pmatrix}$.

e.g. $\overrightarrow{CD}$ represents the vector $\begin{pmatrix} 3 \\ 2 \end{pmatrix}$.

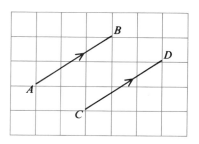

$\overrightarrow{BA}$ means the line in the direction from B to A.

$\overrightarrow{BA} = \begin{pmatrix} -3 \\ -2 \end{pmatrix}$

Vectors can also be represented by small letters in heavy type, such as **a**, **b**, **c**. This is
how they would be shown in printed books.
In handwritten work the letters are underlined instead, as a, b, c, etc.

Equal vectors have the same size and
the same direction.
In this diagram $\overrightarrow{AB}$ and $\overrightarrow{CD}$ are equal
vectors.

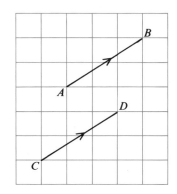

Position vectors

If O is the origin and $\overrightarrow{OA}$ = **a**, then **a** is called the **position vector** of A.

Addition of vectors

1   The rule for addition is $\overrightarrow{AB}$ + $\overrightarrow{BC}$ = $\overrightarrow{AC}$.
         This is shown in the diagram.

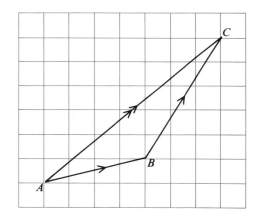

2   To find $\overrightarrow{AB}$ + $\overrightarrow{AD}$ draw $\overrightarrow{AB}$ and $\overrightarrow{AD}$.
         Make a parallelogram $ABCD$ with BC
         equal to AD.
         Then $\overrightarrow{AB}$ + $\overrightarrow{AD}$ = $\overrightarrow{AB}$ + $\overrightarrow{BC}$ = $\overrightarrow{AC}$.
         This is shown in the diagram.

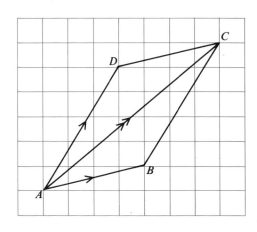

3 Adding numerically.

If $\mathbf{a} = \begin{pmatrix} 4 \\ 1 \end{pmatrix}$ and $\mathbf{b} = \begin{pmatrix} 3 \\ 5 \end{pmatrix}$ then $\mathbf{a} + \mathbf{b} = \begin{pmatrix} 4 \\ 1 \end{pmatrix} + \begin{pmatrix} 3 \\ 5 \end{pmatrix} = \begin{pmatrix} 4 + 3 \\ 1 + 5 \end{pmatrix} = \begin{pmatrix} 7 \\ 6 \end{pmatrix}$

Subtraction of vectors

1 To find $\overrightarrow{AB} - \overrightarrow{BC}$, draw $\overrightarrow{AB}$, and draw
$\overrightarrow{BE}$ equal in length but in the opposite
direction to $\overrightarrow{BC}$.
Then $\overrightarrow{AB} - \overrightarrow{BC} = \overrightarrow{AB} + \overrightarrow{BE} = \overrightarrow{AE}$.
This is shown in the diagram.

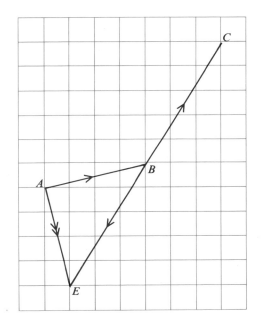

2 To find $\overrightarrow{AB} - \overrightarrow{AD}$.
Since $\overrightarrow{AD} + \overrightarrow{DB} = \overrightarrow{AB}$, then $\overrightarrow{AB} - \overrightarrow{AD} = \overrightarrow{DB}$.
This is shown in the diagram.

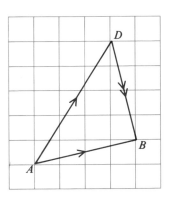

3 Subtracting numerically.

If $\mathbf{a} = \begin{pmatrix} 4 \\ 1 \end{pmatrix}$ and $\mathbf{b} = \begin{pmatrix} 3 \\ 5 \end{pmatrix}$ then $\mathbf{a} - \mathbf{b} = \begin{pmatrix} 4 \\ 1 \end{pmatrix} - \begin{pmatrix} 3 \\ 5 \end{pmatrix} = \begin{pmatrix} 4 - 3 \\ 1 - 5 \end{pmatrix} = \begin{pmatrix} 1 \\ -4 \end{pmatrix}$

Multiplication by a number

If $\overrightarrow{CD} = 2\overrightarrow{AB}$, then $\overrightarrow{CD}$ is a vector twice as long as $\overrightarrow{AB}$ and parallel to $\overrightarrow{AB}$.
If $\overrightarrow{CD} = -3\overrightarrow{AB}$, then $\overrightarrow{CD}$ is a vector three times as long as $\overrightarrow{AB}$, parallel to $\overrightarrow{AB}$ but in the opposite direction because of the minus sign.
These are shown in the diagrams.

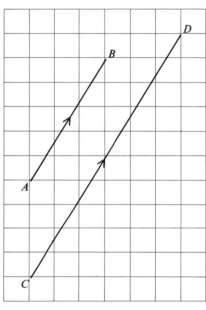

$$\overrightarrow{CD} = 2\overrightarrow{AB}$$

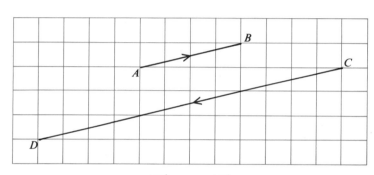

$$\overrightarrow{CD} = -3\overrightarrow{AB}$$

Multiplying numerically.

If $\mathbf{a} = \begin{pmatrix} 3 \\ 5 \end{pmatrix}$ then $2\mathbf{a} = 2 \times \begin{pmatrix} 3 \\ 5 \end{pmatrix} = \begin{pmatrix} 6 \\ 10 \end{pmatrix}$

If $\mathbf{b} = \begin{pmatrix} 4 \\ 1 \end{pmatrix}$ then $-3\mathbf{b} = -3 \times \begin{pmatrix} 4 \\ 1 \end{pmatrix} = \begin{pmatrix} -12 \\ -3 \end{pmatrix}$

Examples

1 If $\mathbf{a} = \begin{pmatrix} 3 \\ 1 \end{pmatrix}$, $\mathbf{b} = \begin{pmatrix} 2 \\ -3 \end{pmatrix}$ and $\mathbf{c} = \begin{pmatrix} 0 \\ 5 \end{pmatrix}$, find the vector $\mathbf{a} + 2\mathbf{b} - \mathbf{c}$, in column form.

$$\mathbf{a} + 2\mathbf{b} - \mathbf{c} = \begin{pmatrix} 3 \\ 1 \end{pmatrix} + 2 \times \begin{pmatrix} 2 \\ -3 \end{pmatrix} - \begin{pmatrix} 0 \\ 5 \end{pmatrix} = \begin{pmatrix} 3 + 4 - 0 \\ 1 - 6 - 5 \end{pmatrix} = \begin{pmatrix} 7 \\ -10 \end{pmatrix}$$

2   If $\mathbf{p} = \begin{pmatrix} 2 \\ 1 \end{pmatrix}$, $\mathbf{q} = \begin{pmatrix} -3 \\ 2 \end{pmatrix}$ and $\mathbf{r} = \begin{pmatrix} 16 \\ 1 \end{pmatrix}$, find numbers m and n such that $m\mathbf{p} + n\mathbf{q} = \mathbf{r}$.

$$m \times \begin{pmatrix} 2 \\ 1 \end{pmatrix} + n \times \begin{pmatrix} -3 \\ 2 \end{pmatrix} = \begin{pmatrix} 16 \\ 1 \end{pmatrix}$$

$$\begin{pmatrix} 2m - 3n \\ m + 2n \end{pmatrix} = \begin{pmatrix} 16 \\ 1 \end{pmatrix}$$

So $2m - 3n = 16$ (1)

$m + 2n = 1$ (2)

These are simultaneous equations, and they can be solved by any suitable method.
Here they are solved by substitution.
From (2), $m = 1 - 2n$
Substitute for m in (1)
$2(1 - 2n) - 3n = 16$
$2 - 4n - 3n = 16$
$-7n = 14$
$n = -2$
Then $m = 1 - 2 \times (-2) = 5$
The numbers are $m = 5$ and $n = -2$.

Exercise 2.2

1. Copy the diagrams on squared paper and for each one show a vector representing $\overrightarrow{AB} + \overrightarrow{BC}$.
    Write the vectors $\overrightarrow{AB}$ and $\overrightarrow{BC}$ in column form and find $\overrightarrow{AB} + \overrightarrow{BC}$. Thus check your answers in the diagrams.

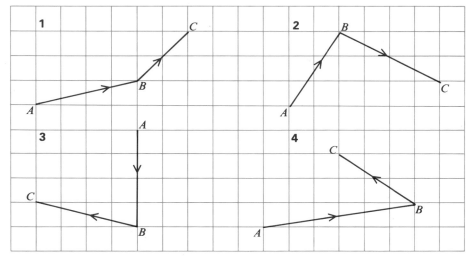

2.   Copy the diagrams and for each one show a vector representing $\overrightarrow{AB} + \overrightarrow{AD}$.
      Write the vectors $\overrightarrow{AB}$ and $\overrightarrow{AD}$ in column form and find $\overrightarrow{AB} + \overrightarrow{AD}$. Thus check
      your answers in the diagrams.

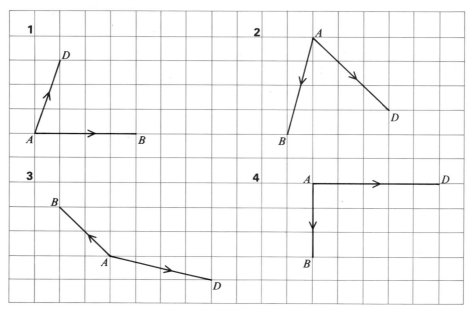

3.   Copy the vectors of question 1 again. For each diagram show a vector
      representing $\overrightarrow{AB} - \overrightarrow{BC}$. Use the vectors in column form to find $\overrightarrow{AB} - \overrightarrow{BC}$, and
      thus check your answers in the diagrams.

4.   Copy the vectors of question 2 again. For each diagram show a vector
      representing $\overrightarrow{AB} - \overrightarrow{AD}$. Use the vectors in column form to find $\overrightarrow{AB} - \overrightarrow{AD}$, and
      thus check your answers in the diagrams.

5.   Draw $\overrightarrow{PQ} = \begin{pmatrix} 5 \\ 2 \end{pmatrix}$, and draw vectors representing $2\overrightarrow{PQ}$, $3\overrightarrow{PQ}$ and $-\overrightarrow{PQ}$.

6.   In the diagram, which vectors
      represent
      1    $\overrightarrow{AB} + \overrightarrow{AD}$,
      2    $\overrightarrow{AB} - \overrightarrow{AD}$,
      3    $2\overrightarrow{AG}$,
      4    $\overrightarrow{AG} + \overrightarrow{GD}$,
      5    $\overrightarrow{AG} - \overrightarrow{AB}$?

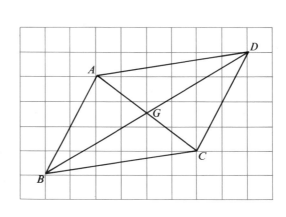

7. *OABC* is a parallelogram, drawn on a unit grid.

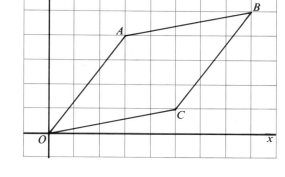

   1   Write down the vectors $\overrightarrow{OA}$ and $\overrightarrow{OC}$ in column form.

   2   Write down a vector equal to $\overrightarrow{AB}$.

   3   Write down a vector equal to $\overrightarrow{OA} + \overrightarrow{AB}$.

   4   Write down a vector equal to $\overrightarrow{OB} - \overrightarrow{CB}$.

   5   State the coordinates of *E* if $\overrightarrow{OE} = 2\overrightarrow{OC}$.

   6   State the coordinates of *F* if $\overrightarrow{OF} = \overrightarrow{BO}$.

8. *A* is the point with coordinates (1, 2).

$$\overrightarrow{AB} = \begin{pmatrix} 3 \\ 9 \end{pmatrix}, \quad \overrightarrow{BD} = \begin{pmatrix} 8 \\ -6 \end{pmatrix}, \quad \overrightarrow{DC} = \begin{pmatrix} 3 \\ 9 \end{pmatrix}.$$

   1   Mark the points *A, B, C, D* on squared paper.

   2   Draw the quadrilateral *ABCD* by joining the points, and draw its diagonals.

   3   If the diagonals intersect at *X*, what are the coordinates of *X* ?

   4   Express $\overrightarrow{AX}$ and $\overrightarrow{XC}$ in column form.

   5   What is the **length** of *BD* ?

9. If $\mathbf{d} = \begin{pmatrix} 3 \\ 1 \end{pmatrix}$, $\mathbf{e} = \begin{pmatrix} 4 \\ 3 \end{pmatrix}$ and $\mathbf{f} = \begin{pmatrix} 0 \\ 7 \end{pmatrix}$, find by drawing or calculation the vector $3\mathbf{d} - \mathbf{e} + 2\mathbf{f}$, in column form.

10. If $\mathbf{p} = \begin{pmatrix} 3 \\ 5. \end{pmatrix}$, $\mathbf{q} = \begin{pmatrix} 2 \\ -1 \end{pmatrix}$ and $\mathbf{r} = \begin{pmatrix} 1 \\ 6 \end{pmatrix}$, find numbers *a* and *b* such that $a\mathbf{p} + b\mathbf{q} = \mathbf{r}$.

11. Draw the *x* and *y* axes labelled from 0 to 70, taking a scale of 2 cm to 10 units. Plot the point *P* (45, 7).

Draw the lines representing these vectors:

$$\overrightarrow{PR} = \begin{pmatrix} -37 \\ 47 \end{pmatrix}, \quad \overrightarrow{RT} = \begin{pmatrix} 58 \\ -17 \end{pmatrix}, \quad \overrightarrow{TQ} = \begin{pmatrix} -57 \\ -19 \end{pmatrix} \text{ and } \overrightarrow{QS} = \begin{pmatrix} 34 \\ 48 \end{pmatrix}.$$

Draw *SP* and state the vector $\overrightarrow{SP}$. Check the answer by calculation. What is the name of the figure you have drawn ?

12. *O* is the origin and *P* is the point (5, 2).

$$\overrightarrow{PQ} = \begin{pmatrix} 0 \\ 5 \end{pmatrix} \text{ and } \overrightarrow{QR} = \begin{pmatrix} 6 \\ -4 \end{pmatrix}$$

Mark the points *P, Q, R* on squared paper, and write down the coordinates of *Q* and *R*.

Find in column form the vector $\overrightarrow{OG}$, where $\overrightarrow{OG} = \frac{1}{3}(\overrightarrow{OP} + \overrightarrow{OQ} + \overrightarrow{OR})$, and mark the position of *G* on the diagram.

Further Examples

1 $PQRS$ is a trapezium with PS parallel to QR and $PS = 2QR$.
Prove that $\overrightarrow{PQ} + \overrightarrow{RS} = \overrightarrow{QR}$.

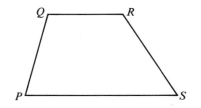

$$\overrightarrow{PS} = \overrightarrow{PQ} + \overrightarrow{QR} + \overrightarrow{RS} \qquad \text{(addition rule)}$$

But $\overrightarrow{PS} = 2\overrightarrow{QR}$

$$2\overrightarrow{QR} = \overrightarrow{PQ} + \overrightarrow{QR} + \overrightarrow{RS}$$

$$\overrightarrow{QR} = \overrightarrow{PQ} + \overrightarrow{RS}$$

2 $\overrightarrow{OA} = \mathbf{a}$, $\overrightarrow{OB} = \mathbf{b}$, $\overrightarrow{OC} = \mathbf{a} + \mathbf{b}$,
and $\overrightarrow{OD} = 2\mathbf{a} + 3\mathbf{b}$.
Express $\overrightarrow{AD}$ and $\overrightarrow{BD}$ in terms of $\mathbf{a}$ and $\mathbf{b}$.
Show that OC is parallel to BD.

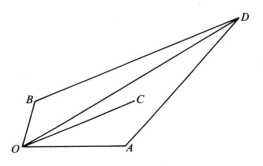

$$\overrightarrow{AD} = \overrightarrow{AO} + \overrightarrow{OD} \qquad \text{(addition rule)}$$

$$= -\mathbf{a} + 2\mathbf{a} + 3\mathbf{b}$$

$$= \mathbf{a} + 3\mathbf{b}$$

$$\overrightarrow{BD} = \overrightarrow{BO} + \overrightarrow{OD}$$

$$= -\mathbf{b} + 2\mathbf{a} + 3\mathbf{b}$$

$$= 2\mathbf{a} + 2\mathbf{b}$$

$$\overrightarrow{BD} = 2(\mathbf{a} + \mathbf{b})$$

$$= 2\overrightarrow{OC}$$

So BD and OC are parallel. (Also $BD = 2OC$.)

3 In $\triangle ABC$, $\overrightarrow{AB} = \mathbf{b}$ and $\overrightarrow{AC} = \mathbf{c}$.
D is a point on BC such that $BD = 2DC$.
Prove that $\overrightarrow{AD} = \frac{1}{3}\mathbf{b} + \frac{2}{3}\mathbf{c}$

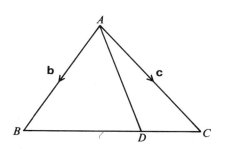

$$\overrightarrow{BC} = \mathbf{c} - \mathbf{b} \qquad \text{(subtraction rule)}$$

$$\overrightarrow{BD} = \tfrac{2}{3}\overrightarrow{BC} = \tfrac{2}{3}(\mathbf{c} - \mathbf{b})$$

$$\overrightarrow{AD} = \overrightarrow{AB} + \overrightarrow{BD}$$

$$= \mathbf{b} + \tfrac{2}{3}(\mathbf{c} - \mathbf{b})$$

$$= \mathbf{b} + \tfrac{2}{3}\mathbf{c} - \tfrac{2}{3}\mathbf{b}$$

$$= \tfrac{1}{3}\mathbf{b} + \tfrac{2}{3}\mathbf{c}$$

Exercise 2.3

1. *ABCD* is a parallelogram whose diagonals intersect at *E*. *M* is the mid-point of *BC*. If $\overrightarrow{AB} = \mathbf{b}$ and $\overrightarrow{AD} = \mathbf{d}$, express in terms of **b** and **d** the vectors

   1 $\overrightarrow{AE}$,

   2 $\overrightarrow{BD}$,

   3 $\overrightarrow{MD}$.

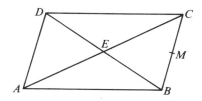

2. In the diagram, $\overrightarrow{EC} = 2\overrightarrow{CB}$ and $\overrightarrow{CD} = 2\overrightarrow{AC}$.
   Find $\overrightarrow{AB}$ and $\overrightarrow{ED}$ in terms of $\overrightarrow{AC}$ and $\overrightarrow{CB}$ and hence show that

   1 *AB* is parallel to *ED*,

   2 $ED = 2AB$.

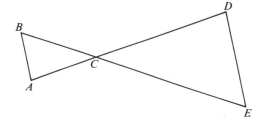

3. In the diagram, $\overrightarrow{AC} = \overrightarrow{BD}$ and $\overrightarrow{BE} = \overrightarrow{AD}$. Prove that *D* is the mid-point of the straight line *CE*.

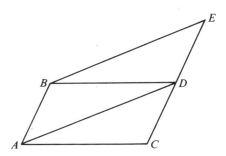

4. In the diagram, $\overrightarrow{XC} = 3\overrightarrow{XA}$, $\overrightarrow{XD} = 3\overrightarrow{XB}$. Show that $\overrightarrow{CD} = 3\overrightarrow{AB}$.

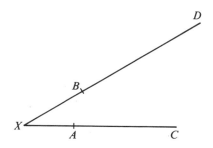

5. $ABCD$ is a parallelogram. $\overrightarrow{AD}$ = **a** and
    $\overrightarrow{AB}$ = **b**. E is the mid-point of BD.
    Express in terms of **a** and/or **b** the
    vectors

    1   $\overrightarrow{DC}$,
    2   $\overrightarrow{CB}$,
    3   $\overrightarrow{BD}$,
    4   $\overrightarrow{AB} + \overrightarrow{BE}$.

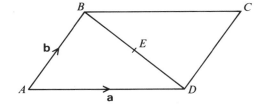

6. In $\triangle ABC$, D is the mid-point
    of BC.
    Prove that $\overrightarrow{AB} + \overrightarrow{AC} = 2\overrightarrow{AD}$.

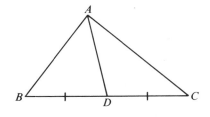

7. In this question, use the result
    of question 6.

    In the quadrilateral $ABCD$, M is the
    mid-point of BD and N is the
    mid-point of AC.
    1   Show that $\overrightarrow{AB} + \overrightarrow{AD} = 2\overrightarrow{AM}$
    2   Simplify $\overrightarrow{CB} + \overrightarrow{CD}$
    3   Simplify $\overrightarrow{AM} + \overrightarrow{CM}$
    4   Show that $\overrightarrow{AB} + \overrightarrow{AD} + \overrightarrow{CB} + \overrightarrow{CD} = 4\overrightarrow{NM}$.

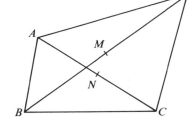

8. In $\triangle ABC$, D, E, F are the mid-points
    of BC, CA and AB respectively.
    Show that $\overrightarrow{AD} + \overrightarrow{BE} + \overrightarrow{CF} = \mathbf{0}$.
    0 is the zero vector.
    (You can use the result of question 6
    in the form $\overrightarrow{AD} = \frac{1}{2}(\overrightarrow{AB} + \overrightarrow{AC})$.)

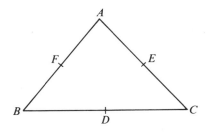

Exercise 2.4   Applications and Activities

1. **To prove the properties of a parallelogram**

    ABCD is a parallelogram.
    (This means only that *AB* is parallel
    to *DC* and *BC* is parallel to *AD*.)
    Prove that triangles *ABC*, *CDA* are
    congruent, and hence that *AB* = *DC*,
    BC = *AD*, ∠*B* = ∠*D* and ∠*BAD* = ∠*BCD*.

    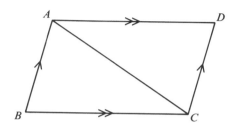

    This proves that
    opposite sides of a parallelogram are equal,
    opposite angles of a parallelogram are equal.

2. *ABCD* is a parallelogram.
    Prove that *AX* = *XC* and *BX* = *XD*.
    (You can assume that opposite
    sides of a parallelogram are
    equal.)

    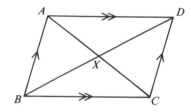

    This proves that the diagonals of
    a parallelogram bisect each other.

3. **Converse properties**

    ABCD is a quadrilateral such that
    AB = *DC* and *AD* = *BC*.
    Prove that it is a parallelogram,
    i.e. prove that both pairs of
    opposite sides are parallel.

    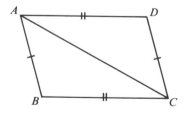

4. *ABCD* is a quadrilateral with one
    pair of sides, *AD* and *BC*, equal
    and parallel.
    Prove that it is a parallelogram,
    i.e. prove that the other pair of
    sides are parallel.

    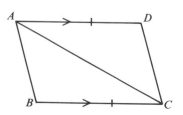

5.   *ABCD* is a quadrilateral whose
     diagonals bisect each other,
     i.e. *AX = XC* and *BX = XD*.
     Prove that it is a parallelogram.

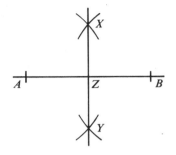

6.   **Proofs of constructions**

     Here is a reminder of the construction
     for bisecting a line *AB*.
     Prove that $\triangle AXY \equiv \triangle BXY$, and hence
     that $\angle AXZ = \angle BXZ$.
     Then use $\triangle AXZ$ and $\triangle BXZ$ to prove
     that *XZY* is the perpendicular
     bisector of *AB*.

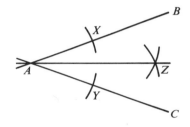

7.   Here is a reminder of the construction
     for bisecting an angle *BAC*.
     Using $\triangle AXZ$ and $\triangle AYZ$, prove that
     AZ bisects $\angle BAC$.

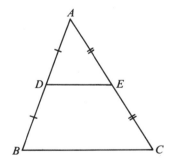

8.   **The mid-point theorem**

     In $\triangle ABC$, *D* is the mid-point of
     AB and *E* is the mid-point of *AC*.
     Prove that *DE* is parallel to *BC*
     and $DE = \frac{1}{2}BC$.

     Produce (extend) *DE* to *F*, such that
     DE = EF. Join *CF*.
     Prove that triangles *ADE*, *CFE* are
     congruent.
     What does this prove about *FC* ?
     What does this prove about $\angle CFE$?
     What sort of figure is *FDBC*, and
     why ?
     What does this prove about *DE* ?

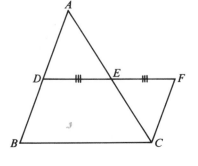

You can also prove this theorem by
using vectors.
Proof using vectors:
If $\overrightarrow{DA} = $ **d** and $\overrightarrow{AE} = $ **e**, express
$\overrightarrow{DE}$ in terms of **d** and **e**.
Express $\overrightarrow{BA}$, $\overrightarrow{AC}$ and $\overrightarrow{BC}$ in terms
of **d** and **e**.
Compare $\overrightarrow{DE}$ with $\overrightarrow{BC}$.
What does this prove about DE ?

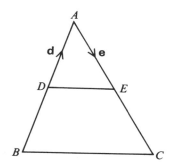

9. **Combining vectors to find distances**

A plane flies from an airfield for 5 km due south, then for 8 km due east, and
finally for 9 km due north-west.
Show the course of the plane on a diagram.
Find the distance and bearing from the airfield of the plane's final position.

10. **Combining vectors to find velocities**

If a boat is travelling across a river which has a current flowing then the velocity
of the boat is affected by the current. The resultant velocity of the boat is a
combination of the actual velocity of the boat and the velocity of the current.
These two velocities are combined using the rules for addition of vectors.

(Velocity is a word used instead of speed when the direction of motion is
included.)

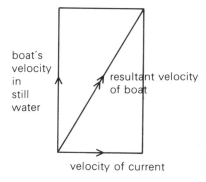

Boat heading at right
angles to the current

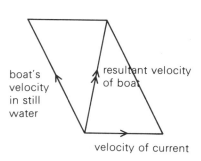

Boat heading
slightly upstream

10.   For parts **1**, **2**, **3**, draw accurate diagrams to show the resultant velocity of the
       boat when the boat is headed in the directions shown. The boat has a speed in
       still water of 24 km/h and the speed of the current is 10 km/h.
       By measurement find the size of the resultant velocity and the angle it makes
       with the direction in which the boat is headed.

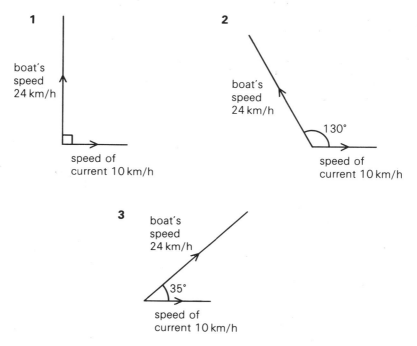

4   A boat heads upstream. At what angle with the bank, θ, should it be headed
       so that the resultant velocity takes the boat directly across the river ? What is
       the size of the resultant velocity ?
       If the river is 125 m wide, how long will it take the boat to cross ?

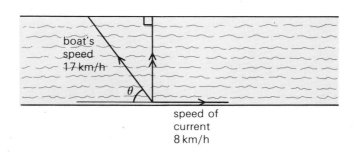

A similar vector rule applies to planes in the air. The resultant velocity is a combination of the plane's velocity due to the effect of the plane's engine, called airspeed, and the wind's velocity. The resultant velocity is called the groundspeed.

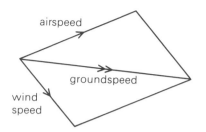

5   If a plane is flying in the direction due east at a speed of 200 km/h, and the wind is blowing from due south with a speed of 50 km/h, draw an accurate diagram to show the resultant velocity (groundspeed) of the plane, and by measurement or calculation find its size, and the bearing on which the plane is travelling.

11.   **Combining vectors to find forces**

Forces are vectors and they are combined using the rules for addition of vectors.

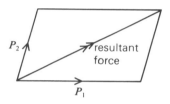

2 forces P_1 and P_2.

For **1**, **2**, **3**, draw accurate diagrams to find the resultant force when the 2 forces are combined, and find the angle the resultant force makes with the larger of the 2 forces. N is the symbol for Newton, which is the unit of force.

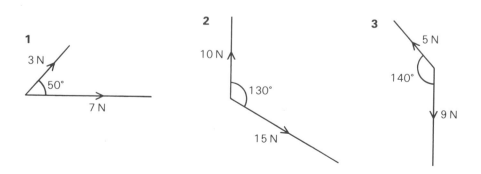

11.   Forces P_1 and P_2 can be
       balanced by a force which
       is equal and in the
       opposite direction to the
       resultant force.

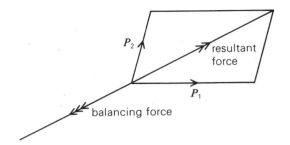

   4   A weight is hanging from 2 strings.
           T_1 and T_2 are the forces of tension
           in the strings.
           The resultant of forces T_1 and T_2
           must be 40 N vertically upwards,
           to balance the weight.

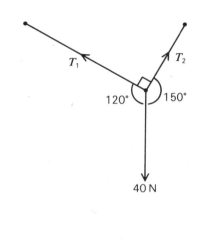

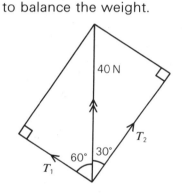

       Use the forces diagram to calculate the sizes of T_1 and T_2, or make an
       accurate drawing of it and find T_1 and T_2 by measurement.

PUZZLES

1.   Stella and Stephen are twins. Stella has twice as many brothers as sisters and Stephen
      has the same number of brothers as sisters.
      How many children are there in the family ?

2.   A farmer has two milk cans. One holds 5 pints and the other holds 3 pints. By using only
      the two cans how can the farmer measure out 1 pint of milk from the churn ?

3. Eight glasses, four of them filled, are in a line on a table. Kevin boasts to his friend that by moving only one glass he can have four filled glasses next to each other. How does he do it ?

4. In our village the butcher's is closed every Monday, the fishmonger's is closed every Tuesday, the greengrocer's is closed every Thursday and the Post Office is only open on Monday, Wednesday and Friday. No shops open on Sundays.
    One afternoon four women went shopping together, each with a different one of the above shops to go to. Here are some of the remarks they made:
    Mrs Grant: I didn't really want to come today but tomorrow the shop would be closed.
    Mrs Hill: I could have come yesterday or the day before if I had had time.
    Mrs Ingham: I too could have come yesterday, and I also could have come tomorrow.
    Mrs Johnson: I needed to get a lift in with Mrs Ingham and this was the first day of the week when we could both do our shopping.

    Which shop did each woman need to visit ?

5. Divide the clock face with two straight lines so that the sum of the numbers in each part are equal.

6. A man having his house modernised said he had paid
        £3500 to the builder and the joiner,
        £2800 to the joiner and the electrician,
        £2700 to the electrician and the plumber,
        £2000 to the plumber and the decorator,
        £3000 to the builder and the decorator.

    What did each man charge ?

7. Two girls were each trying to save £20 to buy some sports equipment. After a few weeks, one girl said to the other, 'Have you got enough money yet ?'
    The other replied, 'Not yet, but if I had twice as much as I have now, plus half as much as I have now, I would have enough.'
    How much had she saved ?

3 Thinking about sampling and

Sampling

If a sample of people was selected from those here, in what ways might it not be a representative sample of the whole population of Britain ?

Random sampling is like choosing the sample by running a raffle. Every person or item has an equal chance of being chosen. The sample can be chosen using electronic equipment.
In this picture, taken in 1957, the machine ERNIE (the **E**lectronic **R**andom **N**umber **I**ndicator **E**quipment) was producing the first-ever winning numbers in the Premium Bond Draw.

To take samples of plants growing in a field, a square frame called a quadrat is used. It usually encloses 1 m². The frame is thrown at random about 20 times in different parts of the field and each time the types of plants in the enclosed area are recorded.

Before a General Election, Public Opinion Polls sample people asking them how they intend to vote. In 1992 the results of the opinion polls did not give a good forecast of the actual election results.
Why are Public Opinion Polls needed ?

presenting data

Presenting data

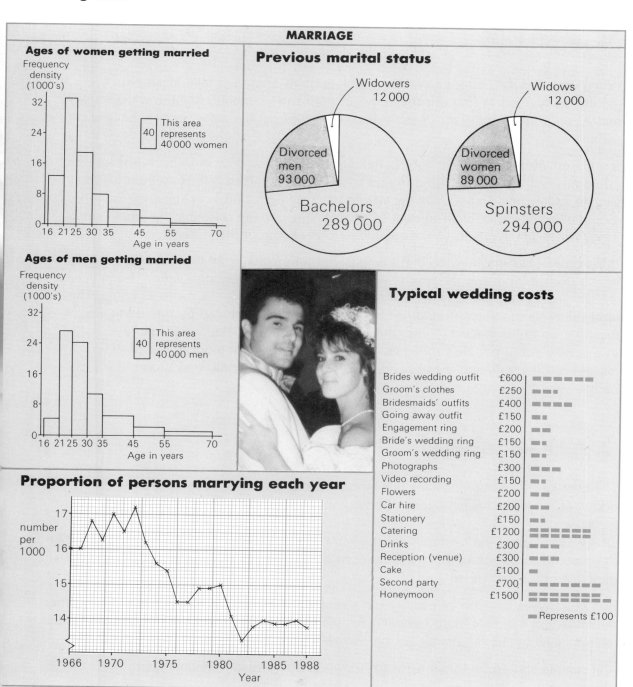

MARRIAGE

Ages of women getting married

Frequency density (1000's)

[Histogram with y-axis values 0, 8, 16, 24, 32 and x-axis: 16 21 25 30 35 45 55 70 — Age in years]

40 — This area represents 40 000 women

Ages of men getting married

Frequency density (1000's)

[Histogram with y-axis values 0, 8, 16, 24, 32 and x-axis: 16 21 25 30 35 45 55 70 — Age in years]

40 — This area represents 40 000 men

Previous marital status

[Pie chart] Widowers 12 000 — Divorced men 93 000 — Bachelors 289 000

[Pie chart] Widows 12 000 — Divorced women 89 000 — Spinsters 294 000

Typical wedding costs

Brides wedding outfit	£600	
Groom's clothes	£250	
Bridesmaids' outfits	£400	
Going away outfit	£150	
Engagement ring	£200	
Bride's wedding ring	£150	
Groom's wedding ring	£150	
Photographs	£300	
Video recording	£150	
Flowers	£200	
Car hire	£200	
Stationery	£150	
Catering	£1200	
Drinks	£300	
Reception (venue)	£300	
Cake	£100	
Second party	£700	
Honeymoon	£1500	

▬ Represents £100

Proportion of persons marrying each year

number per 1000

[Line graph with y-axis values 14, 15, 16, 17 and x-axis: 1966 1970 1975 1980 1985 1988 — Year]

3 Sampling, and presenting data

Sampling

When we need data about a certain population we often just take a sample.
e.g. If you wanted to find out the views of pupils in your school about a particular matter, you might not want to ask everyone, so you would select certain people and ask them.

If a manufacturer of electric light bulbs wanted to know how long his bulbs last, he could not test all of them or he would have no bulbs left to sell. He would just test a sample. Here the population is the whole batch of light bulbs. In statistics the word 'population' does not need to refer to people. It is used to describe the whole set of items which are involved, and a sample involves some of those items.

It is no use choosing a sample if it is biased, that means likely to give unfair results, which do not represent the results which apply to the whole population. For a school matter, you could not just ask your friends whose views are the same as yours. The light bulb manufacturer should not just test the bulbs produced by one particular machine, as bulbs made by other machines may not be of the same quality.
In a survey about people's incomes, names were chosen at random out of the telephone directory, and those people questioned. The sample was biased because people with low incomes are less likely to have telephones.

A random sample

The best kind of sample to take is a random sample. In this, every member of the population has the same chance of being chosen for the sample as every other member.
One way to select the members for the sample is to give each one a number, and then draw numbers out of a hat, or use random number tables or random numbers generated by a computer.

It is not always possible or easy to get a random sample so you may have to use other methods. For example, if you wanted the views of people in your town, you might just have to select your sample by asking people in the street.

The sample should be **large enough** to represent fairly all the varieties in the population.

The sample should **represent fairly** in the right proportions all categories in the population.

e.g. In a survey about a school matter which affects the whole school the sample should include all age groups and, if it is a mixed school, girls and boys.

A stratified sample

For this, the population is divided into different groups called strata (layers), and then samples are taken from each group, in numbers in proportion to the relative sizes of the groups. This method is particularly useful if the population is quite large.

In a school survey, pupils are already divided into groups called forms, classes or tutor groups. If there are roughly equal numbers in each tutor group then you could select a stratified sample by choosing two (or more) pupils from each group. These pupils could be chosen at random.

If you are doing a survey in the street, rather than just stopping people at random, you could choose a stratified sample by choosing equal numbers of men and women, and people of different ages.

The size of the sample

You would have to decide how many items or people you need in your sample. If there are 1000 pupils in your school, a 10% sample would use a sample of 100 pupils and a 5% sample would use a sample of 50 pupils. A smaller sample might not represent the views of the whole school, and a larger sample would make the data collection process take too long.

Systematic sampling

Another way to choose a sample is to list the population in some sort of order, for instance alphabetical order, and then take every 10th or 20th name on the list to form a 10% or 5% sample.

Pupils in your school are already listed in order on class registers. Put the registers in class order and use them as if the names were in one long list. Instead of always starting with the 10th name, choose a random number from 1 to 10 to start with, and then take every 10th name after that.

A survey of school leavers chose a sample by selecting those people whose birthdays were on the 5th, 15th or 25th of the month. This produced a 10% sample.

Exercise 3.1

1. Give reasons why you may not achieve a random sample if you choose your sample by stopping people in the street.

2. A survey is to be made in a school about the pupils' views on out-of-school activities. The school contains 150 pupils in each of 5 years with 5 forms in each year. There are roughly equal numbers of boys and girls in each form. The method of collecting data is to issue a questionnaire to a 20% sample of pupils.
    Explain a method for choosing the sample.

3. In a raffle, a ticket is picked out of a tin, at random.
    In the Premium Bond Lottery, how are the winning numbers produced ?

4. A survey was to be made to find out how pupils of a large school travelled to school. A sample was chosen by asking the first 30 pupils to arrive at school on one morning.
    Explain why this sample is likely to be unsatisfactory, and suggest how a more satisfactory sample could be chosen.

5. In a certain firm there were 3 workshops, with 100 workers in workshop A, 150 workers in workshop B and 200 workers in workshop C. In each workshop, 80% of the workers were male and 20% were female.
    The management decided to conduct a survey about working conditions and decided to select a 10% sample to interview.
    Explain how they could choose the sample so that men and women, and workers from all the workshops, were fairly represented.

6. An interviewer carried out a door-to-door survey one week, on each morning from Monday to Friday, to ask for people's views about unemployment.
    Explain why the sample is likely to be biased.

7. For a survey of children's teeth, the dentist came to school and inspected the teeth of children chosen from every 10th name on the school registers. Some of these children were absent, and the headteacher suggested that in those cases, the dentist looked at the pupil next on the register. However, he was not allowed to substitute different children in that way, as he was told that it would make the sample biased. (The dentist returned two weeks later to check on the children he had missed the first time.)
    Why would the sample have been biased ?

Presenting data

Statistics

Statistics involves numerical data.

Firstly, the data must be collected. Sometimes you carry out an investigation or experiment and collect data for yourself. Sometimes you can use data which someome else has collected. This includes data in government publications, newspapers, scientific textbooks, etc.

Secondly, the data is displayed in the form of a list, a table or a diagram.

Thirdly, it is studied, in order to make conclusions from it, often involving decisions for the future.

A statistical investigation

To carry out a statistical investigation, first of all decide what is the **aim** of the investigation.
Then you can decide where to obtain the data you need, whether you will collect it for yourself or whether you will find it elsewhere.
If you are collecting data for yourself, you will probably need to make a tally table on which to record it.

Example of a tally table

Weight in kg	Tally	frequency
30 to just under 40	II	2
40 to just under 50	ⅼⅼⅼ ⅼⅼⅼ	10
50 to just under 60	ⅼⅼⅼ ⅼⅼⅼ ⅼⅼⅼ ⅼⅼⅼ IIII	24
60 to just under 70	ⅼⅼⅼ ⅼⅼⅼ ⅼⅼⅼ ⅼⅼⅼ ⅼⅼⅼ ⅼⅼⅼ ⅼⅼⅼ	35
70 to just under 80	ⅼⅼⅼ ⅼⅼⅼ ⅼⅼⅼ IIII	19
80 to just under 90	ⅼⅼⅼ I	6
90 to just under 100	IIII	4
		100

When you have carried out the investigation, you should then display your information in an interesting way, so that other people can read about it. Make neat lists or tables, and include statistical diagrams.

Diagrams

You will probably want to draw some statistical diagrams. Here are the kinds of diagrams you can use.

Bar charts, pie charts, pictograms.
For frequency distributions, bar-line graphs, histograms, frequency polygons. You may also need to draw a cumulative frequency graph.
For trends, straight-line graphs (time series graphs).
For correlation or lines of best fit you would draw scatter graphs.

Here are some reminders about these types of diagrams.
N.B. Headings and some other details are not shown.

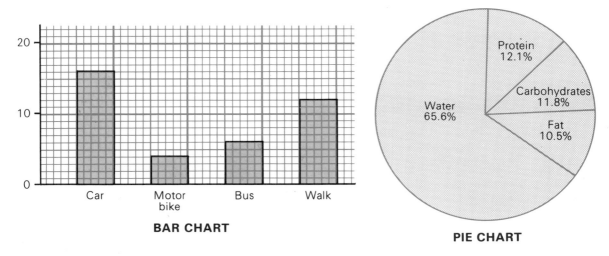

BAR CHART

PIE CHART

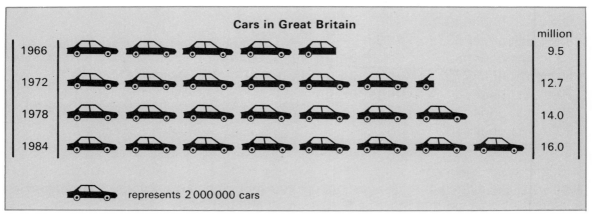

PICTOGRAM

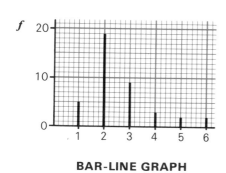

BAR-LINE GRAPH

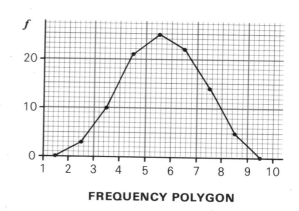

FREQUENCY POLYGON

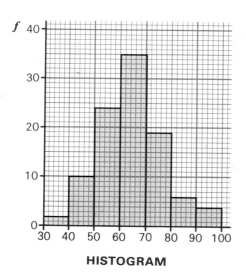

HISTOGRAM

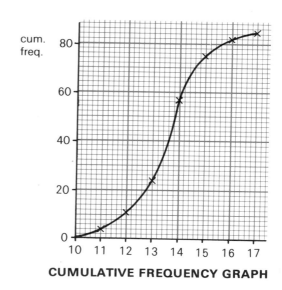

CUMULATIVE FREQUENCY GRAPH

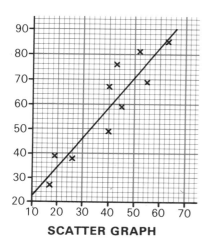

SCATTER GRAPH

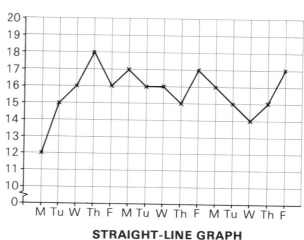

STRAIGHT-LINE GRAPH

Averages

From a set of data, you can find the 3 main averages, mean, median and mode.

Mean. $\bar{x} = \dfrac{\text{sum of the items}}{\text{number of items}} = \dfrac{\Sigma x}{n}$

Median. When the items are arranged in order of size, the median is the value of the middle item, or the value halfway between the middle two if there is an even number of items.

Mode. This is the value which occurs most often.

From a grouped frequency distribution you can find the modal class, and you can use a cumulative frequency graph to find the median.

Mean. $\bar{x} = \dfrac{\Sigma fx}{\Sigma f}$

Dispersion or spread

You can find the **range**, or for a grouped frequency distribution you can use a cumulative frequency graph to find the **interquartile range**.

The range = highest value − lowest value
The interquartile range = value of upper quartile − value of lower quartile

There is another measure of dispersion which is often used. It is called the **standard deviation**, and it is explained in Chapter 8.

Using a computer program

Nowadays there are many types of spreadsheet programs which you can use to present and analyse your data. After you have entered your data, many programs produce a variety of diagrams to illustrate the data, and will work out averages and dispersion. This is very useful, especially if you have a large amount of data.

There are some suggestions for statistical investigations in the next exercise.

Choose a topic which interests you, and carry out a statistical investigation by obtaining data and analysing it. Present your results on a poster, or in a folder, in an interesting way.

Exercise 3.2 Applications and Activities

1. **To investigate the reliability of sampling methods**

   Get a population of 30 potatoes of different sizes. (If you cannot use potatoes, then pebbles of different sizes would do.)
   Each member of the class should choose a sample of 5 which he/she thinks form a representative sample, weigh them and find the average (mean) weight. Make a list of the averages, and by grouping them in suitable classes, make a frequency distribution table, and illustrate it with a histogram.

   When everyone has done this, label the potatoes and ask everyone to choose a sample of 5 using random number tables or an equivalent method. Weigh these samples and find the average weights. List and group these averages, as before.

   Finally, weigh all the potatoes and find their average weight. This is the population mean.

   Compare the sample means with the population mean, and consider whether the first method of sampling was as reliable as the second method. Also consider how reliable a sample of 5 is for a population of 30.

   You can also investigate stratified sampling. Split the potatoes into groups of small, medium or large potatoes and choose at random from those groups. If you had 6 small, 18 medium and 6 large potatoes you would choose your 5 potatoes with 1 from the group of small ones, 3 from the group of medium ones and 1 from the group of large ones.

2. **Previous surveys**

   In past years you have probably carried out surveys using a sample of people.
   For each of these surveys, say what the aim of the investigation was.
   Say what method you used to choose your sample.
   Do you think that this was a good method ? If not, how else could you have chosen the sample ?

3. **A survey of pupils**

   Choose a topic that interests you, and carry out a survey of pupils in your school to ask them for their views.
   Decide how you can choose a representative sample.
   Design a questionnaire and carry out the survey.
   Analyse the results and comment on them.

4. **Estimation skills**

The aim of the investigation is to see whether estimation skills are improved by practice. The skill here is to estimate, by eye, the positions of mid-points of lines.

Draw 10 lines of different lengths, each an exact number of centimetres, arranged randomly on a sheet of A4 paper.
Make 2 photocopies for each person taking part in the investigation. Each person should guess, by eye, what he/she considers to be the mid-point of each line. (Do not use fingers, or pencils, or other aids, to find the mid-points. This is purely by looking.)
Mark all the mid-points in red.
Then find the mid-point of each line by measuring, using a ruler, and mark the true mid-point in blue.
The error is the difference between the red and blue marks.
Find these errors, to the nearest mm, and list them.
Find the average (mean) of the errors.

After a short break, repeat the experiment using a second sheet of paper.

List the average errors of those taking part, from sheet 1, and from sheet 2.
Analyse the results to see whether the 2nd results are better than the 1st ones.

You can plan your own experiments, in a similar way, to check estimation skills for weights, times, numbers of objects, etc.

5. **World Health**

In order to reduce infant mortality, what factors are important, and what is their relative importance ?

Here are data from a sample of countries, chosen by systematic sampling. Examine the data and make a report on it.
This data is obtained, with permission, from *The State of the World's Children* published for UNICEF by Oxford University Press.

You may prefer to obtain your own data, and include other countries, and other factors.

You may prefer to use the data to do a different investigation.

Country	A		B		C	D	E	F
	1	2	1	2				
Mali	369	284	210	164	32	31	41	15
Liberia	310	205	184	134	40	..	55	39
Tanzania	249	170	147	102	91	48	56	76
Togo	305	147	182	90	43	24	71	61
Congo	241	110	143	69	57	24	38	83
Egypt	301	85	179	61	48	13	73	..
Viet Nam	232	65	156	49	88	42	42	80
China	203	42	150	30	73	21	74	90
Malaysia	105	29	73	22	78	..	79	..
Hungary	57	16	51	15	..	..	..	..
Spain	57	10	47	8	95	..	..	..
Netherlands	21	9	18	7	..	..	..	..

A　Under 5 mortality rate per 1000 live births　　　　　A1　1960　　A2　1990
B　Infant (under 1) mortality rate per 1000 births　　　　B1　1960　　B2　1990
C　Adult literacy rate, percentage of persons over 15 who can read and write
D　Percentage of children 0-4 years who are suffering from underweight, moderate or severe
E　Percentage of population with access to safe water
F　Percentage of population with access to health service

A UNICEF programme. Village health workers are monitoring children's weights.

4 Thinking about calculating in solid

We can use trigonometry, or Pythagoras' theorem, to calculate heights, distances and angles in solid figures such as pyramids or cuboids, by using suitable triangles.

Pyramids

The Pyramids of Egypt were built between 2700 and 1900 BC as tombs for the Pharaohs. The biggest is the Great Pyramid of Cheops which has a square base of length about 228 m and height about 146 m. The sides slope at an angle of about 52°, and they face north, south, east or west.

There are also ancient pyramids in Mexico and Guatemala.

Framework of a modern building

The Kephron Pyramid in Egypt

figures

Look for mathematical figures in buildings and structures seen nowadays.

modern pyramid at the Louvre, Paris

4 Calculating in solid figures

You know some methods for calculations in right-angled triangles. Here is a reminder.

1 Pythagoras' theorem

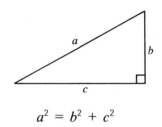

$$a^2 = b^2 + c^2$$

2 Trigonometry

$$\sin \theta = \frac{opp}{hyp}$$

$$\cos \theta = \frac{adj}{hyp}$$

$$\tan \theta = \frac{opp}{adj}$$

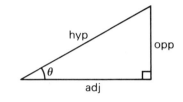

You can use these methods to calculate lengths or angles in solid figures, by taking **plane sections** which can include right-angled triangles.

Plane sections

Here are some examples.

Plane sections of a cuboid

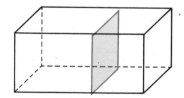

A section parallel to a face

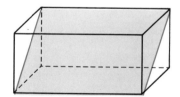

A section diagonally through two parallel edges

Plane sections of a pyramid

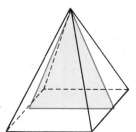
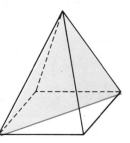

Plane sections of a cylinder

  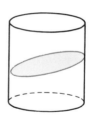

Plane sections of a cone

 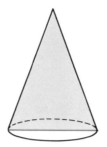 

The angle between a line and a plane

The line meets the plane at point A.
B is another point on the line.

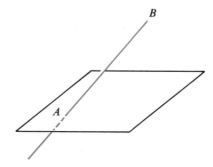

Draw a line from B, perpendicular to
the plane, to meet the plane at C.
Join AC.

AC is called the **projection** of AB on
the plane.
The angle that the line AB makes with
the plane is $\angle BAC$.

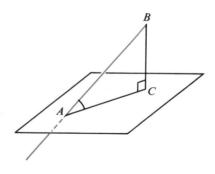

Finding lengths and angles

Examples

1   The cuboid $ABCDEFGH$ has AB = 12 cm, BC = 9 cm and CG = 8 cm. Calculate the length of the diagonal line from A to G.

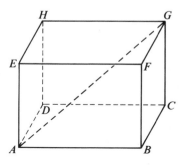

The base is a rectangle and AC can be found using $\triangle ABC$ and Pythagoras' theorem.

$AC^2 = AB^2 + BC^2$

$\qquad = 12^2 + 9^2 \qquad (AC$ in cm)$

$\qquad = 225$

$AC = 15$ cm

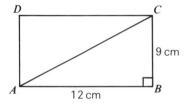

The plane section $ACGE$ is a rectangle. (Since CG is perpendicular to BC and to DC it is perpendicular to all lines on the base, including AC.)

AG can be found using $\triangle ACG$ and Pythagoras' theorem.

$AG^2 = AC^2 + CG^2$

$\qquad = 15^2 + 8^2 \qquad (AG$ in cm)$

$\qquad = 289$

$AG = 17$ cm

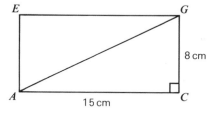

2   In the cuboid of example **1**, find the angle which AG makes with the base $ABCD$.

Since a line from G perpendicular to the base meets the base at C, the angle needed is $\angle GAC$.

In the right-angled triangle GAC,

$$\tan \angle GAC = \frac{\text{opp}}{\text{adj}}$$

$$= \frac{8}{15} \quad (=0.5333\ldots)$$

$$\angle GAC = 28.1°, \text{ to 1 dec. pl.}$$

(It is necessary to find the length of AC, first, as in example **1**. By calculating AG also, you could use the sine ratio or the cosine ratio instead of the tangent ratio, if you prefer to.)

3 $VABCD$ is a pyramid with a square base $ABCD$ and vertex V. The diagonals of the square, AC and BD, intersect at H and VH is perpendicular to the base. $AB = 10\,\text{cm}$ and $VH = 13\,\text{cm}$. Find the size of $\angle VMH$, where M is the mid-point of BC. (This is the angle between the plane VBC and the base.)

To find $\angle VMH$ use the right-angled triangle VMH.

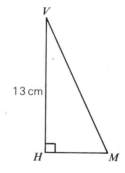

To find HM use the square $ABCD$. $AB = 10\,\text{cm}$ so $HM = 5\,\text{cm}$.

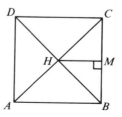

In $\triangle VMH$,

$$\tan \angle VMH = \frac{\text{opp}}{\text{adj}}$$

$$= \frac{13}{5} \quad (=2.6)$$

$$\angle VMH = 69.0°, \text{ to 1 dec. pl.}$$

4   In the pyramid of example **3**, find the angle which *VB* makes with the base.

VH is the perpendicular from *V* to the base, so the angle is ∠*VBH*.

First, we need to find the length of *HB*.
Using Δ*BHM* in the diagram of the square *ABCD*,
and Pythagoras' theorem,

$HB^2 = HM^2 + MB^2$

$\qquad = 5^2 + 5^2 \qquad (HB$ in cm$)$

$\qquad = 50$

$HB = \sqrt{50}$ cm

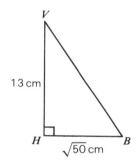

(Unless you are asked to find the length of *HB* it is sufficient to know that it is $\sqrt{50}$ cm.)

In Δ*VAB*,

$\tan \angle VBH = \dfrac{\text{opp}}{\text{adj}}$

$\qquad\qquad = \dfrac{13}{\sqrt{50}}$

Press 13 ÷ 50 √ = inv. tan

$\angle VBH = 61.5°$, to 1 dec. pl.

Note that ∠*VBH* is less than ∠*VMH*.

Exercise 4.1

Give approximate lengths correct to the nearest mm and angles correct to 1 decimal place.

1.   In the diagram, *ABCDEFGH* is a cuboid.
    AB = 16 cm, *BC* = 12 cm, *CG* = 5 cm.
    1   Find the lengths of *AC* and *AG*.
    2   Find the angle which *AF* makes
         with the base *ABCD*.
    3   Find the angle which *AG* makes
         with the base.

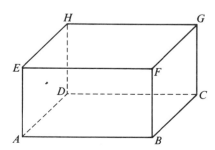

2. *ACBD* is a pyramid which has a
    horizontal base and its vertex
    at *D*. *DA* is perpendicular to
    the base *ABC*. *AB* = *AC* = 7 cm,
    ∠*BAC* = 90° and *DA* = 24 cm.
    E is the mid-point of *BC*.
    Find

    1   the length of *DB*,
    2   the length of *DE*,
    3   the angle between *DB* and the base,
    4   the angle between *DE* and the base.

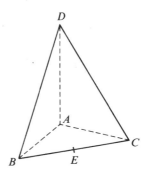

3. *VABCDEF* is a pyramid with vertex *V*
    and horizontal base *ABCDEF* which is
    a regular hexagon with sides of
    length 10 cm.
    The slant edges through *V* are all
    20 cm long. *N* is the point vertically
    below *V* and is the centre of symmetry
    of the hexagon.

    1   State the length of *AN*.
    2   Find the length of *MN*, where *M* is
            the mid-point of *AB*.
    3   Find the vertical height of the
            pyramid.
    4   Find the angle between the face *VAB* and
            the base, i.e. ∠*VMN*.
    5   Find the angle between the edge *VA* and the base.

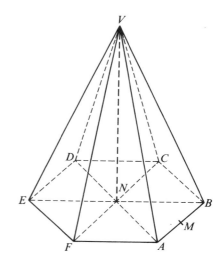

4. The diagram shows a prism with a
    rectangular base *BCFE* which is
    on a horizontal plane, and with
    vertical ends *ABC* and *DEF*, which
    are congruent equilateral
    triangles. *BC* = 8 cm and
    CF = 15 cm. *M* is the mid-point
    of *EF*.
    Find

    1   the length of *DM*,
    2   the length of *DC*,
    3   the angle between the line *DC* and the base.

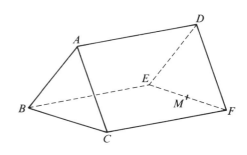

5.   In the diagram, **VABCD** is a pyramid
     on a square base **ABCD**, with vertex
     V vertically above N. **AB** = 8 cm,
     VN = 7 cm. **M** is the mid-point of **AB**.
     1   Find the length of **VM**.
     2   Find the angle which **VM** makes
            with the base.
     3   Find the length of **VA**.
     4   Find the angle which **VA** makes
            with the base.

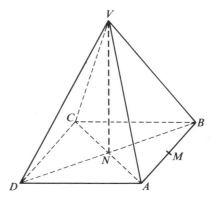

6.   Use the same diagram as in question 5, with measurements **AB** = 10 cm and
     ∠**VMN** = 60°.
     1   Find the height **VN**.
     2   Find the length of **VA**.
     3   Find the angle which **VA** makes with the base.

Exercise 4.2   Applications and Activities

1.   **ABCD** is a rectangular lawn, on level
     ground, and **CE** is a vertical flagpole.
     AB = 60 m and **BC** = 25 m. The angle
     of elevation of the top of the flagpole
     from A, ∠**EAC**, is 6°.
     Find
     1   the length of **AC**,
     2   the height, **CE**, of the flagpole,
     3   the angle of elevation of the
            top of the flagpole from **D**.

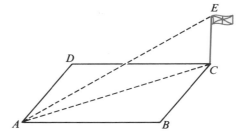

2.   From a point A on the top of a cliff
     80 m high two boats, **B** and **C**, can be seen.
     B is due east at an angle of depression
     of 36°, and C is due south at an
     angle of depression of 48°. **D** is the
     point vertically below A at the edge
     of the sea.
     Find the lengths of **DB** and **DC**, and hence
     find the distance between the boats.

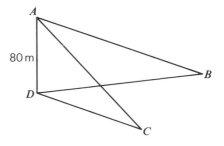

3. The diagram shows the top part of a
    square church tower. *ABCD* is a
    horizontal square with sides 6 m long.
    Each sloping surface makes an angle
    of 50° with the horizontal, i.e.
    ∠ *VMN* = 50°.
    Find

    1   the height of the tip, *V*, above
            ABCD,

    2   the length of the sloping edge *VA*,

    3   the inclination of *VA* to the horizontal.

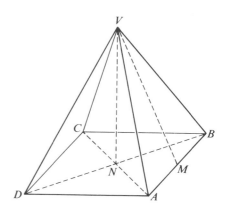

4. Alan is at point *A* and sees a balloon *B*
    due east of him at an angle of
    elevation of 42°.
    The balloon is at a height of 600 m.
    Chris is at point *C*, and at the
    same time he sees the balloon
    due north of him at an angle of
    elevation of 22°.
    If *D* is the point on the ground vertically below the
    balloon, and *A*, *D* and *C* are on level ground, find
    the distances *AD* and *DC*.
    If Chris wants to walk directly to Alan, how far
    must he walk, and on what bearing ?

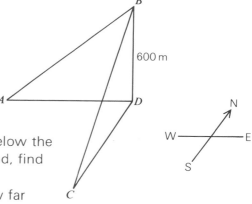

5. The diagram shows the net
    of a box with a rectangular
    horizontal base *BEKN*,
    vertical sides, and a sloping
    lid.

    1   Which points meet with
            point *A* when the box is constructed ?

    2   State the lengths of *AB*,
            EF and *FG*.

    3   When the box is constructed,
            find the angle which the
            line *EM* makes with the base
            of the box.

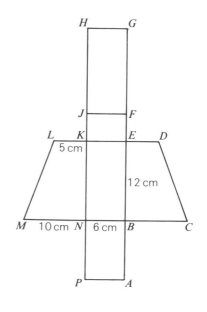

6. A vertical pole *AB*, 5 m tall, stands
    on horizontal ground. The pole is
    supported by four equal wires from
    the top of the pole to corners
    P, Q, R, S of a square of side 6 m
    on the ground.
    Find
    1   the distance *BP*,
    2   the length of each wire,
    3   the angle between two adjacent wires,
    4   the angle each wire makes with the ground.

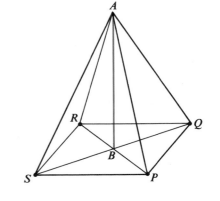

7. A thin stick *AB*, 80 cm long, stands
    slantwise in the corner of a room,
    with its top end, *B*, in the angle
    between two walls. The end, *A*, of
    the stick on the floor is 18 cm from
    one wall and 24 cm from the other
    wall forming the corner.
    Find the angle made by the stick
    with the line *BC*.

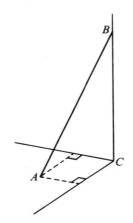

8. *ABCDEFGH* is a rectangular room.
    AB = 6 m, *BC* = 5 m, *CG* = 4 m.
    Temporary wiring is to be
    stretched between *A* and *G*.
    What length of wire is needed
    if it goes directly across the
    room from *A* to *G* ?

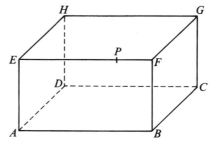

Instead, it is decided to run the wire along the walls of the room. One route is *A*
to *P* and then along the ceiling from *P* to *G*. If *P* is the point on *EF* such that
the distance *AP* + *PG* is as small as possible, find this distance. (It will help to
draw part of the net of the cuboid.)

Similarly, find the least distance going via a point on *BF*, and also the least
distance going via a point on *EH*. Which of these 3 routes uses the least length
of wire ?

9. The diagram shows a triangular field
    ABC on horizontal ground, with a
    right angle at **B**. **AB** = 48 m and
    BC = 14 m.
    CD is a tree at the corner of the
    field. From **A**, the angle of
    elevation of the top, **D**, of the
    tree is 9°.
    Find the height of the tree.

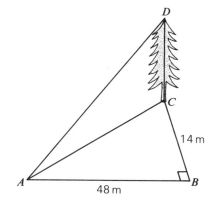

10. **A** and **B** are two radar stations,
    both at sea-level, 6 km apart,
    with **A** due north of **B**.
    An object **C** is observed
    simultaneously from **A** and **B**. It
    is due east of **A** at an angle of
    elevation of 25°.
    From **B** it lies on a bearing of
    055°.
    D is the point at sea-level vertically below **C**.
    Find

    1   the distance **AD**,
    2   the distance **BD**,
    3   the height of **C** above the sea,
    4   the angle of elevation of **C** from **B**.

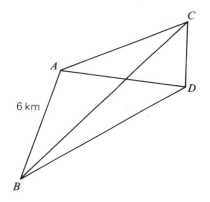

PUZZLE

8. The diagram represents a system of cogwheels that are meshed together. The number on
    each wheel shows how many teeth it has.
    If wheel **A** is revolved 10 times clockwise, how many times will wheel **F** revolve, and will
    it turn clockwise or anticlockwise ?

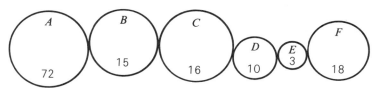

5 Thinking about functions, equations

Graphs of functions

The volume of water in a hemispherical bowl of diameter 20 cm is $\frac{\pi x^2}{3}$ $(30 - x)$ cm^3, when the depth of water is x cm. What is the depth of water when the bowl contains 1 litre ?

How can you find the answer using graphs ?

If you find an approximate solution from a graph, how can you then obtain a more accurate solution ?

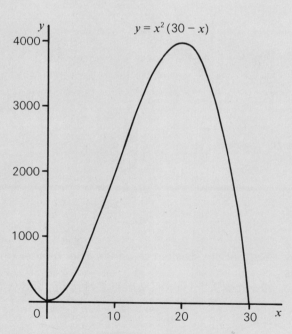

Using the graph of $y = x^2(30 - x)$

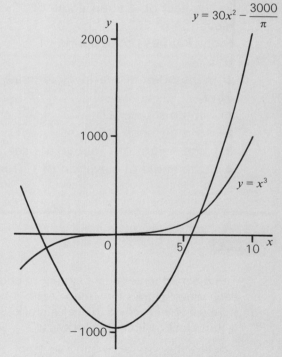

Using the graphs of $y = x^3$ and $y = 3x^2 - \dfrac{3000}{\pi}$

and graphs

The sine and cosine functions

You are familiar with waves. As well as waves in the sea, there are light waves, sound waves, radio waves and many others.
The functions $y = \sin x°$ and $y = \cos x°$, and many related functions, give graphs of wave form.

To produce these graphs using a graphics calculator, press

graph sin EXE or

graph cos EXE

The sine and cosine functions are very important functions which are used in many different situations by mathematicians, scientists and engineers.

The tides

The rise and fall of the sea has always been of importance to sailors, fishermen and other people living near the sea. The depth of water has a sine or cosine equation, and it reaches a maximum depth twice a day, approximately every 12 hours and 25 minutes.

ont St. Michel, in Normandy. It is said that the tide in e bay comes in faster than a horse can gallop.

JUNE ● TIDES

Day	Date	High Tide am	High Tide pm	Low Tide am	Low Tide pm
Sat	1	04 07	04 34	10 40	11 00
Sun	2	04 57	05 23	11 26	11 47
Mon	3	05 47	06 09	** **	00 13
Tues	4	06 35	06 57	00 34	00 58
Wed	5	07 21	07 45	01 22	01 44
Thurs	6	08 09	08 31	02 09	02 29
Fri	7	08 56	09 18	02 59	03 15
Sat	8	09 44	10 09	03 47	04 03
Sun	9	10 34	11 03	04 39	04 55
Mon	10	11 32	** **	05 37	05 59
Tues	11	00 03	00 38	06 42	07 10
Wed	12	01 10	01 47	07 48	08 18
Thurs	13	02 12	02 45	08 47	09 14
Fri	14	03 05	03 34	09 35	09 59
Sat	15	03 52	04 15	10 18	10 38
Sun	16	04 34	04 54	10 56	11 16
Mon	17	05 12	05 30	11 31	11 52
Tues	18	05 49	06 05	** **	00 07
Wed	19	06 26	06 42	00 27	00 43
Thurs	20	07 04	07 20	01 05	01 21
Fri	21	07 45	08 00	01 45	02 00
Sat	22	08 28	08 45	02 27	02 44
Sun	23	09 12	09 33	03 14	03 29
Mon	24	10 04	10 27	04 05	04 24

5 Functions, equations and graphs

Functions

If a set of values, x, is connected to another set of values, y, and for each value of x there is only one value of y, then y is said to be a function of x.

The symbol $f(x)$ means 'function of x' so $y = f(x)$.
Other functions can be identified as $g(x)$, $h(x)$, etc.

A function can be represented by ordered pairs of numbers.
e.g. (1, 1), (2, 4), (3, 9), (4, 16).
The 1st number of each pair is the value of x, the 2nd number is the value of y.

A function can be represented by a mapping diagram.
e.g.

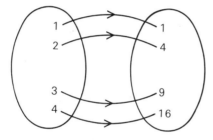

A function can be represented by a table.

e.g.

x	1	2	3	4
y	1	4	9	16

A function can be represented by an equation. The equation for this function is $y = x^2$.
It could also be written as $f(x) = x^2$.
The notation $f : x \mapsto x^2$ can also be used. This is read as 'the function f such that x is mapped onto x^2'.

Using f(x) notation

$f(-1)$ means the value of $f(x)$ when $x = -1$.
e.g. If $f(x) = x^2 + 1$, $f(-1) = (-1)^2 + 1 = 2$

$$f(0) \ \dot= \ 0^2 + 1 = 1$$
$$f(5) \ = \ 5^2 + 1 = 26$$

and so on.

$f(2x)$ means the function related to $f(x)$, with x replaced by $2x$.
If $f(x) = x^2 + 1$, $f(2x) = (2x)^2 + 1 = 4x^2 + 1$

$f(x - 3)$ means the function related to $f(x)$ with x replaced by $x - 3$.
If $f(x) = x^2 + 1$, $f(x - 3) = (x - 3)^2 + 1 = x^2 - 6x + 10$

If the values of x are continuous, the function can
be represented by its graph.
This is the graph of $y = x^2$.

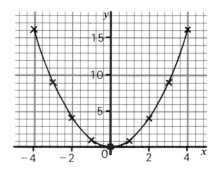

Solving equations using graphs of functions

One method of finding the solution to an equation is to draw a graph of a related
function.

Examples

1   The equation $x^2 - 8x + 10 = 0$ can be solved by drawing the graph of the function
    $y = x^2 - 8x + 10$ and finding the values of x where $y = 0$, that is, where the graph
    cuts the x-axis.

    The same equation can also be solved by drawing the graph of the function
    $y = x^2 - 8x$ and finding the values of x where $y = -10$, since if $x^2 - 8x = -10$,
    then $x^2 - 8x + 10 = 0$.

    The same equation can also be solved by drawing the graphs of the functions
    $y = x^2$ and $y = 8x - 10$. Where these graphs intersect, $x^2 = 8x - 10$,
    i.e. $x^2 - 8x + 10 = 0$.

    There are 2 solutions. They are not integers, so from the graph they could be found
    correct to 1 decimal place, and possibly an estimate of a 2nd decimal place can be
    made. Then trial and improvement methods can be used if more accurate solutions
    are needed. Later, you will learn a formula which you can use to solve quadratic
    equations. However, for cubic equations a graphical method is often necessary.

    You can use the methods above for yourself and check that they all give the same
    2 solutions for x. These solutions can be called the **roots** of the equation.

In each graph, label the x-axis from 0 to 8.
For the graph of $y = x^2 - 8x + 10$, label the y-axis from -6 to 10.
For the graph of $y = x^2 - 8x$, label the y-axis from -16 to 0.

For the graphs of $y = x^2$ and
$y = 8x - 10$, label the y-axis
from -10 to 70.
Here is a sketch graph of this
one, with dotted lines from the
points of intersection to the
x-axis, to read off the
solutions.

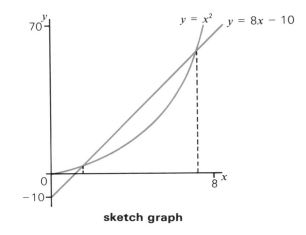

sketch graph

A quadratic equation has either two real solutions, or one, or none. If a line just
touches the curve in one point then the equation is said to have a repeated root.
(There are two solutions but both are the same.)
The line may not meet the curve at all. In that case there are no real solutions.

2 Solve the equation $x^3 = 13x - 9$

1st method
The equation can be solved by drawing the graph of $y = x^3 - 13x + 9$ and finding
the values of x where $y = 0$, since if $x^3 - 13x + 9 = 0$, $x^3 = 13x - 9$.

Copy and complete the table of values for $y = x^3 - 13x + 9$

x	-4	-3	-2	-1	0	1	2	3	4
x^3	-64								
$-13x$	$+52$								
$+9$	$+9$								
y	-3								

Draw the x-axis from -4 to 4 and the y-axis from -10 to 30.
Plot the points and draw the graph.
Find the values of x where $y = 0$, i.e. where the graph cuts the x-axis. Give these
solutions to 1 decimal place.

2nd method

The equation can be solved by drawing the graph of $y = x^3 - 13x$ and finding the values of x where the graph cuts the line $y = -9$.
This graph is similar to the 1st one.
For each value of x, the y-value is 9 less than before.
You could draw the y-axis from -20 to 20, and find the values of x where $y = -9$, since if $x^3 - 13x = -9$, then $x^3 = 13x - 9$.

3rd method

The equation can be solved by drawing the graphs of $y = x^3$ and $y = 13x - 9$ and finding where these intersect.

Draw the x-axis from -4 to 4 and
the y-axis from -70 to 70.
Use the first 2 lines of the previous
table of values to find the points
to plot for $y = x^3$, and
draw the curve.
Find the values of y when
$x = -4$, 0 and 4 for the
straight-line graph of
$y = 13x - 9$,
plot the three points and draw
the line.
Find the points of intersection
of the curve and the line, and
draw dotted lines to the x-axis
to read off the solutions.

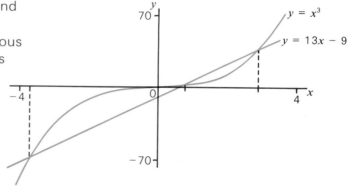

sketch graph

A cubic equation can have 3 real solutions, 2 if the line just touches the curve at one of the points, or 1 only.

3 Which equations are solved by drawing these graphs and finding the values of x at the points of intersection ?

(a) $y = x^3$ and $y = x^2 + 4$
(b) $y = x^3$ and $y = 2x - 9$
(c) $y = 2x^2$ and $y = x + 3$

(a) $x^3 = x^2 + 4$ or $x^3 - x^2 - 4 = 0$
(b) $x^3 = 2x - 9$ or $x^3 - 2x + 9 = 0$
(c) $2x^2 = x + 3$ or $2x^2 - x - 3 = 0$

Using a computer or graphics calculator

If you have the use of a computer then you probably have a graph-plotting program which you can use to plot various graphs of functions. You could also use a graphics calculator, although the graphs are shown much smaller than on a computer screen. One use of plotting the graphs on the computer screen or calculator is so that you can see the general shape of the graph. If you need to find roots of equations from the points of intersection of 2 graphs, you can see where these roots are, approximately. By zooming into an area around a root, or by re-scaling axes to draw that area to a larger scale, you can get a more accurate value for the root. The trace facility will help you to find approximate values of x and y at a point of intersection. This is equivalent to using trial and improvement methods algebraically.

It is also useful to use a computer or calculator to check graphs you have drawn, and the roots of equations you have found.

Exercise 5.1

1. Show these functions for values of x: $-1, 0, 1, 2, 3$, on mapping diagrams, or as ordered pairs.

    1 $f(x) = 3x^2 - 2$

    2 $f(x) = \dfrac{1}{x + 5}$

    3 $f(x) = x(x - 3)(x + 1)$

2. For the function $f(x) = x^2 - 3x$, find the values of $f(0)$, $f(10)$, $f(-2)$, and find expressions for $f(3x)$ and $f(x + 1)$ in their simplest forms.

3. Which equations are solved by drawing these graphs and finding their points of intersection ?

    1 $y = \dfrac{1}{x}$ and $y = 5 - 2x$

    2 $y = x^3$ and $y = 2x^2 + 1$

    Using the graph of $y = 3x^2$, what other graph should be drawn in order to use the graphs to solve these equations ?

    3 $3x^2 - x + 2 = 0$

    4 $x^3 - 3x^2 - 1 = 0$

4. Draw the graph of $y = x^2$ for values of x from -4 to 4, and labelling the y-axis from -4 to 16.

    1 Use your graph to find the solutions of the equation $x^2 = 3$.

    2 Using the same axes, draw the line $4y = 12 - 7x$, and find the values of x at the points where it intersects the curve.
    State the equation which is satisfied by these values of x, and rearrange it into the form $ax^2 + bx + c = 0$, where a, b and c are integers.

    3 By drawing another line on the same axes, use the curve and that line to solve the equation $x^2 - 2x - 2 = 0$.

5. Draw the graph of $y = x^2$ for values of x from -2 to 6, and labelling the y-axis from -10 to 40.

    1 Use the graph to find the positive solution of the equation $2x^2 = 55$.

    2 Using the same axes, draw the line $y = 20 - 5x$, and find the value of x at the point where it intersects the curve.
    State the equation for which this value of x is one of the roots and rearrange it into the form $ax^2 + bx + c = 0$.

    3 By drawing another line on the same axes, use the curve and that line to solve the equation $2x^2 - 5x - 10 = 0$.

6. Draw the graph of $y = x^3$ for values of x from -4 to 4 and labelling the y-axis from -70 to 70.

    1 Use the graph to find the solution of the equation $x^3 = 50$.

    2 Using the same axes, draw the line $y = 10x$, and find the values of x at the points where it intersects the curve.
    State the equation which is satisfied by these values of x.

    3 By drawing another line on the same axes, use the curve and that line to solve the equation $x^3 + 20x + 60 = 0$.

7. **1** Draw the graph of $y = x^3$ for values of x from -4 to 4 and labelling the y-axis from -70 to 90.

    2 On the same axes draw the graph of $y = 90 - 10x^2$, and find the values of x at the points where the graphs intersect.
    State the equation for which these values of x are 2 of the roots.
    There is another root of this equation. Will it be negative or positive?

8.   **1**   Draw the graph of $y = \dfrac{12}{x}$ for values of x from 1 to 8, labelling the x-axis
            from 0 to 10 and the y-axis from 0 to 12.
     2   On the same axes draw the graph of $y = 10 - x$, and find the values of x at
            the points where it intersects the curve.
            State the equation which is satisfied by these values of x and rearrange it in
            the form $ax^2 + bx + c = 0$, where a, b and c are integers, and a is positive.

9.   Draw the graphs of $y = x^2 - 3x - 3$ and $y = 2 - x$, for values of x from -2 to 4.
     Label the y-axis from -6 to 8.

     Use the graphs to find the solutions of
     1 $x^2 - 3x - 3 = 0$,
     2 $x^2 - 2x - 5 = 0$.

Trigonometrical functions

You have used the trigonometrical ratios, $\sin \theta°$, $\cos \theta°$ and $\tan \theta°$ in right-angled
triangles, and probably drawn the graphs of these functions for values of θ from 0 to
90.

However, these functions have uses other than in right-angled triangles, and we need
to define them for angles of any size.

We will give the definitions later, but now we will use a calculator to find the values of
the functions.

Examples

$$\sin 100° = 0.9848$$
$$\cos 150° = -0.8660$$
$$\tan 220° = 0.8391$$
$$\sin (-70°) = -0.9397 \qquad \text{Press 70 } \boxed{^+/_-}\ \boxed{\sin}$$
$$\cos 500° = -0.7660$$
$$\tan 600° = 1.7321$$

All these have been written to 4 decimal places.

In a similar way you can find the values of the trigonometrical functions of any sizes of
angles, except for $\tan \theta°$ when θ is 90 or any odd multiple of 90, positive or negative.

You cannot do the operations in reverse. If you know that sin $\theta°$ = 0.9848 and use the inverse sine key on your calculator it will give you an acute angle.

You may think that it is strange to have a negative angle.
Think of a machine which rotates. If it goes one way you can measure the angle of turning as positive, and the other way as negative.

In Mathematics we measure the angles from the x-axis and we take the anticlockwise direction as positive and the clockwise direction as negative.
(Do not confuse this with bearings which do not follow the mathematical system. There the direction is clockwise and the angles are measured from the north.)

Positive direction of turning

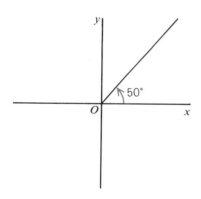

The angle is 50°

Negative direction of turning

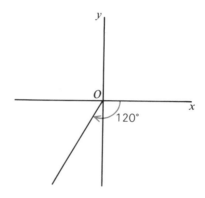

The angle is −120°

Instead of just relying on your calculator to find isolated values of trig. functions, it would be useful to get a general idea of these functions, and draw their graphs.

To draw the graph of y = sin $x°$
for values of x from 0 to 360.

On the x-axis, label from 0 to 360, using a scale of 2 cm to 45.
On the y-axis, label from −1 to 1 using a scale of 4 cm to 1 unit, so that each small 2 mm square represents 0.05.

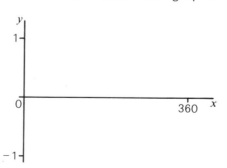

First, plot the points for x from 0 to 90, finding the y-values on your calculator.
y-values for x = 9, 18, 27, . . . , 90 will do. Draw this part of the curve.
Now continue finding y-values for x = 99, 108, 117, . . . , to 180.
What do you notice ?
Draw this part of the curve.

Now continue finding y-values for $x = 189, 198, \ldots$, to 270, and then to 360.
What do you notice ?
Draw the rest of the curve.
Describe the curve you have drawn and describe some of the things you notice
about it.

You can draw the graph of $y = \cos x°$, in a similar way.

Do not draw this on the same axes, it is best drawn separately.
Now compare the graphs of $y = \sin x°$ and $y = \cos x°$ and see what you can notice
about them.

The graph of $y = \tan x°$ is rather different.

Use the same scale as before for x, from 0 to 360.
On the y-axis, label from -5 to 5 using a scale of 2 cm to 1 unit, so that each small
square represents 0.1.
Again, plot the points for x from 0 to 90 first, using values 0, 9, 18, ... You can get as
far as 72, and then 76.5, before the y-values get too big to plot. Draw this part of
the curve.
Next, it is best to go to $x = 180$, and draw the part of the curve between $x = 180$
and 270.
Then, start at 180 and go backwards with $x = 171, 162, \ldots$ until, again, the y-values
go off the graph.
Finally, start at 360 and go backwards towards 270, and draw the rest of the curve.
It is not a continuous curve. It has breaks at 90 and 270.
Describe some of the things you notice about the curve.

You may like to continue this work by drawing the graphs again, using more values for
x, including negative values, and using smaller scales. Alternatively, you may like to
produce these graphs using a graphics calculator or a computer.
If you do not do this, it is important that you know what these graphs look like, so
sketch graphs are given here, and you should copy these.

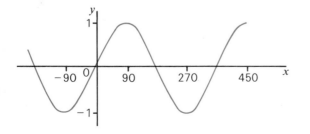

$$y = \sin x°$$

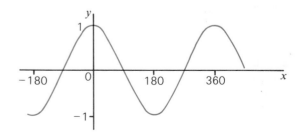

$$y = \cos x°$$

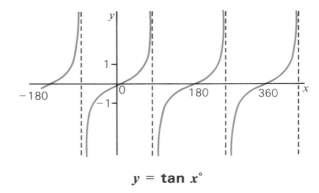

$$y = \textbf{tan } x°$$

Sketch graphs of related functions

Here is a sketch graph of $y = \cos x°$ for x from 0 to 360.

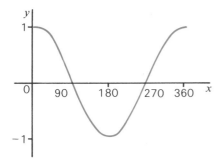

To draw the graph of $y = 2 \cos x°$, every y-value of the graph of $y = \cos x°$ will be multiplied by 2.

Make a table of values to help you.

x	$\cos x°$	$2 \cos x°$
0	1	2
90	0	0
180	−1	−2
270	0	0
360	1	2

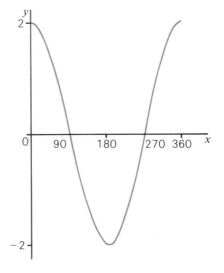

$$y = \textbf{2 cos } x°$$

To draw the graph of $y = 1 + \cos x°$,
every y-value of the graph of
$y = \cos x°$ will have 1 added on.

Make a table of values to help you.

x	$\cos x°$	$1 + \cos x°$
0	1	2
90	0	1
180	−1	0
270	0	1
360	1	2

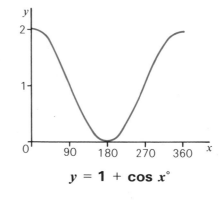

$y = \mathbf{1 + \cos} \, x°$

The graph of $y = -\cos x°$ is the
reflection of the graph of $y = \cos x°$
in the x-axis.

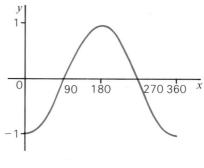

$y = \mathbf{-\cos} \, x°$

To draw the graph of $y = 1 - \cos x°$,
first draw the graph of $y = -\cos x°$,
then add 1 to every y-value.

x	$\cos x°$	$1 - \cos x°$
0	1	0
90	0	1
180	−1	2
270	0	1
360	1	0

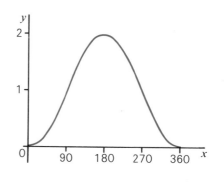

$y = \mathbf{1 - \cos} \, x°$

Exercise 5.2

1. **1** Draw accurately the graph of $y = 5 \cos x°$ for x from 0 to 360.
    Take a scale of 2 cm to 50 on the x-axis, and label from -5 to 5 on the
    y-axis, using a scale of 1 cm to 1 unit.

    2 Draw the line $y = 4$ on your graph.
    Find the solutions of the equation $5 \cos x° = 4$, giving the solutions to the
    nearest 5.

    3 Use your calculator to solve $5 \cos x° = 4$. This will give $x°$ as an acute angle.
    Write this answer correct to the nearest integer, and comparing the answer
    with part **2**, deduce what the other solution is, correct to the nearest integer.

    4 Draw the line $100y + x = 200$ on the same graph and find the values of x at
    the points where the line intersects the curve, giving the answers to the
    nearest 5.
    Show why these are solutions of the equation $500 \cos x° = 200 - x$.

2. **1** Sketch the graph of $y = \sin x°$ for x from 0 to 360.
    Making tables of values for $x = 0, 90, 180, 270, 360$ to help you, and using your
    first sketch also, make sketch graphs of these functions:
    2 $y = 10 \sin x°$
    3 $y = -10 \sin x°$
    4 $y = 10 + 10 \sin x°$
    5 $y = 10 - 10 \sin x°$

3. **1** Sketch the graph of $y = \tan x°$ from $x = 0$ to 360.
    2 Draw the line on your sketch which you would use to find the values of x for
    which $\tan x° = 3$.
    3 Find the solution between 0 and 90, to the nearest whole number, for x
    when $\tan x° = 3$, using your calculator.
    4 Using your sketch, deduce the value of another solution for $\tan x° = 3$.

4. Sketch the graph of $y = 2 \cos x°$ for $x = 0$ to 360. Label the y-axis on your
    sketch from -3 to 3.
    On the same axes, sketch the graph of $y = 2 \cos x° + 1$.
    Show that there are 2 values of x which satisfy the equation $\cos x° = -\frac{1}{2}$, in the
    range from 0 to 360.
    Find one solution using your calculator, and use your sketch to deduce the other
    solution.

5. Copy and complete the table of values for the graph of $y = \sin 3x°$, giving
    approximate values of y correct to 2 decimal places.

x	0	10	20	30	40	50	60
$3x$	0	30					
y	0	0.5					

Draw the graph of $y = \sin 3x°$ for x from 0 to 60, and use your graph to find two
solutions of the equation $\sin 3x° = 0.6$.

Exercise 5.3   Applications and Activities

1. Draw the graphs of $y = x^3$ and $y = 12x - 8$ for values of x from -4 to 4.
    Label the y-axis from -70 to 70.
    Use the graphs to find the solutions of the equation $x^3 - 12x + 8 = 0$, correct to
    1 decimal place.

    Draw new axes with x labelled from 0 to 1, using a scale of 1 cm to 0.1 unit, and
    y labelled from -8 to 4, using a scale of 1 cm to 1 unit.

    Draw the graph of $y = x^3$ for values of x from 0 to 1, plotting points at intervals
    of 0.1. Also draw the graph of $y = 12x - 8$ between $x = 0$ and $x = 1$.
    Use the graphs to find one root of the equation $x^3 - 12x + 8 = 0$, correct to 2
    decimal places.

2. A wire 6 m long is cut into 2 pieces, each of which is then bent to form a circular
    hoop. If one piece is x m long, show that the sum of the areas enclosed by the
    hoops is $\dfrac{x^2 - 6x + 18}{2\pi}$ m².

    Write down an equation to be satisfied if the sum of the areas is to be $\dfrac{6}{\pi}$ m², and
    simplify it.

    Draw the graph of $y = x^2$ for values of x from 0 to 6. Label the y-axis from -10
    to 40.
    Also draw a straight line graph such that the points of intersection of the 2
    graphs give the roots of the equation.
    Find the lengths into which the wire is cut.

3. Draw the graph of $y = x^2$ for values of x from -1 to 4, and the graph of $y = \dfrac{16}{x}$

    for values of x from 1 to 4.
    Label the y-axis from 0 to 16.
    Use the graphs to find the value of $\sqrt[3]{16}$.

4. A cricket ball is thrown vertically upwards from a point A, which is 10 m above
    the ground. The height above A of the ball t seconds after it is thrown is s m,
    where s and t are connected by the equation $s = 10t - 5t^2$.

    Draw the graph of $s = t^2$ for t from 0 to 3, plotting points at intervals of 0.5. Label
    the s-axis from 0 to 9.

    Write down an equation to be satisfied when the ball hits the ground.
    Draw a straight-line graph such that the point of intersection of the two graphs
    gives the root of the equation.
    Find the time at which the ball hits the ground.

5. Sketch the graph of $y = \cos x°$ for values of x from 0 to 90, labelling the y-axis
    from 0 to 2.
    On the same diagram, sketch the graph of $y = \tan x°$ for x from 0 to 60.
    ($\tan 60° = 1.73$.)
    Show that there is a solution of the equation $\cos x° = \tan x°$ for x between 0
    and 45.
    Draw accurately the parts of
    these graphs between $x = 30$
    and $x = 45$, using a scale of
    1 cm to 1 unit on the x-axis
    and labelling y from 0.5 to
    1 using a scale of 2 cm to
    0.1 unit.
    Find the value of x for which
    $\cos x° = \tan x°$.

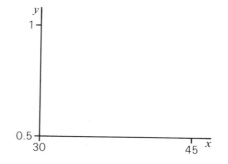

6. The height, y m, of the tide in a harbour above the lowest level is given by the
    equation $y = 2 - 2 \cos 30t°$, where t is the time in hours after low tide.
    Sketch a graph showing the height
    for 24 hours after low tide.
    What is the increase in depth
    of the water between low and
    high tides ?

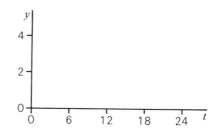

7.   A particle is moving so that t seconds after it started its coordinates (x, y) are
      such that $x = 2 + 6 \cos t°$ and $y = 6 \sin t°$.
      Copy and complete the table of values for x and y, giving approximate values to
      2 decimal places.

t	0	30	60	90	120	150	180
$\cos t°$	1	0.87					
$6 \cos t°$	6	5.20					
x	8	7.20					
$\sin t°$	0	0.5					
y	0	3.0					

Draw the x-axis from -4 to 8 and the y axis from 0 to 6, using equal scales on both
axes.
Plot the points showing the path of the particle. The 1st point is (8, 0) and the 2nd
point is (7.20, 3)
Describe the path of the particle.
Find the distance of the particle from the origin at the point where it crosses the
y-axis.

8.   Copy and complete the table of values for the graph of $y = \cos x° + 2 \sin x°$.

x	0	10	20	30	40	50	60	70	80	90
$\cos x°$	1	0.98								
$2 \sin x°$	0	0.35								
y	1	1.33								

Draw the graph of $y = \cos x° + 2 \sin x°$, taking a scale of 2 cm to 10 units on the x-axis
and labelling y from 0 to 3 taking a scale of 2 cm to 1 unit.
Use the graph to find the maximum value of y in this range, and the value of x for
which this maximum value occurs.
Also use the graph to find the solution of the equation $2 \cos x° + 4 \sin x° = 3$.

PUZZLES

9. Iqbal knows that the new term begins in September but he cannot remember the date. He is told by five friends that term starts on a date which
    (a) is a multiple of 3,
    (b) is before the 18th,
    (c) is an odd number,
    (d) is after his birthday (which is on 13th September),
    (e) is not a square number.

    However, of these 5 statements, only one is true.
    When does the new term begin ?

10. Mrs Wilson keeps ducks and hens. She says that if she had got 5 times as many ducks or 3 times as many hens she would have 70 in all.
    How many of each does she have ?

11. There is a certain 4-figure number that is a square number, the 1st digit is a square, the 2nd digit is a square and the last 2 digits form a square. The 1st and last digits form a square and this square added to the 2nd digit is also a square. The sum of the 1st, 2nd and 4th digits is a square, as is also the number formed by these digits in that order, or in the order of 1st, 4th and 2nd digits, or in that order reversed. Another square is formed by the 3rd, 4th and 1st digits in order, and its square root is the 1st two digits of the number.
    What is the number ?

12. Two clocks in my house were not very accurate. One of them went 2 minutes per hour too slow and the other went 3 minutes per hour too fast. I put them both right at noon and when I looked at them again, the faster one was exactly one hour ahead of the slower one.
    What was the correct time then ?

13. Four men, Norman, Peter, Robert, Sam, and their wives Nora, Pamela, Rhona, Sally, went shopping. Nora spent £10, Pamela spent £20, Rhona spent £30 and Sally spent £40.

    Norman spent the same amount as his wife.
    Peter spent twice as much as his wife.
    Robert spent three times as much as his wife.
    Sam spent four times as much as his wife.
    Three of the men spent the same amount.

    Who was married to Rhona ?

14. Using the digits 1 to 9 once each, make up two numbers which multiply together to give the largest possible product.

15. Buying some Christmas tree decorations I found that each item cost the same price and the number of items was equal to the cost of each item in pence. I gave the cashier a £10 note and received in change a £1 coin and 5 other coins totalling less than £1.
    What were the values of these 5 coins ?

Miscellaneous Section A

Aural Practice

Often in life you will need to do quick calculations without using pencil and paper or calculator. Sometimes you will **see** the numbers written down, and sometimes you will just **hear** the questions. These aural exercises will give you some practice in **listening** to questions.

These aural exercises, A1 and A2, should be read to you, probably by your teacher or a friend, and you should write down the answers only, doing any working out in your head. You should do the 15 questions within 10 minutes.

Exercise A1

1. How many eggs are there in 8 dozen ?

2. How many lines of symmetry has a square ?

3. What is the change from £5 after buying 3 loaves at 62 pence each ?

4. What is the gradient of the line whose equation is $2y = x + 1$?

5. How long will it take to go 6 km when jogging at an average speed of 8 km per hour ?

6. If a car costing £3000 is sold for £2400, what is the percentage loss ?

7. The area of a circle is 24 cm². What is the area of a sector of the circle with an angle of 60° at the centre ?

8. If there are 750 pupils in the school, how many must you select to form a 10% sample ?

9. The sides of a rectangle are 8 cm and 4 cm. What is the approximate length of a diagonal ?

10. What equation is satisfied by the value of x where the curve $y = x^3$ intersects the line $y = 2x + 10$?

11. **1** If 3 sides of one triangle are equal in turn to 3 sides of another triangle, are the triangles congruent ?
    2 If 3 angles of one triangle are equal in turn to 3 angles of another triangle, are the triangles necessarily congruent ?

12.   The total cost of two books is £5.50, with one book costing £1 more than the other. What does the dearer one cost ?

13.   A rectangular piece of paper measuring 40 cm by 30 cm is cut into squares with side 5 cm. How many squares can be made ?

14.   Write down the prime numbers between 20 and 30.

15.   A solid figure is enlarged by a scale factor 2. Its original volume is 5 cm³. What is the new volume ?

Exercise A2

1.   How many 20 pence coins are worth £10 ?

2.   What angle should be used at the centre of a pie chart in a sector representing $\frac{1}{8}$ of the total amount ?

3.   What is the next prime number after 37 ?

4.   If the vector **a** is written in column form as $\begin{pmatrix} 2 \\ -5 \end{pmatrix}$, what is the vector $-2\mathbf{a}$ in column form ?

5.   Write an expression for the nth term of the sequence 3, 9, 27, 81, . . .

6.   Two angles of a triangle are 55° and 65°. What size is the third angle ?

7.   If 1 litre of petrol costs 54 pence, how much will 5 litres cost ?

8.   If a cone has base radius 5 cm and perpendicular height 12 cm, what is the length of the slant height ?

9.   What is left when 0.006 is subtracted from 0.06 ?

10.   For what value of x between 0 and 360, does the graph of $y = \sin x°$ have a maximum value ?

11.   The area of a triangle is 40 cm² and the base is 10 cm long. What is the height ?

12.   If today is 24th November, what will be the date this day next week ?

13.   Three coins are tossed together. What is the chance of getting either three heads or three tails ?

14.   There are 2 parcels with total weight 19 kg. One of them is 4 kg heavier than the other one. What does the heavier parcel weigh ?

15.   A cylinder has a curved surface area of 30 cm², and the circumference of its base is 6 cm. What is the height of the cylinder ?

Exercise A3   Revision

1.   There are two tins of similar shape, one is 12 cm high and the other is 20 cm high. If the smaller one holds 5.4 litres of liquid, how many litres will the larger one hold ?

2.   Calculate the lengths of **AB** and **BC**.

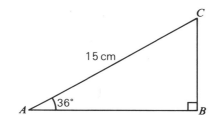

3.   There are four discs in a bag, numbered 1, 2, 3, 4. A disc is drawn and replaced, then a second disc is drawn.
       Make a table to show the possible outcomes.
       What is the probability that
       1   the same number is drawn twice,
       2   the sum of the numbers drawn is a multiple of 3,
       3   the product of the numbers drawn is an odd number ?

4.   A running track is in the form of a circle, centre **O**, with circumference 400 m.
       Chris runs round the track from **A**, for 60 m, to **B**.
       What is the size of $\angle AOB$?

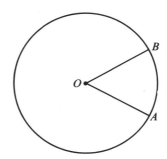

5.   If $f(x) = x^3 - x$, find the values of $f(-2)$, $f(-1)$, $f(0)$, $f(1)$ and $f(2)$.
       Draw a sketch graph of the function.

6. A radio station carried out a telephone poll before 9 am one morning. The question was, 'Should smoking be banned in the workplace ?' People were asked to phone in to register a 'Yes' or a 'No' vote.
Give reasons why a poll taken in this way may not be representative of the views of the whole population.
(The result of the poll was Yes, 86%; No, 14%.)

7. A formula involving energy is $E = \frac{1}{2}mv^2$.
Express this formula in terms in v.

8. Find the value of $\left(\sqrt{25}\right)^2 + 8^{\frac{1}{3}} + 6^0$

9. $\triangle ABC$ is equilateral.
ABP and BCQ are straight lines and $BP = CQ$.
Prove that $AQ = CP$.

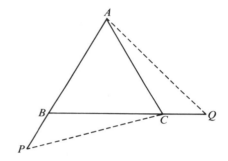

10. Expand these brackets.
   1 $(2x + 3)(2x - 1)$
   2 $(4x + 1)(x - 3)$
   3 $(2x - 3)^2$
   4 $(2x + 1)(2x - 1)$

11. On a map two towns are 1.4 cm apart. The actual distance between the towns is 35 km.
What is the scale of the map in ratio form ?

12. Find the value of x if $\dfrac{1}{x} = \dfrac{1}{8} - \dfrac{1}{10}$.

13. A solid metal cone, radius 5 cm and perpendicular height 9 cm, was melted down and the metal used to make small spheres, each with radius 0.5 cm.
How many spheres could be made ?
(There is no need to substitute for π.)

14. A is the point $(0, 6)$. If $\overrightarrow{AB} = \begin{pmatrix} 3 \\ -6 \end{pmatrix}$ and $\overrightarrow{AC} = \begin{pmatrix} 6 \\ 4 \end{pmatrix}$ write down the coordinates of the points B and C.
E and F are points such that $\overrightarrow{CE} = \frac{1}{3}\overrightarrow{AB}$ and $\overrightarrow{CF} = \frac{1}{2}\overrightarrow{AC}$.
Show that $\overrightarrow{BE} = 2\overrightarrow{EF}$ and state what can be deduced about B, E and F.

15. Explain why triangles *ABC*, *ADE*
     are similar.
     Find the length of *BC*.

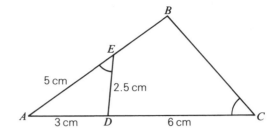

16. If $x^2 + y^2 = 1$, what is the positive value of x when $y = -\frac{4}{5}$?

17. The diagram represents a wooden
     wedge in which the triangular
     faces *ABC* and *DEF* are right-angled
     at *B* and *E*. The other three faces
     are rectangles.
     Find

     1   the angle which the edge *AC*
             makes with the base *ABED*,
     2   the length of *AC*,
     3   the length of the diagonal,
             AF, of the face *ACFD*,
     4   the angle which *AF* makes
             with the base *ABED*.

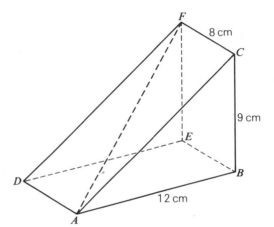

18. Solve the inequalities
     1 $2(x + 1) + 2(x + 8) > 48$
     2 $3x^2 + 2 \leqslant 77$

19. **1**   If $524\,000 = 5.24 \times 10^n$, what is the value of n ?
     2   If $0.000524 = 5.24 \times 10^p$, what is the value of p ?

20. Copy and complete the table of values for the graph of $y = \sin x°$, giving
     approximate values of y correct to 2 decimal places.

x	0	15	30	45	60	75	90
y	0	0.26					

Draw the graph of $y = \sin x°$ for x from 0 to 90.
On the same axes draw the line $y = \frac{1}{120}(x + 30)$.
Find the values of x at the points where the line meets the curve.
Show that these are solutions of the equation $120 \sin x° = x + 30$.

Exercise A4 Activities

1. **Latitude and longitude**

    The Earth is approximately a sphere with a radius of 6370 km.
    If two places lie on the same circle of longitude then the distance over the Earth's surface along the circle of longitude can be calculated.
    This is the shortest distance between the two places over the Earth's surface.

    In the diagram, O is the centre of the Earth.
    A is on latitude $a°$ N, B is on latitude $b°$ S, and A and B lie on the same circle of longitude.
    The angle AOB is $(a + b)°$, and using this angle the length of the arc AB can be calculated.

    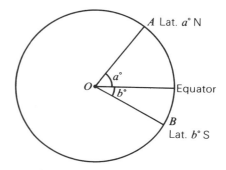

    1 If A is on latitude $53°$ N and B is on latitude $27°$ S, and A and B lie on the same line of longitude, what is the distance from A to B over the Earth's surface ?

    2 Repeat the question if A is on latitude $62°$ N and B is on latitude $17°$ N.

    If two places lie on the same circle of latitude then the distance between them along the circle of latitude can be calculated. (This is not the shortest distance between the two places, unless they lie on the Equator. You can see this by using a globe and stretching a piece of string between the points.)

    Here is a diagram showing the radius XC of the circle of latitude $a°$ N.
    Find a trigonometrical expression for the radius, XC, in terms of the radius OC of the Earth.

    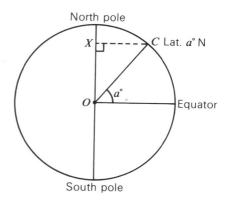

Then you can use this diagram
to find the length of the arc *CD*
along the circle of latitude.

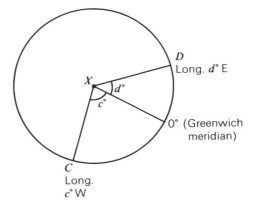

Circle of latitude *a*° N

3   If *C* and *D* lie on the circle of latitude 60° N, and *C* has longitude 10° W, *D*
has longitude 50° E, find the distance between *C* and *D* measured along the
circle of latitude.

4   Repeat the question if *C* is the place 30° S, 70° W; and *D* is the place 30° S,
50° W.

5   From an atlas, find places which lie on the same circle of longitude or
latitude, and calculate the distances between them. (In some atlases, angles
will be given in degrees and minutes. There are 60 minutes in 1 degree, so
6 minutes is 0.1°. You could write the angles in degrees, correct to 1 decimal
place.)

2.   **Areas of parallelograms**

Draw a parallelogram *OABC* on squared
paper, with $\mathbf{a} = \begin{pmatrix} 7 \\ 2 \end{pmatrix}$ and $\mathbf{b} = \begin{pmatrix} 3 \\ 4 \end{pmatrix}$.

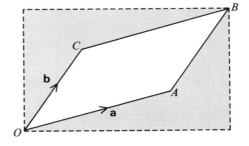

Enclose it in a rectangle, as
shown by the dotted lines.
Find the area of this rectangle.
By drawing lines through *A* and *C*,
find the total area that is shaded in
the diagram, and hence find the area of the parallelogram *OABC*.
Repeat using a parallelogram with different values for **a** and **b**.
Is there any connection between **a** and **b** and the numerical value of the area ?
Can you work out the area algebraically when $\mathbf{a} = \begin{pmatrix} p \\ q \end{pmatrix}$ and $\mathbf{b} = \begin{pmatrix} r \\ s \end{pmatrix}$, to find a
general formula for the area ?

3. **A budget for a year**

Imagine that you plan to move away from home into your own flat, in a few year's time.
This is a big step to take and it deserves proper consideration.
You will have your wages from your work or your grant as a student. Plan how you are going to manage financially.

Firstly, there is necessary spending on the flat, e.g. rent, bills for water, electricity, gas and other fuel, insurance, TV licence, phone bills, etc. If you are over 18 and working you may have to pay a local tax.
Secondly, there is the necessary spending on yourself, e.g. food, travelling expenses (including car expenses if you have a car), clothes, etc.
Then there are all the extras such as things for the flat, holidays, presents, entertainment, sports or hobbies, etc.
If you have borrowed money or bought things on credit you will have regular repayments to make.

Make a complete list of expenditure (what you need to spend) with estimated costs for each item. Find the total amount.
Estimate the total income you will have. If you are working, deductions will be made from your wages for National Insurance contributions and Income Tax.
If the expenditure total exceeds the income total you will have to decide what you can do about it.

(If you prefer, instead of this you can work out a similar budget for a family.)

4. **Pascal's Triangle**

Blaise Pascal was a French Mathematician who lived in the 17th century. Try to find out more about his life and works, from library books.
This triangle of numbers is named after him, although it was known long ago in Ancient China.
Decide how each number is formed from the numbers in the row above, and copy the triangle and continue it for a few more rows. (As a check, a later row is
1   8   28   56   70   56   28   8   1)

What do you notice about the sum of the numbers in each row ?
What do we call the numbers in the diagonal which begins 1, 3, 6, 10 ?
Look for other number patterns in the triangle.
There are many investigations you can do, using the triangle.

Here are some suggestions.

1   Tossing coins

If you toss three coins in turn, there are 8 possible results. HHH, HTH, etc.
which can be summarised like this.

	0 heads	1 head	2 heads	3 heads
Number of ways	1	3	3	1

Investigate the results when 4, or more, coins are tossed.

2

The diagram shows a railway station and the roads which lead to the beach.
From the station, how many ways are there of getting to each access point
A, B, C, D, E or *F* ?
How does this link with Pascal's triangle ?
Why is the beach more crowded in the centre ?

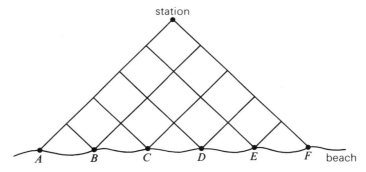

3   The number of selections

Suppose there are *n* people from whom *r* of them have to be selected for
some purpose. How many ways are there of making the selection ?

Begin with 3 people. Find the number of ways of selecting no people, 1
person, 2 people, and 3 people, from the group.
Repeat this with a group of 4 people, and then 5 people.
Can the number of selections be connected with Pascal's triangle ? See if
you can discover a general formula for the number of selections. If so, you
can use the same formula to find terms of Pascal's triangle.

4 Start with Pascal's triangle and move the numbers along so that the first number starts one column further along each time, and find the column totals.

```
              1              →  │ 1 │
           1     1           →  │ 1 │ 1 │
        1     2     1        →  │ 1 │ 2 │ 1 │
     1     3     3     1     →  │ 1 │ 3 │ 3 │ 1 │
  1     4     6     4     1  →  │ 1 │ 4 │ 6 │ 4 │ 1 │
1     5    10    10    5    1 → │ 1 │ 5 │10 │10 │ · │
                                  · │ · │ · │ ·
```

| 1 | 1 | 2 | 3 | 5 | 8 | · | · | · | · |

What do you notice ?

5 **Expanding brackets**

$(x + 1)^2 = x^2 + 2x + 1$
(The coefficients, i.e. numbers in each term, are 1, 2, 1.)

Now $(x + 1)^3 = (x + 1)(x^2 + 2x + 1) = x^3 + 3x^2 + 3x + 1$.
The coefficients are 1, 3, 3, 1.
Note how the powers of x decrease, x^3, x^2, x, 1.
Can you give the expansion of $(x + 1)^4$, and of $(x + 1)^5$?

In a similar way, you can give the expansions of $(x + y)^2$, $(x + y)^3$, $(x + y)^4$, . . .

5. **Definitions of sin $\theta°$, cos $\theta°$, tan $\theta°$**

For sin $\theta°$ and cos $\theta°$ we use a circle with unit radius, centre at the origin.
$\theta°$ is the angle made with the x-axis. Notice the arrow of the angle measurement. If this direction is anticlockwise the angle is positive, otherwise it is negative.

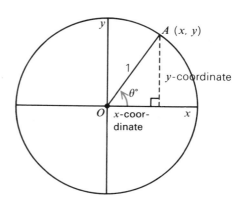

If $\theta°$ is a positive acute angle, you can see from the diagram that

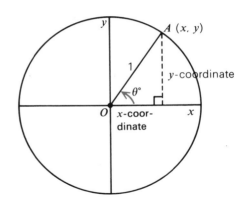

$$\sin \theta° = \frac{\text{opp}}{\text{hyp}} = \frac{y\text{-coordinate of } A}{1}$$

$$\cos \theta° = \frac{\text{adj}}{\text{hyp}} = \frac{x\text{-coordinate of } A}{1}$$

We use these definitions for all values of θ.

So

$\sin \theta°$ = y-coordinate of A
$\cos \theta°$ = x-coordinate of A

As A travels round the circle, the y-coordinate changes from 0, when $\theta = 0$, to 1, when $\theta = 90$, so $\sin \theta$ changes from 0 to 1. Then as θ goes from 90 to 180, $\sin \theta$ changes back from 1 to 0.
When θ goes from 180 to 270, the y-coordinate is negative, so $\sin \theta$ is negative and goes from 0 to -1. From 270 to 360, $\sin \theta$ goes from -1 to 0.

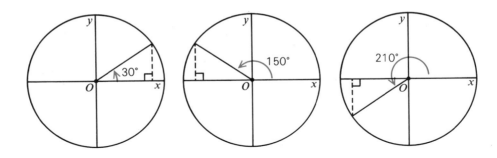

This diagram shows 4 points A, B, C, D with the same numerical y-coordinate, positive for A and B, and negative for C and D.

For A, the y-coordinate = 0.342, so $\sin 20° = 0.342$.
This value has been calculated from a formula, not measured.

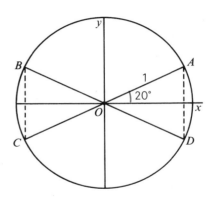

Other angles made by **OA** such as 380°, −340°, and angles made by **OB** such as 160°, 520°, −200° all have the same value for sin θ°.
So sin 160° = sin 20° = 0.342.

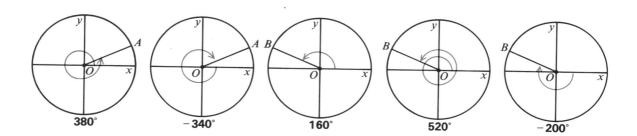

380°   −340°   160°   520°   −200°

Angles made by **OC** or **OD**, such as −20°, −160°, 200° or 340° have the value for sin θ° of −0.342.

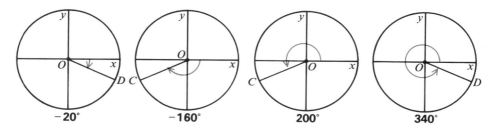

−20°   −160°   200°   340°

In a similar way we can find the sine of any angle.

Decide what happens to cos θ° as **A** travels round the circle, by considering the length of the x-coordinate.
In the diagram on the opposite page angles made by **OA** or **OD** have positive values for cos θ°, and angles made by **OB** or **OC** have negative values for cos θ°.

To define tan θ°, we let $\tan \theta° = \dfrac{\sin \theta°}{\cos \theta°}$.

You can show that this is true for acute angles, and we use it as the definition for all angles.
Thus the sign of tan θ° is positive when sin θ° and cos θ° are both positive or both negative, e.g. as for angles made by **OA** and **OC** in the diagram.
The sign of tan θ° is negative when sin θ° and cos θ° have opposite signs, e.g. as for angles made by **OB** and **OD** in the diagram.

6. **The ninth stellation of the icosahedron**

Here are instructions for making this solid figure.
It is made from 12 star points.

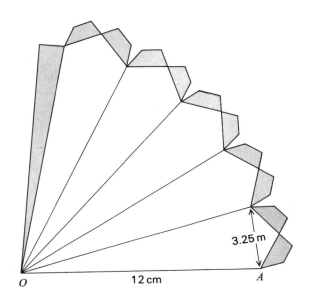

To make a star point:
Draw the pattern on paper.
With centre *O*, draw a faint arc, radius 12 cm.
Starting at *A*, with radius 3.25 cm, mark off 5 more points on the arc.
Using *A* and the other points as centres in turn, with radius 2.05 cm, find the
5 outer points.
Draw all the lines, and add tabs as shown.
If you alter the measurements, keep them in the same proportion.

Transfer the pattern to cardboard. You need 12 pieces altogether. Cut them out.
Score along all the lines on the right side, and bend them away from the side
they were scored on.
Glue the long tab to the opposite face to make a star point.
Then glue 2 pieces together along 2 small tabs of each, one of each on either
side of a long edge.
Glue a third piece in a similar way to each of the first two pieces.
Continue glueing on other pieces until you have a complete, closed model. For
the last star point, you may find it easier to make an incomplete point with 4
faces and tabs on both long edges. Then you can make a single face to glue on
last of all.

7. **The area of a triangle**

Area = $\frac{1}{2}$ × base × height

An alternative formula is

Area = $\frac{1}{2}bc \sin A$

    = $\frac{1}{2}ac \sin B$

    = $\frac{1}{2}ab \sin C$

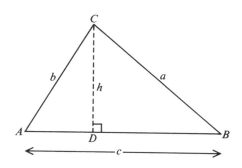

Prove the formula involving sin A, using this diagram.
You can also consider the case when $\angle A$ is obtuse.

Example

Find the area of this triangle.

Area = $\frac{1}{2}ab \sin C$

    = $\frac{1}{2}$ × 9 × 7 × sin 110° cm²

    = 29.6 cm², to 3 sig. fig.

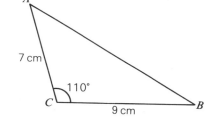

Find the areas of these triangles.

1

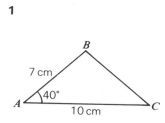

2

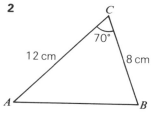

3

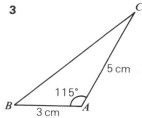

4

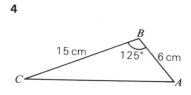

5

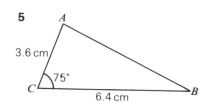

There is a similar formula for the area of a parallelogram.

Area = $ab \sin \theta$

Can you prove this ?

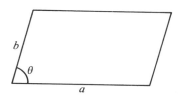

6 Thinking about probability

It is certain to go dark tonight (assuming that you are not in the polar regions). The probability is 1.

There is a 70% chance that it will rain today.

Conditional probability

If you are dealt 3 cards, what is the probability that they are all aces ? What is the probability that there are no aces ? What is the probability that there is at least one ace ?

The marble maze

At each pin, the probability of a marble going left or right is $\frac{1}{2}$. The spacing is such that the marble will then hit the next pin. What is the probability of getting 3 marbles in either of the end holes ?

The possible totals when two dice are thrown

How many equally likely events are there ?
What is the probability of each total score ?

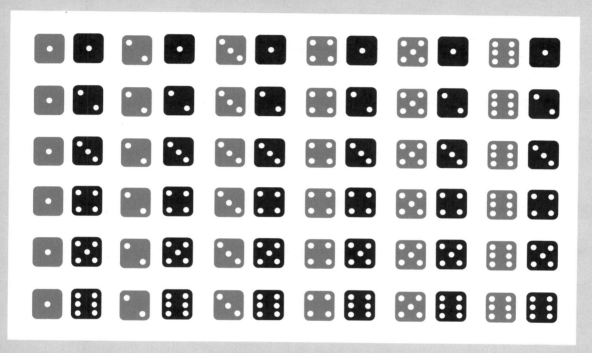

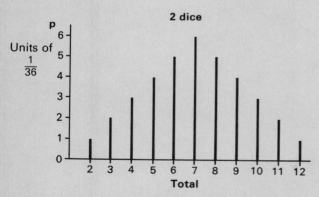

The probabilities of each total when 2 dice are thrown.

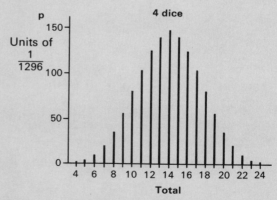

The probabilities of each total when 4 dice are thrown.
Describe the shape of this graph.

6 Probability

Probability is measured on a numerical scale from 0 to 1.

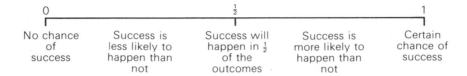

Probability of a successful outcome $= \dfrac{s}{n}$

where n is the total number of equally likely outcomes
and s is the number of successful outcomes.

Mutually exclusive events

When there are two or more outcomes of an event and at each time only one of the outcomes can happen (because if one outcome happens, this prevents any of the other outcomes happening), then the outcomes are called **mutually exclusive events**.

The OR rule

If there are two mutually exclusive events A or B, then the probability of A or B occurring = the probability of A occurring + the probability of B occurring.

$$P(A \text{ or } B) = P(A) + P(B)$$

If there are 3 events, A or B or C, then

$$P(A \text{ or } B \text{ or } C) = P(A) + P(B) + P(C)$$

The rule is similar if there are more than 3 events.

The sum of all possible mutually exclusive events is 1.
The probability of an event happening = 1 − the probability of the event not happening.

Independent events

Two events, where the outcome of the second event does not depend on the outcome of the first event, are called independent events.

The AND rule

If there are two independent events A and B, then the probability of both A and B occurring = the probability of A occurring × the probability of B occurring.

$$P(A \text{ and } B) = P(A) \times P(B)$$

If there are 3 independent events, A, B and C, then

$$P(A \text{ and } B \text{ and } C) = P(A) \times P(B) \times P(C)$$

The rule is similar if there are more than 3 events.

Conditional probabilities

To find the combined probability of 2 events A, B which are not independent:

If A is the 1st event and B the 2nd then the probability of B will depend on the outcome of the 1st event.

The multiplication rule still holds.

$$P(A \text{ and } B) = P(A) \times P(B|A)$$

where $P(B|A)$ is the probability of B, given that event A has occurred.

If B is the 1st event and A the 2nd then the probability of A will depend on the outcome of the 1st event.

$$P(A \text{ and } B) = P(B) \times P(A|B)$$

where $P(A|B)$ is the probability of A given that event B has occurred.

If there are 3 events, in order A, B, C, then

$$P(A \text{ and } B \text{ and } C) = P(A) \times P(B|A) \times P(C|A \text{ and } B)$$

where $P(B|A)$ is the probability of B, given that event A has occurred,
and $P(C|A \text{ and } B)$ is the probability of C, given that events A and B have occurred.

There is a similar rule for more than 3 events.

If the events occur simultaneously, e.g. 3 discs picked out of a bag, imagine that they occur in order one after another, e.g. the 3 discs picked out one at a time.

Examples

1   Two marbles are picked together at random out of a bag which contains 3 red and 5 blue marbles.
    What is the probability that both marbles are red ones ?
    What is the probability that at least one is red ?

If a marble was picked out, its colour noted, and then it was replaced before drawing the 2nd marble, then the two drawings would be independent events.
P(both red) = P(1st red) $\times$ P(2nd red)
$$= \tfrac{3}{8} \times \tfrac{3}{8} = \tfrac{9}{64}$$

But in this question the 1st marble is not replaced before the 2nd one is drawn.
   P(1st red) $= \tfrac{3}{8}$
Now there are only 7 marbles in the bag and 2 of them are red.
   P(2nd red) $= \tfrac{2}{7}$
P(both red) = P(1st red) $\times$ P(2nd red)
$$= \tfrac{3}{8} \times \tfrac{2}{7} = \tfrac{3}{28}$$
In a similar way,
P(both blue) $= \tfrac{5}{8} \times \tfrac{4}{7} = \tfrac{5}{14}$
If the marbles are not both blue then at least one marble is red.
P(at least one red) = 1 $-$ P(both blue)
$$= 1 - \tfrac{5}{14} = \tfrac{9}{14}$$

Here are the different outcomes shown on a tree-diagram.

1st marble	2nd marble		Outcome	Probability

$\frac{3}{8}$ R

$\frac{2}{7}$ R → RR → $\frac{3}{8} \times \frac{2}{7} = \frac{6}{56} = \frac{3}{28}$

$\frac{5}{7}$ B → RB → $\frac{3}{8} \times \frac{5}{7} = \frac{15}{56}$

$\frac{5}{8}$ B

$\frac{3}{7}$ R → BR → $\frac{5}{8} \times \frac{3}{7} = \frac{15}{56}$

$\frac{4}{7}$ B → BB → $\frac{5}{8} \times \frac{4}{7} = \frac{20}{56} = \frac{5}{14}$

2   Peter is aiming at a target. The probability that he hits the target with his first throw is $\frac{1}{3}$. If he misses with his first throw, the probability that he hits the target with his second throw is $\frac{2}{5}$. If he still misses with his second throw, the probability that he hits the target with his third throw is $\frac{1}{2}$.
Find the probability that, if Peter is allowed 3 tries, he hits the target.

Here is the tree-diagram.

1st throw	2nd throw	3rd throw	Outcome	Probability

$\frac{1}{3}$ H → H → $\frac{1}{3}$

$\frac{2}{3}$ M

$\frac{2}{5}$ H → MH → $\frac{2}{3} \times \frac{2}{5} = \frac{4}{15}$

$\frac{3}{5}$ M

$\frac{1}{2}$ H → MMH → $\frac{2}{3} \times \frac{3}{5} \times \frac{1}{2} = \frac{1}{5}$

$\frac{1}{2}$ M → MMM → $\frac{2}{3} \times \frac{3}{5} \times \frac{1}{2} = \frac{1}{5}$

P(Peter hits the target) $= \frac{1}{3} + \frac{4}{15} + \frac{1}{5} = \frac{12}{15} = \frac{4}{5}$

Note: The probability that Peter does not hit the target at all $= \frac{1}{5}$

These two events are mutually exclusive and one or other must happen so the sum of the probabilities = 1.
You could find the second probability and then use $1 - \frac{1}{5}$ to give you the first answer.

3 The probabilities of 3 independent events taking place are $\frac{1}{3}$, $\frac{3}{4}$ and $\frac{2}{5}$, respectively. What is the probability that at least one of these events takes place ?

The simplest way to find this is to first find the probability that none of the events takes place.

The probabilities that the events do not happen are $\frac{2}{3}$, $\frac{1}{4}$ and $\frac{3}{5}$.

P(no event takes place) $= \frac{2}{3} \times \frac{1}{4} \times \frac{3}{5} = \frac{1}{10}$
P(at least one event takes place) $= 1 - \frac{1}{10} = \frac{9}{10}$

You can also solve this question by using a tree-diagram.

Exercise 6.1

Conditional probability questions

1. The probability that Julie is late for school on a Monday morning is $\frac{1}{4}$. If she is late on Monday, she makes more effort to be on time the next day, and the probability that she is late on Tuesday is $\frac{1}{8}$. If she is on time on Monday, the probability that she is late on Tuesday is $\frac{1}{4}$.
    Copy and complete the tree-diagram.
    What is the probability that
    1 Julie is late on both mornings,
    2 Julie is late on one of the two mornings ?

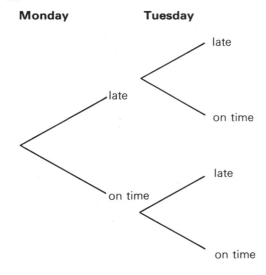

Monday   **Tuesday**

late
on time
late
on time
late
on time

2.   In a pile of 8 cards there are 5 hearts and 3 diamonds.
      If 3 cards are drawn out at random, copy and complete the tree-diagram to
      show the possible outcomes.

1st card   **2nd card**   **3rd card**

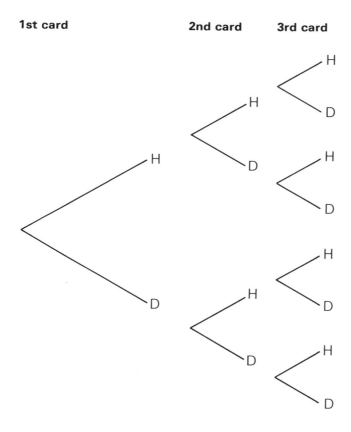

      What is the probability of drawing out
      1   all hearts,
      2   all diamonds,
      3   two cards of 1 suit and one of the other ?

3.   In a class of 30 children, 9 are left-handed and the rest are right-handed.
      If 2 children are chosen at random from this class, what is the probability that
      1   they are both left-handed,
      2   they are both right-handed,
      3   one is left-handed and the other is right-handed ?

4. 3 marbles are taken at random from a bag which contains 6 red and 4 blue marbles. (The marbles are not replaced before the next one is taken out.) Show the results of the 3 drawings on a tree-diagram.
    Find the probability that
    1 all the 3 marbles are red,
    2 2 are red and 1 is blue,
    3 1 is red and 2 are blue,
    4 all 3 are blue.

5. A bag contains 9 discs numbered from 1 to 9. If 3 discs are drawn from the bag, one at a time and not replaced, what is the probability that
    1 the 3 numbers drawn are all odd,
    2 the 3 numbers drawn are all even ?

Miscellaneous questions

6. Three young children, Adam, Bob and Chris, wear identical coats to school. After school, they each put on one of the coats without knowing whether or not it is the right one.
    Calling the children A, B, C and their coats a, b, c, make a list of all the different ways in which the coats could be taken by the children.
    If all these ways are equally likely to happen, what is the probability that all the children will be wearing their own coats ?

7. Manufacturers of a certain make of electric light bulbs find that the probability of a bulb being defective is 0.05. If they test a sample of 3 bulbs, what is the probabiilty that
    1 none of the bulbs are defective,
    2 at least one of the bulbs is defective ?

8. A set of dominoes has spots representing numbers up to double six, e.g. the numbers on the dominoes are 0-0, 0-1, 0-2, . . . , 1-1, 1-2, . . . , 2-2, . . . , 6-6.
    1 How many dominoes are there altogether in the set ?
    The dominoes are put into a bag and one is pulled out at random.
    What is the probability that
    2 it will contain a number 3,
    3 it will be a double (0-0, 1-1, etc.),
    4 the sum of the numbers on the domino will be an odd number ?

9.   Lucy has two purses in the bottom of her shopping bag. In the red purse there
       are 4 20p coins and 3 5p coins. In the brown purse there are 2 20p coins and 8
       5p coins.
       Lucy takes one of the purses out of the bag, at random, and without looking she
       takes out a coin from it.

       Copy and complete the tree-diagram.

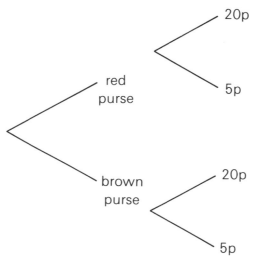

       What is the probability that Lucy takes out
       1   a 20p coin,
       2   a 5p coin ?

10.   The bulbs in a large mixed batch will produce flowers which are either pink,
       yellow, cream or white in the ratio 4:3:2:1.
       If 2 bulbs are chosen at random, what is the probability that
       1   both are pink,
       2   both are the same colour ?
       (Because it is a large batch, the ratios are not altered when one bulb is
       removed.)

11.   Maureen has 3 pairs of similar shoes, black, brown and blue, in a wardrobe.
       She goes to select a pair of shoes, at a time when the light bulb has failed. She
       picks out 2 shoes in the dark, and then takes them into the next room to look at
       them.
       Show the possible combinations of shoes, left or right foot, and black, brown or
       blue, in a list or a table, and find the probability that the 2 shoes selected make
       a pair.
       If the 2 shoes do not make a pair, Maureen returns for a third shoe. What is the
       probability that she then has a pair, from the 3 shoes ?

12. **1**   What is the probability of drawing 2 hearts if 1 card is taken from each of 2 packs of cards ?

   2   If, instead, the 2 packs are placed together and shuffled, and 2 cards are taken from the combined pack, what is the probability of drawing 2 hearts ?

13.   An electrical appliance has 2 components in it and the current will not flow if either component fails. The probability of component A failing is $\frac{1}{10}$ and, independently, the probability of component B failing is $\frac{1}{20}$.

   What is the probability of
   1   both components failing,
   2   one of the two components failing,
   3   both components working ?

14.   There are 5 discs in a bag numbered from 1 to 5. A disc is drawn out of the bag (and not replaced) and then a second disc is drawn out. Make a table of all possible pairs of results and find the probability that
   1   the sum of the numbers on the 2 discs drawn out is even,
   2   the product of the numbers drawn out is even,
   3   the 1st disc drawn out has a higher number than the second one.

15.   When Mr Lambert phones his secretary, the probability that the number is engaged is $\frac{1}{5}$.
   What is the probability that he contacts his secretary
   1   on the 1st attempt,
   2   not on the 1st attempt, but on the 2nd attempt ?

Exercise 6.2   Applications and Activities

1.   In a cricket match, the probability that a certain bowler takes a wicket with any ball is $\frac{1}{20}$.

   What is the probability that in his first over (of 6 balls)
   1   he does not take a wicket,
   2   he takes at least one wicket ?

   3   To get a hat-trick he must get 3 wickets in 3 consecutive balls, not necessarily all in one over.
   What is the probability of this bowler getting a hat-trick after he has taken one wicket ?

2. In a group of 30 girls, 15 play tennis, 18 play badminton and 10 play both games. This information is shown in the diagram.

What is the probability that a girl selected at random from the group
    1   plays tennis but not badminton,
    2   plays badminton but not tennis ?
    3   If a girl is chosen from those who play tennis, what is the probability that she also plays badminton ?
    4   If a girl is chosen from those who do not play badminton, what is the probability that she plays tennis ?

3. A man playing darts can score treble 20 with his first dart with probability $\frac{1}{2}$. If he scores treble 20 with one throw the probability that he scores treble 20 with his next throw is increased to $\frac{3}{5}$.
    If he aims for treble 20 each time, show the results of 3 successive throws on a tree-diagram, using the outcomes 'hit' and 'miss'.

    What is the probability that, in 3 throws,
    1   he scores 180,
    2   he hits treble 20 with 2 darts but not with the other one ?

4. A test has 10 questions, each needing the answer 'yes' or 'no'. If a girl knows the correct answers to 3 of the questions and makes random guesses at the rest, what is the probability of her scoring at least 5 out of 10 ?
    (It is best to first find the probability of her scoring less than 5.)

5. In a certain year-group, all pupils study at least one of the subjects Geography, History or German. The numbers studying each subject are shown in the diagram, e.g. there are 32 + 8 + 5 + 12 pupils who study Geography.

What is the probability that a pupil, chosen at random,
    1   studies only one of these 3 subjects,
    2   studies 2 of these 3 subjects,
    3   studies all three of these subjects ?

    4   If a pupil who studies History is chosen at random, what is the probability that this pupil also studies German ?

6. **An experiment with cards**

Use one suit from a pack of cards and remove the Jack so that there are 12 cards left. Shuffle them well and then turn them over one at a time until a picture card (Queen or King) appears. If it is the first card turned over it counts as 1, if it is the second card turned over it counts as 2, and so on.

Make a grid to record the results on, with space for 200 results.

Before you go further, make two guesses.

1   What will be the most likely number of cards turned over each time (the mode) ?
2   What will be the average (mean) number of cards turned over each time ?

After getting a picture card and recording the result, shuffle the 12 cards and begin again. Repeat the experiment 200 times altogether. You could work in a group and combine your results.

Now make a frequency table of the results.

Number turned over	f
1	
2	
3	
.	
.	
.	
	200

Draw a bar-line graph to show the results and comment on its shape.

What is the mode of the number of cards turned over ?
Find the mean number.
Do your guesses match these averages ?

Now you should compare your results with theoretical results, using probability.

1   What is the probability that a picture card appears first ?
2   What is the probability that another card appears first, then a picture card appears second ?
3   What is the probability that other cards appear first and second, and then a picture card appears third ?

Continue in this way until you have found all the probabilities.

Write them all as fractions with denominator 66, and check that the total of the probabilities is 1.

Now the numbers in the theoretical frequency distribution are these probabilities multiplied by 200. Since 3×66 is nearly 200, they are the numerators multiplied by 3. (If you want to be really accurate, put $\frac{200}{66}$ in the memory of your calculator and multiply the numerators by that.)

Make a bar-line graph of the theoretical frequency distribution.
What is the mode of the distribution ?
Find the mean of the distribution.
Compare your experimental results with the theoretical ones and comment about them.

7. **To find the probability that 2 dominoes will match each other**

Get a set of dominoes which go from
0-0 (double blank) to 6-6 (double
six).

Put the set of dominoes in a bag and draw two out at random. Count it as a success (*s*) if the dominoes match and a failure (*f*) if they do not.

e.g. 2-4 and 3-5 have no number in common and do not match, (*f*),
     2-4 and 4-4 have 4 in common and match, (*s*),
     2-4 and 1-2 have 2 in common and match, (*s*),
     0-0 and 0-6 have 0 in common and match, (*s*).

Before you begin, estimate how many times out of 100 trials the 2 dominoes will match.

Repeat the experiment 100 times, recording your results.

How close was your estimate ?

From your results, find the experimental probability that 2 dominoes will match.

Now to work out the theoretical probability.
The probability that the 2nd domino will match the 1st one depends on whether the 1st domino was a double, or not.
How many of the dominoes are doubles ?
What is the probability that the 1st domino is a double ?
If it is a double, say double 4, how many of the dominoes left in the bag will match it ?
What is the probability of the 2nd domino matching it ?

What is the probability that the 1st domino is not a double ?
If it is not a double, say 1-2, how many of the dominoes left in the bag will match it ?
What is the probability of the 2nd domino matching it ?

Copy and complete this tree-diagram.

1st domino   **2nd domino**   **Probability**

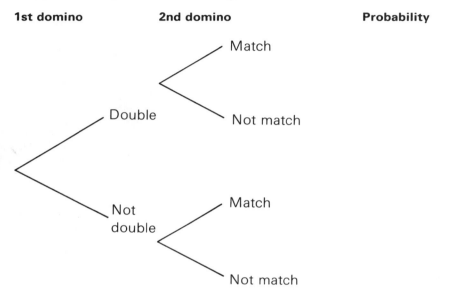

What is the probability of the 2 dominoes matching ?
Do your experimental results agree with the theoretical result ?

If you have a set of dominoes going up to double nine, you can do the experiment with these, and work out the theoretical probability for these.

8. **The Bridge Hand all of one suit**

Occasionally we read in the press about a Bridge player who had been dealt a hand of 13 cards which have turned out to be all of one suit, e.g. spades. The report usually mentions the probability of such an event happening.

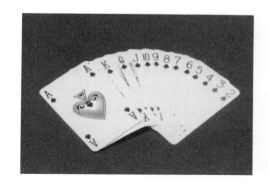

Find the probability that, when 13 cards are dealt to you, they are all of one suit.

The 1st card can be anything. If it is a spade, we need the other 12 spades to follow.

P(2nd card a spade) = $\frac{12}{51}$

P(3rd card a spade) = $\frac{11}{50}$

P(1st 3 cards spades) = $1 \times \frac{12}{51} \times \frac{11}{50}$

Continuing in this way, find the probability that all 13 cards are spades.

The probability is so small that your calculator will give it in standard index form. It is usually given in the press as 1 chance in 158 753 389 900.

You can turn your answer into a similar form by pressing $\boxed{\frac{1}{x}}$.

PUZZLES

16.   The digits of a notable year add up to 13. If you multiply the 1st figure by the 4th figure the answer is 6 more than if you multiply the 2nd figure by the 3rd. Also the 3rd figure is greater than the 2nd figure.
       What year was it and what happened then ?

17.   How many squares and how many triangles are there in this diagram ?

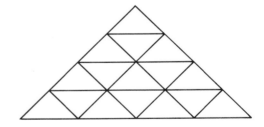

18.   In a park there was a rectangular area of grass which had to be mown by the new worker, Karl. He was told that the job would take two days. On the first day he had to mow the outer half of the area (the shaded part), doing the remainder on the second day.
       How wide should be the strips that he mowed on the 1st day ?

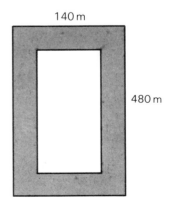

140 m

480 m

7 Thinking about algebraic methods

Expressing a law in symbols

On many cameras nowadays the amount of light entering through the lens is controlled automatically, but on other cameras the light can be controlled by adjusting the radius of the aperture on the lens and the shutter speed.

Here is a table giving the connection between the aperture A and the shutter speed S allowing a fixed amount of light through to the film.

A	4	5.6	8	11	16	22	32
S	$\frac{1}{15}$	$\frac{1}{30}$	$\frac{1}{60}$	$\frac{1}{125}$	$\frac{1}{250}$	$\frac{1}{500}$	$\frac{1}{1000}$

Notice that each aperture number is approximately $\sqrt{2}$ × the previous one, and that each shutter speed is approximately half of the previous one.

Find an approximate formula for S in terms of A.

The difference of 2 squares

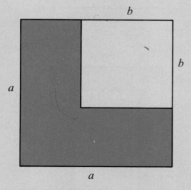

The shaded area is $a^2 - b^2$.

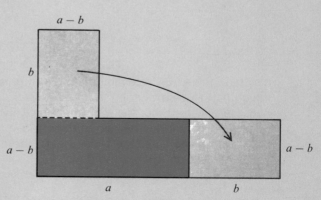

The same shaded area is $(a + b)(a - b)$.
So $a^2 - b^2 = (a + b)(a - b)$.

and numbers

Numbers

$\sqrt{2}$ exists. It is the length shown in this diagram.
But can it be written as an exact (improper) fraction ?

Assume $\sqrt{2} = \dfrac{m}{n}$, where m and n are positive integers with no common factor.

Then square both sides.

$$2 = \left(\frac{m}{n}\right)^2$$

This gives $2n^2 = m^2$.
So m has a factor 2.
Let $m = 2p$, so $m^2 = (2p)^2 = 4p^2$

$$2n^2 = 4p^2$$

Divide both sides by 2.

$$n^2 = 2p^2$$

So n has a factor 2.

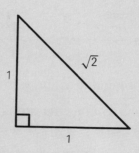

But m and n cannot both have a factor 2 since they have no common factor.

So there is no fraction $\dfrac{m}{n}$ equal to $\sqrt{2}$.

Since 2 cannot be written as an exact fraction it is an irrational number.

Prove in a similar way that $\sqrt{3}$ and $\sqrt{5}$ are irrational numbers.
What about $\sqrt{4}$?

Real numbers

−99·999

20·5̇4̇

5·6

$-2\frac{7}{8}$

$\sqrt[3]{9}$

All real numbers are either rational or irrational.

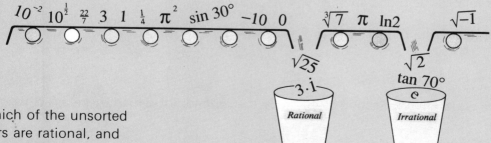

10^{-2} $10^{\frac{1}{2}}$ $\frac{22}{7}$ 3 1 $\frac{1}{4}$ π^2 $\sin 30°$ -10 0 $\sqrt[3]{7}$ π $\ln 2$ $\sqrt{-1}$

$\sqrt{25}$

−3·1̇

Rational

$\sqrt{2}$

$\tan 70°$

e

Irrational

Say which of the unsorted numbers are rational, and which are irrational.

Algebraic methods: Numbers

Laws of connected variables

If there are two variables, x and y, and y is a function of x, then it is often possible to find the equation for the function from a table or ordered pairs of numbers.

e.g.

x	1	2	3	4
y	9	7	5	3

The equation connecting y and x is $y = 11 - 2x$.

The first functions to consider are linear functions, i.e. functions with equations of the form $y = mx + c$, where m and c are numbers. Their graphs are straight lines.

The table above represents a linear function because as x increases by 1 unit, y decreases by 2 units.
So the equation involves $-2x$, and you can soon discover that it is $y = 11 - 2x$, checking that all the pairs of values satisfy this equation.

There are other equations connecting x and y. One of these is
$y = x^4 - 10x^3 + 35x^2 - 52x + 35$. You can check that the values above satisfy this equation. If we had been given more than 4 pairs of values, we might find that this second equation is no longer satisfied.
However, when you find a simple equation connecting y and x, do not look for a more complicated one.

If the function is not linear, other functions to consider are
$y = x^2$, and related functions such as $y = x^2 + 3$, $y = x^2 - x$.
$y = x^3$, and related functions such as $y = x^3 - 5$, $y = x^3 + 2x$.
$y = \dfrac{1}{x}$, and related functions such as $y = \dfrac{20}{x}$, $y = \dfrac{1}{x + 2}$.
$y = 2^x$, and related functions such as $y = 3^x$, $y = 10^x$, $y = 2^x - 1$.

Example

Find the equation connecting y and x for the function of which these are pairs of values.

x	-1	0	1	2	3
y	$1\frac{1}{2}$	2	3	5	9

This is not a linear function as when x increases by 1 unit, y does not increase or decrease by a constant number. The increases are $\frac{1}{2}$, 1, 2, 4, which is the doubling sequence. This suggests that 2^x is involved.

Here is the table for the function $y = 2^x$.

x	-1	0	1	2	3
y	$\frac{1}{2}$	1	2	4	8

Comparing these tables shows that the first function is $y = 2^x + 1$.

Exercise 7.1

Pairs of values of simple functions are given in these tables.
Find the equations connecting y and x.

1.

x	-2	0	2	4
y	-13	-3	7	17

2.

x	0	1	2	3
y	0	1	8	27

3.

x	-1	0	1	2	3
y	0.1	1	10	100	1000

4.

x	1	2	4	6	9
y	36	18	9	6	4

5.

x	2	5	8	11
y	2	-10	-22	-34

6.

x	1	2	3	4
y	3	9	27	81

7.

x	-1	0	1	2	3
y	-1	0	3	8	15

8.

x	1	2	3	4
y	$\frac{1}{4}$	$\frac{1}{5}$	$\frac{1}{6}$	$\frac{1}{7}$

9.

x	-2	0	2	4	6
y	0	-4	0	12	32

10.

x	1	2	3	4	5
y	2	10	30	68	130

Indices

You have already used the rules of indices.

$$a^m \times a^n = a^{m+n}$$
$$a^m \div a^n = a^{m-n}$$
$$(a^m)^n = a^{mn}$$

m and n need not be positive integers (whole numbers).
For the rules above still to be true even if m and n are not positive integers, we give meanings to numbers with other indices, as follows:

$$a^0 = 1$$
$$a^{-n} = \frac{1}{a^n}$$
$$a^{\frac{1}{n}} = \sqrt[n]{a}$$
$$a^{\frac{m}{n}} = \left(\sqrt[n]{a}\right)^m \text{ or } \sqrt[n]{(a^m)}$$

Examples

1 Find the values of 3^0, $4^{\frac{1}{2}}$, 5^{-3}, $8^{\frac{4}{3}}$, $9^{-1\frac{1}{2}}$.

$$3^0 = 1$$

$$4^{\frac{1}{2}} = \sqrt{4} = 2$$

$$5^{-3} = \frac{1}{5^3} = \frac{1}{125}$$

$8^{\frac{4}{3}} = \left(\sqrt[3]{8}\right)^4 = 2^4 = 16$

$9^{-1\frac{1}{2}} = \dfrac{1}{9^{\frac{3}{2}}} = \dfrac{1}{\left(\sqrt{9}\right)^3} = \dfrac{1}{3^3} = \dfrac{1}{27}$

You could check these on your calculator, using the y^x (or x^y) key.
e.g. for $8^{\frac{4}{3}}$, press 8 $\boxed{y^x}$ $\boxed{(}$ 4 $\boxed{\div}$ 3 $\boxed{)}$ $\boxed{=}$

2 Simplify $\dfrac{a^{\frac{1}{2}} \times a^{\frac{2}{3}}}{a^{\frac{1}{6}}}$

This equals $a^{\left(\frac{1}{2}+\frac{2}{3}-\frac{1}{6}\right)} = a^{\frac{3+4-1}{6}} = a^1 = a$

3 Find the value of x if $9^x = 243$.

9 and 243 can both be written as powers of 3.
$\left(3^2\right)^x = 3^5$
$3^{2x} = 3^5$
$2x = 5$
$x = 2\frac{1}{2}$

Exercise 7.2

1. Find the values of
   1 8^{-2} **2** 7^0 **3** 3^{-3} **4** $25^{\frac{1}{2}}$ **5** $32^{\frac{1}{5}}$
   6 $9^{-\frac{1}{2}}$ **7** $81^{\frac{3}{4}}$ **8** $8^{\frac{2}{3}}$ **9** $\left(\frac{1}{2}\right)^{-1}$ **10** 10^{-6}

2. Simplify
   1 $a^3 \times a^{-3}$ **4** $d^{\frac{1}{4}} \times d^{\frac{3}{4}}$
   2 $\dfrac{(b^2)^4}{b \times b^6}$ **5** $e^{\frac{2}{5}} \div e$
   3 $(c^{-3})^{-1}$

3. Find the values of x in these equations.
   1 $2^x = 32$ **5** $5^x = 1$
   2 $3^x = 81$ **6** $9^x = \frac{1}{3}$
   3 $10^x = \frac{1}{100}$ **7** $16^x = 8$
   4 $7^x = \sqrt[3]{7}$ **8** $3^x = \dfrac{(3^4)^2 \times 3^5}{3^{11}}$

4.   Simplify, leaving as a power of 10,

    1 $10^3 \times 10^4$ **4** $\left(10^{\frac{1}{3}}\right)^6$

    2 $10^3 \times 10^{-5}$ **5** $\left(\sqrt{10}\right)^3$

    3 $(10^5)^2$ **6** $100^{\frac{2}{3}} \times 10^{\frac{2}{3}}$

Factorising

You have worked out expressions in brackets to make separate terms,
e.g. $(3x + 4)(2x - 1) = 6x^2 + 5x - 4$

The reverse process turns $6x^2 + 5x - 4$ into $(3x + 4)(2x - 1)$.
$3x + 4$ and $2x - 1$ are factors of $6x^2 + 5x - 4$ and this process is called factorising.
There are different types of factors which you should look for.
You have already found common factors, i.e. factors which belong to all terms of the
expression, and you should always find any common factors first.

Common factors

Examples

    $6x^3 + 2xy^2 = 2x(3x^2 + y^2)$

    $2x$ is a common factor and dividing each term by $2x$ leaves $3x^2 + y^2$.

    $2abc - b^2c = bc(2a - b)$

Difference of two squares

The second type of factor to look for is of the form $A^2 - B^2$.
This is called the difference of two squares and the factors are $A + B$ and $A - B$.

$$A^2 - B^2 = (A + B)(A - B)$$

Check this by multiplying out the right-hand side.

Examples

$$x^2 - 9 = (x + 3)(x - 3)$$
$$4x^2 - 1 = (2x + 1)(2x - 1)$$
$$x^2 - 16y^2 = (x + 4y)(x - 4y)$$
$$3x^2 - 75 = 3(x^2 - 25) = 3(x + 5)(x - 5)$$
(taking out the common factor 3 first.)

Apart from any common factors, there are no factors for the **sum** of two squares.

$A^2 + B^2$ has no factors

Factors by grouping

Usually there are 4 terms and they can be grouped in pairs as a first step, and then there is a common factor of both pairs.
Be careful of signs when you are including brackets.

Examples

$$px + qx - py - qy = x(p + q) - y(p + q)$$
$p + q$ is a common factor
$$= (p + q)(x - y)$$
You can check this, and all answers, by multiplying out the right-hand side.
$$ax - 3ay - 4bx + 12by = a(x - 3y) - 4b(x - 3y)$$
$$= (x - 3y)(a - 4b)$$
$$c^3 - c^2 + c - 1 = c^2(c - 1) + (c - 1)$$
$$= (c - 1)(c^2 + 1)$$

If the 1st and 2nd terms have no common factor, then pair the 1st and 3rd terms together, and then the 2nd and 4th terms will pair together.
$$ap - cq - aq + cp = ap - aq - cq + cp$$
$$= a(p - q) + c(p - q)$$
$$= (p - q)(a + c)$$

Trinomials beginning with x^2

These have x^2, then a term in x, then a number. They are factorised into 2 factors both beginning with x.
(Other letters can be used instead of x.)

Examples

1 $x^2 + 8x + 15 \qquad = (x \ldots)(x \ldots)$

signs both the same, both positive or both negative,
signs same as this, so both positive,
$(x + \ldots)(x + \ldots)$

$x^2 + 8x + 15$

factors of 15, so 15 and 1 or 5 and 3,
which add up to 8, so 5 and 3,

$x^2 + 8x + 15 \qquad = (x + 5)(x + 3)$

2 $x^2 - 6x + 9 \qquad = (x \ldots)(x \ldots)$

signs both the same, both positive or both negative,
signs same as this, so both negative,
$(x - \ldots)(x - \ldots)$

$x^2 - 6x + 9$

factors of 9, so 9 and 1 or 3 and 3,
which add up to 6, so 3 and 3,

$x^2 - 6x + 9 \qquad = (x - 3)(x - 3) = (x - 3)^2$

3 $x^2 + 13x - 30 \qquad = (x \ldots)(x \ldots)$

signs are: one + and one −
$(x + \ldots)(x - \ldots)$

$x^2 + 13x - 30$

factors of 30, so 30 and 1, 15 and 2, 10 and 3, or 6 and 5,
with a difference of 13, so 15 and 2,
to get $+13x$ we need $+15$ and -2,

$x^2 + 13x - 30 \qquad = (x + 15)(x - 2)$

4 $x^2 - 13x - 30$

to get $-13x$ we need $+2$ and -15,
$x^2 - 13x - 30 \qquad = (x + 2)(x - 15)$

5 $x^2 - 13xy - 30y^2 = (x + 2y)(x - 15y)$

Other trinomials

The methods for factorising other trinomials are given here, but try the questions in Exercise 7.3 up to question 4, and make sure that you can do the trinomials of question 4 confidently, before proceeding to trinomials which do not begin with x^2.

Examples

6 $2x^2 - 10x + 8$

Since there is a common factor, deal with this first.
$$2x^2 - 10x + 8 = 2(x^2 - 5x + 4)$$
$$= 2(x - 4)(x - 1)$$

7 $5x^2 - 17x + 6 = (5x \ldots)(x \ldots)$

signs both the same, both positive or both negative,
signs same as this so both negative,
$$(5x - \ldots)(x - \ldots)$$
$$5x^2 - 17x + 6$$

try possible factors of 6, i.e. 6 and 1, or 3 and 2.
There are 4 possibilities,
$$(5x - 6)(x - 1)$$
$$(5x - 1)(x - 6)$$
$$(5x - 3)(x - 2)$$
$$(5x - 2)(x - 3)$$
When multiplied out the middle terms, in order, are $-11x$, $-31x$, $-13x$, $-17x$. The last pair of factors is correct.
$$5x^2 - 17x + 6 = (5x - 2)(x - 3)$$

8 $2x^2 - 7x - 15 = (2x \ldots)(x \ldots)$

signs are: one +, one −
Either $(2x + \ldots)(x - \ldots)$
or $\quad (2x - \ldots)(x + \ldots)$
$$2x^2 - 7x - 15$$

Possible end factors are 15 and 1, or 5 and 3.
There are 8 possibilities,
$(2x + 15)(x - 1)$ middle term is $+13x$
$(2x - 15)(x + 1)$ middle term is $-13x$
$(2x + 1)(x - 15)$ middle term is $-29x$
$(2x - 1)(x + 15)$ middle term is $+29x$
$(2x + 5)(x - 3)$ middle term is $-x$

$(2x - 5)(x + 3)$ middle term is $+x$
$(2x + 3)(x - 5)$ middle term is $-7x$. These are the correct factors
$(2x - 3)(x + 5)$ middle term is $+7x$
$2x^2 - 7x - 15 = (2x + 3)(x - 5)$

It is helpful to know that if you remembered to take out any common factors first, there can be no common factor in any bracket in the answer.

9 $3x^2 + 11x + 6 = (3x + \ldots)(x + \ldots)$
       ⌐——— Possible end factors are 6 and 1, or 3 and 2.
       But $3x + 3$ or $3x + 6$ are not possible factors since there was
       no common factor 3 in the expression.
       So there are 2 possibilities,
$(3x + 1)(x + 6)$ middle term is $+19x$
$(3x + 2)(x + 3)$ middle term is $+11x$. These are the correct factors.
$3x^2 + 11x + 6 = (3x + 2)(x + 3)$

Similarly, $3x^2 + 11xy + 6y^2 = (3x + 2y)(x + 3y)$

10 $10 + 3x - x^2 = (\ldots + x)(\ldots - x)$
       Possible factors at the beginning are 10 and 1, or 5 and 2.
  $10 + 3x - x^2 = (2 + x)(5 - x)$

11 $1 - 4x - 5x^2 = (1 + \ldots)(1 - \ldots)$
       Factors at the end are $5x$ and x.
$(1 + 5x)(1 - x)$ middle term is $+4x$
$(1 + x)(1 - 5x)$ middle term is $-4x$. These are the correct factors.
$1 - 4x - 5x^2 = (1 + x)(1 - 5x)$

Methods for factorising

> **1** Common factors
> **2** Difference of two squares
> **3** Factors by grouping
> **4** Trinomials

1   Always find common factors first.
2   Recognise the difference of two squares, an expression of the form $A^2 - B^2$.
 The factors are $(A + B)(A - B)$.
3   If there are 4 terms they can often be factorised by being grouped in pairs.
4   Trinomials can be factorised into two brackets.

Exercise 7.3

Factorise the following expressions.

1.
1   $a^2 - 4a$
2   $12b^2 + 3$
3   $2c + 6c^2$
4   $d^2 - 2de + d$
5   $fg^2 - g^3$

6   $21h + 7hj^2$
7   $30k - 12km + 24kn$
8   $5p^2q^2 + 5pqr$
9   $6st - 2t^2$
10   $u - 2u^2 + 3u^3$

2.
1   $a^2 - 4$
2   $81 - b^2$
3   $4c^2 - 1$
4   $d^2 - 64$
5   $1 - e^2$

6   $9f^2 - g^2$
7   $16h^2 - 25$
8   $49 - 4j^2$
9   $k^2 - 121$
10   $3m^2 - 3$

11   $81n^2 - 1$
12   $p^2q^2 - 9$
13   $5 - 20r^2$
14   $50s^2 - 2t^2$
15   $36 - 4u^2$

3.
1   $ab - bp + 2ar - 2pr$
2   $3c + 3d + c^2 + cd$
3   $ep - fp - 3eq + 3fq$
4   $gh - 5g + h - 5$
5   $12 - 8k + 15m - 10km$

6   $3p - 3q - ap + aq$
7   $21rs + 12r - 28s - 16$
8   $t^2 - 3t - 2tu + 6u$
9   $x^3 + x^2 + x + 1$
10   $xy - x + y - 1$

4.
1   $a^2 + 9a + 20$
2   $b^2 - 5b + 6$
3   $c^2 + 16c - 80$
4   $d^2 - 4d - 12$
5   $e^2 + 3e - 10$
6   $f^2 - f - 20$
7   $g^2 - 12gh + 32h^2$
8   $h^2 + 4h + 4$
9   $j^2 + 4j - 21$
10   $k^2 - 25k + 144$

11   $m^2 + 2m - 48$
12   $n^2 + 14np + 49p^2$
13   $p^2 - 16p + 60$
14   $q^2 + 19q + 84$
15   $r^2 - 8rs - 20s^2$
16   $s^2 - 16s + 15$
17   $t^2 + tu - 12u^2$
18   $v^2 - 3v - 40$
19   $x^2 + 18x + 45$
20   $y^2 - 2yz - 8z^2$

5.
1   $3x^2 + 5x + 2$
2   $2x^2 - 13xy + 6y^2$
3   $2x^2 + 4x - 30$
4   $2x^2 + xy - 10y^2$
5   $3x^2 - 11x - 20$
6   $3x^2 + 12x + 9$
7   $5x^2 + 6x - 8$
8   $3x^2 - 22x + 7$
9   $3x^2 - 5x - 12$
10   $2x^2 + 12x - 14$

11   $2x^2 + 11x - 6$
12   $3x^2 - 10xy - 32y^2$
13   $2x^2 + 7x + 6$
14   $2x^2 - 13x + 15$
15   $3x^2 - 15x - 42$
16   $3x^2 + xy - 2y^2$
17   $5x^2 + 16x + 12$
18   $4x^2 - 8xy + 4y^2$
19   $2x^2 + 12x + 18$
20   $3x^2 - 7x - 6$

6.
1	$9a^3 - 24a^2$		**11**	$2x^2 - 8$
2	$3b^2 - 11b - 4$		**12**	$6x^2 + 7x + 2$
3	$cp - dp + 2cq - 2dq$		**13**	$x^3 + 16x$
4	$2e^2 + 6e - 36$		**14**	$2xy - 4y + x - 2$
5	$5f^2 - 20g^2$		**15**	$3x^2 + 2xy - 8y^2$
6	$h^2 - 9h$		**16**	$18x^2 - 8y^2$
7	$1 - 3k - 4k^2$		**17**	$12 + 4x^2$
8	$2m^2 + 7mn - 4n^2$		**18**	$2x^2 - 5xy - 3y^2$
9	$3p^2 - p - 2$		**19**	$2x^2 + 16xy - 18y^2$
10	$15s^2 + 10st - 3s - 2t$		**20**	$4x^2 + 11x - 3$

Completing the square

This is a process which we will use later when solving quadratic equations.
It involves an expression such as $x^2 + 10x$ and the aim is to add a number so that the whole expression can be written as a square.

Diagramatically:

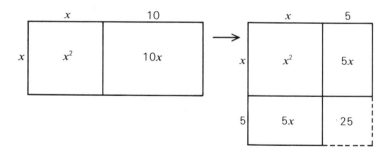

The number to be added is 25,
i.e. $x^2 + 10x + 25 = (x + 5)^2$

25 came from (half of 10) squared.

Similarly, $x^2 - 8x + \ldots$
(Half of 8) squared $= 4^2 = 16$
$x^2 - 8x + 16 = (x - 4)^2$

$x^2 + x + \ldots$
(Half of 1) squared $= (\frac{1}{2})^2 = \frac{1}{4}$
$x^2 + x + \frac{1}{4} = (x + \frac{1}{2})^2$

Exercise 7.4

Add a number to complete the square in these expressions, and write the complete expression as a square.

1. $x^2 + 18x$ 4. $x^2 - x$
2. $x^2 - 6x$ 5. $x^2 + 9x$
3. $x^2 + 5x$

Fractions

Remember that you use the same methods for algebraic fractions as you use for numerical fractions.

Examples

Addition and subtraction

1 $\dfrac{3x}{4} + \dfrac{x - 2y}{6} - \dfrac{2x - y}{12}$

$= \dfrac{9x + 2(x - 2y) - (2x - y)}{12}$

The lowest common denominator is 12.

$\dfrac{3x}{4} = \dfrac{9x}{12}$, $\dfrac{x - 2y}{6} = \dfrac{2(x - 2y)}{12}$, $\dfrac{2x - y}{12}$ still has a bracket.

$= \dfrac{9x + 2x - 4y - 2x + y}{12}$

$= \dfrac{9x - 3y}{12}$

You cannot cancel at this stage.

$= \dfrac{\cancel{3}(3x - y)}{\cancel{12}\,_4}$

There is a common factor 3 which will cancel.

$= \dfrac{3x - y}{4}$

2 $\dfrac{4}{x-4} - \dfrac{3}{x-3}$

$= \dfrac{4(x-3) - 3(x-4)}{(x-4)(x-3)}$

The common denominator is $(x-4)(x-3)$

$\dfrac{4}{x-4} = \dfrac{4(x-3)}{(x-4)(x-3)}, \quad \dfrac{3}{x-3} = \dfrac{3(x-4)}{(x-4)(x-3)}$

$= \dfrac{4x - 12 - 3x + 12}{(x-4)(x-3)}$

$= \dfrac{x}{(x-4)(x-3)}$

You cannot cancel by x as there is no common factor x in the denominator. The denominator is usually left in factor form.

Multiplication and division

3 $\dfrac{x^2 + 4x + 4}{2x - 8} \div \dfrac{2x + 4}{x^2 - 4x}$

Turn the divisor upside down, and multiply. But also, factorise the expressions as far as possible.

$x^2 + 4x + 4 = (x + 2)^2$
$2x - 8 = 2(x - 4)$
$2x + 4 = 2(x + 2)$
$x^2 - 4x = x(x - 4)$

$= \dfrac{\cancel{(x+2)^2}^{\,x+2}}{2\cancel{(x-4)}} \times \dfrac{x\cancel{(x-4)}}{2\cancel{(x+2)}}$

Cancel by $x - 4$, which is a factor.
Cancel by $x + 2$, which is a factor.

$= \dfrac{x(x + 2)}{4}$

You cannot cancel by 2 as there is no common factor 2 in the numerator.

4 $\dfrac{x^2 - y^2}{x^2 - 9} \times \dfrac{2x + 6}{y - x} = \dfrac{(x+y)\cancel{(x-y)}^{-1}}{\cancel{(x+3)}(x-3)} \times \dfrac{2\cancel{(x+3)}}{\cancel{y-x}}$

$= -\dfrac{2(x + y)}{x - 3}$

Note that $y - x$ cancels into $x - y$, giving -1, since $x - y = -(y - x)$

Equations with fractions

Remove the fractions by multiplying.

5 Solve the equation $\dfrac{4}{5x - 3} = \dfrac{1}{x + 3}$

Multiply both sides by $(5x - 3)(x + 3)$

$\dfrac{4}{5x - 3} \times (5x - 3)(x + 3) = 4(x + 3)$

$\dfrac{1}{x + 3} \times (5x - 3)(x + 3) = 5x - 3$

$4(x + 3) = 5x - 3$
$4x + 12 = 5x - 3$
$\quad\quad 15 = x$
$\text{i.e. } x = 15$

You can check this solution by substituting $x = 15$ into each side of the original equation separately.

Exercise 7.5

1. Simplify these expressions.

1 $\dfrac{2}{x} - \dfrac{3}{2x} + \dfrac{4}{3x}$

2 $\dfrac{3x - 1}{2y} + \dfrac{5}{3y} - \dfrac{2x}{y}$

3 $\dfrac{3}{2x - 1} - \dfrac{1}{x + 1}$

4 $\dfrac{2x^2}{x - 3} - \dfrac{6x}{x - 3}$

5 $\dfrac{2}{x + 3} - \dfrac{x - 9}{x^2 - 9}$

2. Simplify these expressions.

1 $\dfrac{x^2 + 3x - 10}{x^2 + 5x}$

2 $\dfrac{3x - 6}{18 - 9x}$

3 $\dfrac{2x^2 - 7x + 3}{x^2 - 9}$

4 $\left(\dfrac{4}{x} + \dfrac{3}{y}\right) \div \dfrac{6}{xy}$

5 $\dfrac{x^2 - 6x + 5}{3x} \times \dfrac{12}{x^2 - 4x + 3} \times \dfrac{x^2 - 4x}{x - 5}$

3. Solve these equations.

1 $\dfrac{x - 2}{3x + 4} = \dfrac{3}{4}$

2 $\dfrac{1}{3x - 8} = \dfrac{5}{x + 2}$

3 $\dfrac{x - 1}{3} - \dfrac{2x + 1}{4} = 0$

4 $\dfrac{x - 2}{2} - \dfrac{2x - 1}{3} + 1 = 0$

5 $\dfrac{2x - 1}{6} + \dfrac{x + 1}{8} = 2\tfrac{1}{4}$

Sequences

Exercise 7.6

Say what the next 2 terms are in each of these sequences, and explain the rule for generating each sequence.

1. 5, 10, 15, 20, 25, . . .
2. 4, 0 −4, −8, −12, . . .
3. 4, 2, 1, 0.5, 0.25, . . .
4. 3, 6, 12, 24, 48, . . .
5. 2, 0.2, 0.02, 0.002, 0.0002, . . .
6. $\frac{1}{25}, \frac{1}{5}$, 1, 5, 25, . . .
7. 81, 54, 36, 24, 16, . . .
8. 4, −8, 16, −32, 64, . . .
9. $2 + \frac{1}{2}, 2 - \frac{1}{4}, 2 + \frac{1}{8}, 2 - \frac{1}{16}, 2 + \frac{1}{32}, \ldots$
10. $\frac{3}{1}, \frac{4}{2}, \frac{5}{3}, \frac{6}{4}, \frac{7}{5}, \ldots$

Convergent sequences

The sequence 4, 2, 1, 0.5, 0.25, . . . gets closer and closer to the value 0 as the number of terms increases.
We could show this on a sketch graph.

The crosses show the values of
the terms.
It is useful to draw the curve,
but the other points on the
curve have no meaning.

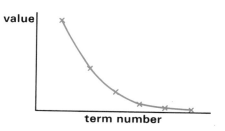

The sequences 2, 0.2, 0.02, 0.002, 0.0002, . . . and 81, 54, 36, 24, 16, . . . also get
closer and closer to the value 0 as the number of terms increases.

The sequence $2 + \frac{1}{2}$, $2 - \frac{1}{4}$, $2 + \frac{1}{8}$,
$2 - \frac{1}{16}$, $2 + \frac{1}{32}$, . . . gets closer and
closer to the value 2 as the number
of terms increases. Alternate values
are greater and less than 2 and
the diagram looks like this:

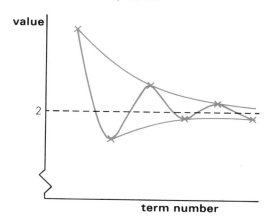

The sequence $\frac{3}{1}$, $\frac{4}{2}$, $\frac{5}{3}$, $\frac{6}{4}$, $\frac{7}{5}$, . . . gets closer and closer to the value 1 as the number of
terms increases.

If a sequence gets closer and closer to a certain value, called the **limit**, as the number
of terms increases, then the sequence is called a **convergent sequence**. The numbers
converge onto the limit.

Any sequence which does not converge to a limit is called a **divergent sequence**.

The sequences 5, 10, 15, 20, 25, . . .; 4, 0, -4, -8, -12, . . .; 3, 6, 12, 24, 48, . . .;
$\frac{1}{25}$, $\frac{1}{5}$, 1, 5, 25, . . .; 4, -8, 16, -32, 64, . . . are all divergent sequences.
Here are sketch graphs for three of these sequences.

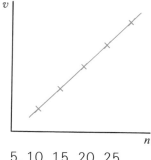

5, 10, 15, 20, 25, . . .

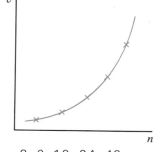

3, 6, 12, 24, 48, . . .

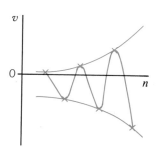

4, -8, 16, -32, 64, . . .

Iterative sequences

These are sequences where every term can be found using the preceding term or terms.
The terms of the sequence are denoted by u_1, u_2, u_3, u_4, . . . the nth term is u_n and the
one after u_n is u_{n+1}.
Other letters can be used instead of u.

Examples

1   The sequence where $u_1 = 1$ and $u_{n+1} = u_n + n + 1$

$u_1 = 1$

$u_2 = u_1 + 1 + 1 = 1 + 1 + 1 = 3$

$u_3 = u_2 + 2 + 1 = 3 + 2 + 1 = 6$

$u_4 = u_3 + 3 + 1 = 6 + 3 + 1 = 10$

and so on.

The sequence is 1, 3, 6, 10, 15, . . . and this is the sequence of triangular numbers.
It is a divergent sequence.
You can use your calculator, or a computer program, to find further terms of the
sequence.

2   The sequence where $u_1 = 1$, $u_2 = 1$ and $u_{n+1} = u_{n-1} + u_n$

$u_3 = u_1 + u_2 = 1 + 1 = 2$

$u_4 = u_2 + u_3 = 1 + 2 = 3$

$u_5 = u_3 + u_4 = 2 + 3 = 5$

and so on.

The sequence is 1, 1, 2, 3, 5, 8, . . . and this is the Fibonacci sequence.
It is a divergent sequence.

3   The sequence where $u_1 = 1$ and $u_{n+1} = 1 + \dfrac{1}{u_n}$

$u_1 = 1$

$u_2 = 1 + \dfrac{1}{u_1} = 1 + 1 = 2$

$u_3 = 1 + \dfrac{1}{u_2} = 1 + \tfrac{1}{2} = 1\tfrac{1}{2} = \tfrac{3}{2}$

$u_4 = 1 + \dfrac{1}{u_3} = 1 + \tfrac{2}{3} = 1\tfrac{2}{3} = \tfrac{5}{3}$

$$u_5 = 1 + \frac{1}{u_4} = 1 + \tfrac{3}{5} = 1\tfrac{3}{5} = \tfrac{8}{5}$$

and so on.

Notice that this sequence is formed from the Fibonacci sequence.

If the successive terms are written as decimals, to 3 decimal places, they are

$u_1 = 1$

$u_2 = 2$

$u_3 = 1.5$

$u_4 = 1.667$

$u_5 = 1.6$

$u_6 = 1.625$

$u_7 = 1.615$

$u_8 = 1.619$

$u_9 = 1.618$

$u_{10} = 1.618$

. . .

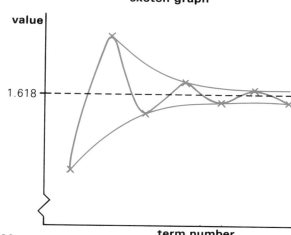

The sequence is a convergent sequence.
The limit is approximately 1.618.

Exercise 7.7

1. Write down the next 2 terms in each of these sequences.
   Say whether each sequence is convergent or divergent.
   For those which are convergent, say what the limit is.

   1   2, 7, 12, 17, . . .

   2 $3 - 2, 3 - \tfrac{2}{3}, 3 - \tfrac{2}{9}, 3 - \tfrac{2}{27}, \ldots$

   3 $1 + 1, 4 + 1, 9 + 1, 16 + 1, \ldots$

   4 $-8, 4, -2, 1, -\tfrac{1}{2}, \ldots$

   5 $10 + 1, 10 - 0.1, 10 + 0.01, 10 - 0.001, \ldots$

   6   1, 2, 6, 24, 120, . . .

   7 $\tfrac{60}{1}, \tfrac{60}{2}, \tfrac{60}{3}, \tfrac{60}{4}, \ldots$

   8 $\tfrac{3}{4}, \tfrac{8}{9}, \tfrac{15}{16}, \tfrac{24}{25}, \ldots$

   9   1, 2, 4, 7, 11, . . .

   10 $\tfrac{4}{1}, \tfrac{7}{2}, \tfrac{10}{3}, \tfrac{13}{4}, \tfrac{16}{5}, \ldots$

2.   Work out the first 10 terms of these sequences and say whether the sequence is convergent or divergent. For those which are convergent, say what the limit is. If the limit cannot be found exactly, give it correct to 2 decimal places.
(Keep as many figures as are available on your calculator but record each term to 4 decimal places. If you use a computer program or graphics calculator you can record the terms to more decimal places, and maybe work out more terms.)

1 $u_{n+1} = 5u_n - 3, \quad u_1 = 1$

2 $u_{n+1} = \dfrac{4}{u_n} + 3, \quad u_1 = 2$

3 $u_{n+1} = \sqrt{2u_n + 1}, \quad u_1 = 1.5$

4 $u_{n+1} = \dfrac{5}{u_n + 3}, \quad u_1 = -2$

5 $u_{n+1} = 3u_n - 2n - 1, \quad u_1 = 5$

6 $u_{n+1} = \dfrac{u_n}{n}, \quad u_1 = 10$

7 $u_{n+1} = 3u_n - 2u_{n-1}, \quad u_1 = 4, u_2 = 5$

8 $u_{n+1} = \dfrac{u_n + u_{n-1}}{2}, \quad u_1 = 3, u_2 = 1$

Numbers

These can be classified into different sets.

Natural numbers

These are the numbers 1, 2, 3, 4, . . .
They can also be called positive integers. (Integer means whole number.)

Positive integers and zero

0, 1, 2, 3, 4, . . .

Negative integers

$-1, -2, -3, -4, . . .$

Integers

. . . , $-4, -3, -2, -1, 0, 1, 2, 3, 4, . . .$

Rational numbers

These are fractions and mixed numbers, as well as the integers.

Any number that can be written as $\frac{m}{n}$, where m and n are integers, is called a rational number.

e.g. -4, $-1\frac{1}{3}$, $-\frac{8}{9}$, 0, $\frac{1}{6}$, $\frac{7}{8}$, 1, $3\frac{4}{5}$, 7, 10.03.

Written as $\frac{m}{n}$, these are $\frac{-4}{1}$, $\frac{-4}{3}$, $\frac{-8}{9}$, $\frac{0}{1}$, $\frac{1}{6}$, $\frac{7}{8}$, $\frac{1}{1}$, $\frac{19}{5}$, $\frac{7}{1}$, $\frac{1003}{100}$.

The fractional part of a rational number can be written as a decimal. If the denominator of the fraction includes only powers of 2 and/or 5, then the decimal will be exact.

e.g. $\frac{3}{8} = 0.375$, $\frac{1}{25} = 0.04$, $\frac{7}{5000} = 0.0014$.

For fractions with other denominators, the decimal will be a recurring decimal.

e.g. $\frac{2}{3} = 0.66666\ldots$ $\frac{1}{22} = 0.0454545\ldots$

$\frac{5}{7} = 0.714285714285\ldots$ $\frac{12}{13} = 0.923076923\ldots$

If you want to show that a decimal is a recurring one, then you write dots over the first and last number of the recurring pattern.

$0.\dot{7}$ means $0.77777\ldots$ $0.\dot{2}9\dot{3}$ means $0.293293293\ldots$

$0.1\dot{6}$ means $0.166666\ldots$ $0.31\dot{2}8\dot{5}$ means $0.31285285285\ldots$

$0.\dot{4}\dot{1}$ means $0.414141\ldots$ $0.9\dot{7}\dot{2}$ means $0.9727272\ldots$

All numbers which end in an exact decimal or a recurring decimal are rational numbers.

Irrational numbers

There are other numbers which are not rational numbers $\left(\text{they cannot be written in the form } \frac{m}{n}\right)$. These are called irrational numbers.

Examples are:

Square roots of numbers which are not perfect squares, e.g. $\sqrt{2}$, $-\sqrt{2.1}$, $\sqrt{26.52}$.

Cube roots of numbers which are not perfect cubes, e.g. $\sqrt[3]{4}$, $-\sqrt[3]{7.3}$.

π, and expressions involving π such as $\frac{\pi}{2}$, π^2, $\pi + 4$.

Most trig. functions where the angle is a rational number of degrees, e.g. $\sin 20°$, $\cos 85.1°$, $\tan 60°$.
(Certain trig. functions are exact and rational, e.g. $\sin 30°$, $\tan 45°$, $\cos 60°$, $\cos 90°$.)

Real numbers

All the rational numbers and irrational numbers combined form the set of real numbers. (Later on you may learn about other numbers which are called imaginary numbers and complex numbers.)

Here are real numbers shown on a number line.

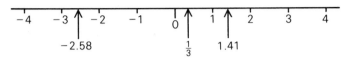

Between the integers there are fractions and mixed numbers, i.e. the rest of the rational numbers.

Between the rational numbers there are the irrational numbers,
e.g. $\sqrt{2}$ is greater than 1.414213
$\sqrt{2}$ is less than   1.414214
Somewhere between the rational numbers 1.414213 and 1.414214 there is the number $\sqrt{2}$.

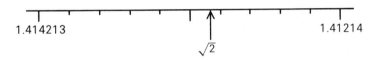

Somewhere between the rational numbers 3.141592 and 3.141593 there is the number π.

Surds

Irrational numbers such as $\sqrt{2}$, $\sqrt{3}$, $\sqrt{5}$ are also called surds.

These rules apply:

$$\sqrt{ab} = \sqrt{a} \times \sqrt{b}$$

$$\sqrt{\frac{a}{b}} = \frac{\sqrt{a}}{\sqrt{b}}$$

Examples

$$\sqrt{44} = \sqrt{4 \times 11} = \sqrt{4} \times \sqrt{11} = 2\sqrt{11}$$

$$\sqrt{6} \times \sqrt{24} = \sqrt{6 \times 24} = \sqrt{144} = 12$$

$$\frac{\sqrt{98}}{\sqrt{2}} = \sqrt{\frac{98}{2}} = \sqrt{49} = 7$$

$$\tfrac{1}{2} \text{ of } \sqrt{28} = \tfrac{1}{2} \times \sqrt{4 \times 7} = \tfrac{1}{2} \times \sqrt{4} \times \sqrt{7} = \sqrt{7}$$

$$\sqrt{6\tfrac{1}{4}} = \sqrt{\frac{25}{4}} = \frac{\sqrt{25}}{\sqrt{4}} = \frac{5}{2} = 2\tfrac{1}{2}$$

Exercise 7.8

1. Say which of these numbers are
    1   natural numbers,
    2   integers,
    3   rational numbers which are not integers,
    4   irrational numbers,
    5   real numbers.

    $2\tfrac{9}{11}, \quad -4, \quad 3.72, \quad \sqrt{20}, \quad \sqrt[3]{1000}, \quad 3\pi, \quad \sqrt[3]{7}, \quad 0, \quad -3\tfrac{1}{2}, \quad 2.\dot{2}0\dot{1}.$

2. In these equations, say whether the solutions are
    (a) natural numbers,
    (b) integers,
    (c) rational numbers which are not integers,
    (d) irrational numbers.

    1 $3(x - 2) = x + 9$

    2 $\dfrac{3x}{4} - \dfrac{5x}{2} = 7$

    3 $x^2 + 1 = 4$

3. Express these fractions as exact or recurring decimals, and then write the recurring decimals correct to 3 decimal places.

    1 $\frac{2}{3}$ **2** $\frac{7}{8}$ **3** $\frac{5}{11}$ **4** $\frac{12}{125}$ **5** $\frac{50}{111}$ **6** $\frac{4}{13}$

4. Simplify these surds.

1 $\sqrt{\dfrac{16}{25}}$ **4** $\sqrt{2} \times \sqrt{3} \times \sqrt{6}$

2 $\sqrt{3\tfrac{1}{16}}$ **5** $\dfrac{\sqrt{45}}{\sqrt{5}}$

3 $\tfrac{1}{3}$ of $\sqrt{162}$ **6** $\dfrac{\sqrt{750}}{\sqrt{30}}$

5. Simplify these numbers, writing them correct to 3 decimal places if they are not exact numbers. Say whether they are rational or irrational.

1	$\tfrac{1}{2}$ of $\sqrt{8}$	**6**	$10^{\frac{1}{2}}$
2	π^2	**7**	10^{-1}
3	$\sin 45°$	**8**	$\sqrt{2} + 3$
4	$\tan 45°$	**9**	$\sqrt{12} \times \sqrt{3}$
5	$0.\dot{5}$	**10**	$\sqrt[3]{27}$

Exercise 7.9   Applications and Activities

1. Pairs of values of related variables are given in these tables.
   Find the equations connecting the variables.

   1 The speed v m/s of a stone dropped and falling through the air, at various times t seconds.

t sec	0	1	2	3	4	5
v m/s	0	9.8	19.6	29.4	39.2	49

   2 The weight W g of a set of discs of different radii r cm but with the same thickness.

r cm	0	1	2	3	4	5
W g	0	15	60	135	240	375

   3 A light bar with a fixed load at one end is pivoted near that end and balanced by different weights W kg hung in turn from different distances d cm along the bar from the pivot.

W kg	1	2	2.5	4	5
d cm	32	16	12.8	8	6.4

4   There is a drop in temperature from that at sea-level as the height above sea-level increases. Here is the approximate relationship between the height h m and temperature $t°C$, when the temperature at sea-level was 10°C.

h m	0	100	200	300	400	500
$t°C$	10	9.4	8.8	8.2	7.6	7.0

5   The weight W g of a set of similar solid model pyramids of different heights h cm.

h cm	0	5	10	15	20
W g	0	100	800	2700	6400

2.   1   The table shows some values of x and y which are linked by the equation $y = 10x^n$.

x	-2	-1	0	1	2
y	-80	-10	0	10	80

Find the value of n.
Find the value of y when $x = \frac{1}{2}$.
Find x when $y = 17.28$.

2   Here are some values of x and y which are linked by the equation $y = 5x^n$.

x	0	1	4	9
y	0	5	10	15

Find the value of n.
Find y when $x = 12.96$.
Find x when $y = 2.5$.

3.   Find the values of the following:

1    $4^{\frac{1}{2}} \times 4^{\frac{3}{2}}$ 6 $\left(\frac{1}{3}\right)^{-2}$

2    $9^{-\frac{1}{2}} \times 16^{\frac{3}{4}}$ 7 $32^{\frac{3}{5}}$

3    $25^{\frac{3}{2}} + 8^{\frac{1}{3}}$ 8 $36^{\frac{1}{2}} + 10^{-2}$

4    $(3^2 + 4^2)^{-\frac{1}{2}}$ 9 $(3^2)^{-1}$

5    $\left(\frac{1}{8}\right)^{\frac{1}{3}} - 2^{-3}$ 10 $\left(5\frac{4}{9}\right)^{\frac{1}{2}}$

4.   Factorise $4a^2 - 4a + 1$ and hence factorise $4a^2 - 4a + 1 - b^2$.

5. The internal volume of this
    hollow metal pipe is given by the
    expression $\pi r^2 h$.
    The total volume (volume of pipe + internal
    volume) is given by $\pi(r + t)^2 h$.
    Find an expression for the volume
    of the metal pipe, giving your
    answer in factorised form.
    If h = 20 cm, t = 1 cm and r = 6.5 cm,
    find the volume of the pipe,
    without using your calculator,
    taking π as $\frac{22}{7}$.

6. Flats are squares of edge x cm. Rods are rectangles x cm long and 1 cm wide.
    Small squares have edge 1 cm.

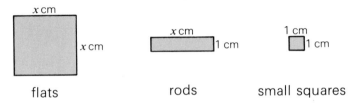

    flats   rods   small squares

    6 flats, 7 rods and 2 small squares are to be arranged to form a rectangle.
    By factorising $6x^2 + 7x + 2$, decide how the pieces can be arranged, and show
    the arrangement on a sketch diagram.

7. Pythagoras' theorem when used to
    find a side other than the
    hypotenuse is given as $c^2 = a^2 - b^2$

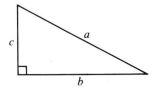

    Write the right-hand side in factors.
    Use the factorised form to calculate side c, without using your calculator, if
    1 a = 25 cm, b = 24 cm,
    2 a = 61 cm, b = 60 cm,
    3 a = 37 cm, b = 35 cm,
    4 a = 17 cm, b = 15 cm,
    5 a = 2.5 cm, b = 1.5 cm.

8. If a regular polygon has n sides, the size of each interior angle is $\dfrac{180(n - 2)°}{n}$.

    Find the number of sides of a regular polygon if each interior angle is 162°.

9. Two numbers are in the ratio $3:4$. When 10 is added to each number, the ratio of the new numbers is $5:6$.
    Find the two original numbers.
    (Let them be $3x$ and $4x$.)

10. Ken cycles to school every morning in 40 minutes. On one day he set off 10 minutes later than usual, so he increased his speed by 5 km/h, and reached school at the normal time.
    If his usual speed is v km/h, write down two expressions for the distance to school, and use them to find his usual speed.

11. The nth term of a sequence is $\dfrac{6n + 5}{n + 7}$. Which term of the sequence is equal to $4\frac{3}{20}$?

12. **1** This sequence can be used to find an approximation for the square root of a number N. The limit of the sequence is $\sqrt{N}$.
    $$u_{n+1} = \frac{1}{2}\left(u_n + \frac{N}{u_n}\right)$$
    Use the sequence to find the square root of 70, correct to 4 decimal places, starting with $u_1 = 7$.

    2 This sequence can be used to find an approximation for the cube root of a number N. The limit of the sequence is $\sqrt[3]{N}$.
    $u_{n+1} = (Nu_n)^{\frac{1}{4}}$.
    For $x^{\frac{1}{4}}$, enter x then press the square root key twice in succession.
    Use the sequence to find the cube root of 100, correct to 4 decimal places, starting with $u_1 = 5$.

13. Use the diagram of an equilateral triangle to find the values of sin 30°, cos 30°, tan 30°, sin 60°, cos 60°, tan 60°.
    Say which of them are rational.

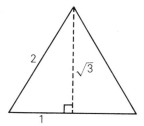

PUZZLE

19. How high is a tree which is 5 m shorter than a pole which is three times as tall as the tree ?

8 Thinking about data and

A histogram with unequal class intervals

The distribution of prices of 600 houses advertised for sale in a local newspaper during a week in 1992 is shown in this histogram.
Notice that the class intervals are unequal, and that the **area** of each block is proportional to the frequency.

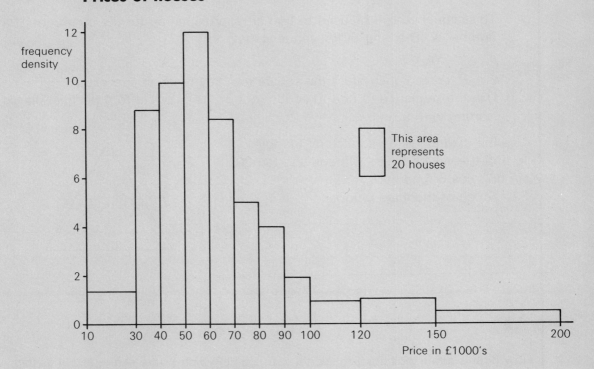

Prices of houses

This area represents 20 houses

distributions

Mean and standard deviation

The numbers of goals scored by 22 football teams in 8 home matches are as follows:
14, 15, 13, 17, 15, 16, 10, 9, 9, 12, 16, 20, 16, 11, 11, 9, 4, 9, 16, 8, 10, 4.
What is the mean number of goals scored ?
Here are the numbers represented on a number line.

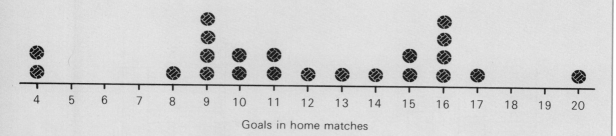

Goals in home matches

The numbers of goals scored by the same teams in 8 away matches are:
16, 8, 11, 9, 7, 10, 13, 8, 11, 9, 10, 10, 8, 7, 5, 7, 9, 5, 7, 10, 10, 8.
What is the mean number of goals scored ?
Here are the numbers shown on a number line. Compare it with the other line.

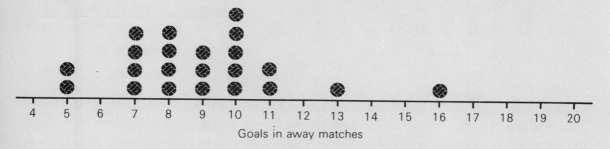

Goals in away matches

You can see that there is a bigger spread of goals in the home matches.

Standard deviation is a measurement of spread (or dispersion). The standard deviation for the home goals is 4.08, and the standard deviation for the away goals is 2.43. You can check these values for yourself, later.

8 Data and distributions

Histograms

The most suitable diagram for representing a frequency distribution with grouped data is a histogram.

In a histogram, the **area** of each block represents the frequency.

Histograms with class intervals of equal width

Example

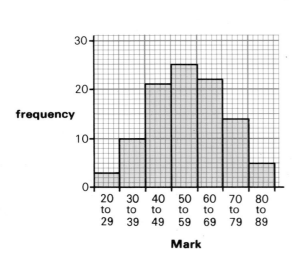

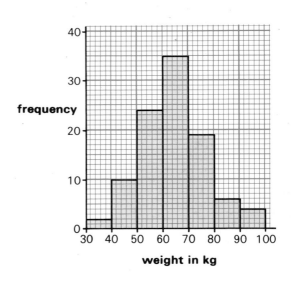

In these histograms, the class intervals are of equal width, so the heights of the columns are in proportion to their frequencies, and can be labelled to represent the frequencies.

Histograms with unequal class intervals

A histogram can have unequal class intervals. In such cases the heights of the columns must be adjusted so that the areas of the blocks are in proportion to their frequencies.

To calculate the heights of the columns,
which are rectangles,
area = height × width of class interval.

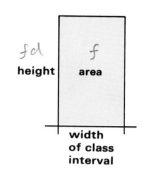

The area represents the frequency, so

$$\text{height} = \frac{\text{frequency}}{\text{width of class interval}}$$

This height can be labelled 'frequency
density', so

$$\text{frequency density} = \frac{\text{frequency}}{\text{width of class interval}}$$

$fd \times w = f$

Example

A check was made of the hours of overtime worked by 400 employees in a certain
firm. Here are the figures:

annual overtime (hours)	0 to <5	5 to <10	10 to <20	20 to <30	30 to <40	40 to <60	60 to <100
frequency (number of employees)	14	22	73	137	95	43	16

In the histogram

area (frequency)	14	22	73	137	95	43	16
class width	5	5	10	10	10	20	40
height $= \dfrac{\text{frequency}}{\text{width}}$	2.8	4.4	7.3	13.7	9.5	2.15	0.4

Histogram

Draw the horizontal axis from 0 to 100, labelling the values for the edges of the
blocks at 0, 5, 10, 20, 30, 40, 60, 100.

Draw the vertical axis from 0 to 14.
Draw each block to the height given in the table.

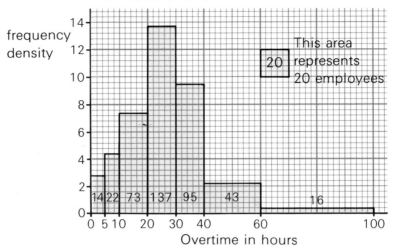

**Histogram to show the distribution
of hours of overtime worked**

Complete the histogram with a title and label the axes.

It is helpful to write the actual frequencies in the blocks as they cannot be read from the vertical axis.

You should also give a key to show how much a certain area represents. Here we have made the block in the key 10 units wide as that is the width of 3 of the central blocks in the histogram. We have drawn it with a height of 2 units, so that in this case it represents a frequency of 20, but we could have made it any suitable height.

Exercise 8.1

1. A survey of 200 cars gave the following distribution of ages.

Age (years)	frequency
0 to <1	18
1 to <2	24
2 to <4	41
4 to <6	32
6 to <8	29
8 to <10	22
10 to <12	20
12 to <15	13

Work out the heights of the columns for a histogram.

Draw the histogram.

Comment briefly on its shape.

2.   A large company made a survey of the income received over a certain period at a sample of 100 of its branches.

Amount (£100 000's)	Number of branches
0-4	11
4-6	22
6-7	19
7-8	15
8-10	18
10-14	15

Draw a histogram of this distribution.

Comment briefly on its shape.

3.   The population of a district was estimated to be as follows:

Age (years)	Population in 1000's
0-4	18
5-14	33
15-64	201
65-74	36
75-94	32
	320

Draw a histogram of the distribution and comment briefly on its shape.

(0-4 means 0 to under 5 and the class interval is 5 years, similarly 5-14 means 5 to under 15 and the class interval is 10 years.)

Dispersion

You already know two measures of dispersion, the range and the interquartile range.

The range = highest value − lowest value

The interquartile range = value of upper quartile − value of lower quartile.

Standard deviation

This is another measure of dispersion. In advanced methods of statistics it is much more useful than the other two measures.

To find the standard deviation

We shall describe this by taking a simple example of 5 variables, which are
1, 2, 6, 7, 9.

First, find the mean. $\bar{x} = \dfrac{\Sigma x}{n} = \dfrac{25}{5} = 5$

Find the deviation of each variable from the mean.
$1 - 5, 2 - 5, 6 - 5, 7 - 5, 9 - 5$; giving $-4, -3, 1, 2, 4$.
The sum of these deviations is 0, because they are deviations from the mean.

Square the deviations.
$(-4)^2, (-3)^2, 1^2, 2^2, 4^2$; giving 16, 9, 1, 4, 16.
Add up these. $16 + 9 + 1 + 4 + 16 = 46$
Find the average. $\frac{46}{5} = 9.2$
Take the square root. $\sqrt{9.2} = 3.03$, to 2 dec. pl.

This is the standard deviation of the set of numbers. It gives a measure of the 'average'
deviation of each number from the mean, although by squaring the deviations, values
further away from the mean affect the answer more than values nearer to the mean.

Here are the instructions, again.

To find the standard deviation of a set of numbers

Find the mean.
Find the deviation of each variable from the mean.
(Check that the sum of the deviations is 0.)
Square the deviations, and find the sum of the squares.
Find the average of the squares.
Take the square root of the average.

Here is the formula for the standard deviation of a set of numbers.

$$s = \sqrt{\dfrac{\Sigma(x - \bar{x})^2}{n}}$$

Here is the working set down in columns.

x	$x - \bar{x}$	$(x - \bar{x})^2$
1	-4	16
2	-3	9
6	1	1
7	2	4
9	4	16
25	0	46

$$\bar{x} = \frac{\Sigma x}{n} = \frac{25}{5} = 5$$

$$s = \sqrt{\frac{\Sigma(x - \bar{x})^2}{n}}$$

$$= \sqrt{\frac{46}{5}} = 3.03, \text{ to 2 dec. pl.}$$

check that this total is 0

When the data is given in whole numbers, work out the mean to 1 decimal place and the standard deviation to 2 decimal places.

Here is another example. Again, we have only taken 6 items, for simplicity. Usually there would be more.

Example

The lengths of 6 rods are 55 cm, 56 cm, 57 cm, 63 cm, 67 cm, 68 cm.

x	$x - \bar{x}$	$(x - \bar{x})^2$
55	-6	36
56	-5	25
57	-4	16
63	2	4
67	6	36
68	7	49
366	0	166

$$\bar{x} = \frac{\Sigma x}{n} = \frac{366}{6} \text{ cm} = 61 \text{ cm}$$

$$s = \sqrt{\frac{\Sigma(x - \bar{x})^2}{n}} = \sqrt{\frac{166}{6}} \text{ cm}$$

$$= \sqrt{27.666\ldots} \text{ cm}$$
$$= 5.26 \text{ cm, to 2 dec. pl.}$$

Remember to give the units, in this case, cm.

If the mean is not exact, it is easier to use an alternative formula for the standard deviation.

$$s = \sqrt{\frac{\Sigma x^2}{n} - \left(\frac{\Sigma x}{n}\right)^2}$$

It can be proved algebraically that this formula is correct.

We will do the previous example using this formula.

x	x^2
55	3025
56	3136
57	3249
63	3969
67	4489
68	4624
366	22492

$$s = \sqrt{\frac{\Sigma x^2}{n} - \left(\frac{\Sigma x}{n}\right)^2}$$

$$= \sqrt{\frac{22492}{6} - \left(\frac{366}{6}\right)^2} \quad \text{cm}$$

$$= \sqrt{27.666\ldots} \quad \text{cm}$$

$$= 5.26\,\text{cm, to 2 dec. pl.}$$

In using this formula for standard deviation, we can measure the x-numbers from any chosen number, not necessarily from 0. The chosen number is called an assumed mean and it is written as x_0.

In this example, suppose the readings were all taken from an assumed mean of 60 cm. Then 55 cm would be written as -5 cm, 68 cm would be $+8$ cm, etc. This will simplify the working, which now looks like this:

Old x	New x with $x_0 = 60$	x^2
55	-5	25
56	-4	16
57	-3	9
63	$+3$	9
67	$+7$	49
68	$+8$	64
	$+6$	172

To find the mean, add x_0 to the formula

$$\bar{x} = x_0 + \frac{\Sigma x}{n}$$

$$= (60 + \tfrac{6}{6}) \quad \text{cm}$$

$$= 61\,\text{cm}$$

$$s = \sqrt{\frac{\Sigma x^2}{n} - \left(\frac{\Sigma x}{n}\right)^2}$$

$$= \sqrt{\frac{172}{6} - \left(\tfrac{6}{6}\right)^2} \quad \text{cm}$$

$$= \sqrt{27.666\ldots} \quad \text{cm}$$

$$= 5.26\,\text{cm, to 2 dec. pl.}$$

If you are asked to find the standard deviation of a set of data, **showing your working**, then you should use one of the above methods, setting down the values in columns as shown.

You can use your calculator, as usual, to work out any calculations needed.

At other times, or for checking answers, you can use a statistical calculator or a computer program. You enter the data, and the program will calculate the value of the mean and the standard deviation.

There is some confusion over notation.
We have used $\bar{x}$ for the mean.
Actually, $\bar{x}$ should be used if it is the mean of a sample.
μ (the Greek letter mu) should be used if it is the population mean.
Similarly,
s should be used for the standard deviation of a sample.
σ (the small Greek letter sigma) should be used if it is the population standard deviation.

These differences are unimportant except in more advanced work. We will continue to use $\bar{x}$ and s.

However, if you use a statistical calculator or a computer to find the standard deviation, it calculates the standard deviation of a **sample** using a slightly different formula. You will not get the same value of the answer if you use the $\boxed{s}$ key. Instead you should use the key $\boxed{\sigma}$.

To do the last example using a statistical calculator:
Set the calculator to work in statistical mode.
Press 55 DATA 56 DATA 57 DATA 63 DATA 67 DATA 68 DATA

Then if you press Σx you will get 366.
If you press Σx^2 you will get 22 492.
If you press $\bar{x}$ you will get 61.   (This is the mean.)
If you press σ you will get 5.2599. . .   (This is the standard deviation.)

Exercise 8.2

For the following sets of data, find the mean and the standard deviation.

1. The numbers of matches in 10 boxes.
    52   45   47   50   51   53   46   52   46   48

2. The temperature in London on 7 days of a week, in °C.
    15°,   17°,   16°,   14°,   13°,   17°,   20°.

3. The times taken by a mechanic to do 5 jobs, in minutes.
    36   45   26   55   40

4. The ages of 11 footballers, in years.
    38   29   26   31   27   24   29   26   30   26   22

5. The heights of 6 pupils.
    1.66 m,   1.48 m,   1.70 m,   1.56 m,   1.62 m,   1.46 m.

6. The weekly wages of 4 people in an office.
    £101,   £84,   £118,   £127.

7. The weights of 8 packets of tea, in grams.
    503   510   507   500   504   507   501   500

8. The attendances of a class on 5 days.
    25   26   28   27   23

9. The heights of 6 plants, in cm.
    31   28   29   26   33   30

10. The marks of 10 students in an examination.
    60   63   72   91   55   75   80   68   50   84

Shapes of histograms

We often draw a histogram because we can deduce things from its general shape.
Here are some examples.

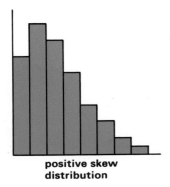

positive skew distribution

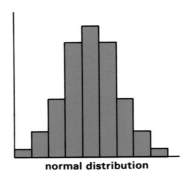

normal distribution

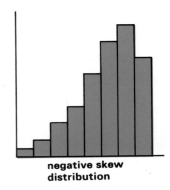

negative skew distribution

If we replace the histogram with a smooth curve, which encloses the same area
between the curve and the x-axis as is enclosed by the histogram, then these
histograms can be replaced by these frequency curves.

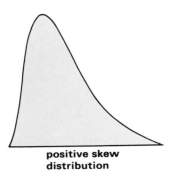

positive skew distribution

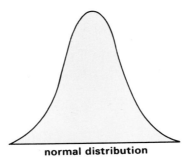

normal distribution

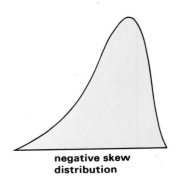

negative skew distribution

On these distributions, the positions of the mean, median and mode are roughly as shown:
The mode is at the peak of the curve.
The median divides the curve into two equal areas.

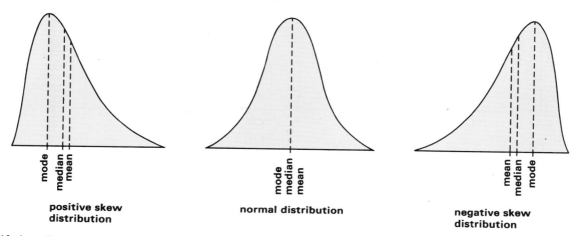

**positive skew
distribution**   **normal distribution**   **negative skew
distribution**

If the distribution is skewed, the median is often a better average to use than the mean, as the mean is affected by extreme values.

Examples of a positively skewed distribution:
The number of children in families,
the number of goals scored in football matches,
exam marks when the exam was too hard.

Examples of a negatively skewed distribution:
Exam marks when the exam was too easy,
speed of traffic on a motorway.

The Normal Distribution

The word 'normal' here implies a distribution with this bell-shaped curve.
It is symmetrical about the line through its peak, which gives the position of the mean, median and mode.

Many observations are normally distributed, or nearly so.
Examples are:
Heights of people,
lengths of leaves from a tree,
exam marks when the exam is set to match the ability of the pupils,
lifetimes of light bulbs,
weights of manufactured products, e.g. bags of sugar,
estimates of length.

Another property of the normal distribution curve is the relationship between the curve, the mean and the standard deviation.

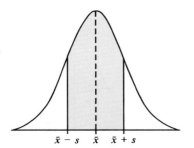 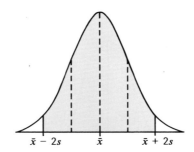 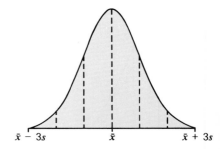

The curve is symmetrical about the mean so there is 50% of its area on either side of the mean.

About 68% (roughly $\frac{2}{3}$) of its area lies within 1 standard deviation of the mean on either side.

About 95% of its area lies within 2 standard deviations of the mean.

About 99.8% of its area lies within 3 standard deviations of the mean.
(This is **nearly all**,—only 0.2% of the area lies outside this range, 0.1% on either side.)

The curve tails off at both ends.

We can use these facts to estimate the percentage of the population in each part.

Example

The weights of a large number of pupils in the same age-group have been recorded, and the weights are found to be normally distributed. The mean weight is 46 kg and the standard deviation is 3 kg.

Using the properties of the normal distribution curve, here are the estimated percentages of pupils whose weights are within various ranges.

The distribution is symmetrical about the mean.

50% of the pupils weigh less than 46 kg and 50% weigh more than 46 kg.

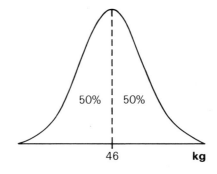

68% of the weights lie within 1
standard deviation on either
side of the mean.

This leaves 16% of the pupils
weighing less than 43 kg and
16% weighing over 49 kg.

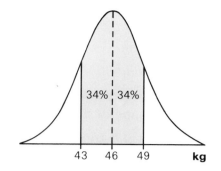

95% of the weights lie within 2
standard deviations on either
side of the mean.

This leaves $2\frac{1}{2}$% of the pupils
weighing less than 40 kg and $2\frac{1}{2}$%
weighing over 52 kg.

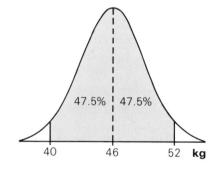

Nearly all the weights are within
3 standard deviations on either
side of the mean.

Only 1 pupil out of 1000 would
weigh less than 37 kg, and only
1 pupil out of 1000 would weigh
more than 55 kg.

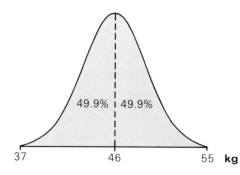

Exercise 8.3

Questions 1 to 8.
Here are data of some distributions. Sketch (roughly) the frequency distribution curves and describe the shape of the distributions.

1.   The times taken by runners in a 10-mile road race.

	Number of runners
50 min but less than 1 hour	57
1 hr but less than 1 hr 10 min	221
1 hr 10 min but less than 1 hr 20 min	276
1 hr 20 min but less than 1 hr 30 min	163
1 hr 30 min but less than 1 hr 40 min	51
1 hr 40 min but less than 1 hr 50 min	16
1 hr 50 min but less than 2 hr	8
2 hr but less than 2 hr 10 min	5
2 hr 10 min but less than 2 hr 20 min	3

2.   The ages of the population of the UK in 1901.

Age (years)	Number of people
0-under 10	8 500 000
10-under 20	7 800 000
20-under 30	7 000 000
30-under 40	5 300 000
40-under 50	4 000 000
50-under 60	2 800 000
60-under 70	1 800 000
70-under 80	800 000
80 and over	200 000

3.   The examination marks of a year-group of children.

Mark	20-29	30-39	40-49	50-59	60-69	70-79	80-89	90-99
Number of pupils	2	3	8	18	21	29	14	5

4. The heights of a group of girls.

Height in cm	f
110 – <120	5
120 – <130	27
130 – <140	70
140 – <150	66
150 – <160	26
160 – <170	4

5   The times of pupils' arrival at school.

Time	Number of pupils
8.15-8.25	20
8.25-8.35	50
8.35-8.45	150
8.45-8.55	240
8.55-9.05	140
9.05-9.15	50
9.15-9.25	10
	660

6. The weights of 100 small animals.

Weight in g	frequency
70-<80	3
80-<90	6
90-<100	12
100-<110	18
110-<120	21
120-<130	18
130-<140	13
140-<150	7
150-<160	2
	100

7.   The distribution of the number of heads when 10 coins are tossed 1024 times.

Number of heads	0	1	2	3	4	5	6	7	8	9	10
Frequency	1	10	45	120	210	252	210	120	45	10	1

8.   The number of children in 150 families.

Number of children	0	1	2	3	4	5	6
Number of families	80	27	25	11	4	2	1

9.   Here is the distribution of times spent by 60 teenagers watching television on a particular day.

Time in hours	Number of teenagers
0 to just under 1	12
1 to just under 2	22
2 to just under 3	17
3 to just under 4	7
4 to just under 5	2

Sketch roughly the frequency distribution curve.
The mode of the distribution is 1.7 hours.
The median of the distribution is 1.8 hours.
The mean of the distribution is 1.9 hours.
Show these averages in their approximate positions on the sketch.

10.   The birth weights of a large number of babies born in the local hospital were recorded. The distribution was approximately normal with mean weight 7.6 lb and standard deviation of weights 1.1 lb.

Approximately what percentage of the babies
1   weighed less than 7.6 lb,
2   weighed between 6.5 lb and 8.7 lb,
3   weighed between 5.4 lb and 9.8 lb ?
4   Between which weights were most of the babies ?

11.   The marks in a particular examination were approximately normally distributed
       with mean 60 and standard deviation 12.

       Approximately, what percentage of candidates
       1   scored between 48 and 72 marks,
       2   scored less than 48 marks,
       3   scored between 36 and 84 marks,
       4   scored between 72 and 84 marks,
       5   scored over 84 marks ?

Exercise 8.4   Applications and Activities

1.   The age distribution of the population of the UK in 1989 is given in the table. The
      figures are in 100 000's.
      Draw two histograms, one for males, one for females.
      Comment on the shapes of your graphs, and their similarities and differences.

Age (years)	males	females
0-4	19.5	18.6
5-9	18.6	17.7
10-14	17.4	16.5
15-19	20.9	19.9
20-29	47.0	45.7
30-39	39.0	38.7
40-49	36.9	36.8
50-59	30.0	30.6
60-69	27.6	31.1
70-79	16.0	23.3
80-94	6.1	14.5

(A few people in the last group are 95 or over.)

2.   The heights of 2000 men were measured. These heights were found to be
      normally distributed with a mean of 172 cm and a standard deviation of 6 cm.

      Approximately, how many of these men,
      1   had heights between 166 cm and 178 cm,
      2   had heights between 160 cm and 172 cm,
      3   had heights between 172 cm and 190 cm,
      4   were taller than 190 cm,
      5   were smaller than 160 cm ?

3. Here is data about the heights of a class of Year 8 pupils in a local school. All the heights were measured to the nearest cm.

Boys' heights (in cm): 164, 155, 150, 159, 146, 150, 149, 167, 156, 156, 170, 172, 161, 160, 155, 158.

Girls' heights (in cm): 150, 159, 156, 153, 152, 159, 156, 150, 170, 154, 160, 160, 159, 159, 162, 160, 167.

Find
1   the mean of the boys' heights,
2   the standard deviation of the boys' heights,
3   the mean of the girls' heights,
4   the standard deviation of the girls' heights.
Comment on the results.

You can do a similar survey of the heights of the pupils in your class, or of pupils in a Year 8 class if you want to compare the data with that above.

4. **The binomial distribution for $n = 10$**

There is a large quantity of red beads and blue beads in a box. Random samples of 10 are taken and the numbers of red beads in the samples are counted.

Here are the results of 200 samples.

Number of red heads	0	1	2	3	4	5	6	7	8	9	10
Number of samples	5	25	47	53	40	20	8	2	0	0	0

Draw a bar-line graph of the distribution, and use it to draw an approximate frequency curve. Comment on the shape of the curve.

If the proportion of beads which are red is P, then the mean number of red beads per sample is $10P$.
Calculate the mean of the distribution, and hence find the proportion of red beads in the box.
Also find the median and the mode of the distribution.

5. **1**   8 pupils travel to school by bus and their fares are (in pence),

29   32   35   36   39   40   45   48

Find the mean and standard deviation of the fares.

   2   Each pupil also travels home by bus, at a similar fare.
State, or find, the mean and standard deviation of the total fares for the double journey, to and from school.

   3   The bus company has announced that it is going to increase all the above fares by 4p each.
State, or find, the mean and standard deviation of the new fares for travelling to school.

PUZZLES

20.   If a tennis ball is dropped from a height of 25 m, and on each rebound rises to $\frac{1}{5}$ of its previous height, what distance will it travel before it comes to rest ?

21.   Of 3 people sitting at a table in a cafe, 2 have ordered cups of tea, 2 have ordered sandwiches and 2 have ordered scones. One who is not having a cup of tea is not having a sandwich, either. One who is not having a scone is not having a cup of tea. What is each person going to have ?

22.   Khalid won a fishing competition by catching a huge fish. When I asked him what it weighed, he replied, 'To twice the weight (in pounds), add 10 more than the square root of twice the weight. This amount added to its square is equal to 1640.'
How heavy was the fish ?

23.   40 people went together to an amusement park. The price for adults was £4 each more than the price for children.
The total price was £312, of which £60 was for the children.
How many on the trip were children ?

24.   Can you decode this calculation, where each letter stands for a different figure ?

```
                    T  R  Y
         Y  E ) M  A  T  H  S
               M  M  M
               Y  H  H
               Y  Y  Y
                  S  S  S
                  S  S  S
```

25.   On a camping expedition, every two people shared a tin of soup, every three people shared a tin of meat and every four people shared a tin of fruit. How many people were on the expedition if 78 tins altogether were opened ?

9 Thinking about accuracy and error

Mount Everest

This is the world's highest mountain, and it is on the Tibet–Nepal border. It was surveyed between 1845 and 1850. There were problems because the survey had to be done from a distance of about 120 miles away. It was surveyed from six stations and the heights found varied from 28 990 feet to 29 026 feet, with an average of 29 002 feet.

To quote the height to the nearest 10 feet might have been sensible, normally, but in this case, that would be 29 000 feet, which might have suggested that the height was only an estimate to the nearest 1000 feet. So the figure of 29 002 feet was adopted, and you will find this given on old maps.

The mountain was surveyed from a nearer distance between 1952 and 1955, and the height is now quoted at 29 028 feet ± 25 feet, (8848 m), above sea level.

The Channel Tunnel

A recent situation where measurements have to be made to great accuracy is in the construction of the Channel Tunnel.

The breakthrough. English and French workers meet.

A view of Mount Everest.

Accuracy in weighing

You could try this recipe for chocolate fudge:
100 g plain chocolate
100 g butter or margarine
450 g icing sugar
45 ml milk
Place everything in a large ovenproof dish and microwave on high for 3 minutes or until the chocolate has melted.
Alternatively, use a pan and melt the ingredients over a low heat, stirring continuously, and adding the icing sugar when the butter and chocolate have melted.
Beat well until smooth.
Pour into a greased dish, 20 cm by 15 cm.
Using a sharp knife, mark into squares.
Leave for 1 to 2 hours to set.

How accurately would you need to weigh or measure the ingredients ?

Calculating area

The diagram shows the effect on the area of a rectangular field *ABCD* when using the lower bounds, or the upper bounds, of the length and breadth.

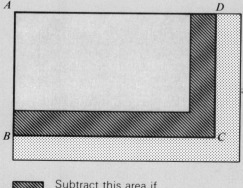

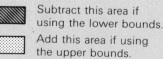

Subtract this area if using the lower bounds.

Add this area if using the upper bounds.

When weighing precious metals great accuracy is needed.

9 Accuracy and error

In counting large numbers of items, it is sometimes not necessary to be completely accurate. An approximate total may be sufficient. For example, the number of people visiting a fair can be estimated. The exact number of people is not needed and would be difficult to obtain. On the other hand, the exact number of people attending an exhibition where they had to pay and enter through turnstiles is much easier to find. Even so, it might be sufficient to know that about 3000 people attended on one day, rather than knowing that the exact number was 3279. If the figure of 3000 was not sufficiently accurate for a purpose, then 3300 might be good enough.

Upper and lower bounds of numbers

If we are expressing numbers correct to the nearest whole number, then
7.49 to the nearest whole number is 7,
6.51 to the nearest whole number is 7.
In fact, 7.49, 7.499, 7.4999, . . . are all 7, to the nearest whole number.
These numbers get nearer and nearer to 7.5, so 7.5 is the **upper bound** (boundary) of numbers which are corrected to 7.

6.51, 6.501, 6.5001, 6.50001, . . . are also all 7, to the nearest whole number.
These numbers get nearer and nearer to 6.5, so 6.5 is the **lower bound** of numbers which are corrected to 7.

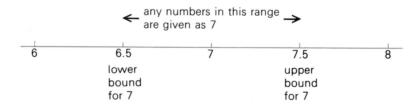

Similarly, 13 to the nearest whole number can represent any number from 12.5 to 13.5
Then, 14 to the nearest whole number can represent any number from 13.5 to 14.5.
You can see that a number such as 13.5 which is exactly on the boundary can either be corrected down or corrected up. We normally correct it up. However, this is just a rule made for convenience. Other rules can be made which are just as acceptable, but we will not confuse you by mentioning them here. Just work to the usual rule.

Work to one more figure than you need.
If that figure is 5 or more, correct up.
If that figure is 4 or less, do not correct up.

However, now we are considering this procedure in reverse and we have to **include the upper and lower bounds** as possible original numbers.

e.g. 7 to the nearest whole number can represent a number lying anywhere between 6.5 and 7.5 inclusive.

13 to the nearest whole number can represent a number lying anywhere between 12.5 and 13.5 inclusive.

9 to the nearest whole number can represent a number lying anywhere between 8.5 and 9.5 inclusive.

A similar idea works with numbers which are given correct to 1 decimal place.

8.7 can represent a number lying anywhere between 8.65 and 8.75 inclusive.

20.2 can represent a number lying anywhere between 20.15 and 20.25 inclusive.

9.0 can represent a number lying anywhere between 8.95 and 9.05 inclusive.

These next numbers are correct to 2 decimal places.

2.34 can represent a number lying anywhere between 2.335 and 2.345 inclusive.

8.99 can represent a number lying anywhere between 8.985 and 8.995 inclusive.

9.00 can represent a number lying anywhere between 8.995 and 9.005 inclusive.

Notice the differences with the boundaries for 9 (to the nearest whole number), 9.0 (to 1 dec. pl.) and 9.00 (to 2 dec. pl.).

If you correct a number to 1 decimal place, and the number in this decimal place is 0, you should still write it in the answer to show that you are working correct to 1 decimal place.

e.g. $16.1 \div 4 = 4.025$

       $= 4.0$, correct to 1 dec. pl.

If you correct a number to 2 decimal places and the number in the 2nd decimal place is 0, you should still write it in the answer to show that you are working correct to 2 decimal places.

e.g. $3 \times \tan 25° = 1.3989 . . .$

       $= 1.40$, correct to 2 dec. pl.

By writing 1, 2 or more decimal places we can tell how accurate we have made the number.

With numbers of tens, i.e. 10, 20, 30, etc. it is not possible to tell whether they have been corrected to the nearest whole number, with a units figure which just happens to be 0, or corrected to the nearest ten.

20 to the nearest whole number can represent a number lying anywhere between 19.5 and 20.5 inclusive.

20 to the nearest ten can represent a number lying anywhere between 15 and 25 inclusive.

There are similar difficulties for hundreds, thousands, etc.

500 to the nearest whole number can represent a number lying anywhere between 499.5 and 500.5 inclusive.
500 to the nearest ten can represent a number lying anywhere between 495 and 505 inclusive.
500 to the nearest hundred can represent a number lying anywhere between 450 and 550 inclusive.

Significant figures

The rules for correcting up to 1, 2, 3, . . . significant figures are similar to the rules for correcting up to whole numbers or to so many decimal places.
Significant figures are the figures of the number not counting any 0's which are just filling in spaces at the beginning or end of the number.

329 correct to 3 sig. fig. can lie between 328.5 and 329.5 inclusive.

6.04 correct to 3 sig. fig. can lie between 6.035 and 6.045 inclusive.

0.069 correct to 2 sig. fig. can lie between 0.0685 and 0.0695 inclusive.

9620 correct to 3 sig. fig. can lie between 9615 and 9625 inclusive.

9620 correct to 4 sig. fig. can lie between 9619.5 and 9620.5 inclusive.

Exercise 9.1

1.   Write these numbers to the accuracy stated.

1	2.254	to 1 dec. pl.
2	10.87	to 3 sig. fig.
3	9.723	to 2 dec. pl.
4	0.416	to 2 sig. fig.
5	0.0723	to 3 dec. pl.
6	12.37	to the nearest whole number
7	144.9	to the nearest ten
8	250.4	to the nearest hundred
9	4237	to 2 sig. fig.
10	0.8076	to 3 sig. fig.

2.   Give the lower and upper bounds of these numbers.

1	4.21	**6**	120	(given to the nearest ten)
2	0.69	**7**	22.0	
3	3.259	**8**	3400	(given to the nearest hundred)
4	15	**9**	92.00	
5	7.83	**10**	2100	(given to 3 sig. fig.)

3.   The numbers or measurements in these statements have been given to several
      figures.
      For each statement, correct the figures to what **you consider** to be a sensible
      degree of accuracy, state the degree of accuracy that you are using, and then
      state the lower and upper bounds of your number.

   1   The girl's height is 1.605 m.
   2   The time taken to fill a tank was 3 h 44 min 22.3 s.
   3   The attendance at a show was 7592 people.
   4   The distance of the Sun from the Earth is 92 955 829 miles.
   5   The capacity of a car's fuel tank is 40.914 ℓ.
   6   The area of a paddock is 1979.0575 m^2.
   7   The weight of the man is 120.765 kg.
   8   The average amount per child spent by 7 children was 78.57143 p.
   9   The average age of the 7 children was 10 years 8.57143 months.
   10   The amount of wheat produced was 11716.583 tonnes.
   11   The population of the town is 28 807.
   12   The length of the race (5 miles) is 8.0465 km.

Calculations involving approximate numbers

Addition

If you add two approximate numbers then the total is also approximate.

Example

   2.75 and 3.17 are each given to 2 decimal places.

   2.75 + 3.17 = 5.92

Normally, we give the answer as 5.92, and you should continue to do this in most
questions.

However, it is sometimes important to realise that the answer may differ from 5.92, and you may be asked to find the lower and upper bounds of the answer.

Lower bound.   2.75 has a lower bound of 2.745
                    3.17 has a lower bound of 3.165
                                              5.910

The lower bound of the sum is 5.91, written to 2 dec. pl.

Upper bound.   2.75 has an upper bound of 2.755
                    3.17 has an upper bound of 3.175
                                              5.930

The upper bound of the sum is 5.93, written to 2 dec. pl.

Subtraction

Using the same numbers as above, for 3.17 − 2.75,

3.17	3.165	3.175
2.75	2.755	2.745
0.42	0.410	0.430

The usual answer would be 0.42, but the answer can range from 0.41 (lower bound) to 0.43 (upper bound).

Notice that to find the least difference, we take the lower bound of the larger number and the upper bound of the smaller number.
To find the greatest difference, we take the upper bound of the larger number and the lower bound of the smaller number.
This is shown in a diagram.

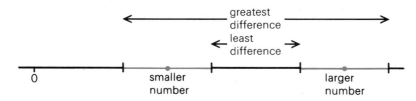

Multiplication

    3.17 × 2.75   = 8.7175   = 8.72, to 2 dec. pl.

Lower bound:
3.165 × 2.745 = 8.687925 = 8.69, to 2 dec. pl.
Upper bound:
3.175 × 2.755 = 8.747125 = 8.75, to 2 dec. pl.

The usual answer would be 8.72, to 2 dec. pl., or 8.7, to 1 dec. pl.
2 decimal places would be suitable as the original numbers are given to 2 decimal places, but 1 decimal place might be better, considering that the possible answers can range from 8.69 to 8.75.

Division

3.17 ÷ 2.75   = 1.1527. . . = 1.153, to 3 dec. pl.
3.165 ÷ 2.755 = 1.1488. . . = 1.149, to 3 dec. pl.
3.175 ÷ 2.745 = 1.1566. . . = 1.157, to 3 dec. pl.

The usual answer would be 1.153, to 3 dec. pl. For the possible answers the lower bound is 1.149 and the upper bound is 1.157.

3 decimal places would be suitable for a division question as the original number to be divided was given to 2 decimal places, but 2 decimal places might be better, considering the possible range of answers.

Notice that to find the lowest possible answer, divide the lower bound of the first number by the upper bound of the second number.
To find the highest possible answer, divide the upper bound of the first number by the lower bound of the second number.

Multiplication or division of an approximate number by an exact number

Examples

1 28.3 × 100

If 28.3 is a number correct to 1 decimal place then the lower bound is 28.25 and the upper bound is 28.35.
If 100 is an exact number, then
28.3 × 100 = 2830
28.25 × 100 = 2825
28.35 × 100 = 2835

The usual answer is 2830, the lower bound is 2825 and the upper bound is 2835.

Notice that the possible error in 28.3 is ±0.05, and when this is multiplied by 100 the possible error in the result is 100 times as large.
±0.05 × 100 = ±5.

Error used here does not mean mistake, it means the difference between the stated result and the true result.

2 $63 \div 5$

If 63 is a number correct to the nearest whole number then the lower bound is 62.5 and the upper bound is 63.5.

If 5 is an exact number, then

$63 \div 5 \quad = 12.6$
$62.5 \div 5 = 12.5$
$63.5 \div 5 = 12.7$

The usual answer is 12.6, the lower bound is 12.5 and the upper bound is 12.7.

Notice that the possible error in 63 is ± 0.5, but when this is divided by 5, the possible error is $\frac{1}{5}$ of this.

$\pm 0.5 \div 5 = \pm 0.1$

Exercise 9.2

1. Work out these calculations, where each number is given to 2 decimal places. Give the usual answer, and also the lower and upper bounds of the possible answers, all to 2 decimal places.

    1 $5.12 + 2.53$ **4** 35.42×7.81
    2 $8.66 - 4.47$ **5** 8.67^2
    3 14.02×5.29

2. Work out these calculations, where each number is given to the nearest whole number. Give the usual answer, and also the lower and upper bounds of the possible answers, all to 2 significant figures.

    1 $46 + 29$ **4** $19 \div 70$
    2 $60 - 30$ **5** $53 \div 12$
    3 12×7

3. Work out these calculations, where each number is given to 1 decimal place. Give the usual answer, and also the lower and upper bounds of the possible answers, all to 3 significant figures.

    1 $10.3 + 5.2$ **4** $10.7 \div 5.8$
    2 $22.0 - 3.7$ **5** $22.3 \div 9.9$
    3 31.5×8.6

4. Work out these calculations, where the first number is given correct to 3 significant figures, and the second number is an exact number. Give the usual answer and also the lower and upper bounds of the possible answers, all to 3 significant figures.

    1 5.37 × 16   **4** 2.96 ÷ 8
    2 12.9 ÷ 30   **5** 56 700 ÷ 6
    3 0.505 × 12

Accuracy of measurements

Since measurements are continuous, i.e. they go up gradually, not in jumps, all measurements are approximations.
e.g. If the length of a line is given as 10.8 cm then this has been measured to the nearest mm and the actual length can lie anywhere between 10.75 cm and 10.85 cm.
If the length was measured more accurately and given as 10.77 cm, the actual length could lie between 10.765 cm and 10.775 cm.

Exercise 9.3   Applications and Activities

In questions 1 to 12, give answers to what you consider to be a sensible degree of accuracy.

1. Two sides of a rectangle were measured to the nearest mm, as 8.7 cm and 5.2 cm.
    1 Find the least and greatest possible values of the perimeter.
    2 Find the least and greatest possible values of the area.

2. A metal rod was measured as 155.3 cm. After a length was cut off, its new length was 89.9 cm. The measurements were made to the nearest mm. What are the least and greatest values of the reduction in length ?

3. The weight of 1 cm^3 of silver is stated to be 10.6 g, to 3 significant figures. What are the lower and upper bounds for the weight of 50 cm^3 of silver ?

4. 5 sample packages were weighed, each to the nearest gram, and their weights were 495 g, 501 g, 486 g, 499 g and 502 g. What are the lower and upper bounds for
    1 the total weight,
    2 the average (mean) weight, of the packages ?

5. A square courtyard has sides of length 35 m, correct to the nearest metre. What are the lower and upper bounds for
   1 the perimeter,
   2 the area, of the courtyard ?

6. Javid tried to find the value of π by measuring the circumference and diameter of a wheel. To the nearest cm these lengths were 151 cm and 48 cm respectively.
   What are the lower and upper bounds for the experimental value he obtained for π ?

7. The population of a region per km^2 is given as 42 to the nearest whole number. The area of the region is given as 5290 km^2, to the nearest 10 km^2.
   What are the lower and upper bounds for the actual population of the region ?

8. If 24 marbles weigh 720 g, correct to the nearest 10 g, what are the lower and upper bounds for the average weight of one marble ?

9. An empty jar weighs 329 g and when it is full of water it weighs 872 g. If each measurement is correct to the nearest gram, what are the lower and upper bounds for the weight of the water ?

10. The average daily rainfall for a month of 30 days was given as 0.38 cm, to 0.01 cm. What are the lower and upper bounds of the total rainfall for the month ?

11. Pauline tried to find the height of a tower by standing 50 m from its foot on level ground and measuring the angle of elevation of the top of the tower, which she found to be 21°.
    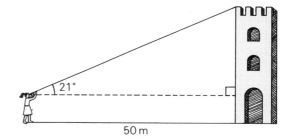
    If the length of 50 m was correct to the nearest metre and the angle of elevation was given to the nearest degree, and Pauline's eye-level is 1.52 m from the ground, to the nearest cm, find the lower and upper bounds for Pauline's estimated height of the tower.
    What do you suggest Pauline should give as a sensible answer for her estimate ?

12. A cyclist worked out his average speed by timing himself over a distance of 1 mile.
    If the distance of 1 mile was accurate to within ± 0.05 mile, and the time of 2 minutes 30 seconds was accurate to the nearest 10 seconds, find the calculated speed, and also the lower and upper bounds of the speed, in miles per hour.

13.   **Approximations in terms of error**

If a number is given to the nearest whole number, e.g. 12, then the lower bound is 11.5 and the upper bound is 12.5.
The number can be written as 12 ± 0.5. The maximum error is 0.5.
Similarly, 2.8, correct to 1 decimal place, can be written as 2.8 ± 0.05.

Calculations can be carried out with numbers in this notation.
e.g. In the example on page 173, the numbers are 2.75 and 3.17. These can be written as 2.75 ± 0.005 and 3.17 ± 0.005.

Addition

Usual answer	lower bound	upper bound
2.75	2.75 − 0.005	2.75 + 0.005
3.17	3.17 − 0.005	3.17 + 0.005
5.92	5.92 − 0.01	5.92 + 0.01

The answer could be given as 5.92 ± 0.01

Subtraction

Usual answer	lower bound	upper bound
3.17	3.17 − 0.005	3.17 + 0.005
2.75	2.75 + 0.005	2.75 − 0.005
0.42	0.42 − 0.01	0.42 + 0.01

The answer could be given as 0.42 ± 0.01

Multiplication

We use the rules for multiplying out brackets, and ignore the term 0.005×0.005 as it is so small.

Usual answer: $3.17 \times 2.75 = 8.7175$
Lower bound: $(3.17 - 0.005)(2.75 - 0.005)$
                 $= 8.7175 - (0.005 \times 3.17) - (0.005 \times 2.75)$
                 $= 8.7175 - 0.0296$
Upper bound: $(3.17 + 0.005)(2.75 + 0.005)$
                 $= 8.7175 + (0.005 \times 3.17) + (0.005 \times 2.75)$
                 $= 8.7175 + 0.0296$

The answer could be given as 8.72 ± 0.03, to 2 dec. pl.

It is not so easy to adapt this method for division.

Try some of the questions 1, 2, 3 of Exercise 9.2, page 176, (except the division questions) using this method, and compare your answers with those obtained by using the other method.

14.   **Absolute error and percentage error**

> **The error**, or **absolute error**, is the difference between
> the estimated value and the true value.

e.g. If the true value is £82.55 and the estimated value is £80, the absolute error
is £82.55 − £80 = £2.55.

The absolute error is in the same units as the true value, and it is always
positive.

> **The relative error** $= \dfrac{\text{absolute error}}{\text{true value}}$

e.g. If the true value is £82.55 and the estimated value is £80, the relative error
is $\dfrac{2.55}{82.55} = 0.031$ to 2 significant figures.

The relative error is often expressed as a percentage and this is called a
percentage error.

> **Percentage error** $= \dfrac{\text{absolute error}}{\text{true value}} \times 100\%$

In the example above, the percentage error = 3.1%, to 1 dec. pl.

Example

If you measure a line to the nearest mm, and get 7.8 cm, then the upper
bound is 7.85 cm and the lower bound is 7.75 cm.
The maximum absolute error is 0.05 cm.

Since we do not know the true length, we use the measured length as an
approximation for the true length in the formula for the percentage error.

Approximate maximum percentage error $= \dfrac{0.05}{7.8} \times 100\% = 0.6\%$, to 1 dec. pl.

Find the maximum absolute error and the approximate value for the maximum
percentage error in these estimations.
1   A length of 2.2 cm, correct to the nearest mm.
2   A weight of 1.38 kg, to 2 dec. pl.
3   £580, correct to the nearest £10.
4   9 months, correct to the nearest month.

Find the percentage error in these estimations.

5 A measured length was 7.9 cm; the true length was calculated as 7.72 cm.

6 A measured weight was 12.3 kg; the true weight was calculated as 12.25 kg.

7 π was estimated as 3.14. A closer approximation to the true value is 3.14159.

8 $\sqrt{2}$ was estimated as 1.41. Use the value given by your calculator as an approximation for the true value.

9 Small components each weighed 2.3 g. Find the maximum absolute error and the approximate maximum percentage error for one component. 50 components were packed together. What is their total weight ? What is the maximum absolute error and the approximate maximum percentage error of this total weight. Comment on the answers.

10 A side of a field was 240 m long, to the nearest 10 metres. Find the maximum absolute error and the approximate maximum percentage error for this length. The length was divided into 20 equal parts, for building plots. How long was one plot ? Find the maximum absolute error and the approximate maximum percentage error for the lengths of the plots. Comment on the answers.

15. Unrealistic accuracy

Having learnt that numbers, amounts and measurements are subject to error, do not think that you have to analyse all future answers in this way.

Only if you are asked to, should you work out the lower and upper bounds or the error for an answer.

However, these ideas should make you aware that if you give answers to a large number of figures, then your answers may not be realistic.

In an examination, it is sometimes necessary to give an exact answer, to show that you can do a correct calculation, in cases where an approximate answer would be more sensible. You can make sure that you do not lose marks by approximating too soon by **writing down** the answer to a calculation to several figures, in case it is wanted, and then correcting it up to what you consider to be sensible for that question. Often, answers correct to 3 significant figures are appropriate for a final answer.

Here is an extract from a newspaper giving information about preparations for the Olympic Games of 1992.
Decide whether any of the figures are exact ones, and say how accurately you think each of the others are expressed.

The 25th Olympic Games opened in Barcelona on Friday 25/7/92 before the King of Spain, more than 20 heads of state and a television audience of 3.5 billion. The opening ceremony in the 65 000 capacity stadium involved 9000 people and cost £15 million. Competitors came from 172 countries to take part in 257 events.

The Olympic torch had been carried in a 4000 mile relay from Greece. The Olympic flame was lit by a flaming arrow shot by an archer, Antonio Rebello, who had practised the 70 metre shot more than 1000 times.

Security at the Games was tight. 46 000 security men, police and soldiers outnumbered the 15 000 competitors, 14 500 journalists and 15 000 officials. Security costs were high—£200 million —though small compared with the £4.6 billion it cost to stage the Games.

PUZZLES

26.   Mrs Kaye has 4 children, Anton, Bernard, Corin and Denise.
      Corin is twice as old as Denise.
      Denise and Bernard together are twice as old as Corin.
      Corin and Anton together are twice as old as Denise and Bernard together.
      Denise, Bernard and Mrs Kaye together are twice as old as Corin and Anton together.
      If Mrs Kaye is 36 years old, how old are her children?

27. **1** A cube is such a size that the number of cm^3 in its volume is the same as the number of cm^2 in its surface area. What is the length of an edge ?

     2 A sphere is such a size that the number of cm^3 in its volume is the same as the number of cm^2 in its surface area. What is the length of a diameter ?

         (The surface area of a sphere is given by $S = 4\pi r^2$.)

28. Three men entered a cafe and asked for a meal, but as the time was late and the cook would have to work overtime the manager said that the meal would cost them £30. Each man then paid £10.

     After the manager reconsidered, he decided that he had overcharged the men. He called the waiter and instructed him, 'Take this £5 note back to those three men. Tell them that I overcharged them and that they should divide the £5 among themselves'.

     The waiter thought that dividing £5 among 3 men would not go exactly so he decided to keep £2 for himself. Then he returned £1 to each man, so that the actual cost to each man was £9.

     Now, 3 × £9 = £27, and the £2 the waiter kept makes £29.

     What happened to the other £1 ?

29. A young man, Lee, has two girl friends, Paula who lives at Appleton, and Sharon who lives at Birchwood.

     To visit either girl, Lee travels by train. He goes to the station where trains run north every 10 minutes to Appleton, and run south every 10 minutes to Birchwood. He goes to the station at random times, and then catches the first train to arrive. He thinks that in this way he will spend half his evenings with Paula and half of them with Sharon. However, on average he sees Paula on 4 evenings out of 5, and Sharon only on 1 evening out of 5.

     Can you explain why this is ?

30.

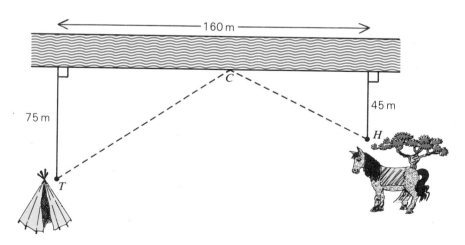

A cowboy had pitched his tent near a river, as shown on the sketch. He wanted to get some water from the river and take it to his horse.

Where is point *C* on the river bank from where he should get the water, so as to make the distance he needs to walk (*TC* + *CH*) as short as possible? And then, how far does he have to walk ?

10 Thinking about rates of change,

World Population

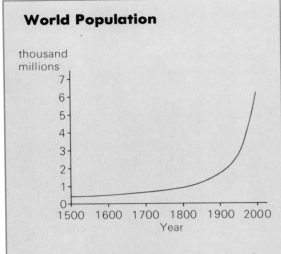

Comment on the rate of growth of the World Population over the last 500 years.

If the treads of the steps are 30 cm long and the risers are 16 cm, what is the gradient of the staircase ?

Approximate area

A scale drawing of a field is shown here. It is bounded by straight fences on 3 sides and the 4th side is bounded by a stream.
Find an approximate value for the area of the field.

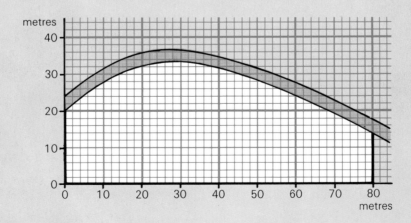

gradients and areas

Speed or velocity is the rate of change of distance over time.

Acceleration is the rate of change of velocity over time.

actor pulling is an unusual sport. The tractors
ve powerful engines and can pull about
0 tons. When not pulling, the tractors can
celerate from 0 to 60 mph in 2 seconds.

A thrilling ride

10 Rates of change, gradients and areas

Rates of change

In this curve, between A and E, the y-value is increasing. Between A and B, it increases slowly, between B and C it increases at a greater rate, between C and D the rate of increase is less and between D and E y is increasing very slowly.

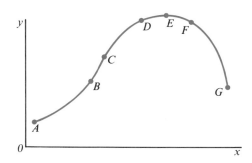

At E the rate of increase is zero and between E and F there is a slow decrease. Between F and G there is a greater rate of decrease.

The slope of the curve shows the rate of change of y, which can be a rate of increase or decrease.

Gradients

Gradient of line $= \dfrac{\text{increase in } y}{\text{increase in } x}$

$= \dfrac{y_2 - y_1}{x_2 - x_1}$

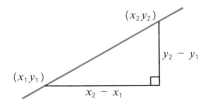

Example

1 Find the gradient of the line.

Choose 2 points A, B on the line. It is more accurate to choose points far apart rather than near together, and it simplifies the working if you choose x_1 and x_2 as exact numbers.

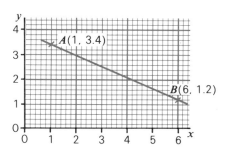

$$\text{Gradient} = \frac{y_2 - y_1}{x_2 - x_1}$$

$$= \frac{1.2 - 3.4}{6 - 1} = \frac{-2.2}{5} = -0.44$$

The gradient is negative because on the line, as x increases, y decreases.

The average rate of increase or decrease of y between two points on a graph, can be found from the gradient of the **chord** joining these points.

Example

2   Find the average rate of
     increase of y between
     A and B.

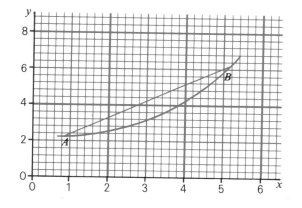

Gradient of chord AB

$$= \frac{y_2 - y_1}{x_2 - x_1}$$

$$= \frac{6.2 - 2.2}{5.2 - 0.9}$$

$$= \frac{4}{4.1} = 0.98, \text{ to 2 dec. pl.}$$

The average rate of increase between A and B = 0.98 units of y per unit of x.

Tangents to a curve

A tangent is a line which just touches
a curve.

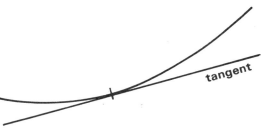

To construct a tangent at a point

(1) By eye

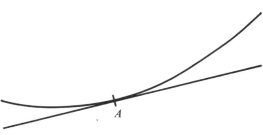

(2) Using a mirror.
The mirror is placed so that the curve
and its reflection form one smooth
curve.
Draw along the line of the mirror.
This line is called the **normal** to
the curve at the point A and it is
perpendicular to the tangent.
Draw the line at right angles
to the normal, through A, and
this will be the tangent.

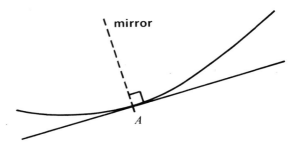

Rate of change

To find the rate of change of y
at any point, find the gradient of
the tangent to the curve at that point.

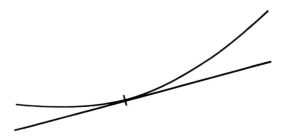

Examples

3   Find the rate of increase of the value of y at point A.

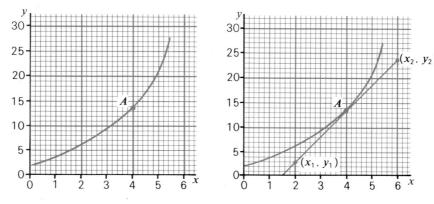

Draw a tangent to the curve touching it at A.
Select 2 points on the tangent, to calculate its gradient.
(You can select A as one of them if convenient.)

$$\text{Gradient} = \frac{y_2 - y_1}{x_2 - x_1} = \frac{23.5 - 3.0}{6 - 2} = \frac{20.5}{4} = 5.13$$

At A, y is increasing at the rate of 5.13 units of y per unit of x.

4   Find the rate of change of the value of y at **B**.

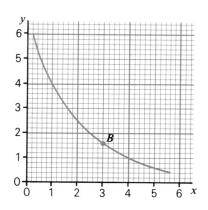 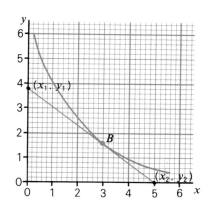

$$\text{Gradient} = \frac{y_2 - y_1}{x_2 - x_1} = \frac{0 - 3.8}{5 - 0} = -0.76$$

The rate of change of y at **B** is -0.76 units of y per unit of x.
i.e. At **B**, y is decreasing at the rate of 0.76 units of y per unit of x.

Maximum and minimum points

At these points the gradient of the tangent is 0.

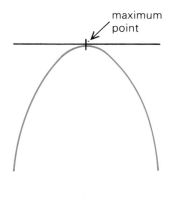

maximum
point

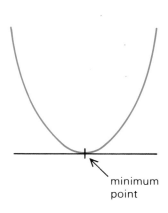

minimum
point

Exercise 10.1

1. Find the gradients of the
    lines in the diagram.

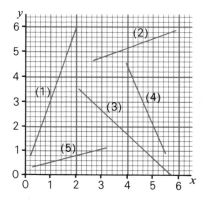

2. Find the average rates of
    change of y on this curve
    1   between A and B,
    2   between C and D.

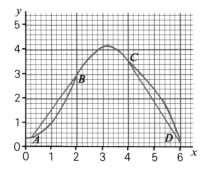

3. Find the gradient of the
    tangent to the curve at A.

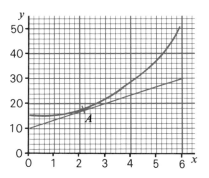

4.   Draw the graph of $y = x^2$ for x from 0 to 8.
      Label the x-axis from 0 to 8 using a scale of 2 cm to 1 unit.
      Label the y-axis from 0 to 70 using a scale of 2 cm to 10 units.
      Draw tangents to the curve at the points where $x = 2$, $x = 4$ and $x = 6$, and find
      their gradients.
      What is the gradient of the tangent at (0, 0) ?

      List your results on a table and see if there is any pattern. (The pattern may not
      be obvious as there could be inaccuracies in drawing the curve and the tangents.)

x	0	2	4	6
Gradient				

5.   Draw the graph of $y = \dfrac{48}{x}$ for x from $\frac{1}{2}$ to 8.

      Label the x-axis from 0 to 8 using a scale of 2 cm to 1 unit.
      Label the y-axis from 0 to 100 using a scale of 2 cm to 10 units.
      Plot points with x-values $\frac{1}{2}$, 1, $1\frac{1}{2}$, 2, 3, 4, 5, 6, 7, 8.
      Draw tangents to the curve at the points where $x = 1$, $x = 2$, $x = 4$ and $x = 6$,
      and find their gradients.

      List the results on a table. Include the values of $x^2 \times$ gradient and see if you can
      discover any pattern.

x	1	2	4	6
gradient				
$x^2 \times$ gradient				

Distance-time graphs

The rate at which distance is travelled is called **speed**.
Velocity is a word used instead of speed when the direction of motion is included, so
that if one direction is regarded as positive, a speed in the opposite direction will have
a negative velocity.

To find velocity from a distance-time graph

The average velocity from A to B
is given by the gradient of the
chord AB.

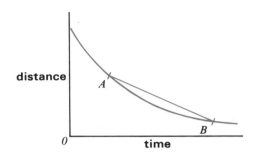

The actual velocity at A is given by
the gradient of the tangent
to the curve, at A.
On this diagram the velocity is
negative. This means that the
object is travelling in the
opposite direction to that in
which the distance is measured.
The speed has the same
numerical value as the velocity,
but it is positive. e.g. If the
velocity is -5 m/s, the speed is 5 m/s.

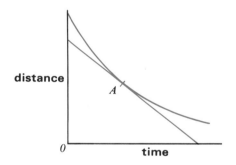

On a distance-time graph, if at any
point the gradient of the tangent to the
curve is 0, at that time the object is
at rest, possibly just for an
instant, as at points C and D on
this sketch graph.

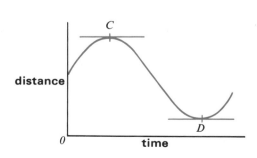

Example

Here is the distance-time graph of a particle moving along a straight line.

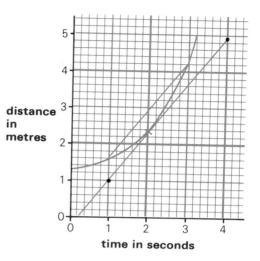

distance in metres

time in seconds

1   Find the average velocity between times $t = 1$ and $t = 3$.
2   Find the actual velocity at time $t = 2$.

Average velocity = gradient of chord

$$= \frac{\text{increase in distance}}{\text{increase in time}}$$

$$= \frac{4.2 - 1.6}{3 - 1} \text{m/s} = 1.3 \text{m/s}$$

Velocity at time $t = 2$, = gradient of tangent

$$= \frac{4.9 - 1.0}{4 - 1} \text{m/s}$$

$$= 1.3 \text{m/s}$$

Velocity-time graphs

The rate at which velocity increases with time is called **acceleration**. A negative acceleration is called a retardation or deceleration.

$$\text{acceleration} = \frac{\text{increase in velocity}}{\text{increase in time}}$$

If velocity is given in m/s and time in seconds then the acceleration is measured in metres per second, per second, which is written in symbols as m/s^2 or ms^{-2}.

To find acceleration from a velocity-time graph

The acceleration at A is given by the
gradient of the tangent at A.

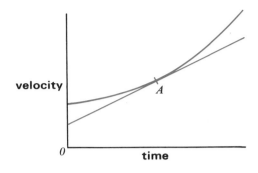

On a velocity-time graph, if at a point
the gradient of the tangent is 0, at
that time the object has no acceleration.

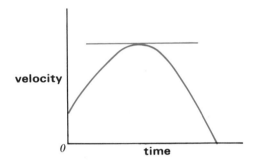

Example

Here is a velocity-time graph
of a particle moving along a
straight line.
Find the acceleration at time
$t = 3$.

acceleration = gradient of tangent

$$= \frac{\text{increase in velocity}}{\text{increase in time}}$$

$$= \frac{38 - 11}{4 - 2} \text{cm/s}^2$$

$$= 13.5 \text{ cm/s}^2$$

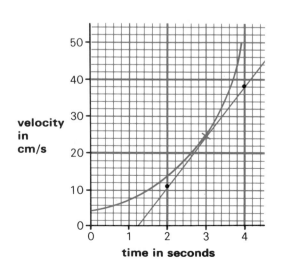

Examples of other curves

Growth of bacteria

The rate of growth at any time is
given by the tangent to the curve
at that time, and it increases as
time increases.

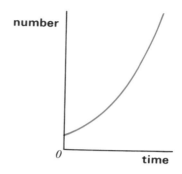

Radioactive decay

The rate of decay at any time is
given by the tangent to the
curve at that time, ignoring
the negative sign, and it
slows down as time increases.

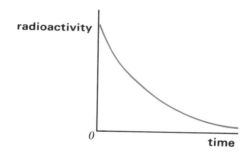

Exercise 10.2

1. An object is projected upwards and its height s metres at time t seconds is given
    by the equation $s = 60t - 10t^2$.
    Draw the graph of this function for values of t from 0 to 6, using a scale on the
    t-axis of 2 cm to 1 unit.
    Label the s-axis from 0 to 100 using a scale of 2 cm to 10 units.
    Plot values for t at $\frac{1}{2}$ unit intervals.
    Use your graph to answer these questions.
    1 At what time is the object momentarily at rest ?
    2 Find the velocity of the object at times $t = 1$ and $t = 4$, and deduce the
        velocities of the object at times $t = 2$ and $t = 5$.
    3 List the velocities at times $t = 1, 2, 3, 4, 5$ in a table and see if there is any
        pattern.

2. An object is projected along a line so that its velocity, v cm/s, at time t seconds is
    given by the equation $v = t^2 + 6t$.
    Draw a graph of this function for values of t from 0 to 7, using a scale on the
    t-axis of 2 cm to 1 unit. Label the v-axis from 0 to 100 using a scale of 2 cm to
    10 units.
    1   Use your graph to find the acceleration at times $t = 2$, $t = 4$ and $t = 6$.
    2   The acceleration initially (at time $t = 0$) is 6 cm/s^2.
            List the accelerations at times $t = 0, 2, 4, 6$ and see if there is any pattern in
            the values.

3. The velocity of a particle is given by the equation $v = 20t - 5t^2$, with v in m/s
    and t in seconds.
    Draw the graph of v against t for values of t from -1 to 5, using a scale on the
    t-axis of 2 cm to 1 unit.
    Label the v-axis from -25 to 25, using a scale of 2 cm to 5 units.

    1   The particle starts from rest when $t = 0$. After how many seconds does it
            come to instantaneous rest ?
    2   What is the acceleration of the particle at the start of its motion ?
    3   At what time is the acceleration momentarity zero ?
    4   What is the acceleration at time $t = 3$?

4. The table shows the growth of a culture of bacteria at different times, t hours.
    N is the number of bacteria present.
    Draw a graph showing this information.
    Find the rate of growth when $t = 3$.

t	0	1	2	3	4	5
N	10	15	23	34	51	76

5. The table shows the temperature, $T°C$, of a liquid which is cooling, at different times,
    t minutes.
    Draw a graph showing this information.
    Find the rate of cooling at time $t = 4$.

t	0	2	4	6	8	10	12
T	90	79	70	62	55	50	45

To find the area under a curve

When we refer to the area under a curve we
mean the area between the curve and the
x-axis. So the area under the curve between the
lines $x = a$ and $x = b$ is shown shaded in the sketch.

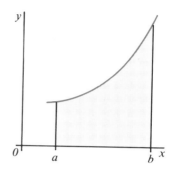

The area under this straight line is in the shape of
a trapezium.
If the heights are y_0 and y_1 and the width is
$b - a$,

area = $\frac{1}{2}$ (sum of parallel sides)
        × distance between them

   = $\frac{1}{2}(y_0 + y_1)(b - a)$

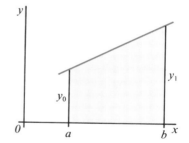

Example

1   Find the area under the line
    $y = 2x + 5$ between the points
    $(2, 9)$ and $(6, 17)$.

    The heights (parallel sides) are
    9 and 17.
    The distance between them
    = 6 − 2 = 4
    Area = $\frac{1}{2}$ × (9 + 17) × 4
         = 52 unit^2

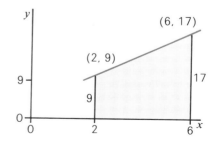

The area under a curve can be estimated.

Finding the area by counting squares

Count the number of squares on the grid.
For part squares, if the area included is half or
more of a square, count it as a whole square,
and if the area included is less than half of a
square, ignore it. The errors by taking these
approximations should balance each other
fairly well.
This is a rather tedious method.
Here there are approximately 153 small squares.
25 of these make 1 unit square.

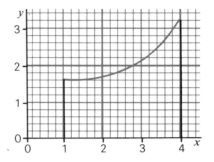

Area $= \frac{153}{25} = 6.1$ unit^2 approximately.

Finding the area by using the trapezium rule

If we divide the total area into thin vertical
strips of equal widths, each strip has
approximately the shape of a trapezium. We can
calculate the areas of these trapeziums.

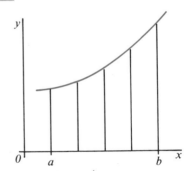

area divided into 4 strips

(The more strips we use,
the more accurate will be
the result.)

1st strip is nearly a trapezium.
Find the total width $b - a$ and hence find the value of x_1.
Find the y-values when $x = a$ and when $x = x_1$.

Area of trapezium $= \frac{1}{2}(y_0 + y_1)(x_1 - a)$

Similarly, find the other areas and add
them together to find the total area.

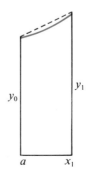

The areas all added together give the general formula for *n* strips:

$$\text{The area under curve} \approx \frac{h}{2}\,(y_0 + 2y_1 + 2y_2 + 2y_3 + \cdots + 2y_{n-1} + y_n)$$

where h = width of a strip = $\dfrac{b - a}{n}$

and the y-values in order are $y_0, y_1, y_2, y_3, \ldots, y_{n-1}, y_n$.
$\approx$ means 'is approximately equal to'.

Example

2   Find the area under this curve
    between $x = 1$ and $x = 9$, by
    dividing it into 4 trapeziums.

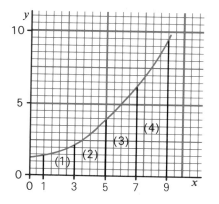

1st method. Working out the area
of each trapezium separately.

Each strip is 2 units wide.
Read off the y-values from the graph.

x	1	3	5	7	9
y	1.3	2.1	3.7	6.1	9.3

1st trapezium.   Area = $\frac{1}{2}$ × (1.3 + 2.1) × 2 =   3.4
2nd trapezium.   Area = $\frac{1}{2}$ × (2.1 + 3.7) × 2 =   5.8
3rd trapezium.   Area = $\frac{1}{2}$ × (3.7 + 6.1) × 2 =   9.8
4th trapezium.   Area = $\frac{1}{2}$ × (6.1 + 9.3) × 2 = $\underline{15.4}$
                                                              34.4

Total area = 34.4
The area under the curve is approximately 34 unit².

2nd method. Using the formula.

$h = 2$, $y_0 = 1.3$, $y_1 = 2.1$, $y_2 = 3.7$, $y_3 = 6.1$, $y_4 = 9.3$.

$$\text{Area under curve} \approx \frac{h}{2}\,(y_0 + 2y_1 + 2y_2 + 2y_3 + y_4)$$
$$= \tfrac{2}{2} \times (1.3 + 2 \times 2.1 + 2 \times 3.7 + 2 \times 6.1 + 9.3)$$
$$= 34.4 \text{ unit}^2$$

Why will the approximate area, in this case, be slightly **greater** than the actual area ?

To find distance from a velocity-time graph

The area under the graph (i.e. between the graph and the time axis) gives the distance travelled between the two times.
If the velocity is in m/s and the time in seconds then the distance will be in metres.

Graphs showing steady velocity or steady acceleration

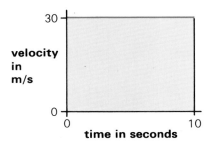

An object moving at 30 m/s for 10 seconds will have travelled 300 metres. This is represented by the area of the rectangle.

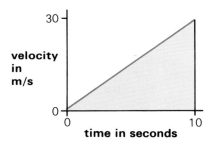

An object starting from rest and increasing speed steadily over 10 seconds to 30 m/s will have travelled 150 metres. This is represented by the area of the triangle.

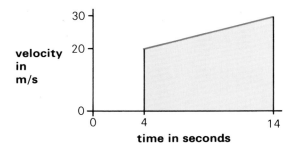

An object moving with steadily increasing speed from 20 m/s at time 4 seconds to 30 m/s at time 14 seconds will have travelled between those times a distance represented by the area of the trapezium.

Area $= \frac{1}{2}$ (sum of parallel sides)
$\qquad \times$ distance between them
$\quad = \frac{1}{2} \times (20 + 30) \times (14 - 4)$
$\quad = 250$
Distance $= 250$ m

Graphs with variable velocity and acceleration

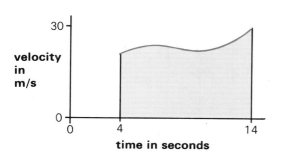

The distance travelled between times 4 seconds and 14 seconds is represented by the area under the curve between these times. This area can be estimated.

Examples

3 A car increases velocity at a steady rate from 50 km/h to 70 km/h over 6 seconds.
What is the distance travelled during this time ?

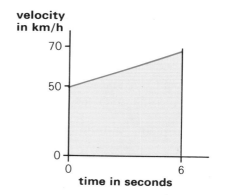

Distance = shaded area

$$= \tfrac{1}{2}(y_0 + y_1)h$$

$$= \tfrac{1}{2} \times (50 + 70) \times \frac{6}{60 \times 60} \text{ km}$$

$$= \tfrac{1}{10} \text{ km} = 100 \text{ m}$$

(Since the velocity was given in km/h, to correspond, the time had to be given in hours, so it was $\dfrac{\cdot 6}{60 \times 60}$ hours, and then the distance was given in km.

Alternatively, the velocities could have been changed into km/s and the time left in seconds.)

4 The speed of a racing car during the first minute after starting from rest is given in this table.

Time in seconds	0	10	20	30	40	50	60
Speed in m/s	0	28	46	51	47	43	46

Draw the velocity-time graph, joining the points with a smooth curve. By dividing the area under the graph into 6 trapeziums of equal width, estimate the distance travelled in the first minute.

Width of each trapezium or
triangle = 10

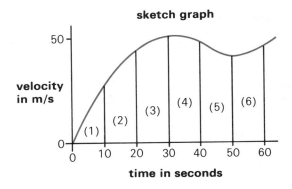

sketch graph

Triangle (1).   Area $= \frac{1}{2} \times 28 \times 10$ $=$ 140
Trapezium (2). Area $= \frac{1}{2} \times (28 + 46) \times 10 =$ 370
Trapezium (3). Area $= \frac{1}{2} \times (46 + 51) \times 10 =$ 485
Trapezium (4). Area $= \frac{1}{2} \times (51 + 47) \times 10 =$ 490
Trapezium (5). Area $= \frac{1}{2} \times (47 + 43) \times 10 =$ 450
Trapezium (6). Area $= \frac{1}{2} \times (43 + 46) \times 10 =$ $\underline{445}$
                                              2380

Total area = 2380.
Estimated distance travelled = 2400 m = 2.4 km, to 2 significant figures.

Or, using the formula,

area under curve $\approx \dfrac{h}{2} (y_0 + 2y_1 + 2y_2 + 2y_3 + 2y_4 + 2y_5 + y_6)$

$$= \frac{10}{2} (0 + 2 \times 28 + 2 \times 46 + 2 \times 51 + 2 \times 47 + 2 \times 43 + 46)$$

$$= 2380$$

Estimated distance travelled = 2400 m = 2.4 km, to 2 sig. fig.

Other graphs of rates of change

If you have a graph showing
acceleration against time, then
since acceleration is the rate
of change of velocity, the area
under the curve between two times
gives the increase in velocity
during that time interval.

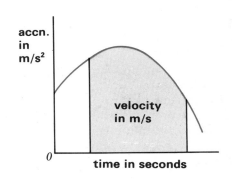

Similarly with other graphs.

From a graph showing rate of
change of volume against time,
the area under the curve
between two times gives the
increase in volume during
that time interval.

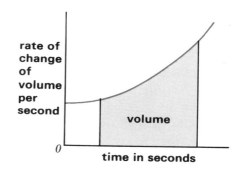

Exercise 10.3

1. Draw sketch graphs of these lines and calculate the area between the line, the
    x-axis and the lines $x = a$ and $x = b$.

    1 $y = 3x + 5$, between $x = 2$ and $x = 4$.
    2 $y = 100 - 6x$, between $x = 0$ and $x = 10$.
    3 $y = 7x$, between $x = 1$ and $x = 6$.

2. Find the approximate area
    enclosed by the curve, the x
    and y axes and the line $x = 6$.

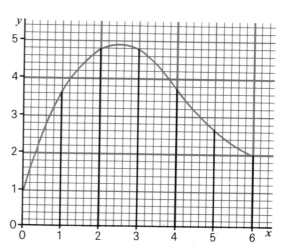

3. Draw a sketch graph of the function $y = x^3$ for values of x from 0 to 4.
    Find the approximate area between the curve, the x-axis and the line $x = 4$, by
    dividing it into 4 areas using the lines $x = 1$, $x = 2$, $x = 3$.

4. The velocity of an object is given by the equation $v = 75 - 25t$.
    v is in m/s, t is in seconds.
    Draw a sketch graph of this function.
    1   Find the distance travelled in the 1st 3 seconds.
    2   Find the distance travelled between the 1st and 2nd seconds.

5. The velocity of a particle is given by the equation $v = 3t^2 + 6t$.
   v is in cm/s, t is in seconds.
   Draw a graph of this function for values of t from 0 to 6, using a scale of 2 cm to 1 unit on the t-axis, and labelling the v-axis from 0 to 160 using a scale of 2 cm to 20 units.
   Find an approximate value for the distance travelled between the times $t = 2$ and $t = 5$, by also using the lines $t = 3$ and $t = 4$.

6. The velocity of a car is given by this table of values.

t (seconds)	0	5	10	15	20	25	30	35	40	45	50	55	60
v (m/s)	0	4	5	9	13	14	14	12	9	8	4	1	0

   Draw a graph showing the velocity of the car during the 60 seconds.
   1 Estimate the time when the acceleration is 0.
   2 Using the lines $t = 10, 20, 30, 40, 50$, find an estimate for the distance the car travels before coming to rest.

7. The acceleration of an object is given by the equation $a = 4 + 5t$.
   a in cm/s^2, t is in seconds.
   Sketch the graph of the function for values of t from 0 to 5.
   By finding areas under the curve, find the velocity of the object at times $t = 1, 2, 3, 4, 5$, assuming that it started from rest at time $t = 0$.

   Using these values for the velocity, draw a sketch graph of velocity against time, for the first 5 seconds of motion.
   Use the values on the sketch graph to find an approximation for the total distance travelled during the first 3 seconds of motion.

Exercise 10.4   Applications and Activities

1. A particle moves along a straight line and its distance s cm from its starting point in the line after t seconds is given by the equation $s = 8t - t^2$.
   Draw the graph of this function, for t from 0 to 8.

   1 What is the maximum distance of the particle from the starting point ?
   2 After how many seconds does the particle arrive back at the starting point ?
   3 After how many seconds from the start is the particle momentarily at rest ?
   4 Draw the tangent to the graph at the point where $t = 3$, and find the velocity of the particle after 3 seconds.
   5 Find the velocity of the particle after 6 seconds.

2. A motorist travelling along a road at a steady speed sees traffic lights at red in front of him. He immediately reduces speed and then travels at a steady speed until the lights are green. He then accelerates until he reaches a steady speed 5 s after passing the lights.
    The graph of this information is shown below.

    1 At what steady speed was the motorist travelling before he saw the red light ?
    2 To what steady speed did he reduce his speed ?
    3 For how many seconds did he slow down ?
    4 What distance did he travel while he was slowing down ?
    5 At what rate did he accelerate when the lights changed to green ?
    6 At what speed was he travelling when he passed the lights ?

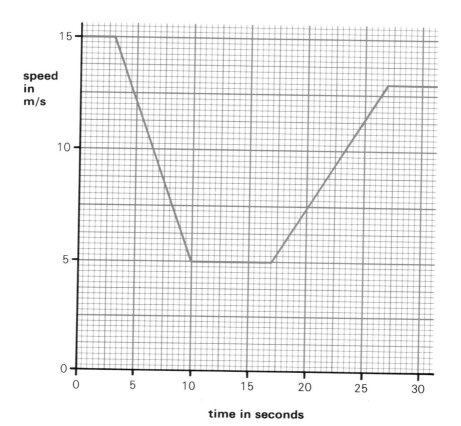

time in seconds

3.　A car moves away from traffic lights and travels with constant acceleration for 6 seconds, and reaches a speed of 12 m/s. It then travels at constant speed for 15 s and then travels with uniform retardation for 9 s to come to a stop at a junction.
   1　Draw a velocity-time graph for the car.
   2　Find the acceleration of the car in the first 6 s, and the retardation as it approaches the junction.
   3　Find the distance from the traffic lights to the junction.

4.　A lift moves from rest at one floor level to rest at another floor level. After it has been moving for t seconds its velocity, v m/s, is given by the equation $v = t - \frac{1}{12}t^2$.
   1　Draw the graph of v against t, for values of t from 0 to 12 seconds.
   2　What is the time taken to travel between the two floors ?
   3　Find the acceleration when $t = 4$.
   4　Estimate the distance between the two floors, using the lines $t = 3$, $t = 6$ and $t = 9$.

5.　Liquid from a tank is being pumped out at such a rate that t minutes after the start the volume of liquid, V m³, remaining in the tank is given by the formula $V = 144 - 48t + 4t^2$.

   1　What is the volume of liquid in the tank at the start ?
   2　Verify that the tank is emptied after 6 minutes.
   3　Draw a graph of V against t for $t = 0$ to 6.
   4　Find the rate, in m³/minute, at which the liquid is flowing out of the tank after 2 minutes (i.e. at time $t = 2$).

6.　Water is poured into a container, which is initially empty.
   There is V cm³ of water in the container after t seconds, such that the rate of increase of volume is given by the equation Rate $= 80 - 2t$, in cm³/s.
   Sketch the graph showing the rate of increase of volume during the first 40 seconds.
   By finding the area under the graph, find the volume of the container, if it takes 40 seconds to fill.
   What fraction of the volume is filled in the first 20 s ?

7.　Sketch the graph of $y = \cos x°$ for values of x from 0 to 90.
   Using lines at $x = 15$, 30, 45, 60 and 75, find an approximate value of the area between the curve and the x and y axes.
   Explain why this approximation is slightly **less** than the true area.
   The true area is $\dfrac{180}{\pi}$ unit². Find the value of this to check that your answer is reasonable.

8. Draw the graph of $y = 180 \sin x°$ for values of x from 0 to 90, taking 2 cm to represent 15 units on the x-axis.
   Label the y-axis from 0 to 200, taking a scale of 1 cm to 20 units.
   Find the gradients of the curve at points with x-values 15, 30, 45, 60 and 75, giving the answers to 2 decimal places.
   State the value of the gradient at the point where $x = 90$.
   The gradient at the origin is 3.14.

   Show the results in a table, also showing the values of $\dfrac{\text{gradient}}{\pi}$.

   Draw a second graph showing the relationship between $\dfrac{\text{gradient}}{\pi}$ and x, for x between 0 and 90.
   Comment on the shape of this graph.

9. Draw axes with x from -8 to 8 and y from -6 to 6, taking 1 cm to 1 unit on both axes.
   Plot these points and join them to form a curve.
   (0, 6), (1, 6), (2, 5.8), (3, 5.6), (4, 5.2), (5, 4.7), (6, 4.0), (7, 2.9), (8, 0).
   Find the approximate area between this curve and the x and y axes.
   The curve is part of an ellipse, which is symmetrical about the x and y axes.
   Draw the rest of the ellipse and find its approximate area.
   The formula for the area of an ellipse is Area $= \pi ab$. In this ellipse, $a = 8$ and $b = 6$. Use the formula to check that your answer is reasonable.

10. The table shows the percentage of activity remaining in a radioactive substance at different times.

time in days	0	1	2	3	4	5	6	7	8	9	10
% remaining	100	92	84	77	71	65	60	55	50	46	42

   Show this information on a graph.
   Use the graph to find the **rate** of decrease of activity after 2, 4, 6 and 8 days.
   Find the values of $\dfrac{\text{rate of decrease}}{\text{% remaining}}$ at these times, as decimals correct to 2 decimal places, and hence verify, approximately, that for a radioactive substance, the rate of decrease of activity is proportional to the activity remaining.

Miscellaneous Section B

Aural Practice

These aural exercises, B1 and B2, should be read to you, probably by your teacher or a friend, and you should write down the answers only, doing any working out in your head. You should do the 15 questions within 10 minutes.

Exercise B1

1. There are 48 eggs in a box. One-twelfth are cracked. How many are whole ?

2. What is the name of a quadrilateral which has all four sides equal but has no right angles ?

3. What is the mean of the numbers 8, 12 and 28 ?

4. What is the square root of $\frac{4}{9}$?

5. Which of the following numbers is a rational number:
    $\sqrt{80}$, $\sqrt{81}$, $\sqrt{90}$, $\sqrt{91}$?

6. When a 10% surcharge is added to £12, what is the new price ?

7. If £1 is equal to 170 pesetas, how many pesetas will I get for £20 ?

8. Write the expression $x^2 + 10x + 9$ in factorised form.

9. If 25 equal packages weigh 100 kg, what is the weight of one package ?

10. On a distance-time graph, what is represented by the gradient of the graph ?

11. If £42 is divided in the ratio 3:4, what is the larger share ?

12. What is the total surface area of a cube of edge 3 cm ?

13. If two events A and B are mutually exclusive events with probabilities of success 0.4 and 0.5 respectively, what is the probability of either event A or event B occurring ?

14. What is the smallest number into which 5, 6 and 8 divide exactly ?

15. If a rectangular block in a histogram with unequal intervals represents a frequency of 12 and has a width of 10 units, what height should it have ?

Exercise B2

1. How many hours are there from 8 am to 12 midnight ?

2. How many edges has a triangular pyramid ?

3. The temperature during the night was $-6°$ Celsius. During the day the temperature rose to $12°$ Celsius. Through how many degrees did the temperature rise ?

4. A rectangle 8 cm by 5 cm is cut out of a square piece of paper of side 11 cm. What area is left ?

5. The number of people attending an exhibition is given as 12 700, to the nearest hundred. What are the lower and upper bounds of the number ?

6. What is the value of $3^5 \div 3^2$?

7. What is 0.05 as a fraction in its lowest terms ?

8. On a velocity-time graph, what is represented by the area between the graph and the time axis ?

9. What number must be added to $x^2 + 14x$ to make an expression which is a perfect square ?

10. What is 13 less than $\frac{1}{4}$ of 80 ?

11. Write $\frac{7}{9}$ as a decimal, correct to 3 decimal places.

12. A man is normally paid £6 per hour. How much does he earn for 3 hours work on a Saturday when he is paid at 'time and a half' ?

13. Two fair dice are thrown together. What is the probability of scoring a 1 on one die and a 2 on the other ?

14. Give an approximate value for the square root of $7^2 + 7^2$.

15. The distance between the Earth and the Sun is 93 million miles. Write this number in standard index form.

Exercise B3   Revision

1. In the diagram, $AB = AD$, $AC = AE$
    and $BC = DE$.
    1   Explain why triangles ABC, ADE
         are congruent.
    2   Name the angle equal to $\angle BAC$.
    3   Show that $\angle BAE = \angle DAC$.
    4   Prove that $BE = DC$.

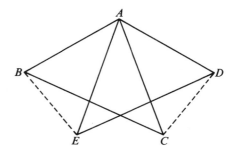

2. Say whether these numbers are rational or irrational:
    $\sqrt{5}$,   3.142, $\sqrt[3]{8}$, $\pi + 5$, $\sqrt{1\frac{7}{9}}$, $0.\dot{7}1428\dot{5}$, $3^{\frac{1}{3}}$, $\frac{3}{4} + \frac{1}{12}$, π^2, $6^0 \times 6^{-2}$.

3. Three containers are as follows:
    (1) a cylinder, radius 10 cm, height 50 cm,
    (2) a cone, base radius 20 cm, perpendicular height 60 cm,
    (3) a sphere, radius 15 cm.
    Find the ratio of their volumes in its simplest form.

4. The total amount, £A, received when £P is invested at 8% Simple Interest for
    1 year is given by the table.

P	100	200	300	400	500	600
A	108	216	324	432	540	648

    Find the equation connecting A and P.

5. A bus moves from rest with constant acceleration until it attains a certain speed,
    then moves for a time with constant speed and then slows down with constant
    retardation until it comes to rest at the next stop.

    The table gives details of its speed.

time in s	0	5	10	15	20	30	40	50	55	60
speed in m/s	0	4	8	12	12	12	12	12	6	0

    Plot a velocity-time graph, taking 2 cm to represent 10 s on the time axis and 2 cm
    to represent 2 m/s on the velocity axis.

    Use the graph to find
    1   the acceleration during the first part of the journey, in m/s²,
    2   the distance travelled by the bus at constant speed,
    3   the distance between the two stops.

6. Jodi's netball team has a 0.7 chance of winning a home match, and a 0.4 chance of winning an away match. If the team play 2 matches, one at home and one away, what are their chances of
   1 winning both,
   2 not winning either,
   3 winning one of them ?
   Assume that the result of the second match is independent of the result of the first match.

7. Find the first 6 terms of these sequences and say whether each sequence is convergent or divergent.
   If a sequence is convergent, say what the limit is, giving it correct to 3 decimal places.
   1 $u_{n+2} = 4u_{n+1} - 3u_n,\quad u_1 = 0.1,\quad u_2 = 0.3$
   2 $u_{n+1} = \dfrac{1}{4 + 3u_n},\quad u_1 = 0.1$

8. $ABCD$ is a parallelogram whose diagonals intersect at E. M is the mid-point of BC and N is the mid-point of CD. If $\overrightarrow{AB} = 2\mathbf{b}$ and $\overrightarrow{AD} = 2\mathbf{d}$, express in terms of $\mathbf{b}$ and $\mathbf{d}$ the vectors

   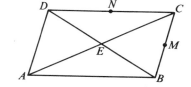

   1 $\overrightarrow{AC}$ **2** $\overrightarrow{AE}$ **3** $\overrightarrow{BD}$ **4** $\overrightarrow{BE}$
   5 $\overrightarrow{AM}$ **6** $\overrightarrow{AN}$ **7** $\overrightarrow{MN}$

   What can you deduce about MN and BE ?

9. Simplify
   1 $a^{\frac{2}{3}} \times a^{\frac{1}{2}} \div a^{\frac{1}{6}}$
   2 $(b^3)^{\frac{4}{3}}$
   3 $\left(c^{\frac{1}{4}}\right)^{10} \times c^0 \times c^{-\frac{1}{2}}$

10. A square board $ABCD$ is supported in a horizontal position by 4 chains VA, VB, VC, VD each 50 cm long, from a point V on the ceiling. The sides of the square are 30 cm long. Find
    1 the length of AC,
    2 the angle between the chains VA and VB,
    3 the angle VA makes with the board,
    4 the height of V above the board.

    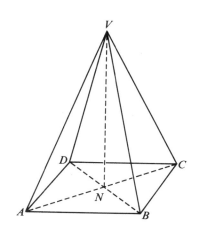

11. A survey of distances travelled by a particular type of tyre gives these results:

Distance (in 1000 km)	Number of tyres
0 to 20	11
20 to 30	18
30 to 40	38
40 to 50	52
50 to 60	42
60 to 90	39
	200

Work out the heights of the columns for a histogram.

Draw the histogram.

Comment briefly on its shape.

12. Draw the graph of $y = x^3$ for values of x from -3 to 3, and labelling the y-axis from -30 to 30.
     Using the same axes, draw the line $y = 7x + 3$ and find the values of x at the points where it intersects the curve.
     State the equation which is satisfied by these values of x.

13. Imagine that you are making a survey of pupils in your school about some important matter which would affect all the pupils, and you have to select a 10% sample of pupils to interview.
     Describe three different methods of choosing this sample and for each method state any advantages or disadvantages.

14. On a scale drawing, Tanya measured a distance as 4.6 cm, to the nearest mm. Give the lower and upper bounds of this measurement.
     If the scale of the drawing is '1 cm represents 80 m', find the actual distance represented, giving the usual answer and also the lower and upper bounds of the possible answers, each to the nearest metre.

15. Factorise these expressions.
     1 $x^2 - 9x$
     2 $x^2 - 9$
     3 $x^2 - 9x + 14$
     4 $x^2 - 9x - 70$

16. Arc AB is part of a circle, centre O, radius 9 cm.
     Arc CD is part of a circle, centre O, radius 5 cm.
     $\angle AOB = 135°$.
     Find the shaded area.

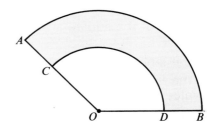

17. **1**   Sketch the graph of $y = \cos x°$ for x from 0 to 360.
     2   Draw the line on your sketch which you would use to find the values of x for which $\cos x° = 0.6$.
     3   Find the solution for x between 0 and 90, to the nearest whole number, for which $\cos x° = 0.6$, using your calculator.
     4   Using your sketch, deduce another value of x for which $\cos x° = 0.6$.

18. The numbers of goals scored by the top 8 teams in the football league in 1991-1992 are as follows:

| 74 | 63 | 62 | 81 | 61 | 47 | 48 | 60 |

Find the mean and standard deviation of the numbers of goals scored.

19. Two bags contain coloured marbles. The first bag contains 5 red and 4 blue marbles, the second contains 2 red and 3 blue marbles.

     A marble is taken at random out of the first bag and placed in the second bag, then a marble is taken at random out of the second bag.
     What is the probability that both these marbles are
     1   red ones,
     2   blue ones ?

20. Copy and complete the table of values for $y = x(8 - x)$.

x	0	1	2	3	4	5	6	7	8
$8 - x$		7			4				
$y = x(8 - x)$		7			16				

Draw the graph of $y = x(8 - x)$ for values of x from 0 to 8, taking 2 cm to represent 1 unit on the x-axis and 2 cm to represent 2 units on the y-axis.

By dividing the area under the curve into 4 strips, each of width 2 units along the x-axis, calculate an approximate value of the area under the curve (i.e. between the curve and the x-axis).
Explain why this approximate value will be slightly less than the true value of the area.

Exercise B4   Activities

1.   **Reuleaux Curves**

The shape of the 20 pence coin and the
50 pence coin is a curved regular
heptagon.
This type of figure is called a
Reuleaux Curve, named after a German,
Franz Reuleaux, who wrote about such
curves about 100 years ago.

You can investigate some properties of Reuleaux Curves.

A simpler figure is made from an equilateral
triangle, so begin by studying that.
Draw an equilateral triangle *ABC*.
With centre *A*, radius *AB*, draw an
arc from *B* to *C*.
Draw similar arcs using centres
B and *C*.

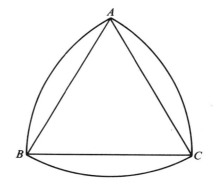

1   The breadth of the figure is defined
as the distance across the figure between
any two parallel lines which just touch
the perimeter.
Prove that this breadth is constant
(regardless of the direction of the
parallel lines), and is equal to the
length of *AB*.

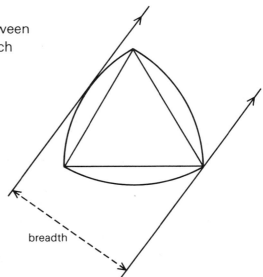

breadth

This means that although the shape cannot be used as a wheel, since it has not got a constant radius, it can be used in situations where a constant breadth is needed. It will fit exactly in a square with sides equal to its breadth.

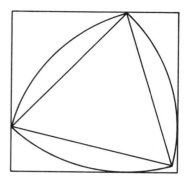

2   Find the perimeter of the figure, in terms of its breadth, and show that it is equal to the circumference of a circle with diameter equal to the breadth.

3   Find the area of the figure in terms of its breadth, and show that it is less than the area of a circle with diameter equal to the breadth.

4   You can repeat the investigation for the 7-sided Reuleaux curve.

For the coins, the property of a constant breadth is useful when the coins are used in a coin-operated machine. They will roll down a slope, guided by two grooves, one above the other, just as easily as circular coins.

It is not so easy to find the area of the 7-sided Reuleaux curve so here is a formula for it.

Area $= \dfrac{b^2}{2}\left(\pi - 7 \tan \frac{90°}{7}\right)$, where b is the breadth of the figure.

Use the formula to find what percentage of metal is saved by making coins of the Reuleaux curve shape, rather than making them circular, with diameter equal to the breadth of the curved coin.

2.   Maximum and minimum values

Using the method of completing the square, $x^2 + 2x + 13$ can be written as $(x + 1)^2 + 12$.

The first term of this expression is always positive, except when $x = -1$, when it is 0.

Thus the value of the complete expression is always greater than 12, except when $x = -1$, when it is 12.

So the minimum value of the expression is 12.

For $15 + 10x - x^2$, this can be written as
$-(x^2 - 10x) + 15$
$= -(x^2 - 10x + 25) + 25 + 15$
$= 40 - (x - 5)^2$

$(x - 5)^2$ is always positive, except when $x = 5$, when it is 0.

Thus the value of the complete expression is always less than 40, except when $x = 5$, when it is 40.

So the maximum value of the expression is 40.

Find the maximum or minimum values of these expressions.
1    $x^2 - 6x + 2$
2    $x^2 + 9x - 40$
3    $18 + 12x - x^2$
4    $4 - x - x^2$
5    $2x^2 - 16x + 1$, i.e. $2(x^2 - 8x) + 1$

3.   The gradient of the graph of $y = x^2$

To calculate the gradient of the chord AB, when A is the point $(3, 9)$.

$$\text{Gradient} = \frac{y\text{-step}}{x\text{-step}}$$

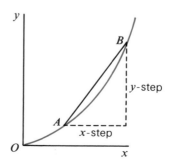

Point B	x-step	y-step	gradient
(4, 16)	1	7	7
$(3\frac{1}{2}, 12\frac{1}{4})$	$\frac{1}{2}$	$3\frac{1}{4}$	$6\frac{1}{2}$
(3.1, 9.61)	0.1	0.61	6.1
(3.01, 9.0601)	0.01	0.0601	6.01
(3.001, 9.006001)	0.001	0.006001	6.001

From the pattern, you can see that if the x-step is h, the gradient is $6 + h$.
If h is very small then
1   the two points A and B are very close together,
2   the gradient of the chord is very similar to the gradient of the tangent at the
       point A.

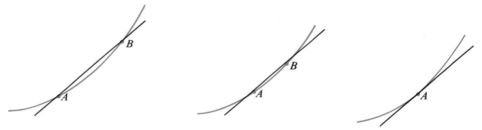

3   The gradient of the chord is approximately 6.
4   There is no chord through A with gradient 6, they are all 6 + something.
5   The line through A with gradient 6 is not a chord so it is the tangent at A.

You can find the gradients of the curve at points where $x = 1, 2, 4$ and 5 in a
similar way.

Put the results in a table and find the general result.

x	0	1	2	3	4	5	x
gradient	0			6			

The **calculation** of gradients from the equations of functions uses formulae worked
out by this method. This subject is called calculus, and the process of using the rules
to find gradients is called differentiation.

Do a similar investigation for the curve $y = x^3$, and see if you can find a general result.
What is the gradient of the line $y = x$?
Use the general results for the functions $y = x$, $y = x^2$ and $y = x^3$ to see if you can
predict the general results for gradients of $y = x^4$, $y = x^5$, and $y = x^n$.
You can use the formulae you have found to check the gradients you have found by
drawing in other questions.

4.   **The mean and standard deviation of a frequency distribution**

You already know how to find the mean of a frequency distribution. Here is an example, using the heights of a group of children.

Height in cm	frequency	x centre of interval	fx
110 to <120	6	115	690
120 to <130	17	125	2125
130 to <140	32	135	4320
140 to <150	26	145	3770
150 to <160	19	155	2945
	100		13850

$$\bar{x} = \frac{\Sigma fx}{\Sigma f} = \frac{13850}{100} \text{ cm} = 138.5 \text{ cm}$$

It is also possible to find the mean using an assumed mean x_0. This is particularly useful if you also wish to find the standard deviation.

Here is the same example. We use one of the centres of interval as the assumed mean, usually one near the middle of the list. Here we are choosing 135. For the standard deviation we also need a column fx^2. Note that fx^2 is not the same as $(fx)^2$. It is the fx column multiplied by the x column.

Height in cm	f	C of I	New x $x_0 = 135$	fx	fx^2
110-120	6	115	−20	−120	2400
120-130	17	125	−10	−170	1700
130-140	32	135	0	0	0
140-150	26	145	+10	+260	2600
150-160	19	155	+20	+380	7600
	100			+350	14300

$$\bar{x} = x_0 + \frac{\Sigma fx}{\Sigma f} = (135 + \tfrac{350}{100}) \text{ cm}$$

$$= (135 + 3.5) \text{ cm}$$

$$= 138.5 \text{ cm}$$

To find the standard deviation use the formula

$$s = \sqrt{\frac{\Sigma fx^2}{\Sigma f} - \left(\frac{\Sigma fx}{\Sigma f}\right)^2}$$

$$s = \sqrt{\frac{14300}{100} - \left(\frac{350}{100}\right)^2} \text{ cm}$$

$$= \sqrt{143 - 12.25} \text{ cm}$$

$$= \sqrt{130.75} \text{ cm}$$

$$= 11.43 \text{ cm, to 2 dec. pl.}$$

It is useful as a check to work out the values of 3 standard deviations below and above the mean, as most of the data should lie in that range.

Here, those values are approximately 104 cm and 173 cm, and all the data lies between those values.

Find the mean and standard deviation of these distributions.

1   The number of phone calls received in an office each hour over a period of 100 working hours.

Number of calls	0	1	2	3	4	5	6
frequency	15	30	23	18	10	4	0

2   The number of hours of tuition needed by 50 pupils of a driving school, before passing the test.

Number of hours	8	9	10	11	12	13	14
Number of pupils	2	3	8	12	11	10	4

3   The number of heads when 10 coins are tossed 1024 times. The data is on page 164, question 7.
(Check that the answers satisfy the formulae, mean = np and standard deviation = $\sqrt{npq}$, where $p = q = \frac{1}{2}$ and $n = 10$.)

4   The lengths of a sample of 60 bars, which were cut by a machine, which was set to cut to a length of 70 cm.

length (mm)	697	698	699	700	701	702	703
frequency	3	7	11	24	10	3	2

5   A survey to find the annual distances travelled by a sample of 40 cars.

Distance (in 1000 km)	f
9 - <11	5
11 - <13	6
13 - <15	9
15 - <17	14
17 - <19	4
19 - <21	2
	40

6   The lengths of 100 leaves from a certain type of plant.

Length (mm)	f
20 - <24	4
24 - <28	17
28 - <32	33
32 - <36	25
36 - <40	13
40 - <44	8
	100

5.   **Matrices**

A matrix is an array of numbers enclosed in a bracket. It is used to store information.

One use of matrices is to define certain transformations, and that is why we are introducing them here.

Column vectors can be used to define translations.
These are 2 × 1 (2 by 1) matrices. They have 2 rows and 1 column. They can also be called column matrices.

We can also express the coordinates of a point as a column matrix.

e.g. the point (4, 3) can be expressed as $\begin{pmatrix} 4 \\ 3 \end{pmatrix}$.

Addition or subtraction of column matrices

You have already added or subtracted vectors numerically.
Simply add or subtract the corresponding terms in each position.

e.g. $\begin{pmatrix} 5 \\ 7 \end{pmatrix} + \begin{pmatrix} -6 \\ 3 \end{pmatrix} = \begin{pmatrix} 5 + (-6) \\ 7 + 3 \end{pmatrix} = \begin{pmatrix} 5 - 6 \\ 7 + 3 \end{pmatrix} = \begin{pmatrix} -1 \\ 10 \end{pmatrix}$

$\begin{pmatrix} 4 \\ 9 \end{pmatrix} - \begin{pmatrix} -1 \\ 6 \end{pmatrix} = \begin{pmatrix} 4 - (-1) \\ 9 - 6 \end{pmatrix} = \begin{pmatrix} 4 + 1 \\ 9 - 6 \end{pmatrix} = \begin{pmatrix} 5 \\ 3 \end{pmatrix}$

Work out these matrices.

1 $\begin{pmatrix} 3 \\ 2 \end{pmatrix} + \begin{pmatrix} -1 \\ 3 \end{pmatrix}$

4 $\begin{pmatrix} 1 \\ 0 \end{pmatrix} - \begin{pmatrix} -1 \\ 2 \end{pmatrix}$

2 $\begin{pmatrix} 4 \\ 6 \end{pmatrix} + \begin{pmatrix} -2 \\ 2 \end{pmatrix}$

5 $\begin{pmatrix} 3 \\ 6 \end{pmatrix} + \begin{pmatrix} -7 \\ -2 \end{pmatrix}$

3 $\begin{pmatrix} 3 \\ 8 \end{pmatrix} - \begin{pmatrix} 9 \\ -4 \end{pmatrix}$

We will also use 2 × 2 (2 by 2) matrices. They have 2 rows and 2 columns.

Examples are $\begin{pmatrix} 5 & 4 \\ 7 & 9 \end{pmatrix}, \begin{pmatrix} 1 & 0 \\ 0 & 1 \end{pmatrix}, \begin{pmatrix} 5 & -7 \\ -2 & 3 \end{pmatrix}, \begin{pmatrix} 0.6 & -0.8 \\ -1.4 & 2.2 \end{pmatrix}$.

We need to learn how to multiply two 2 × 2 matrices.

Multiplication of two matrices

This does **not** follow the same method as addition.

e.g. $\begin{pmatrix} 4 & 9 \\ 5 & 8 \end{pmatrix} \times \begin{pmatrix} 2 & 1 \\ 3 & 7 \end{pmatrix}$ is **NOT** $\begin{pmatrix} 4 \times 2 & 9 \times 1 \\ 5 \times 3 & 8 \times 7 \end{pmatrix}$.

The rule is as follows.
Use the **1st row** of the 1st matrix (4 9) and the **1st column** of the 2nd matrix $\begin{pmatrix} 2 \\ 3 \end{pmatrix}$ and combine them thus: (4 × 2) + (9 × 3) = 8 + 27 = 35.

This number goes in the 1st row, 1st column of the answer. $\begin{pmatrix} 35 & \cdot \\ \cdot & \cdot \end{pmatrix}$

Now use the **1st row** of the 1st matrix (4 9)

and the **2nd column** of the 2nd matrix $\begin{pmatrix} 1 \\ 7 \end{pmatrix}$.

(4 × 1) + (9 × 7) = 4 + 63 = 67.

This number goes in the 1st row, 2nd column. $\begin{pmatrix} 35 & 67 \\ \cdot & \cdot \end{pmatrix}$

Next use the **2nd row** of the 1st matrix (5   8)

and the **1st column** of the 2nd matrix $\begin{pmatrix} 2 \\ 3 \end{pmatrix}$.

$(5 \times 2) + (8 \times 3) = 34$.

This number goes in the 2nd row, 1st column. $\begin{pmatrix} 35 & 67 \\ 34 & \cdot \end{pmatrix}$

Finally, use the **2nd row** of the 1st matrix (5   8)

and the **2nd column** of the 2nd matrix $\begin{pmatrix} 1 \\ 7 \end{pmatrix}$.

$(5 \times 1) + (8 \times 7) = 61$.

This number goes in the 2nd row, 2nd column. $\begin{pmatrix} 35 & 67 \\ 34 & 61 \end{pmatrix}$

Note that you only use the **rows** of the 1st matrix and the **columns** of the 2nd matrix.

Two matrices can only be multiplied if there is the same number of columns in the 1st matrix as rows in the 2nd matrix.

The order of multiplication affects the result.

$\begin{pmatrix} 2 & 1 \\ 3 & 7 \end{pmatrix} \times \begin{pmatrix} 4 & 9 \\ 5 & 8 \end{pmatrix}$ is not the same as $\begin{pmatrix} 4 & 9 \\ 5 & 8 \end{pmatrix} \times \begin{pmatrix} 2 & 1 \\ 3 & 7 \end{pmatrix}$.

Check for yourself that $\begin{pmatrix} 2 & 1 \\ 3 & 7 \end{pmatrix} \times \begin{pmatrix} 4 & 9 \\ 5 & 8 \end{pmatrix} = \begin{pmatrix} 13 & 26 \\ 47 & 83 \end{pmatrix}$.

If **A** and **B** are matrices, **A** × **B** ≠ **B** × **A**, in general.

Work out these matrices. Note that the multiplication sign can be omitted.

6 $\begin{pmatrix} 3 & 4 \\ 2 & 6 \end{pmatrix} \times \begin{pmatrix} -1 & -2 \\ 3 & 2 \end{pmatrix}$

11 $\begin{pmatrix} 4 & 2 \\ -3 & 1 \end{pmatrix} \begin{pmatrix} 1 & 0 \\ 0 & 1 \end{pmatrix}$

7 $\begin{pmatrix} 3 & 1 \\ 8 & 0 \end{pmatrix} \times \begin{pmatrix} 9 & -1 \\ -4 & 2 \end{pmatrix}$

12 $\begin{pmatrix} 3 & 7 \\ 2 & 5 \end{pmatrix} \begin{pmatrix} 5 & -7 \\ -2 & 3 \end{pmatrix}$

8 $\begin{pmatrix} 2 & 5 \\ -1 & 1 \end{pmatrix} \times \begin{pmatrix} 3 & 1 \\ 6 & 4 \end{pmatrix}$

13 $\begin{pmatrix} 5 & -7 \\ -2 & 3 \end{pmatrix} \begin{pmatrix} 3 & 7 \\ 2 & 5 \end{pmatrix}$

9 $\begin{pmatrix} 1 & -1 \\ 2 & 3 \end{pmatrix} \times \begin{pmatrix} 3 & 1 \\ 6 & -2 \end{pmatrix}$

14 $\begin{pmatrix} 3 & -4 \\ -8 & 11 \end{pmatrix} \begin{pmatrix} 11 & 4 \\ 8 & 3 \end{pmatrix}$

10 $\begin{pmatrix} 1 & 0 \\ 0 & 1 \end{pmatrix} \times \begin{pmatrix} 4 & 2 \\ -3 & 1 \end{pmatrix}$

15 $\begin{pmatrix} 11 & 4 \\ 8 & 3 \end{pmatrix} \begin{pmatrix} 3 & -4 \\ -8 & 11 \end{pmatrix}$

You will notice from questions **10** and **11** that multiplying a matrix by the matrix $\begin{pmatrix} 1 & 0 \\ 0 & 1 \end{pmatrix}$ leaves the other matrix unchanged.

The matrix $\begin{pmatrix} 1 & 0 \\ 0 & 1 \end{pmatrix}$ is denoted by **I** and is called the identity matrix (for 2 × 2 matrices).

If **A** is any matrix then **A** × **I** = **A** and **I** × **A** = **A**.

You will notice in questions **12–15** that the result is **I**.
If 2 matrices multiplied together give the matrix **I** then they are inverse matrices.
If **A** is one matrix, the other is denoted by **A**$^{-1}$ and
A × **A**$^{-1}$ = **I**, also **A**$^{-1}$ × **A** = **I**.

To find the inverse of the matrix $\begin{pmatrix} a & b \\ c & d \end{pmatrix}$.

If **A** = $\begin{pmatrix} a & b \\ c & d \end{pmatrix}$ and $ad - bc = 1$, then the rule for finding **A**$^{-1}$ is
1   interchange a and d,
2   change b into $-b$ and c into $-c$.

A^{-1} = $\begin{pmatrix} d & -b \\ -c & a \end{pmatrix}$

e.g. **A** = $\begin{pmatrix} 3 & 7 \\ 2 & 5 \end{pmatrix}$
$ad - bc = (3 \times 5) - (7 \times 2) = 1$.
Interchange 3 and 5.
Change 7 into -7 and 2 into -2.

Then **A**$^{-1}$ = $\begin{pmatrix} 5 & -7 \\ -2 & 3 \end{pmatrix}$

Check for yourself that **A** × **A**$^{-1}$ = $\begin{pmatrix} 1 & 0 \\ 0 & 1 \end{pmatrix}$ and **A**$^{-1}$ × **A** = $\begin{pmatrix} 1 & 0 \\ 0 & 1 \end{pmatrix}$.

If $ad - bc$ is not 1, the same rule is used but the new matrix is, divided by $ad - bc$.
$ad - bc$ is called the **determinant** of the matrix.

$$\mathbf{A}^{-1} = \frac{1}{ad - bc}\begin{pmatrix} d & -b \\ -c & a \end{pmatrix}$$

e.g. **A** = $\begin{pmatrix} 11 & 4 \\ 7 & 3 \end{pmatrix}$
$ad - bc = (11 \times 3) - (4 \times 7) = 5$.

Then **A**$^{-1}$ = $\dfrac{1}{5}\begin{pmatrix} 3 & -4 \\ -7 & 11 \end{pmatrix} = \begin{pmatrix} \frac{3}{5} & -\frac{4}{5} \\ -\frac{7}{5} & \frac{11}{5} \end{pmatrix} = \begin{pmatrix} 0.6 & -0.8 \\ -1.4 & 2.2 \end{pmatrix}$.

Check for yourself that $\mathbf{A} \times \mathbf{A}^{-1} = \begin{pmatrix} 1 & 0 \\ 0 & 1 \end{pmatrix}$ and $\mathbf{A}^{-1} \times \mathbf{A} = \begin{pmatrix} 1 & 0 \\ 0 & 1 \end{pmatrix}$.

If $ad - bc = 0$, the matrix has no inverse.

Use the rule to find the inverse matrices to these matrices.
If a matrix is $\mathbf{A}$ and its inverse is $\mathbf{A}^{-1}$, check that $\mathbf{A} \times \mathbf{A}^{-1} = \mathbf{I}$ and $\mathbf{A}^{-1} \times \mathbf{A} = \mathbf{I}$.

16 $\begin{pmatrix} 3 & 4 \\ 2 & 3 \end{pmatrix}$ 19 $\begin{pmatrix} 10 & -5 \\ -3 & 2 \end{pmatrix}$

17 $\begin{pmatrix} 2 & 3 \\ -2 & -1 \end{pmatrix}$ 20 $\begin{pmatrix} 6 & 8 \\ 1 & 3 \end{pmatrix}$

18 $\begin{pmatrix} 2 & 1 \\ -1 & 0 \end{pmatrix}$

Here is an example of a 2 × 2 matrix multiplying a 2 × 1 matrix.

$$\begin{pmatrix} 5 & 2 \\ -1 & 8 \end{pmatrix}\begin{pmatrix} 3 \\ -6 \end{pmatrix} = \begin{pmatrix} 5 \times 3 & + & 2 \times -6 \\ -1 \times 3 & + & 8 \times -6 \end{pmatrix} = \begin{pmatrix} 3 \\ -51 \end{pmatrix}$$

These cannot be multiplied in the reverse order since there has to be the same number of columns in the 1st matrix as rows in the 2nd matrix.

Work out these matrices.

21 $\begin{pmatrix} 1 & 3 \\ 4 & 2 \end{pmatrix}\begin{pmatrix} -2 \\ -1 \end{pmatrix}$ 24 $\begin{pmatrix} -1 & 0 \\ 0 & -1 \end{pmatrix}\begin{pmatrix} 5 \\ -2 \end{pmatrix}$

22 $\begin{pmatrix} 2 & 3 \\ 0 & 6 \end{pmatrix}\begin{pmatrix} 7 \\ -3 \end{pmatrix}$ 25 $\begin{pmatrix} 2 & 0 \\ 0 & 2 \end{pmatrix}\begin{pmatrix} -3 \\ 1 \end{pmatrix}$

23 $\begin{pmatrix} 2 & 3 \\ 3 & 1 \end{pmatrix}\begin{pmatrix} -3 \\ 1 \end{pmatrix}$

This is just a brief introduction to matrices, which will be used in Chapter 14.

6. The Binomial Distribution

If there is an experiment where there is a constant probability of an event being successful, and the results of the separate events are independent from each other, and the event is repeated twice in all, then the number of successes can be 0, 1 or 2.
We can find formulae for the probabilities of 0, 1 or 2 successes, and the complete list of probabilities is called a binomial distribution.

Example

A die is thrown and a six is counted as a success. If the die is thrown twice, find the probabilities of 0, 1 or 2 successes.

The throws are independent events.
$P(six) = \frac{1}{6}$, $P(not\ six) = \frac{5}{6}$

1st throw	2nd throw		Result	Probability

six — $\frac{1}{6}$ — six — SS — $\frac{1}{6} \times \frac{1}{6} = \frac{1}{36}$

$\frac{5}{6}$ — not six — SN — $\frac{1}{6} \times \frac{5}{6} = \frac{5}{36}$

not six — $\frac{1}{6}$ — six — NS — $\frac{5}{6} \times \frac{1}{6} = \frac{5}{36}$

$\frac{5}{6}$ — not six — NN — $\frac{5}{6} \times \frac{5}{6} = \frac{25}{36}$

$P(0\ sixes) = \frac{25}{36}$

$P(1\ six) = \frac{5}{36} + \frac{5}{36} = \frac{10}{36} = \frac{5}{18}$

$P(2\ sixes) = \frac{1}{36}$

Note that the probabilities add up to 1 as it is certain that one of these events must happen.

To get the general formula, let the probability of success be p, and the probability of failure be q, where $q = 1 - p$.

Then $P(0) = q^2$

$\qquad P(1) = 2qp$

$\qquad P(2) = p^2$

The sum of the probabilities is $q^2 + 2qp + p^2 = (q + p)^2$ which equals 1 since $q + p = 1$.

When the event is repeated three times in all, then the number of successes can be 0, 1, 2 or 3.

Example

There is a large batch of light bulbs and 0.3 of them are faulty. If 3 bulbs are picked out at random, then the sample can contain 0, 1, 2 or 3 faulty ones.

The results of the 3 bulbs, faulty or not, are independent events.
Here, being faulty is taken to be the successful event.
The probability, 0.3, is constant, since the bulbs are taken from a large batch.
The probability of a bulb not being faulty is $1 - 0.3 = 0.7$.

1st bulb	2nd bulb	3rd bulb	Outcome	Probability

		0.3 F	FFF	0.3^3
	0.3 F	0.7 N	FFN	0.7×0.3^2
F	0.7 N	0.3 F	FNF	0.7×0.3^2
0.3		0.7 N	FNN	$0.7^2 \times 0.3$
		0.3 F	NFF	0.7×0.3^2
0.7	0.3 F	0.7 N	NFN	$0.7^2 \times 0.3$
N	0.7 N	0.3 F	NNF	$0.7^2 \times 0.3$
		0.7 N	NNN	0.7^3

F → faulty
N → not faulty

P(0 faulty) $= 0.7^3 = 0.343$
P(1 faulty) $= 3 \times 0.7^2 \times 0.3 = 0.441$
P(2 faulty) $= 3 \times 0.7 \times 0.3^2 = 0.189$
P(3 faulty) $= 0.3^3 = 0.027$

If the probability of success is p, and the probability of failure is q, then
$P(0) = q^3$
$P(1) = 3q^2p$
$P(2) = 3qp^2$
$P(3) = p^3$

You may already know that $q^3 + 3q^2p + 3qp^2 + p^3 = (q + p)^3$, which equals 1.

You may like to work out for yourself the probabilities when the event is repeated 4 times in all.

The general results are
$P(0) = q^4$
$P(1) = 4q^3p$
$P(2) = 6q^2p^2$
$P(3) = 4qp^3$
$P(4) = p^4$

These are the terms in order when $(q + p)^4$ is expanded.

We will not go further, with the experiment repeated 5, 6, ... , n times, but you may like to investigate these for yourself, and link the probabilities with terms of $(q + p)^5$, ... , $(q + p)^n$, and maybe find a pattern for these terms, using Pascal's Triangle, (see page 97).

Here are some questions for you to try. You can either use tree-diagrams, or use the formulae given above.

1   4 coins are tossed. Find the probabilities of 0, 1, 2, 3 or 4 heads.

2   A marksman's chances of hitting a target with each of his shots is 0.6. If he fires 3 shots, find the probabilities of 0, 1, 2 or 3 hits.

3   A pack of cards is cut twice. What is the probability of the result being a heart 0, 1 or 2 times ?

4   In a multi-choice test each question has 5 possible answers A, B, C, D, E. One pupil answers 3 questions by random guessing.
What is the probability of getting 0, 1, 2 or 3 answers correct ?
What is the probability of getting at least 2 answers correct ?

5   In a workshop there are 4 machines and the probability of any machine breaking down on a particular day is $\frac{1}{10}$.
On one day, find the probabilities that
(a) all the machines work perfectly,
(b) at least 3 machines work perfectly.

11 Thinking about quadratic equations

Solving quadratic equations by using factors

If there are 2 numbers a and b and $ab = 0$, what can you say about the numbers ?

The quadratic equation $x^2 - 10x + 9 = 0$ can be written as $(x - 9)(x - 1) = 0$.

What can you say about $x - 9$ or $x - 1$?

What values of x satisfy the equation ?

A problem which can be solved by using a quadratic equation

Owing to track repairs a train covers a distance of 240 miles at an average speed of 12 mph less than the normal average speed, and so takes 1 hour longer than usual.
Find the normal average speed.

Let the normal average speed be x mph.
How long does the journey normally take ?
What is the average speed on this slower journey ?
How long does this journey take, in terms of $x - 12$?
Since this is 1 hour more than usual, write down an equation.
Simplify the equation and show that it can be rearranged to give $x^2 - 12x - 2880 = 0$.
Solve this equation to find the normal average speed.

Solving quadratic equations by using the general formula

To solve the equation $x^2 - 10x + 9 = 0$, the general formula (page 233) gives the solution

$$x = \frac{10 \pm \sqrt{(-10)^2 - 4 \times 1 \times 9}}{2 \times 1}$$

Find the 2 values for the solutions.

Two more problems which can be solved by using quadratic equations

Buying oranges

Rachael bought some oranges for £2.52, but she found that 2 of them were bad. She calculated that, as a result, each good orange had cost her 3p more than she had expected.

How many oranges did she buy ?

Let Rachael buy x oranges.
Obtain an equation involving x and show that it can be rearranged to give
$x^2 - 2x - 168 = 0$.
Solve this equation to find the number of oranges bought.

How many people ?

Of the people in an airport departure lounge, the square root of 10 times the number of people went on the first plane, and then $\frac{4}{5}$ of the original number went on the second plane, leaving 12 behind. How many people were there at first ?

Let there be x people at first.
Obtain an equation involving x, and rearrange it to give $\sqrt{10x} = \frac{1}{5}x - 12$.
Square both sides of this equation, and rearrange it again to give
$x^2 - 370x + 3600 = 0$.
Solve this equation to find the number of people who were there at first.

11 Quadratic Equations

A quadratic equation is an equation of the form $ax^2 + bx + c = 0$, where a, b, c are constant numbers and a is not 0, i.e. the highest power of x is x^2.

Solving equations by using factors

If there are two numbers p and q, and $pq = 0$, then either $p = 0$ or $q = 0$.
This fact leads to the method of solving quadratic equations by factorising.

Examples

1   Solve the equation $x^2 = 5x + 36$

Make the right-hand side zero.

$x^2 - 5x - 36 = 0$

Factorise the left-hand side

$(x + 4)(x - 9) = 0$

Since the two factors multiplied together have product 0, one of them must be 0.

Either $x + 4 = 0$ or $x - 9 = 0$

$\qquad\qquad x = -4$ or $x = 9$

You can check both these solutions in the original equation.

When $x = -4$, LHS $= x^2 = (-4)^2 = 16$
RHS $= 5x + 36 = 5 \times (-4) + 36 = -20 + 36 = 16$
Both sides are the same, so the equation checks when $x = -4$.

Check the solution $x = 9$ in a similar way.

The answers to an equation may be called the **roots** of the equation.
Here the roots are -4 and 9.

2   Solve the equation $4x^2 + 5x - 6 = 0$

Factorise the left-hand side

$(4x - 3)(x + 2) = 0$

Either $4x - 3 = 0$ or $x + 2 = \quad 0$

$\qquad\qquad 4x = 3$ or $\qquad x = -2$

$\qquad\qquad x = \frac{3}{4}$ or $\qquad x = -2$

Exercise 11.1

1. Solve these equations, which have been written in factor form.

    1 $(x - 5)(x - 3) = 0$
    2 $(2x - 1)(x + 4) = 0$
    3 $(2x + 3)(3x - 2) = 0$
    4 $(x + 1)(x + 9) = 0$
    5 $x(3x - 4) = 0$
    6 $(4x - 1)(4x - 7) = 0$

2. Solve these equations by the method of using factors.

    1 $x^2 - 3x - 10 = 0$
    2 $x^2 + 5x + 6 = 0$
    3 $x^2 + 11x + 10 = 0$
    4 $x^2 + 6x - 16 = 0$
    5 $x^2 + 7x + 12 = 0$
    6 $x^2 + 5x - 6 = 0$
    7 $x^2 - 4x = 0$
    8 $x^2 - 11x - 60 = 0$
    9 $x^2 - 3x - 4 = 0$
    10 $x^2 + 14x + 24 = 0$

3. Solve these equations by the method of using factors.

    1 $2x^2 + 9x + 10 = 0$
    2 $2x^2 - 11x + 15 = 0$
    3 $2x^2 + x = 0$
    4 $3x^2 + 13x + 4 = 0$
    5 $2x^2 + 5x - 3 = 0$
    6 $5x^2 + 14x - 3 = 0$
    7 $3x^2 - 2x = 0$
    8 $2x^2 - x - 3 = 0$
    9 $3x^2 + x - 2 = 0$
    10 $4x^2 + 8x - 5 = 0$

4. Solve these equations by writing them in the form $ax^2 + bx + c = 0$, and then using the method of factors.

    1 $x^2 - 17x = 60$
    2 $x^2 = 16x - 48$
    3 $x^2 + 8 = 6x$
    4 $x^2 + 144 = 25x$
    5 $2x^2 = 5x + 3$
    6 $3x^2 + 16x = 12$

The equation $x^2 = d$

The solution of this equation is $x = \pm\sqrt{d}$

Examples

1 Solve the equation $9x^2 = 16$

Divide both sides by 9
$$x^2 = \tfrac{16}{9}$$
Take the square root of both sides
$$x = \pm\tfrac{4}{3}$$
$$x = 1\tfrac{1}{3} \text{ or } -1\tfrac{1}{3}$$

2 Solve the equation $3x^2 = 10$, giving the roots correct to 2 decimal places.

Divide both sides by 3
$$x^2 = \tfrac{10}{3}$$
$$x = \pm\sqrt{\tfrac{10}{3}}$$
$$= \pm 1.825\ldots \qquad \text{(using your calculator)}$$
$$x = 1.83 \text{ or } -1.83, \text{ to 2 dec. pl.}$$

3 Solve the equation $(x + 4)^2 = 5$, giving the roots correct to 2 decimal places.

Take the square root of both sides
$$x + 4 = \pm\sqrt{5}$$
Subtract 4 from both sides
$$x = -4 \pm \sqrt{5}$$
$$= -4 + \sqrt{5} \quad \text{or} \quad -4 - \sqrt{5}$$
$$= -1.763\ldots \quad \text{or} \quad -6.236\ldots \qquad \text{(using your calculator)}$$
$$= -1.76 \text{ or } -6.24, \text{ to 2 dec. pl.}$$

This last example leads to a general method for solving quadratic equations, called 'completing the square', which is explained later, and also leads to the general formula for the solution of quadratic equations.

Solving equations by using the general formula

The equation $ax^2 + bx + c = 0$ has the solution

$$x = \frac{-b \pm \sqrt{b^2 - 4ac}}{2a}$$

This is the general formula which gives the two roots.

Examples

4 Solve the equation $6x^2 + 11x - 35 = 0$

Comparing this equation with $ax^2 + bx + c = 0$,
$a = 6, b = 11, c = -35$.

The solution is

$$x = \frac{-b \pm \sqrt{b^2 - 4ac}}{2a}$$

$$= \frac{-11 \pm \sqrt{11^2 - 4 \times 6 \times (-35)}}{2 \times 6}$$

You can use your calculator at this stage to work out $\sqrt{11^2 - 4 \times 6 \times (-35)}$

$$x = \frac{-11 \pm 31}{12}$$

$$= \frac{-11 + 31}{12} \quad \text{or} \quad \frac{-11 - 31}{12}$$

$$= \tfrac{20}{12} \text{ or } -\tfrac{42}{12}$$

$$= 1\tfrac{2}{3} \text{ or } -3\tfrac{1}{2}$$

Since the number under the square root is a perfect square, the square root is exact and the answers are rational numbers. In this case they are often given in fractional form, rather than as approximate decimals.

An equation where the number under the square root is a perfect square could have been solved by factorising.

5   Solve the equation $3x^2 - 5x + 1 = 0$, giving your solutions correct to 2 decimal places.

($3x^2 - 5x + 1$ cannot be factorised so you cannot use the method of factorisation. Often a clue to this is when you are asked to give an approximate answer.)

Comparing the equation with $ax^2 + bx + c = 0$, $a = 3, b = -5, c = 1$.

$$x = \frac{-b \pm \sqrt{b^2 - 4ac}}{2a}$$

$$= \frac{-(-5) \pm \sqrt{(-5)^2 - 4 \times 3 \times 1}}{2 \times 3}$$

Use your calculator to work out $\sqrt{(-5)^2 - 4 \times 3 \times 1}$
Since the result is not exact, save it in the memory of the calculator.

$$x = \frac{5 \pm \sqrt{13}}{6}$$

$$= \frac{5 + \sqrt{13}}{6} \quad \text{or} \quad \frac{5 - \sqrt{13}}{6}$$

Press 5 $\boxed{+}$ $\boxed{\text{RM}}$ $\boxed{=}$ $\boxed{\div}$ 6 $\boxed{=}$
then 5 $\boxed{-}$ $\boxed{\text{RM}}$ $\boxed{=}$ $\boxed{\div}$ 6 $\boxed{=}$

$x = 1.434 \ldots$ or $0.232 \ldots$
   $= 1.43$ or 0.23, to 2 dec. pl.

Exercise 11.2

1.   Solve these equations. If the answers are not exact, give them correct to 2 decimal places.

    1 $x^2 = 121$ **4** $10x^2 = 3$
    2 $4x^2 = 49$ **5** $(x - 3)^2 = 81$
    3 $2x^2 = 17$ **6** $(x + 7)^2 = 2$

2.   Solve these equations using the general formula, giving the answers in fractional form.

    1 $10x^2 - 11x - 6 = 0$ **4** $8x^2 - 58x + 77 = 0$
    2 $4x^2 + 7x + 3 = 0$ **5** $3x^2 - 19x - 72 = 0$
    3 $6x^2 + 7x - 3 = 0$ **6** $6x^2 + 7x - 10 = 0$

3.   Solve these equations using the general formula, giving the answers correct to
     2 decimal places.

     1 $x^2 + x - 3 = 0$ **6** $5x^2 - 3x = 4$

     2 $3x^2 + 4x - 2 = 0$ **7** $x^2 - 2x - 1 = 0$

     3 $2x^2 - 7x + 4 = 0$ **8** $2x^2 + 6x = 3$

     4 $5x^2 - 9x - 4 = 0$ **9** $x^2 + 9x - 30 = 0$

     5 $2x^2 - 9x + 3 = 0$ **10** $4x^2 = 2 - x$

4.   Solve these fractional equations.

     1 $\dfrac{2}{x - 5} - \dfrac{3}{x + 3} = \dfrac{1}{4}$

     2 $\dfrac{2}{x} = 2 - \dfrac{7}{12 - x}$

     3 $\dfrac{2x}{x + 4} = \dfrac{x + 3}{x - 2}$

Exercise 11.3   Applications and Activities

1.   A polygon of n sides has $\frac{1}{2}n(n - 3)$ diagonals. How many sides has a polygon
     with 54 diagonals ?

2.   A rectangular lawn 30 m by 24 m is
     surrounded by a concrete path of uniform
     width. If the area of the path is half the
     area of the lawn, write down an equation
     involving x, where x m is the width of the
     path, and solve it to find how wide the
     path is.

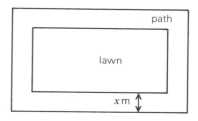

3.   A group of children decide to buy a computer game costing £18, to share
     among them. On working out what they will each have to pay, they realise that,
     if they invite 3 more children to join the group they will each have to pay £1
     less.
     If there are x children originally, write down an equation using this information,
     and solve it to find the value of x.
     How many children were there originally ?

4.   A rectangular enclosure of area $12\,m^2$ is to be made to keep pet rabbits in.
     If one side is $x\,m$ long, show that the length of wire netting needed to enclose
     the area is $2\left(x + \dfrac{12}{x}\right)m.$
     If there is $18\,m$ of wire netting available, write down an equation in x, and solve
     it to find the measurements of the enclosure with area $12\,m^2$ which uses the
     $18\,m$ of netting. Give these measurements in metres, correct to 1 decimal place.

5.   A train travels 75 miles at an average speed of $x\,$mph and then 100 miles at an
     average speed of $(x - 15)\,$mph. Find an expression for the total time taken for
     the journey.
     If the total time was 5 hours, write down an equation and solve it to find the
     value of x.

6.   In the right-angled triangle ABC, $\angle B = 90°$, AB is 1 cm longer than BC and AC
     is 8 cm longer than AB.
     Write down an equation in terms of x, where $BC = x\,$cm, and solve it to find the
     lengths of the sides of the triangle.

7.   A rectangular block has a height $h\,$cm
     and a square base of side $x\,$cm. Show
     that the total surface area, $A\,cm^2$,
     is given by $A = 2x^2 + 4xh$.

     If the total surface area is $600\,cm^2$
     and the height is 12 cm, find the
     length of an edge of the base,
     correct to the nearest mm.

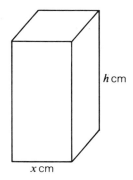

8.   In the diagram, $ABCD$ is a rectangle.
     P is a point on DC $x\,$cm from D.
     Write down expressions for AP^2 and
     BP^2.
     If $AP = 2BP$, what is the connection
     between AP^2 and BP^2?
     Write down an equation involving x
     and solve it to find the value of x.

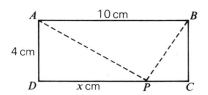

9. **Solving equations by completing the square**

In Chapter 7 you learnt about completing the square. This technique can be used in solving quadratic equations. It is the method from which the general formula is obtained.

Example

Solve the equation $3x^2 - 5x + 1 = 0$
(This equation was solved using the formula on page 234.)

Subtract 1 from both sides.
$$3x^2 - 5x = -1$$
Divide both sides by 3.
$$x^2 - \tfrac{5}{3}x = -\tfrac{1}{3}$$
Complete the square by adding $\left[\tfrac{1}{2} \text{ of } \left(-\tfrac{5}{3}\right)\right]^2$ to both sides.
$$x^2 - \tfrac{5}{3}x + \tfrac{25}{36} = \tfrac{25}{36} - \tfrac{1}{3}$$
$$\left(x - \tfrac{5}{6}\right)^2 = \tfrac{13}{36}$$
Take the square root of both sides.
$$x - \tfrac{5}{6} = \pm \frac{\sqrt{13}}{6}$$
Add $\tfrac{5}{6}$ to both sides.
$$x = \frac{5 \pm \sqrt{13}}{6}$$
$$= 1.43 \text{ or } 0.23, \text{ to 2 dec. pl.}$$

Completing the square is a good method to use when the equation starts with x^2 and the term in x has an even number, i.e. $a = 1$ and b is even.

Example

Solve the equation $x^2 + 8x + 5 = 0$
$$x^2 + 8x = -5$$
Add $\left(\tfrac{1}{2} \text{ of } 8\right)^2$ to both sides
$$x^2 + 8x + 16 = 11$$
$$(x + 4)^2 = 11$$

Take the square root of both sides

$x + 4 = \pm\sqrt{11}$

$x = -4 \pm \sqrt{11}$

$\quad = -4 + \sqrt{11}$ or $-4 - \sqrt{11}$

$\quad = -0.683\ldots$ or $-7.316\ldots$

$\quad = -0.68$ or -7.32, to 2 dec. pl.

Solve these equations using the method of completing the square, giving answers correct to 2 decimal places.

1 $x^2 - 10x - 6 = 0$

2 $x^2 + 2x = 4$

3 $x^2 - 12x + 10 = 0$

You can also solve some of the equations of Exercise 11.2, question 3 on page 235, by completing the square. Then you can decide which method you prefer to use.

You can prove that the general formula is correct by beginning with $ax^2 + bx + c = 0$ and solving it by completing the square. (Begin by dividing by a.)

10. Solving quadratic equations by iteration

Example

To solve the equation $x^2 + 2x - 2 = 0$

Rewrite it as $x^2 + 2x = 2$

$$x(x + 2) = 2$$

$$x = \frac{2}{x + 2}$$

Use the iteration formula $x_{n+1} = \dfrac{2}{x_n + 2}$

If you begin with $x_1 = 5$,

$$x_2 = \frac{2}{x_1 + 2} = \frac{2}{5 + 2} = \frac{2}{7} = 0.2857\ldots$$

Put the answer in the memory of the calculator.

$$x_3 = \frac{2}{x_2 + 2} = 0.875$$

Press 2 ÷ (RM + 2) = and put the answer in the memory to use next.

$$x_4 = \frac{2}{x_3 + 2} = 0.6957$$

$$x_5 = \frac{2}{x_4 + 2} = 0.7419$$

Using a graphics calculator you can find the values of x_2, x_3, x_4, . . . by pressing

5 EXE	This enters $x_1 = 5$
2 ÷ (ANS + 2) EXE	This calculates x_2
EXE	This calculates x_3
EXE	This calculates x_4

and press EXE to find x_5, x_6, . . .

Here are the first 12 terms of the sequence.

$x_1 = 5$	$x_7 = 0.7328$
$x_2 = 0.2857$	$x_8 = 0.7319$
$x_3 = 0.875$	$x_9 = 0.7321$
$x_4 = 0.6957$	$x_{10} = 0.7320$
$x_5 = 0.7419$	$x_{11} = 0.7321$
$x_6 = 0.7294$	$x_{12} = 0.7320$

The sequence converges to 0.732, correct to 3 decimal places, and this is the approximate value for a root of the equation.
Try this method again, starting with different values for x_1.
You will find that it is not possible to get any further if you get any value of x_n to be -2, since the denominator of the fraction would then be zero.

A different iteration formula can be used to solve the same equation, $x^2 + 2x - 2 = 0$.

Rewrite it as $2x = 2 - x^2$

$$x = \frac{2 - x^2}{2}$$

Use the iteration formula $x_{n+1} = \frac{2 - x_n^2}{2}$

If you begin with $x_1 = 5$, you will not get a convergent sequence.

If you begin with $x_1 = 0.5$,

$$x_2 = \frac{2 - x_1^2}{2} = \frac{2 - 0.5^2}{2} = 0.875$$

Put the answer in the memory of the calculator.

$$x_3 = \frac{2 - x_2^2}{2} = 0.6172$$

Press $\boxed{(}\ 2\ \boxed{-}\ \boxed{RM}\ \boxed{x^2}\ \boxed{)}\ \boxed{\div}\ 2\ \boxed{=}$ and put the answer in the memory to use next.

$$x_4 = \frac{2 - x_3^2}{2} = 0.8095$$

Using a graphics calculator you can press

0.5 $\boxed{EXE}$ This enters $x_1 = 0.5$

$\boxed{(}\ 2\ \boxed{-}\ \boxed{ANS}\ \boxed{x^2}\ \boxed{)}\ \boxed{\div}\ 2\ \boxed{EXE}$ This calculates x_2

and press $\boxed{EXE}$ to find $x_3, x_4, x_5, \ldots$

Here are the first 12 terms of the sequence.

$x_1 = 0.5$	$x_7 = 0.7005$
$x_2 = 0.875$	$x_8 = 0.7547$
$x_3 = 0.6172$	$x_9 = 0.7152$
$x_4 = 0.8095$	$x_{10} = 0.7442$
$x_5 = 0.6723$	$x_{11} = 0.7231$
$x_6 = 0.7740$	$x_{12} = 0.7386$

The sequence has not converged quickly enough to find the solution of the equation correct to 3 decimal places. It is necessary to work out more terms, until it becomes clear that the limiting value of the sequence, correct to 3 decimal places, is 0.732.

By using a different formula it may be possible to find the second root of the equation.
For this equation, $x^2 = 2 - 2x$

$$x = \frac{2}{x} - 2$$

Use the iteration formula $x_{n+1} = \frac{2}{x_n} - 2$, with $x_1 = 5$, to find the second root of the equation.

What quadratic equation can be solved by using the iteration formula
$$x_{n+1} = \frac{2}{10 - x_n} ?$$

At the limiting value, $x_{n+1} = x_n = x$

The equation is $x = \dfrac{2}{10 - x}$

$$x(10 - x) = 2$$
$$10x - x^2 = 2$$
i.e. $x^2 - 10x + 2 = 0$

In these questions, show that the limiting values of the iteration formulae will give roots of the corresponding quadratic equations.

Solve the equations, finding one root of each, correct to 2 decimal places.

1 $x^2 - 2x - 4 = 0$.   Use $x_{n+1} = \dfrac{4}{x_n - 2}$ and let $x_1 = 1$.

2 $x^2 - 6x - 10 = 0$.   Use $x_{n+1} = \dfrac{x_n{}^2 - 10}{6}$ and let $x_1 = 5$.

3 $2x^2 - 4x + 1 = 0$.   Use $x_{n+1} = \dfrac{1}{4 - 2x_n}$ and let $x_1 = 3$.

4 $3x^2 + 4x - 2 = 0$.   Use $x_{n+1} = \dfrac{2 - 3x_n{}^2}{4}$ and let $x_1 = -0.2$.

5 $2x^2 + 6x + 3 = 0$.   Use $x_{n+1} = -\dfrac{3}{2x_n + 6}$ and let $x_1 = -4$.

PUZZLES

31.   A speedboat went between two jetties in 6 minutes when going along at full power, with the current of the river. It took 9 minutes to return, going against the current. How long would it take to travel the same distance in still water ?

32.   A conifer tree when planted was 2 m high and it grew by an equal amount each year. At the end of the 7th year it was $\frac{1}{8}$ taller than it was at the end of the 6th year. How tall was the tree at the end of the 10th year ?

33.   On her stall at a fair, Mavis sold dolls at £10 each, teddy bears at £2.50 each and fluffy spiders at 50p each. During the afternoon, Mavis sold exactly 100 articles, and her takings were exactly £100. How many of each article did she sell ?

12 Thinking about circle properties

Angles in circles

You have already used circles. You know about the relationship between the circumference and radius, or the area and radius. You have used symmetrical properties. In this chapter we look (mainly) at some properties of angles in circles.

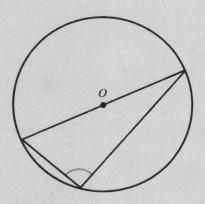
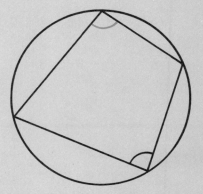

Draw diagrams similar to these and by measurement see if you can discover any facts about the marked angles.
Draw slightly different diagrams and see if the relationships still hold.
Then see if you can prove that the relationships are true.

Look for circles in the home, in manufactured objects, or in nature.

lica of a 600-year old clock

Concentric circles

big wheel in Vienna

Wheels on display

12 Circle properties

A circle is the locus of a point which moves at a constant distance from a fixed point.

In the diagram, *A* is the fixed point, and is the centre of the circle. *r* units is the constant distance, and is the radius of the circle.

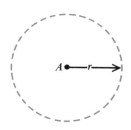

Here are the names of some of the parts of a circle.

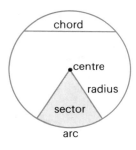

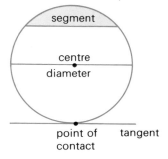

Circles which have the same centre are called concentric circles.

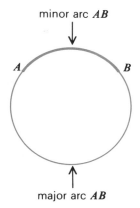

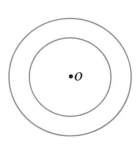

Here are some formulae for calculations involving circles.

$C = 2\pi r = \pi d$

$A = \pi r^2$

Length of arc $= \dfrac{\theta}{360} \times 2\pi r$

Area of sector $= \dfrac{\theta}{360} \times \pi r^2$

π is approximately 3.142.

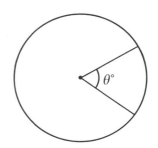

Some symmetrical properties of chords and tangents

Chord property

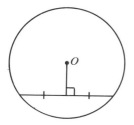

The line from the centre to the mid-point of a chord is perpendicular to the chord.

Tangent property

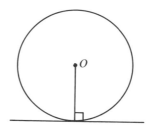

The radius to the point of contact is perpendicular to the tangent.

Equal chords

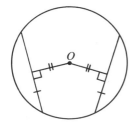

Chords of equal length are equidistant (the same distance) from the centre.

Tangents from an external point

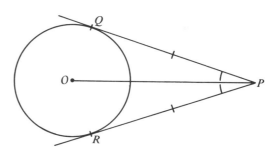

They are equal, i.e. $PQ = PR$
Also OP bisects $\angle QPR$

Some properties of angles in circles

Angle at the centre

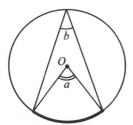

The angle at the centre is twice as big as the angle at the circumference (standing on the same arc).

$a = 2b$

An angle in a semicircle

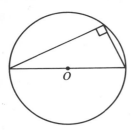

The angle in a semicircle is a right angle.

Angles on the same arc

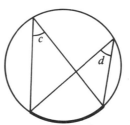

Angles at the circumference (standing on the same arc) are equal.
(These are sometimes called angles in the same segment.)

$c = d$

Cyclic quadrilaterals

A quadrilateral whose 4 vertices lie on a circle is called a cyclic quadrilateral.

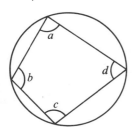

Opposite angles add up to 180°.

$a + c = 180°$

$b + d = 180°$

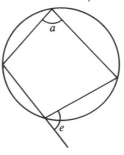

An exterior angle is equal to the opposite interior angle.

$e = a$

The alternate segment theorem

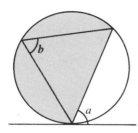

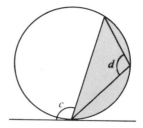

The angle between a tangent and a chord is equal to any angle made by that chord in the alternate segment (i.e. the shaded part) of the circle.

$$a = b \qquad\qquad\qquad c = d$$

Examples.

1 The circle has radius 10 cm and the chord AB is 8 cm from the centre O. Find the length of AB.

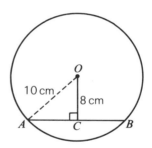

If C is the mid-point of AB, the line OC is perpendicular to AB, so $OC = 8$ cm. In the right-angled triangle OAC,

$OA^2 = AC^2 + OC^2$ Pythagoras' theorem

$10^2 = AC^2 + 8^2$ (AC in cm)

$AC^2 = 10^2 - 8^2$

$AC = 6$ cm

$AB = 12$ cm

2 In the diagram, PS and PT are tangents to the circle, touching it at Q and R. What is the size of $\angle PQR$?

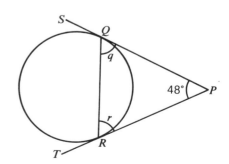

Since PQ and PR are tangents, $PQ = PR$. $\triangle PQR$ is isosceles and $q = r$.

$q + r + 48° = 180°$ angles of triangle

$q + r = 132°$

$q = 66°$

i.e. $\angle PQR = 66°$

3   In the diagram, O is the centre of
the circle.
Find the sizes of a and b.

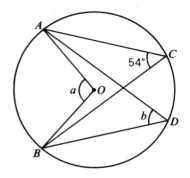

$a = 108°$ $\angle AOB$ = angle at centre on
arc $AB = 2 \times \angle ACB$

$b = 54°$ $\angle ACB = \angle ADB$, angles on
the same arc AB

4   Find the value of x.

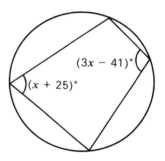

$x + 25 + 3x - 41 = 180$ opposite angles
of cyclic
quadrilateral

$$4x - 16 = 180$$
$$4x = 196$$
$$x = 49$$

(Substituting for x gives angles of 74° and 106°. You can check that these add up
to 180°.)

5 PTQ is a tangent touching the
circle at T.
Find the sizes of c and d.

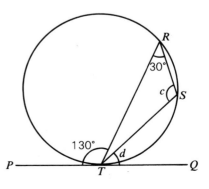

$c = 130°$ angle in alternate
segment = $\angle PTR$

$d = 30°$ angle in alternate
segment = $\angle QTS$

6 In the diagram, **AB** is a diameter of
the circle.

AB = 9 cm, **AC** = 2 cm.

Calculate the size of ∠**ABC**.

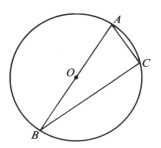

Since **AB** is a diameter,

∠**C** = 90°   angle in a semicircle

Triangle **ABC** is right-angled at **C**.

$$\sin \angle ABC = \frac{\text{opp}}{\text{hyp}}$$

$$= \tfrac{2}{9}$$

∠**ABC** = 12.8°, to 1 dec. pl.

Exercise 12.1

1. In the diagram, **O** is the centre of
the circle.
If **AC** = **CB** = 4 cm and **OC** = 3 cm,
find the radius of the circle.

2. Using the same diagram as in question 1,
if the circle has a radius 12 cm and
OC = 7 cm, find the size of ∠**OAC**,
to the nearest degree.

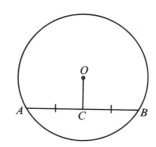

3. In the diagram, **O** is the centre
of the circle. **PT** is a tangent
touching the circle at **T**.
If **OA** = 8 cm and **AP** = 9 cm,
find the length of **PT**.

4. Using the same diagram as in
question 3, if the circle has
radius 6 cm and ∠**TOP** = 72°,
find the length of **PT**, to the
nearest mm.

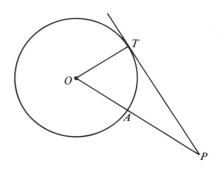

5. Find the sizes of the unknown marked angles in these diagrams. O is the centre of the circle. PT and PS are tangents touching the circle at T and S.
Give brief reasons for your answers.

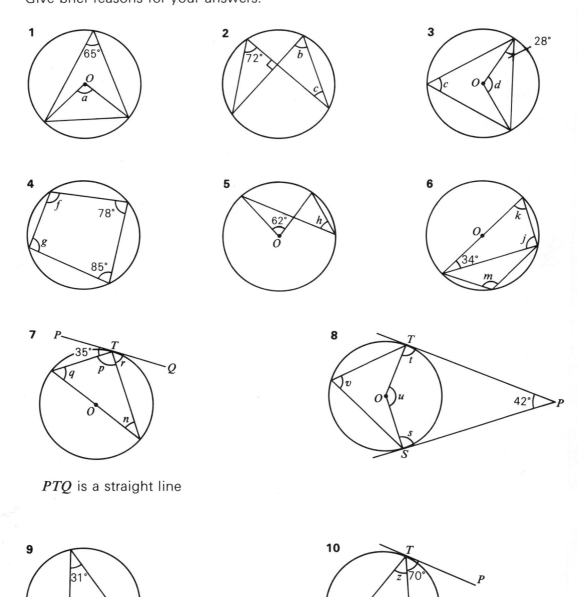

PTQ is a straight line

6.   Find the sizes of the unknown marked angles in these diagrams. *O* is the centre of the circle. *PT* and *PS* are tangents touching the circle at *T* and *S*. Give brief reasons for your answers.

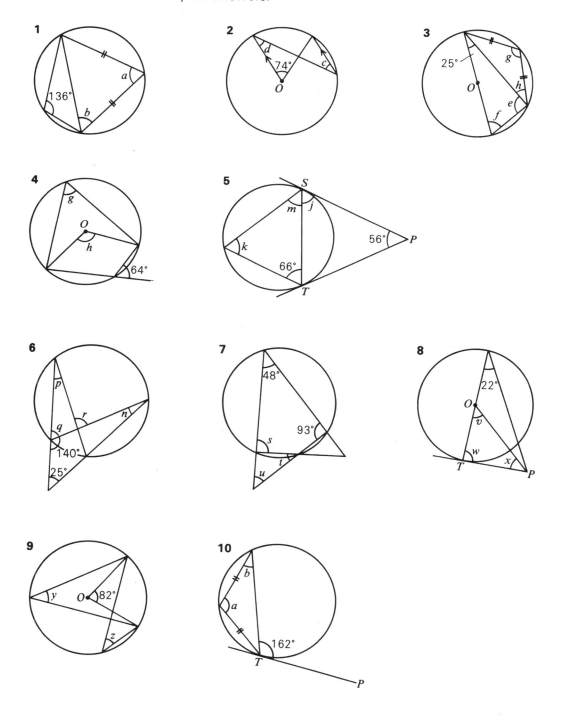

Exercise 12.2   Applications and Activities

1. Write down the equation connecting x and y in these diagrams. O is the centre
    of the circle. PT is a tangent touching the circle at T.

1
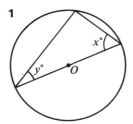

2
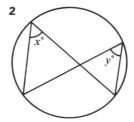

3
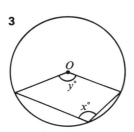

4
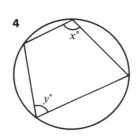

5
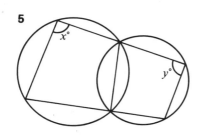

6
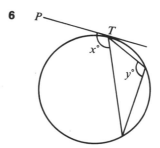

2. In the diagram PAX and QAY
    are straight lines.
    Prove that $\angle PBQ = \angle XBY$.

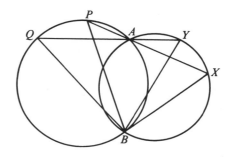

3. In the diagram, $\angle PXQ = 108°$
and $\angle PXR = 124°$.
Find the size of $\angle BAC$.

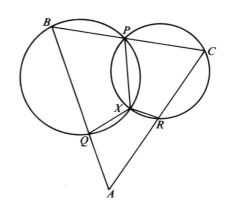

4. In the diagram, $ABCD$ is a trapezium
with AB parallel to DC.
$AB = 24$ cm, $CD = 10$ cm and the
radius of the circle is 13 cm.
Find the distance between AB and DC.

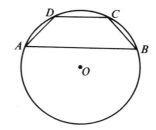

5. AB is a fixed line and P is a point
such that $\angle APB = 90°$.
State the locus of P.

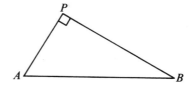

6. In the diagram, AB is the diameter of
the semicircle ACB. XC is a tangent
touching the semicircle at C, and X
is the point such that AX is
perpendicular to XC.
Prove that the triangles AXC and ACB
are similar.

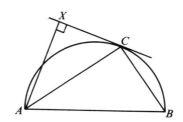

Hence show that $\dfrac{\text{area } \Delta AXC}{\text{area } \Delta ABC} = \dfrac{AC^2}{AB^2}$

7. *A, B, C, D, E* are 5 points on the circumference of the circle, centre *O*. ∠*AOB* = 100°.
    Prove that ∠*BCD* + ∠*DEA* = 230°

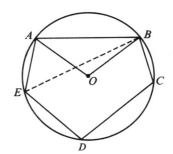

8. In the diagram, *AB* = *BE* and *AC* is a diameter of the circle. ∠*E* = 25°.
    Prove that *AC* = *CE*, and find the size of ∠*DAC*.

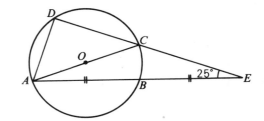

9. In the diagram, *TP* and *TQ* are tangents touching the circle at *P* and *Q*.
    The chords *PR* and *RQ* are equal.
    Find the size of ∠*PQR*.

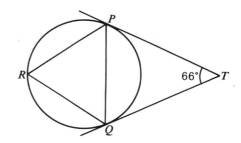

10. In the diagram, *O* is the centre of the circle.
    Find the size of ∠*AOC*.

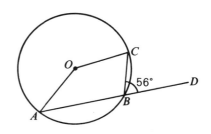

11. In the diagram, *BD* is a diameter of the circle and *A* is a point on the circumference such that ∠*ABD* = 30°. The tangent to the circle at *A* meets *BD* produced at *C*.
    Prove that *AC* = *AB*.

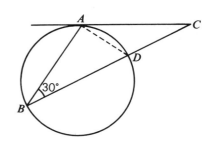

12. The diagram shows a tight string
    passing round a horizontal circular
    disc, centre *A*, and round a peg *B*
    on the same level. The string
    forms tangents to the disc at *T*
    and *S*.
    If *AB* = 20 cm and *AT* = 10 cm,
    find

    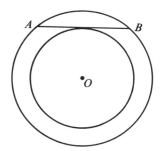

    1 the length of *TB*,
    2 the size of ∠*TAS*,
    3 the length of the **major arc** *ST*,
    4 the total length of the string.

13. In the diagram, the circles have
    the same centre, and the radius
    of the smaller circle is 12 cm.
    AB is a chord of the larger
    circle and is a tangent to the
    smaller circle. *AB* = 18 cm.
    Find the radius of the larger
    circle.

    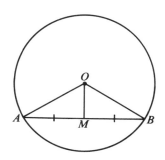

14. **Proofs by using congruent triangles**

    In these diagrams, *O* is the centre of the circle.

    1 To prove that the line from
    the centre of a circle to the
    mid-point of a chord is
    perpendicular to the chord.

    Explain why Δ*OAM*, Δ*OBM* are
    congruent.
    What does this prove about
    ∠*OMA* ?

    The converse of this theorem is also true, and you could prove it, that the
    line from the centre of a circle perpendicular to a chord bisects the chord.

2 To prove that equal chords are equidistant from the centre.

AB and *CD* are equal chords. *E* and *F* are the mid-points of these chords, so *EB* = *FC*. Assume the result of part **1** and explain why Δ*OEB*, Δ*OFC* are congruent. What does this prove about *OE* ?

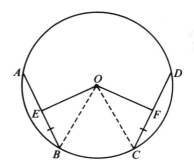

The converse of this theorem is also true. Chords which are equidistant from the centre of a circle are equal.

3 To prove that tangents from an external point are equal.

Assume that a tangent is perpendicular to the radius at the point of contact. Explain why Δ*POQ*, Δ*POR* are congruent. What does this prove about *PQ* ? What does this prove about ∠*QPO* ?

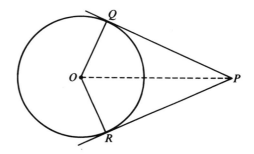

15. To prove the angle properties of circles

In these diagrams, *O* is the centre of the circle.

1 To prove that the angle at the centre is twice as big as the angle at the circumference, standing on the same arc.

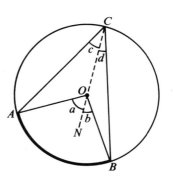

Join *CO* and produce (extend) it to a point *N*.
What kind of triangle is Δ*OAC* ?
Using Δ*OAC*, express *a* in terms of *c*.
Using Δ*OBC*, express *b* in terms of *d*.
Hence express *a* + *b* in terms of *c* + *d*.
What does this prove about ∠*AOB* ?

If *C* is nearer to *A* or *B*, how can
this proof be adapted for the
second diagram ?

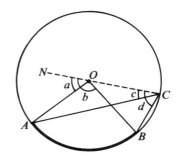

2   To prove that angles at the
circumference standing on
the same arc are equal.

Assume the result of part **1**.
Express *c* in terms of *a*.
Express *d* in terms of *a*.
What does this prove about
c and *d* ?

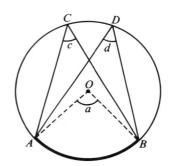

3   To prove that the angle in a
semicircle is a right angle.

Assume the result of part **1**.
Express *c* in terms of *a*.
What does this prove about *c* ?

Maybe you can find an
alternative proof by joining
OC and using Δ*OAC* and Δ*OBC*.

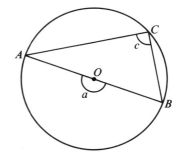

4   To prove that opposite angles
of a cyclic quadrilateral add
up to 180°, and an exterior
angle is equal to the opposite
interior angle.

Assume the result of part **1**.
Express *a* in terms of *y*, and
c in terms of *x*.
What does this prove about *a* + *c* ?
Use this result to prove that *a* = *d*.

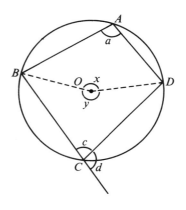

5 To prove that the angle between a tangent and a chord is equal to any angle made by that chord in the alternate segment of the circle.

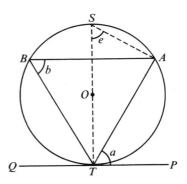

First, use the diameter *TOS* through the point of contact *T*, to prove that *a* = *e*.
Hence prove that *a* = *b*.
Assume the results of parts **2** and **3**.

Maybe you can find an alternative proof, using the angles of Δ*OTA*.

To prove that *c* = *d*,
write down an equation connecting *a* and *c*,
write down an equation connecting *b* and *d*.
Hence prove that *c* = *d*.

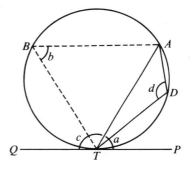

16. Converse theorems

1 If *A*, *B*, *C*, *D* are the 4 points shown, such that *c* = *d*, prove that *A*, *B*, *C* and *D* lie on a circle.

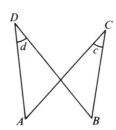

There is only one circle which passes through *A*, *B* and *C*.
Suppose *D* lies outside this circle.
Let the circle cut *AD* at *E*.
By using the angles of Δ*BDE*, show that this is not possible, so *D* cannot be outside the circle.
Show in a similar way that *D* cannot be inside the circle.
What does this prove ?

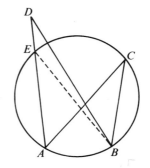

2   If *A*, *B*, *C*, *D* are the 4 points
shown, such that *b* + *d* = 180°,
prove that *A*, *B*, *C* and *D* lie
on a circle.

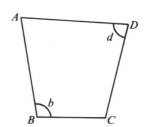

Prove this in a similar way.
Begin by drawing the circle
through *A*, *B* and *C* and
suppose *D* is outside the
circle, which cuts *AD* at *E*.

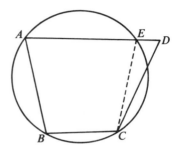

PUZZLES

34.   Two girls set off at the same time from their villages at Westby and Eastby, each going to
the other village. By the time they met, on the way, Sasha had walked 2 km further than
Trudy. After they had spent some time together, they continued their journeys, walking at
the same speeds as before. Sasha took another 1 hour 36 minutes to reach Eastby, Trudy
took $2\frac{1}{2}$ hours to reach Westby.
How far was it from Westby to Eastby ?

35.   Suppose you have a large wooden cube with all six faces painted red. This large cube is
then cut up by 6 straight cuts into 27 smaller cubes.
How many of these small cubes have 3 red faces, 2 red faces, 1 red face, no red faces ?
These 27 small cubes are now placed in a bag and shaken up. One is taken out at
random and rolled.
What is the probability that, when it comes to rest, its upper face will be red ?

36.   Mr Adam, Mr Berry, Mr Chadwick and Mr Davis owned, though not necessarily
respectively, the butcher's shop, the chemist's, the jeweller's and the tailor's. They each
drove a car and these were coloured red, cream, black and green, again, not necessarily
respectively.

Mr Adam often beat the butcher at snooker.
Mr Berry and the jeweller often played golf with the men whose cars were black and red.
Mr Chadwick and the tailor both envied the man with the red car, but this was not the
chemist, whose car was green.

Who was the owner of each shop, and what colour of cars did they drive ?

13 Thinking about the sine and

Right-angled triangles

Trigonometry can be used in right-angled triangles . . .

. . . to find heights.

Explain how you could use trigonometry to find the height of the spire.

. . . to find distances.

Explain how you could use trigonometry to find the width of the river.

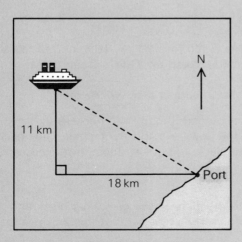

. . . to find angles.

Explain how you could use trigonometry to find the bearing on which the ship must sail, to return to port.

cosine rules

Other triangles

Trigonometry can also be used in other triangles, using the sine rule or the cosine rule . . .

. . . to find heights.

Explain how you could use trigonometry to find the height of the lighthouse above sea level.

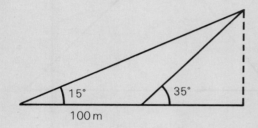

15°   35°
100 m

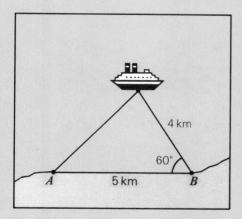

4 km

60°

A   5 km   *B*

. . . to find distances.

How can you find the distance of the ship from *A* ?

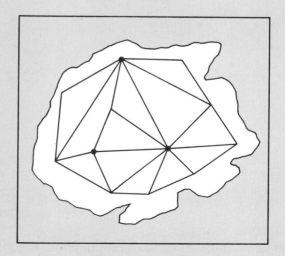

A surveyor maps out an area by triangulation. The angles of the triangles are measured very accurately, base lengths are also measured, and other distances are calculated, using trigonometry.

13 Sine and cosine rules

The sine and cosine rules can be used to calculate lengths or angles in any triangle. They are particularly useful when the triangle is not right-angled or isosceles.

Labelling a triangle

The small letter a refers to the side opposite angle A, the small letter b refers to the side opposite angle B, the small letter c refers to the side opposite angle C.

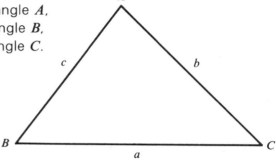

(Write C and c clearly so that you can tell which is which. Capital letters refer to angles, small letters refer to sides, so C refers to angle C, c refers to the side opposite angle C.)

Sine rule

$$\frac{a}{\sin A} = \frac{b}{\sin B} = \frac{c}{\sin C}$$

This can be rearranged as

$$\frac{\sin A}{a} = \frac{\sin B}{b} = \frac{\sin C}{c}$$

Cosine rule

$$a^2 = b^2 + c^2 - 2bc \cos A$$
or $b^2 = a^2 + c^2 - 2ac \cos B$
or $c^2 = a^2 + b^2 - 2ab \cos C$

These can be rearranged as

$$\cos A = \frac{b^2 + c^2 - a^2}{2bc}$$

$$\cos B = \frac{a^2 + c^2 - b^2}{2ac}$$

$$\cos C = \frac{a^2 + b^2 - c^2}{2ab}$$

These rules can be used in any triangle, but you would not use them in a right-angled triangle, in which the usual ratios, $\sin \theta = \dfrac{\text{opp}}{\text{hyp}}$, $\cos \theta = \dfrac{\text{adj}}{\text{hyp}}$, $\tan \theta = \dfrac{\text{opp}}{\text{adj}}$, are simpler and easier to use.

The usual method of calculating sides or angles in an isosceles triangle is to split it into two congruent right-angled triangles, rather than using the rules given above.

Using the sine rule to find the length of a side

You must know the length of one other side, and the sizes of two of the angles.

Examples

1   To find side b.

Use the part of the sine rule
involving a and b.

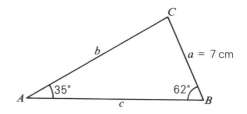

$$\frac{b}{\sin B} = \frac{a}{\sin A}$$

$$\frac{b}{\sin 62°} = \frac{7}{\sin 35°} \quad (b \text{ in cm})$$

$$b = \frac{7 \times \sin 62°}{\sin 35°} \text{ cm}$$

$$= 10.77\ldots \text{ cm}$$

$$= 10.8 \text{ cm, to 3 sig. fig.}$$

On your calculator, make sure that it is set to work in degrees, then press
7 $\boxed{\times}$ 62 $\boxed{\sin}$ $\boxed{\div}$ 35 $\boxed{\sin}$ $\boxed{=}$ getting 10.77. . .

If you want to find side c, use $\dfrac{c}{\sin C} = \dfrac{a}{\sin A}$
You need to know the size of $\angle C$.
$\angle C = 180° - (35° + 62°) = 83°$
Check that $c = 12.1$ cm.

You could use $\dfrac{c}{\sin C} = \dfrac{b}{\sin B}$ instead, since you have previously found b, but it is
safer to use a in case you have made a mistake in calculating b.

Check that your answers seem reasonable. In this triangle, $\angle C$ is the largest angle
so c will be the largest side. $\angle A$ is the smallest angle so a will be the smallest side.

Obtuse angles

Sometimes one of the angles in a triangle will be greater than 90°. However, the
calculator will give you its correct value. e.g. sin 106° = 0.9613 and
cos 106° = −0.2756.

2   To find side *a*.

$$\frac{a}{\sin A} = \frac{c}{\sin C}$$

$$\frac{a}{\sin 106°} = \frac{11}{\sin 42°} \qquad (a \text{ in cm})$$

$$a = \frac{11 \times \sin 106°}{\sin 42°} \text{ cm}$$

$$= 15.80. . . \text{ cm}$$

$$= 15.8 \text{ cm, to 3 sig. fig.}$$

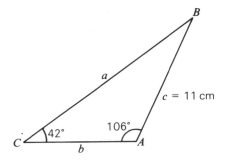

Exercise 13.1

Use the sine rule to find the stated sides in these triangles. Give the answers correct to 3 significant figures.

1.

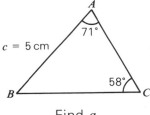

Find *a*

2.

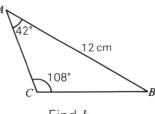

Find *b*

3.

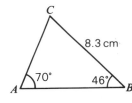

Find *c*

4.

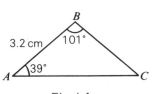

Find *b*

5.

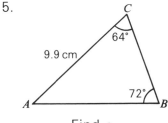

Find *c*

6.

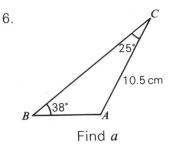

Find *a*

7.

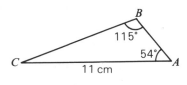

Find *BC*

8.

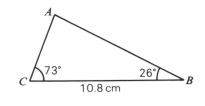

Find *AB*

9.

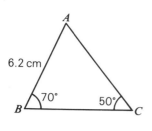

Find AC

10.

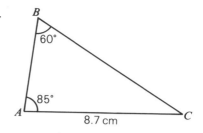

Find AB and BC

Using the sine rule to find an angle

You must know the lengths of two sides and an angle opposite to one of those sides.

3 To find $\angle C$.

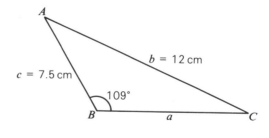

$$\frac{\sin C}{c} = \frac{\sin B}{b}$$

$$\frac{\sin C}{7.5} = \frac{\sin 109°}{12}$$

$$\sin C = \frac{7.5 \times \sin 109°}{12}$$

$$= 0.5909\ldots$$

$$\angle C = 36.2°, \text{ to 1 dec. pl.}$$

On your calculator, make sure that it is set to work in degrees then press
7.5 $\boxed{\times}$ 109 $\boxed{\sin}$ $\boxed{\div}$ 12 $\boxed{=}$ $\boxed{\text{inverse sin}}$ getting 36.22. . .

Now that you know the sizes of angles B and C, you can find $\angle A$ by subtraction.
$\angle A = 180° - (109° + 36.2°) = 34.8°$

If the length of side a is needed, you can now use the sine rule again, to find it.

A calculator will give an inverse sine as an acute angle. As long as you are not
finding the largest angle in the triangle, you know that the angle must be an acute
angle.
There could be complications if you use the sine rule to find the largest angle in a
triangle, as you would not know whether it was an acute angle or an obtuse angle.
Since there are two possible answers, you should not be asked to solve such problems
at this stage.

Exercise 13.2

Use the sine rule to find the stated angles in these triangles. (They are all acute angles.) Give the answers in degrees, correct to 1 decimal place.

1.
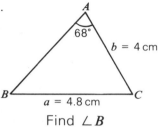
Find ∠B

2.
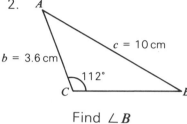
Find ∠B

3.
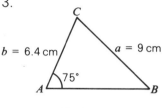
Find ∠B

4.
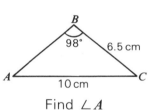
Find ∠A

5.
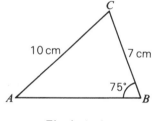
Find ∠A

6.
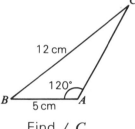
Find ∠C

7.
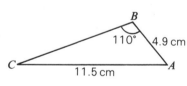
Find ∠C

8.
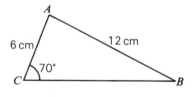
Find ∠B

9.
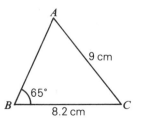
Find ∠A and hence
find ∠C

10.
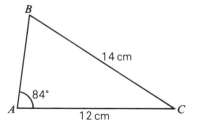
Find ∠B and hence
find ∠C

Using the cosine rule to find the length of a side

You must know the lengths of the other two sides and the size of the angle included between them.

4   To find side a.

Use $a^2 = b^2 + c^2 - 2bc \cos A$

$\qquad = 9^2 + 6^2 - 2 \times 9 \times 6 \times \cos 65°$ (a in cm)

$\qquad = 71.357...$

$\quad a = \sqrt{71.357...}$ cm

$\qquad = 8.447...$ cm

$\qquad = 8.4$ cm, to the nearest mm

$\qquad$ (or 8.45 cm, to 3 sig. fig.)

On your calculator you can do the complete calculation.
Make sure that it is set to work in degrees then press

$9\; \boxed{x^2}\; \boxed{+}\; 6\; \boxed{x^2}\; \boxed{-}\; 2\; \boxed{\times}\; 9\; \boxed{\times}\; 6\; \boxed{\times}\; 65\; \boxed{\cos}\; \boxed{=}\; \boxed{\sqrt{}}$

You may prefer to do some of the working without using your calculator.

$a^2 = 9^2 + 6^2 - 2 \times 9 \times 6 \times \cos 65°$ (a in cm)

$\quad = 81 + 36 - 108 \times \cos 65°$

$\quad = 117 - 108 \times \cos 65°$

Now $108 \times \cos 65°$ must be worked out before subtracting it from 117 so you will probably use your calculator at this stage, getting the same answer as above.

Having found the length of side a you can use the sine rule, or the cosine rule, if you need to find $\angle B$ or $\angle C$. The third angle can be found by subtraction.

5   To find side c

$c^2 = a^2 + b^2 - 2ab \cos C$

$\quad = 3^2 + 5^2 - 2 \times 3 \times 5 \times \cos 106°$ (c in cm)

$c = 6.501...$ cm

$\quad = 6.5$ cm, to the nearest mm

$\quad$ (or 6.50 cm, to 3 sig. fig.)

On your calculator, press $3\; \boxed{x^2}\; \boxed{+}\; 5\; \boxed{x^2}\; \boxed{-}\; 2\; \boxed{\times}\; 3\; \boxed{\times}\; 5\; \boxed{\times}\; 106\; \boxed{\cos}\; \boxed{=}\; \boxed{\sqrt{}}$

There is a minus sign in the formula, and $\cos 106°$ is also a negative number. This means that the last term, $-2 \times 3 \times 5 \times \cos 106°$, is **added** to $3^2 + 5^2$. The calculator will automatically do this by changing $- \times -$ into $+$.

Exercise 13.3

Use the cosine rule to find the 3rd sides in these triangles. Give the answers to the nearest mm.

1.

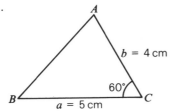

2.

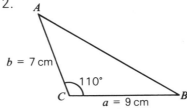

3.

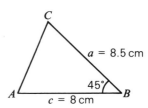

4.

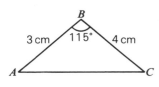

5.

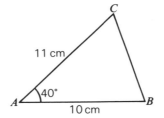

6.

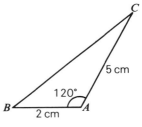

7.

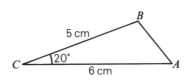

8.

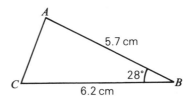

9.

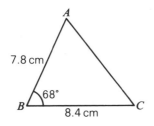

10.

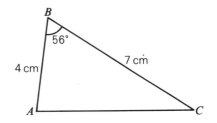

Using the cosine rule to find an angle

You must know the lengths of all three sides.

6   To find $\angle A$.

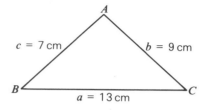

Use $\cos A = \dfrac{b^2 + c^2 - a^2}{2bc}$

$\qquad = \dfrac{9^2 + 7^2 - 13^2}{2 \times 9 \times 7}$

$\qquad = -0.3095\ldots$

$\angle A = 108.0°$, to 1 dec. pl.

You can do the complete calculation on your calculator. Press

$9\ \boxed{x^2}\ \boxed{+}\ 7\ \boxed{x^2}\ \boxed{-}\ 13\ \boxed{x^2}\ \boxed{=}\ \boxed{\div}\ 2\ \boxed{\div}\ 9\ \boxed{\div}\ 7\ \boxed{=}\ \boxed{\text{inverse cos}}$

If you need to find all three angles, find the largest one first, i.e. the angle opposite the largest side, using this method. Then you know that the other two angles must be acute angles and you can use the sine rule to find one of them, although you can use the cosine rule instead if you prefer it. You can then find the third angle by subtraction.

Exercise 13.4

Use the cosine rule to find the stated angles in these triangles. Give the answers in degrees, correct to 1 decimal place.

1.

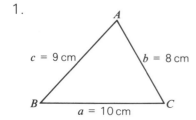

Find $\angle A$

2.

$b = 3\,cm$

Find $\angle C$

3.

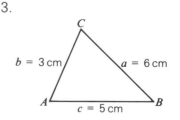

Find $\angle C$

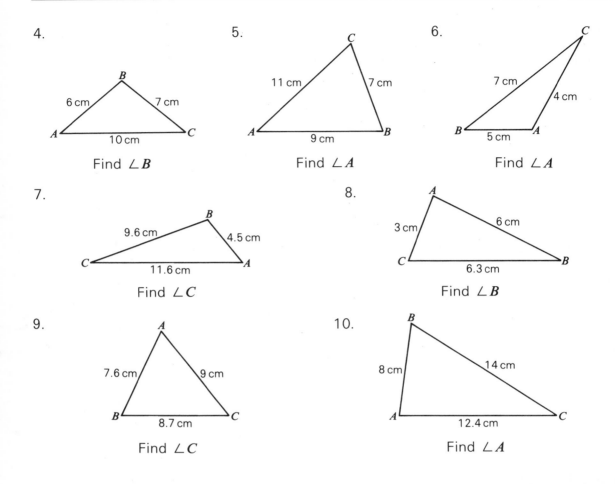

4.

6 cm, 7 cm, 10 cm, A, B, C

Find ∠B

5.

11 cm, 7 cm, 9 cm, A, B, C

Find ∠A

6.

7 cm, 4 cm, 5 cm, B, A, C

Find ∠A

7.

9.6 cm, 4.5 cm, 11.6 cm, C, B, A

Find ∠C

8.

3 cm, 6 cm, 6.3 cm, C, A, B

Find ∠B

9.

7.6 cm, 9 cm, 8.7 cm, A, B, C

Find ∠C

10.

8 cm, 14 cm, 12.4 cm, B, A, C

Find ∠A

Exercise 13.5

Use the sine or cosine rule, as appropriate to find the stated sides or angles in these triangles. Give lengths correct to 3 significant figures and angles in degrees correct to 1 decimal place.

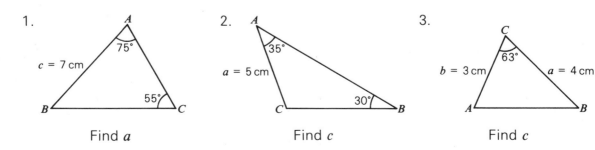

1.

$c = 7$ cm, 75°, 55°, A, B, C

Find a

2.

$a = 5$ cm, 35°, 30°, A, B, C

Find c

3.

$b = 3$ cm, 63°, $a = 4$ cm, C, A, B

Find c

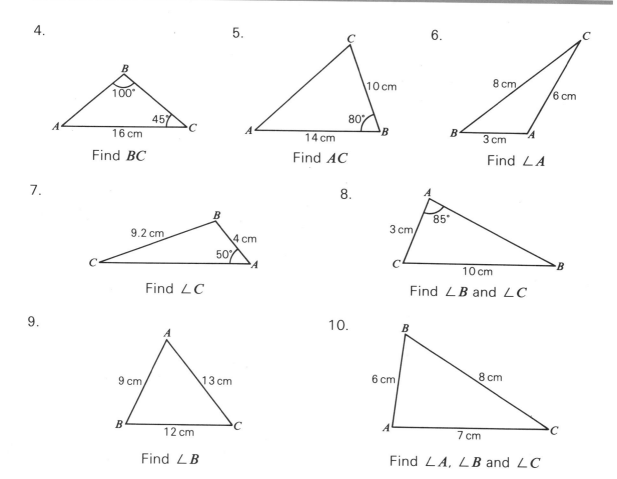

4.

B

100°

A   45°
       16 cm   *C*

Find *BC*

5.

C

10 cm

80°

A   14 cm   *B*

Find *AC*

6.

C

8 cm   6 cm

B   3 cm   *A*

Find ∠*A*

7.

B

9.2 cm   4 cm

50°

C   *A*

Find ∠*C*

8.

A

85°

3 cm

C   10 cm   *B*

Find ∠*B* and ∠*C*

9.

A

9 cm   13 cm

B   12 cm   *C*

Find ∠*B*

10.

B

6 cm   8 cm

A   7 cm   *C*

Find ∠*A*, ∠*B* and ∠*C*

Exercise 13.6   Applications and Activities

1.   The diagram shows a circular clock face,
     centre *O*, and the hands *OA* and *OB* are
     12 cm and 10 cm long respectively.
     Find the shortest distance between *A*
     and *B* at 4 pm.

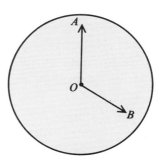

2. An airfield runway runs west to east.
    A and *B* are 2 points on the runway
    and *B* is 800 m east of *A*.
    From *A* the bearing of the control
    tower is 048° and from *B* it is 300°.

    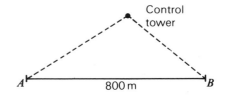

    1 Find the distance of the control
           tower from point *A*.
    2 A plane travels due east along the runway, starting at *A*. How far is it from
           the control tower when it is due south of it ?

3. *A* and *B* are 2 points 100 m apart
    on one bank of a river and *P* is
    a point on the opposite bank,
    80 m from *A*. ∠*APB* = 78°.
    Find

    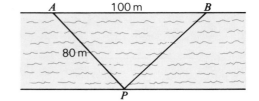

    1 ∠*PAB*,
    2 the width of the river.

4. From a coastguard station a lighthouse is 10 km away on a bearing of 055° and
    a buoy is 7 km away on a bearing of 130°.
    Draw a sketch diagram to show this information.
    Calculate the distance of the lighthouse from the buoy.

5. *A*, *B*, *C* are 3 landmarks on a level plain. *A* is 8 km due north of *B*. *C* is to the
    west of *AB*, the distance *AC* is 6.5 km and *BC* is 5 km.
    Draw a sketch diagram to show this information.
    Calculate ∠*BAC* and state the bearing of *C* from *A*.

6. A man walking along a straight
    road notices a hut *H* in a field
    on one side of the road. At
    one point *A* he observes that the
    line *AH* makes an angle of 16°
    with his direction of motion.
    After walking another 200 m to
    a point *B* he observes that *BH*
    makes an angle of 39° with the
    direction of motion.
    Find

    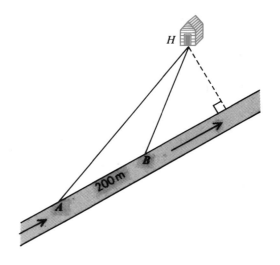

    1 the distance *BH*,
    2 the shortest distance from
           the hut to the road.

7.   In the diagram, *ABC* is a triangle on
     horizontal ground and *CD* is a
     vertical tower of height 32 m.
     The angle of elevation of *D* from
     A is 32°, and from *B* it is 25°.
     A is due west of *C* and *B* is
     south-west of *C*.
     Find

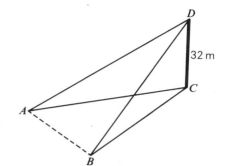

     1   the distance *AC*,
     2   the distance *BC*,
     3   the distance *AB*.

8.   A plane *P* is observed simultaneously from 2
     observation posts *S* and *T*, both at sea-level,
     T being 60 km south-west of *S*.
     From *S* the bearing of the plane is
     280° and it is at an angle of
     elevation of 10°, while from *T* the
     bearing of the plane is 017°.
     X is the point at sea-level vertically below *P*.
     Using Δ*SXT* find the lengths of *XT* and *XS*.
     Find the height of the plane above sea-level.
     Find the angle of elevation of the plane from *T*.

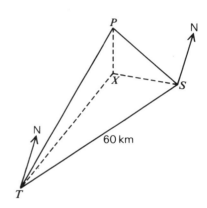

9.   **To prove the formula for the sine rule**

     Express *h* in terms of sin *A*.
     Express *h* in terms of sin *B*.
     Hence find an equation not
     involving *h*.
     Rearrange this to give
     $$\frac{a}{\sin A} = \frac{b}{\sin B}.$$

     Using angles *A* and *C* in a
     similar way will give
     $$\frac{a}{\sin A} = \frac{c}{\sin C}.$$

     So $\dfrac{a}{\sin A} = \dfrac{b}{\sin B} = \dfrac{c}{\sin C}.$

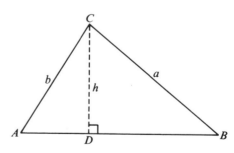

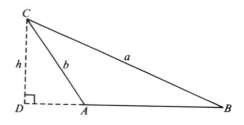

     In the second diagram, use
     $\sin A = \sin(180° - A) = \sin \angle DAC.$

A different method

If the circumcircle of $\triangle ABC$ is
drawn, let the diameter through
C meet the circle at D.

Prove that $\dfrac{a}{\sin A} = 2R$, where R
is the radius of the circumcircle.
In a similar way it can be proved

that $\dfrac{b}{\sin B} = 2R$ and $\dfrac{c}{\sin C} = 2R$.

You can also consider the case when
$\angle A$ is an obtuse angle.

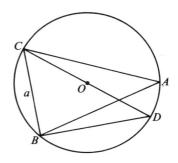

10. **To prove the formula for the cosine rule**

To prove that $a^2 = b^2 + c^2 - 2bc \cos A$.

Use Pythagoras' theorem in $\triangle ADC$.
Use Pythagoras' theorem in $\triangle BDC$.
Use these 2 equations to eliminate
h (and p^2 will also be eliminated).
Write p in terms of $\cos A$ and
substitute this expression instead
of p in the equation.

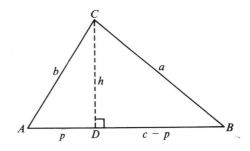

You can also consider the case when
$\angle A$ is an obtuse angle.
Use $\cos A = -\cos(180° - A)$.

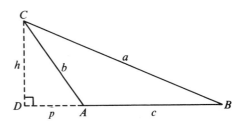

Show that you can rearrange the cosine rule to give $\cos A = \dfrac{b^2 + c^2 - a^2}{2bc}$.

11.   **'The ambiguous case'**

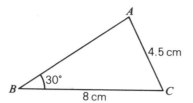
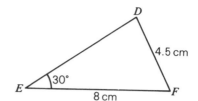

You know that these triangles need not be congruent, since you only know the
lengths of two sides and the non-included angles.
Construct accurately a triangle with the measurements of $\triangle ABC$, and show that
there are two possible positions for A.
Measure the size of $\angle BAC$ for each possible angle, and also use the sine rule to
calculate $\angle BAC$, showing how it is possible for there to be two answers.

PUZZLES

37.   What is the smallest number which, when divided by 3 leaves a remainder of 1, when
divided by 5 leaves a remainder of 3 and when divided by 7 leaves a remainder of 5 ?

38.   Three men and a monkey were shipwrecked on a deserted island, where they found some
palm trees, and with some difficulty they gathered a pile of coconuts. They decided to
divide this collection, which was less than 100 coconuts, into 3 equal shares, but by that
time it was evening so they went to sleep and left the pile of coconuts to be shared out
on the next day.
During the night, one man woke up and he decided that he would take his share of $\frac{1}{3}$.
There was one coconut left over, so he gave it to the monkey. He then went back
to sleep.
Then a second man awoke and he decided that we would take his share, so he took $\frac{1}{3}$ of
the pile of coconuts remaining. Again, there was one coconut left over, and he gave that
one to the monkey.
After the second man had gone back to sleep also, the third man awoke and he also took
a share of $\frac{1}{3}$ of the pile that remained. Again, there was one coconut left over, which he
gave to the monkey.
When the men got up next morning, they each noticed that the pile of coconuts was
much smaller than it had been originally, but none of them dared admit that they had
already taken some. So they divided the remaining coconuts into 3 shares, and one was
left over, which they gave to the monkey.
Now, how many coconuts had they collected originally ?

14 Thinking about transformations

Transformations include translation, reflection, rotation and enlargement.

Reflection

Describe this tile pattern in terms of reflections and rotations.

Windmills for generating electricity at Palm Springs, California.

277

ranslation ?

argement ?

Describe the transformations used in this old
vehicle. How does rotation lead to translation ?

SONAR

SONAR stands for <u>so</u>und <u>na</u>vigation <u>r</u>anging.
A ship uses sonar to find the depth of the
sea-bed, and it can also be used to search for
underwater objects such as submarines,
wrecks or rocks.
Fishing vessels use sonar to locate shoals of
fish.
A sound pulse is sent from the ship and it is
reflected from the sea-bed or underwater
object. The time taken for the pulse to travel
out and back is used to work out the distance
it has travelled.

14 Transformations

Here are details of three kinds of transformation: translation, reflection and rotation.

Translation

The dotted lines show the translation of the triangles when every point has been moved an equal distance in the same direction.

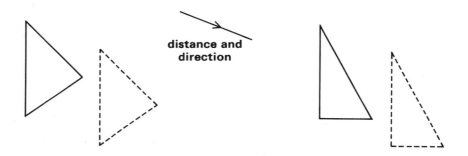

**distance and
direction**

Example

The translation 4 units in the
x-direction, 1 unit in the
y-direction.

A (2, 1) is transformed into
A' (6, 2).

B (3, 2) is transformed into
B' (7, 3).

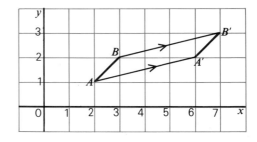

The translation can be represented by the vector $\begin{pmatrix} 4 \\ 1 \end{pmatrix}$.

A' is called the **image** of A, B' is the image of B and the line $A'B'$ is the image of the line AB.

Reflection

The dotted lines show the reflections of the triangles in the line **AB**, which is an axis of symmetry of the completed figure.

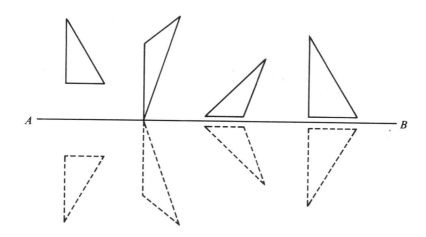

Each dotted triangle is called the **image** of the original triangle.

Reflection in the x-axis

A (2, 1) is transformed into A' (2, −1).
B (3, 2) is transformed into B' (3, −2).

The line **AB** is reflected into the line **A'B'**.
AB and **A'B'** are equal in length and the x-axis is a line of symmetry between **AB** and **A'B'**.

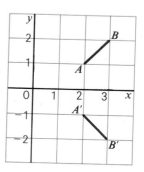

Reflection in the y-axis

A (2, 1) is transformed into A' (−2, 1).
B (3, 2) is transformed into B' (−3, 2).

The line **AB** is reflected into the line **A'B'**.
AB and **A'B'** are equal in length and the y-axis is a line of symmetry between **AB** and **A'B'**.

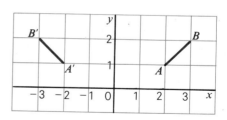

Reflection in the line $y = x$

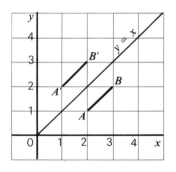

A (2, 1) is transformed into A' (1, 2).
B (3, 2) is transformed into B' (2, 3).

The line AB is reflected into the line $A'B'$.
AB and $A'B'$ are equal in length and the line
$y = x$ is an axis of symmetry between AB and
$A'B'$.

Reflection in the line $y = -x$

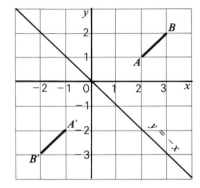

A (2, 1) is transformed into A' (−1, −2).
B (3, 2) is transformed into B' (−2, −3).

The line AB is reflected into the line $A'B'$.
AB and $A'B'$ are equal in length and the line
$y = -x$ is an axis of symmetry between AB
and $A'B'$.

Reflections in other lines
e.g. Reflection in the line $y = 3$.

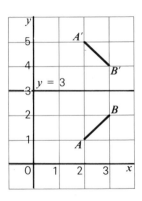

A (2, 1) is transformed into A' (2, 5).
B (3, 2) is transformed into B' (3, 4).

AB and $A'B'$ are equal in length and $y = 3$ is an axis of
symmetry between AB and $A'B'$.

Rotation

The dotted lines show the new position of the triangles when they have been rotated about the point marked •

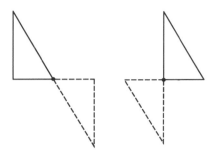 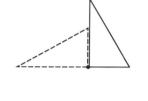 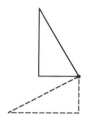

Rotations through 180°   **Rotations through 90° anticlockwise**

---

3 things are needed to define a rotation.
1 A centre of rotation.
2 An amount of turn.
3 A direction of turn.

Rotation about the origin through 90° anticlockwise ($\frac{1}{4}$ turn)

A (2, 1) is transformed into *A'* (−1, 2).
B (3, 2) is transformed into *B'* (−2, 3).

The line *AB* is rotated into the line *A'B'*.
AB and *A'B'* are equal in length.

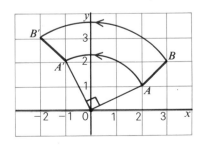

Rotation about the origin through 180° ($\frac{1}{2}$ turn)

A (2, 1) is transformed into A' (-2, -1).
B (3, 2) is transformed into B' (-3, -2).

The line AB is rotated into the line $A'B'$.
AB and $A'B'$ are equal in length.
O is a point of symmetry between AB and
$A'B'$.

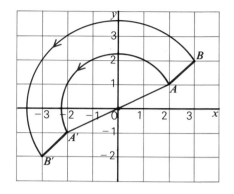

Rotation about the origin through 90° clockwise ($\frac{1}{4}$ turn)

A (2, 1) is transformed into A' (1, -2).
B (3, 2) is transformed into B' (2, -3).

The line AB is rotated into the line $A'B'$.
AB and $A'B'$ are equal in length.

A rotation of 90° clockwise is the
same as a rotation of 270° anticlockwise.

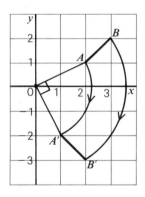

Rotations can be made about other points.
e.g. AB rotated through 90° anticlockwise about point A.

A is unaltered.
B (3, 2) is transformed into B' (1, 2).

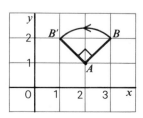

Exercise 14.1

1. On graph paper or squared paper, label the x and y axes from -6 to 6, using equal scales on both axes.
    Draw the triangle with vertices (1, 2), (1, 5), (2, 5) and label the triangle A.
    Draw also the line $y = x$.
    Draw triangles B to H and label them, following these transformations, each one on triangle A.
    1 ΔA is reflected in the x-axis to make ΔB.
    2 ΔA is rotated through 90° clockwise about the origin to make ΔC.
    3 ΔA is translated -4 units in the x-direction and 1 unit in the y-direction to make ΔD.
    4 ΔA is reflected in the line $y = x$ to make ΔE.
    5 ΔA is rotated through 180° about the origin to make ΔF.
    6 ΔA is reflected in the line $x = -2$ to make ΔG.
    7 ΔA is translated 3 units in the x-direction and -8 units in the y-direction to make ΔH.

2. State which single transformation will map (i.e. transform)
    1 A into B,
    2 A into C,
    3 A into D,
    4 A into E,
    5 A into F,
    6 A into G,
    7 A into H,
    8 B into G,
    9 B into E,
    10 D into F.

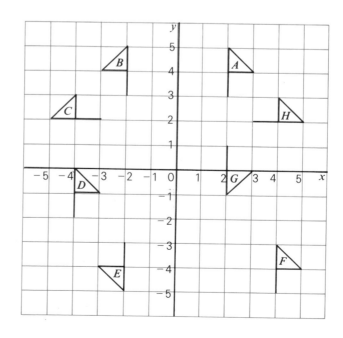

3. In the diagram ΔOAB is rotated clockwise about the origin through 90° into triangle OA_1B_1. ΔOA_1B_1 is reflected in the y-axis into ΔOA_2B_2. Draw the 3 triangles on your own diagram.

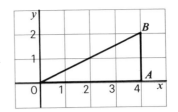

What single transformation would map ΔOA_2B_2 into ΔOAB ?

4. A transformation is described as, translate 3 units parallel to the x-axis then reflect the image point in the line $y = x$.

    1 What is the final position of the point $(2, 4)$?
    2 What is the point whose final position is $(5, 3)$?

In questions 5 to 8 begin each question by drawing x and y axes from -8 to 8, using equal scales on both axes. Draw the triangle ABC with A $(1, 1)$, B $(4, 3)$ and C $(3, 6)$.

5. Translate triangle ABC to triangle $A_1B_1C_1$ by moving each point 2 units in the x direction and then -3 units in the y direction. What are the coordinates of the image points A_1, B_1, C_1 ?
    Transform triangle $A_1B_1C_1$ to triangle $A_2B_2C_2$ by translating each point -6 units in the x direction and then 2 units in the y direction.
    What are the coordinates of the image points A_2, B_2, C_2 ?
    What single transformation would map triangle ABC into triangle $A_2B_2C_2$?

6. Reflect triangle ABC about the line $y = 1$. What are the coordinates of the image points A_1, B_1, C_1 ?
    Reflect triangle $A_1B_1C_1$ about the line $y = x$. What are the coordinates of the image points A_2, B_2, C_2 ?
    What single transformation would map triangle ABC into triangle $A_2B_2C_2$?

7. Reflect triangle ABC about the x-axis. What are the coordinates of the image points A_1, B_1, C_1 ?
    Rotate triangle $A_1B_1C_1$ about the origin through 180°. What are the coordinates of the image points A_2, B_2, C_2 ?
    What single transformation would map triangle ABC into triangle $A_2B_2C_2$?

8. Rotate triangle ABC anticlockwise about the origin through 90°. What are the coordinates of the image points A_1, B_1, C_1 ?
    Reflect triangle $A_1B_1C_1$ about the x-axis. What are the coordinates of the image points A_2, B_2, C_2 ?
    What single transformation would map triangle ABC into triangle $A_2B_2C_2$?

9. **Inverses of transformations**

Draw x and y axes from -3 to 3 using equal scales on both axes.
Draw the triangle A with vertices (1, 0), (2, 3) and (0, 2).

1   Reflect ΔA in the y-axis to make ΔB.
        The inverse transformation transforms ΔB back into ΔA.
        Describe this inverse transformation.

2   Rotate ΔA through 90° clockwise about the origin to make ΔC.
        The inverse transformation transforms ΔC back into ΔA.
        Describe this inverse transformation.

3   Translate ΔA by -2 units in the x-direction and -3 units in the y-direction to
        make ΔD.
        The inverse transformation transforms ΔD back into ΔA.
        Describe this inverse transformation.

Enlargement

A figure and its enlargement are similar figures.
The scale factor of the enlargement is the number of times the original has been
enlarged.

The centre of enlargement

X is the centre of enlargement
and k is the scale factor of
the enlargement.
If the image of A is A' and
the image of B is B', then

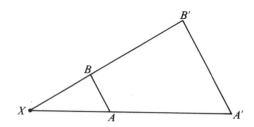

$XA' = k \times XA$, with XAA' being a straight line.
$XB' = k \times XB$, with XBB' being a straight line.

2 things are needed to define an enlargement.
1   A centre of enlargement.
2   A scale factor.

Examples

The dotted lines show the new positions of the triangles when they have been enlarged with the point X as the centre of enlargement.

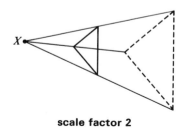

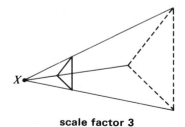

scale factor 2   **scale factor 3**

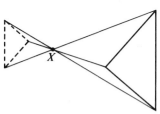

scale factor −1   **scale factor $-\frac{1}{2}$**

Enlargement with scale factor 2, and centre of enlargement O (0, 0).

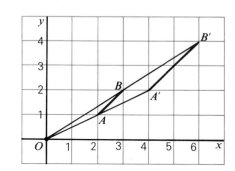

A (2, 1) is transformed into A' (2 × 2, 2 × 1), i.e. (4, 2).
B (3, 2) is transformed into B' (6, 4).
The line AB is transformed into the line $A'B'$.
AB and $A'B'$ are parallel and
length $A'B' = 2 \times$ length AB.

Triangles $OA'B'$ and OAB are similar with lengths in the ratio 2 : 1, and areas in the ratio 4 : 1.

If the scale factor is 3 then
A (2, 1) is transformed into A' (3 × 2, 3 × 1), i.e. (6, 3).
B (3, 2) is transformed into B' (9, 6).
The line AB is transformed into the line $A'B'$.
AB and $A'B'$ are parallel and length $A'B' = 3 \times$ length AB.

Triangles $OA'B'$ and OAB are similar with lengths in the ratio 3 : 1, and areas in the ratio 9 : 1.

Enlargements can have centres of enlargement other than the origin.
e.g. Enlargement with scale factor 2 and centre of
enlargement C (3, 0).

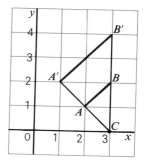

A (2, 1) is transformed into A' (1, 2).
B (3, 2) is transformed into B' (3, 4).

AB and $A'B'$ are parallel and length $A'B' = 2 \times$ length AB.

Triangles $CA'B'$ and CAB are similar with lengths in the
ratio 2 : 1.

Exercise 14.2

1.   Draw the x-axis from 0 to 6 and the y-axis from 0 to 9.
      Plot the points A (1, 1), B (2, 1), C (1, 3) and draw $\triangle ABC$.
      Using the origin as centre of enlargement, enlarge $\triangle ABC$ with scale factor 3,
      transforming it into triangle $A'B'C'$.
      State the coordinates of A', B', C'.
      What is the ratio of length $B'C'$: length BC ?

2.   Draw the x-axis from 0 to 8 and the y-axis from -3 to 6. Taking C (2, 3) as
      centre of enlargement, A (6, -1) is mapped into A_1 (8, -3). What is the scale
      factor of the enlargement ?
      Using this same transformation B (4, 5) is mapped into B_1. What are the
      coordinates of B_1 ?
      What is the ratio length $A_1 B_1$: length AB ?

3.   Draw the x-axis from 0 to 12 and the y-axis from 0 to 20.
      Plot the points A (1, 1), B (3, 3), C (2, 5) and draw $\triangle ABC$.
      Using the origin as centre of enlargement, enlarge $\triangle ABC$ with scale factor 4,
      mapping it into $\triangle A'B'C'$.
      What is the ratio of length $A'B'$: length AB ?
      What is the ratio of area $\triangle A'B'C'$: area $\triangle ABC$?
      What is the scale factor of the enlargement (reduction) which will transform
      $\triangle A'B'C'$ into $\triangle ABC$?

4.   Draw x and y axes from 0 to 12.
      Plot the points A (2, 2), B (4, 6), C (6, 0), D (12, 12).
      Join AB and CD.
      What is the scale factor of the enlargement which maps AB into CD ?
      On your diagram find E, the centre of enlargement, and state the coordinates of E.

5. If a triangle ABC is enlarged, using the origin as centre of enlargement, with scale factor 2, mapping it into $\Delta A_1 B_1 C_1$, and then $\Delta A_1 B_1 C_1$ is enlarged, using the origin as centre of enlargement, with scale factor $2\frac{1}{2}$, into $\Delta A_2 B_2 C_2$, what is the scale factor which would transform ΔABC into $\Delta A_2 B_2 C_2$?

Exercise 14.3   Applications and Activities

The questions in this exercise involve matrices, which were introduced in Exercise B4, question 5, page 220, and so that question should be done first; followed by these questions in order.

Computers or calculators can be programmed to do calculations with matrices, which is why matrices are useful for defining transformations.

1. **Using matrices to define transformations**

    Examples here use the line AB, where A is (2, 1) and B is (3, 2).

    Translations

    e.g. The translation (4, 1) can be represented by the vector $\begin{pmatrix} 4 \\ 1 \end{pmatrix}$.

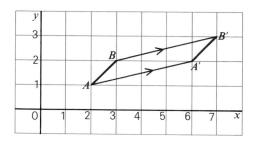

    If each point (a, b) to be translated is represented by the vector $\begin{pmatrix} a \\ b \end{pmatrix}$ then the

    image point (a', b') is such that $\begin{pmatrix} a' \\ b' \end{pmatrix} = \begin{pmatrix} a \\ b \end{pmatrix} + \begin{pmatrix} 4 \\ 1 \end{pmatrix}$.

    If A is (2, 1), then for A', $\begin{pmatrix} 2 \\ 1 \end{pmatrix} + \begin{pmatrix} 4 \\ 1 \end{pmatrix} = \begin{pmatrix} 6 \\ 2 \end{pmatrix}$; A' is (6, 2).

    If B is (3, 2), $\begin{pmatrix} 3 \\ 2 \end{pmatrix} + \begin{pmatrix} 4 \\ 1 \end{pmatrix} = \begin{pmatrix} 7 \\ 3 \end{pmatrix}$; B' is (7,3).

Reflections about lines passing through the origin.

Reflection in the x-axis

The matrix giving this transformation is $\begin{pmatrix} 1 & 0 \\ 0 & -1 \end{pmatrix}$.

So for A', $\begin{pmatrix} 1 & 0 \\ 0 & -1 \end{pmatrix}\begin{pmatrix} 2 \\ 1 \end{pmatrix} = \begin{pmatrix} 2 \\ -1 \end{pmatrix}$; A' is $(2, -1)$.

For B', $\begin{pmatrix} 1 & 0 \\ 0 & -1 \end{pmatrix}\begin{pmatrix} 3 \\ 2 \end{pmatrix} = \begin{pmatrix} 3 \\ -2 \end{pmatrix}$; so B' is $(3, -2)$.

For a general point P (x, y), P' is $(x, -y)$.

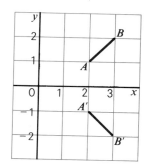

Reflection in the y-axis

The matrix giving this transformation is $\begin{pmatrix} -1 & 0 \\ 0 & 1 \end{pmatrix}$.

For a general point P (x, y), P' is $(-x, y)$.

Reflection in the line $y = x$

The matrix giving this transformation is $\begin{pmatrix} 0 & 1 \\ 1 & 0 \end{pmatrix}$.

So for A', $\begin{pmatrix} 0 & 1 \\ 1 & 0 \end{pmatrix}\begin{pmatrix} 2 \\ 1 \end{pmatrix} = \begin{pmatrix} 1 \\ 2 \end{pmatrix}$; A' is $(1, 2)$.

For B', $\begin{pmatrix} 0 & 1 \\ 1 & 0 \end{pmatrix}\begin{pmatrix} 3 \\ 2 \end{pmatrix} = \begin{pmatrix} 2 \\ 3 \end{pmatrix}$; B' is $(2, 3)$.

For a general point P (x, y), P' is (y, x).

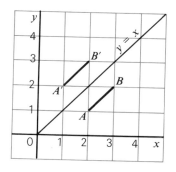

Reflection in the line $y = -x$

The matrix giving this transformation is $\begin{pmatrix} 0 & -1 \\ -1 & 0 \end{pmatrix}$.

For a general point P (x, y), P' is $(-y, -x)$.

Rotations about the origin

Rotation about the origin through 90° anticlockwise

The matrix giving this transformation is $\begin{pmatrix} 0 & -1 \\ 1 & 0 \end{pmatrix}$.

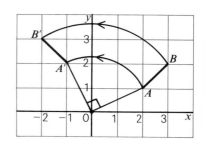

So for A', $\begin{pmatrix} 0 & -1 \\ 1 & 0 \end{pmatrix}\begin{pmatrix} 2 \\ 1 \end{pmatrix} = \begin{pmatrix} -1 \\ 2 \end{pmatrix}$; A' is $(-1, 2)$.

For B', $\begin{pmatrix} 0 & -1 \\ 1 & 0 \end{pmatrix}\begin{pmatrix} 3 \\ 2 \end{pmatrix} = \begin{pmatrix} -2 \\ 3 \end{pmatrix}$; B' is $(-2, 3)$.

For a general point $P\ (x, y)$, P' is $(-y, x)$.

Rotation about the origin through 180°

The matrix giving this transformation is $\begin{pmatrix} -1 & 0 \\ 0 & -1 \end{pmatrix}$.

For a general point $P\ (x, y)$, P' is $(-x, -y)$.

Rotation about the origin through 270° anticlockwise (90° clockwise)

The matrix giving this transformation is $\begin{pmatrix} 0 & 1 \\ -1 & 0 \end{pmatrix}$.

For a general point $P\ (x, y)$, P' is $(y, -x)$.

Enlargements with the origin as centre of enlargement.

If the scale factor is k, the matrix giving the transformation is $\begin{pmatrix} k & 0 \\ 0 & k \end{pmatrix}$.

If the scale factor is 2,

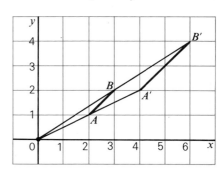

for A', $\begin{pmatrix} 2 & 0 \\ 0 & 2 \end{pmatrix}\begin{pmatrix} 2 \\ 1 \end{pmatrix} = \begin{pmatrix} 4 \\ 2 \end{pmatrix}$, A' is $(4, 2)$.

For B', $\begin{pmatrix} 2 & 0 \\ 0 & 2 \end{pmatrix}\begin{pmatrix} 3 \\ 2 \end{pmatrix} = \begin{pmatrix} 6 \\ 4 \end{pmatrix}$, B' is $(6, 4)$.

For a general point $P\ (x, y)$ and scale factor k, P' is (kx, ky).

In the diagram, give the
matrices or vectors which
transform

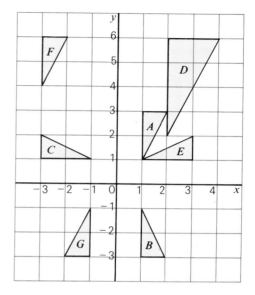

1   ΔA into ΔB,
2   ΔA into ΔC,
3   ΔA into ΔD,
4   ΔA into ΔE,
5   ΔA into ΔF,
6   ΔA into ΔG.

7   ΔPQR has vertices P (3, −5),
     Q (2, 6), R (−1, 4). Use the
     matrix $\begin{pmatrix} 1 & 0 \\ 0 & -1 \end{pmatrix}$ to find the
     coordinates of the points P′, Q′,
     R′ if ΔPQR is reflected in the
     x-axis. (Do not draw a diagram.)
     Repeat this using the relevant matrix if ΔPQR is
8   reflected in the line $y = -x$.
9   rotated about the origin through 90° clockwise,
10   rotated about the origin through 180°,
11   enlarged with scale factor 5, with the origin as centre of enlargement,
12   enlarged with scale factor −3, with the origin as centre of enlargement.

2.   **Combined transformations, using matrices**

If points are reflected in the x-axis, this transformation is represented by the
matrix $\begin{pmatrix} 1 & 0 \\ 0 & -1 \end{pmatrix}$.

If the image points are then rotated about the origin through 90° anticlockwise,
this transformation is represented by the matrix $\begin{pmatrix} 0 & -1 \\ 1 & 0 \end{pmatrix}$.

The combined transformation is represented by $\begin{pmatrix} 0 & -1 \\ 1 & 0 \end{pmatrix}\begin{pmatrix} 1 & 0 \\ 0 & -1 \end{pmatrix}$.

Notice that the matrix representing the 2nd transformation is written first, before
the matrix representing the 1st transformation.

Multiplying these matrices gives $\begin{pmatrix} 0 & 1 \\ 1 & 0 \end{pmatrix}$. You can check this for yourself.

$\begin{pmatrix} 0 & 1 \\ 1 & 0 \end{pmatrix}$ represents the transformation, reflection in the line $y = x$.

You can check that this is the combined transformation, beginning with the line AB where A is $(2, -3)$ and B is $(4, -2)$. Draw x and y axes from -4 to 4.

Use matrices to find the combined transformations in these situations.

1 Points rotated about the origin through $180°$ and then reflected in the line $y = -x$.

2 Points reflected in the y-axis and then rotated about the origin through $90°$ anticlockwise.

3 Points reflected in the line $y = x$, then reflected in the x-axis.

4 Points enlarged with scale factor 3, then enlarged with scale factor $-\frac{1}{3}$.

3. **One way stretch**

One way stretch parallel to the x-axis, with scale factor 2, from the y-axis

A $(2, 1)$ is transformed into A' $(2 \times 2, 1)$ i.e. $(4, 1)$.
B $(3, 2)$ is transformed into B' $(2 \times 3, 2)$ i.e. $(6, 2)$.

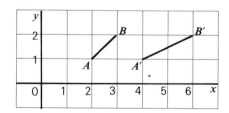

The matrix giving this transformation is $\begin{pmatrix} 2 & 0 \\ 0 & 1 \end{pmatrix}$.

If the scale factor is k, the matrix is $\begin{pmatrix} k & 0 \\ 0 & 1 \end{pmatrix}$.

One way stretch parallel to the y-axis, with scale factor k, from the x-axis

The matrix giving this transformation is $\begin{pmatrix} 1 & 0 \\ 0 & k \end{pmatrix}$.

What is the combined result of a one way stretch from the y-axis parallel to the x-axis followed by a one-way stretch from the x-axis parallel to the y-axis, both with scale factor 3 ?

4.   **Transformations on the unit square**

It is possible to find what transformation

results from any matrix $\begin{pmatrix} a & b \\ c & d \end{pmatrix}$ by

investigating the effect on the unit
square $OABC$ where O is the origin,
A is $(1, 0)$, B is $(1, 1)$ and C is $(0, 1)$.

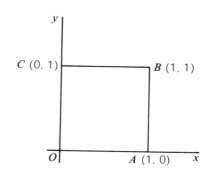

Example

Investigate the transformation

given by the matrix $\begin{pmatrix} 6 & 2 \\ 1 & 4 \end{pmatrix}$.

A is mapped into A'.

$\begin{pmatrix} 6 & 2 \\ 1 & 4 \end{pmatrix}\begin{pmatrix} 1 \\ 0 \end{pmatrix} = \begin{pmatrix} 6 \\ 1 \end{pmatrix}$ so A' is $(6, 1)$.

B is mapped into B' $(8, 5)$.
C is mapped into C' $(2, 4)$.
O is mapped into itself.
The unit square $OABC$ is
mapped into $OA'B'C'$ which is
a parallelogram.

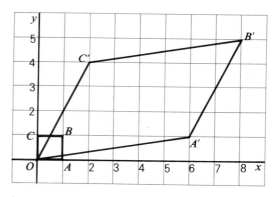

Investigate the transformations resulting from these matrices by finding the effect
on the unit square.

1   $\begin{pmatrix} 3 & 7 \\ 2 & 5 \end{pmatrix}$ 2 $\begin{pmatrix} 11 & 4 \\ 7 & 3 \end{pmatrix}$ 3 $\begin{pmatrix} 2 & -2 \\ 3 & -1 \end{pmatrix}$

If the unit square is transformed into a quadrilateral $OA'B'C'$, is this quadrilateral
always a parallelogram ?

Calculate the area of $OA'B'C'$ for each of the above questions, (by enclosing it in
a rectangle with sides parallel to the axes and subtracting the unwanted areas).
Try to find a link between the area and the matrix.

5. Inverse transformations

If points are transformed using the matrix **A** then the inverse transformation to return the points to their original positions has the matrix $\mathbf{A}^{-1}$.

1   Points P (3, -4) and Q (-1, 2) are transformed using the matrix
$\mathbf{A} = \begin{pmatrix} 5 & 2 \\ 7 & 3 \end{pmatrix}$.
State the coordinates of P' and Q'.
Find $\mathbf{A}^{-1}$, the inverse of **A**.
Transform P' and Q' using the matrix $\mathbf{A}^{-1}$ and show that they are transformed to P and Q.

2   Repeat part **1** with the matrix $\mathbf{A} = \begin{pmatrix} 3 & 4 \\ 2 & 6 \end{pmatrix}$.

3   If points are transformed using the matrix $\mathbf{A} = \begin{pmatrix} 2 & 4 \\ -1 & 3 \end{pmatrix}$, what matrix gives the inverse transformation ?

4   If points are transformed using the matrix $\mathbf{A} = \begin{pmatrix} 3 & 2 \\ 7 & 5 \end{pmatrix}$, and the image points are then transformed using the matrix $\mathbf{B} = \begin{pmatrix} -4 & 3 \\ 2 & -4 \end{pmatrix}$, what is the matrix **C** which gives the combined transformation ?
What matrix gives the inverse of the combined transformation ? If this is denoted by $\mathbf{C}^{-1}$, show that $\mathbf{C}^{-1} = \mathbf{A}^{-1}\mathbf{B}^{-1}$.

PUZZLES

39.   The ladder is 5 m long and just touches the barrel, which has diameter 1.2 m.
How far from the wall does the ladder touch the ground ?

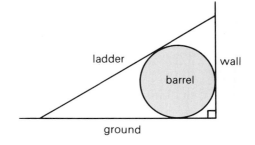

40. **A sliding-block puzzle**
     Copy this diagram on thick cardboard.
     Cut out the pieces and discard the
     shaded rectangle. (If you prefer,
     you can make the pieces out of wood.)
     Make a square base of the same size
     to put the pieces on.
     By sliding the pieces into empty
     spaces and keeping them inside the
     square of the base, you should
     score a goal by moving the large
     square into the bottom right-hand
     corner.

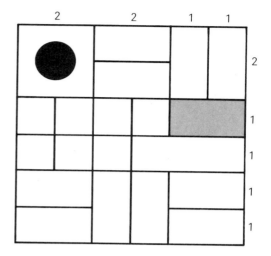

41. Tony decided to withdraw exactly half of the money in his savings account, to spend on
     Christmas presents. He noticed that after he had withdrawn the money, the number of
     pence left in the account was the same as the number of £'s he had had in before, and
     the number of £'s left in the account was half the number of pence there were before.
     How much had he to spend ?

42. Two ferry boats, the old boat and the new boat, start moving at the same time from
     opposite sides of the river, each going to the opposite bank. The new boat is faster than
     the old boat, and the boats meet at a point 120 yards from the nearest bank. When they
     arrive at their destinations, each remains there for 5 minutes while unloading and loading
     cars and passengers, then starts on the return trip. On this trip the boats meet at a point
     60 yards from the other bank.
     How wide is the river ?

43. *ABCD* is a rectangle inscribed in
     a circle.
     Semicircular arcs are drawn on the
     sides of the rectangle.

     Is the total shaded area greater
     than, less than or equal to the
     area of the rectangle ?

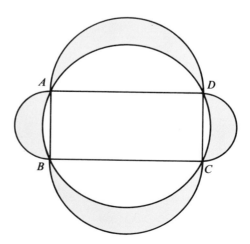

15 Thinking about graphs and

Families of curves

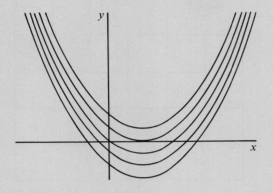

These graphs have equations
$y = x^2 - 2x - 2$
$y = x^2 - 2x - 1$
$y = x^2 - 2x$
$y = x^2 - 2x + 1$
$y = x^2 - 2x + 2$

Which is which ?
Draw some similar graphs on a graphics calculator.

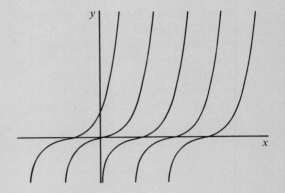

These graphs have equations
$y = (x + 2)^3$
$y = x^3$
$y = (x - 2)^3$
$y = (x - 4)^3$
$y = (x - 6)^3$

Which is which ?
Draw some similar graphs on a graphics calculator.

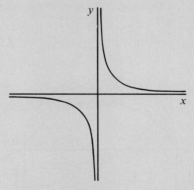

This graph has equation $y = \dfrac{1}{x}$.

Plot it on a graphics calculator and also plot graphs of functions such as $y = \dfrac{1}{x^2}$, $y = \dfrac{1}{x^3}$, to compare them.

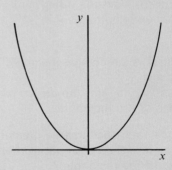

This graph has equation $y = x^2$.
Plot it on a graphics calculator and also plot graphs of functions such as $y = 2x^2$, $y = \frac{1}{2}x^2$, $y = -x^2$, to compare them.

other diagrams

Linear programming

Here is an example of a problem which can be solved using this method.

A boat owner runs pleasure cruises. His boat will carry 60 passengers, but of these at least half of them, but not more than three-quarters of them, must be children. The fares charged are £3 for an adult and £2 for a child. To cover expenses the fares on any trip must be at least £75.

If there are x children and y adults on a particular trip, write down 4 inequalities satisfied by x and y. Draw a graph showing the region satisfying all these inequalities. Use the graph to find the greatest possible amount that could be taken in fares on the trip.

Critical path diagrams

A building firm can use a critical path diagram to plan the work so that the various craftsmen (electricians, joiners, plumbers, etc.) are fully employed at certain times, and the building is completed in the least possible time.

15 Graphs and other diagrams

Sketch graphs of functions

A sketch graph should show the main shape of the graph and perhaps also the coordinates of a few important points on it, such as where it crosses the axes, and any maximum or minimum points.

It may be helpful to make a table of values to get an idea of the general shape of the graph, but do not plot unimportant points for just a few values of x near the origin. Consider what happens to the graph when x is a very big positive or negative number.

You will find it easier to understand how to draw sketch graphs if you draw them yourself.

If you can use a computer graph plotting program, or a graphics calculator, you can investigate the shape of a graph and other related graphs quite quickly.

Some basic functions

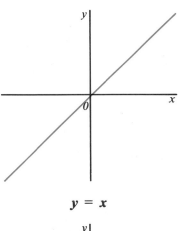

$y = x$

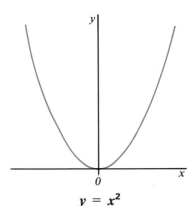

$y = x^2$

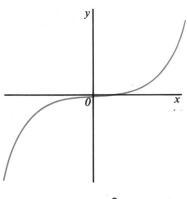

$y = x^3$

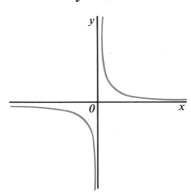

$y = \dfrac{1}{x}$

The graph of $y = \dfrac{1}{x^2}$

Look at the graph of $y = x^2$ and you will see that y is always positive, except when $x = 0$, where $y = 0$.

So $\dfrac{1}{x^2}$ will always be positive, except when $x = 0$, where there is no value, since dividing by 0 is not possible.

As x gets very large, x^2 is larger and so $\dfrac{1}{x^2}$ gets very small and approaches 0.

When x is between 0 and 1, x^2 is less than 1 and is very small when x is near 0. So $\dfrac{1}{x^2}$ is greater than 1 and is very large when x is near 0.

The graph of $y = x^2$ is symmetrical about the y-axis, and so is the graph of $y = \dfrac{1}{x^2}$.

Using this information, here is a sketch graph of $y = \dfrac{1}{x^2}$.

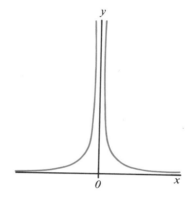

The graphs of $y = x^4$ and $y = \dfrac{1}{x^4}$

These can be sketched in a similar way.

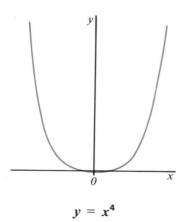

$$y = x^4$$

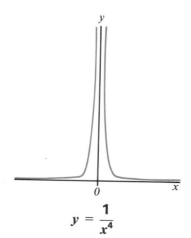

$$y = \dfrac{1}{x^4}$$

$y = x^4$ is flatter near the origin, so is more U-shaped, than $y = x^2$.

Compare this graph with that of $y = \dfrac{1}{x^2}$.

The graph of $y = \dfrac{1}{x^3}$

Look at the graph of $y = x^3$ and you will see that y is positive when x is positive, and negative when x is negative. So $\dfrac{1}{x^3}$ is positive when x is positive and negative when x is negative.

When $x = 0$ there is no value.

When x is very large, x^3 is larger and so $\dfrac{1}{x^3}$ gets very small and approaches 0.

When x is between 0 and 1, x^3 is less than 1 and so $\dfrac{1}{x^3}$ is greater than 1, and is very large when x is near 0.

The graph of $y = x^3$ is symmetrical about the origin, and so is the graph of $y = \dfrac{1}{x^3}$.

Here is the sketch graph.

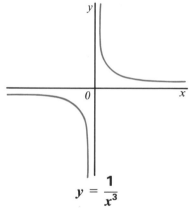

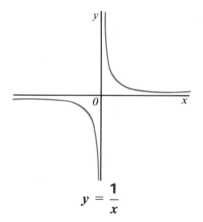

$y = \dfrac{1}{x^3}$

$y = \dfrac{1}{x}$

Compare this graph with that of $y = \dfrac{1}{x}$.

Straight-line graphs

The general equation of a straight line is $y = mx + c$.
The gradient is m and the line cuts the y-axis at $(0, c)$.
c is called the **intercept** on the y-axis.

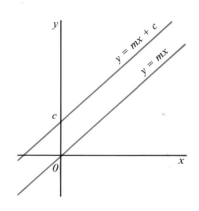

Graphs of quadratic functions

The general equation of a quadratic function is $y = ax^2 + bx + c$.
The shape of the graph is a parabola.

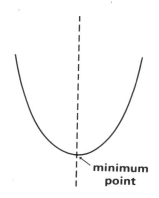

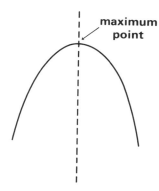

curve when a is positive   curve when a is negative

The graph cuts the x-axis at the points where x satisfies the equation
$ax^2 + bx + c = 0$.
The graph cuts the y-axis at $(0, c)$.
The line of symmetry is the line $x = -\dfrac{b}{2a}$.

Example

Sketch the graph of the function $y = 5 + 4x - x^2$.

It is of the form $y = ax^2 + bx + c$ with $a = -1$, $b = 4$, $c = 5$.
a is negative so the graph has a maximum point.
The graph cuts the x-axis at the points where $5 + 4x - x^2 = 0$
i.e. $x^2 - 4x - 5 = 0$
$\qquad (x + 1)(x - 5) = 0$
$\qquad x + 1 = 0 \quad$ or $\quad x - 5 = 0$
$\qquad x = -1$ or $x = 5$
The graph cuts the y-axis at $(0, 5)$.

The line of symmetry is the line
$x = -\dfrac{b}{2a} = -\dfrac{4}{-2} = 2$

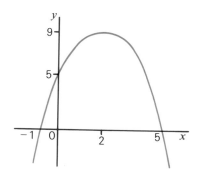

When $x = 2$, $y = 5 + 4 \times 2 - 2^2 = 9$,
so the maximum point has coordinates $(2, 9)$.

Exercise 15.1

1. **Straight-line graphs**

    Using graph paper draw axes with x from -4 to 4 and y from -4 to 6, taking a scale of 2 cm to 1 unit on both axes.
    Draw these lines on the same graph, and label them. Draw as much of each line as fits on the paper.

    1 $y = x$
    2 $y = 2x$
    3 $y = 2x + 3$
    4 $y = -\frac{1}{2}x$
    5 $y = 5 - \frac{1}{2}x$

    Comment on the difference between the graphs of $y = x$, $y = 2x$ and $y = -\frac{1}{2}x$.

    Comment on the difference between the graphs of $y = 2x$ and $y = 2x + 3$, also between $y = -\frac{1}{2}x$ and $y = 5 - \frac{1}{2}x$.

2. Without using graph paper, draw axes as shown and, assuming that you are using equal scales on each axis, draw sketch graphs of these functions and label them. (Use a ruler to draw straight lines, do not draw them freehand.)

    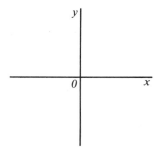

    1 $y = x$
    2 $y = x + 4$
    3 $y = 3x$

    On a separate diagram draw sketch graphs of these functions.
    4 $y = 3x$
    5 $y = 3x - 2$
    6 $y = 6 - 3x$
    Label the points where any of the lines cut the y-axis.

3. **Quadratic functions**

   1 Using graph paper, draw axes with x from -4 to 4 and y from 0 to 16.
   Make a table of values for the graph of $y = x^2$, for x from -4 to 4 including
   $x = -\frac{1}{2}$ and $x = \frac{1}{2}$. Plot the points and draw the curve.
   Notice that y is always positive except when $x = 0$.
   When x is a fraction between 0 and 1, x^2 is a smaller fraction.
   As x gets very large, x^2 is even larger.
   The graph is symmetrical about the y-axis.

   2 Sketch the graph of $y = x^2$, not on graph paper.

   3 Make a table of values for the graph of $y = 3x^2$ for x from -4 to 4, and use
   this and the sketch graph of $y = x^2$ to sketch the graph of $y = 3x^2$.

   4 Make a table of values for the graph of $y = x^2 + 5$, for x from -4 to 4, and
   use this and the sketch graph of $y = x^2$ to sketch the graph of $y = x^2 + 5$.

   5 Copy and complete this table of values for the graph of $y = (x - 3)^2$.

x	-1	0	1	2	3	4	5	6	7
$x - 3$	-4								
$(x - 3)^2$	16								

   Use this and the sketch graph of $y = x^2$ to sketch the graph of $y = (x - 3)^2$.

4. This question uses the quadratic function $y = 2x^2 - 2x - 24$.
   1 Has the graph of the function got a maximum point or a minimum point ?
   2 Find the coordinates of the points where the graph cuts the x-axis.
   3 Find the coordinates of the point where the graph cuts the y-axis.
   4 Sketch the graph of the function.

5. Repeat question 4 for the quadratic function $y = 4 + 7x - 2x^2$.

6. **Cubic functions**

   1 Using graph paper, draw axes with x from -3 to 3 and y from -30 to 30.
   Make a table of values for the graph of $y = x^3$, for x from -3 to 3, including
   $x = -\frac{1}{2}$ and $x = \frac{1}{2}$. Plot the points and draw the curve.

   Notice that when x is positive, y is positive; when x is negative, y is negative.
   When x is a fraction between 0 and 1, x^3 is a smaller fraction.
   As x gets very large, x^3 is much larger,
   The graph is symmetrical about the origin.

   2 Sketch the graph of $y = x^3$.

6. **3**   Make a table of values for the graph of $y = 2x^3$ for x from -3 to 3, and use this and the sketch graph of $y = x^3$ to sketch the graph of $y = 2x^3$.

   4   Make a table of values for the graph of $y = x^3 - 8$ for x from -3 to 3, and use this and the sketch graph of $y = x^3$ to sketch the graph of $y = x^3 - 8$.

   5   Copy and complete this table of values for the graph of $y = (x + 2)^3$.

x	-5	-4	-3	-2	-1	0	1
$x + 2$	-3						
$(x + 2)^3$	-27						

   Use this and the sketch graph of $y = x^3$ to sketch the graph of $y = (x + 2)^3$.

Related functions

In the previous exercise you sketched one graph by noticing its relationship to another graph. The main ideas are summarised here, with further examples.
You will find it helpful to sketch the graphs yourself.
If you cannot sketch a graph by discovering its relationship to another graph, remember that you can always make a table of values to get an idea of its general shape.

The relationship between $y = f(x)$ and $y = f(x) + a$, where a is a constant number.
The graph of $y = f(x) + a$ will be a translation of the graph of $y = f(x)$, of a units in the y-direction.

Examples

   $y = 3x$
   $y = 3x + 1$
   The 2nd graph is 1 unit higher in the y-direction.

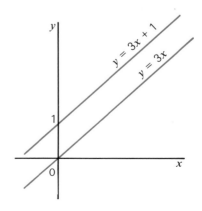

$y = x^2$
$y = x^2 + 2$
The 2nd graph is 2 units higher.

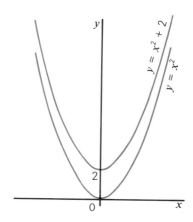

$y = x^2 - 3x$
$y = x^2 - 3x - 4$
The 2nd graph is 4 units lower.

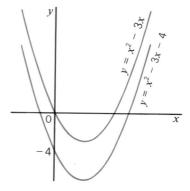

The relationship between $y = f(x)$ and $y = f(x - a)$

The graph of $y = f(x - a)$ will be a translation of the graph of $y = f(x)$, of a units in the x-direction.

Examples

$y = 3x$
$y = 3(x - 2)$ $y = 0$ $3(x - 2) = 0$
(i.e. $y = 3x - 6$) $3x = 6$
The 2nd graph is 2 units further $x = 2$
along in the x-direction.

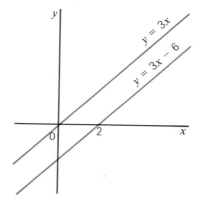

$y = x^2$
$y = (x - 3)^2$
(i.e. $y = x^2 - 6x + 9$)
The 2nd graph is 3 units further
along.

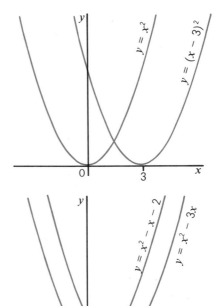

$y = x^2 - 3x$
$y = (x + 1)^2 - 3(x + 1)$
(i.e. $y = x^2 - x - 2$)
The 2nd graph is 1 unit
backwards in the
x-direction.

The relationship between $y = f(x)$ and $y = af(x)$

The graph of $y = af(x)$ will have the y-values of the function $y = f(x)$ multiplied by a
factor a.

Examples

$y = 3x + 1$
$y = 4(3x + 1)$
(i.e. $y = 12x + 4$)

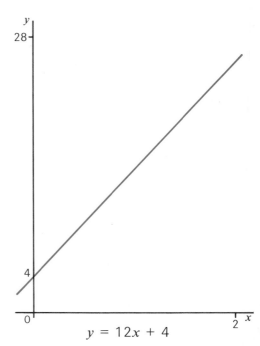

$y = 12x + 4$

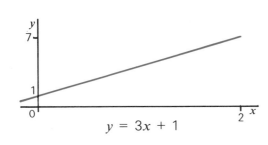

$y = 3x + 1$

$y = x^2 + x - 2$
$y = 3(x^2 + x - 2)$
(i.e. $y = 3x^2 + 3x - 6$)

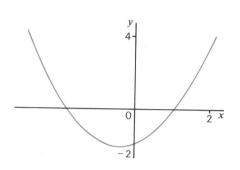

$y = x^2 + x - 2$

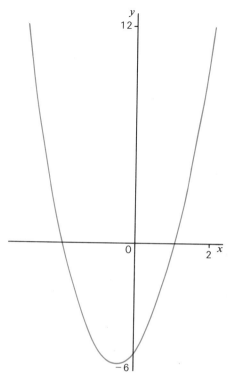

$y = 3x^2 + 3x - 6$

$y = x^3 + 1$
$y = 2(x^3 + 1)$
(i.e. $y = 2x^3 + 2$)

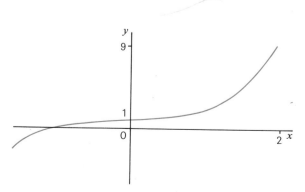

$y = x^3 + 1$

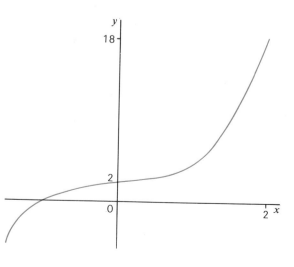

$y = 2x^3 + 2$

The relationship between $y = f(x)$ and $y = f(ax)$

The graph of $y = f(ax)$ will have the x-values of the function $y = f(x)$ divided by a $\left(\text{or multiplied by } \dfrac{1}{a}\right)$.

Examples

$y = 3x + 1$
$y = 3(4x) + 1$
(i.e. $y = 12x + 1$)

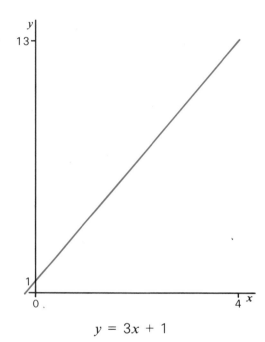

$y = 3x + 1$

$y = 12x + 1$

$y = x^2 + x - 2$
$y = (2x)^2 + (2x) - 2$
(i.e. $y = 4x^2 + 2x - 2$)

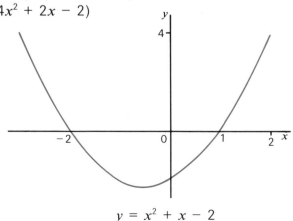

$y = x^2 + x - 2$

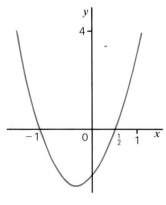

$y = 4x^2 + 2x - 2$

$y = x^2 - 6x$
$y = (3x)^2 - 6(3x)$
(i.e. $y = 9x^2 - 18x$)

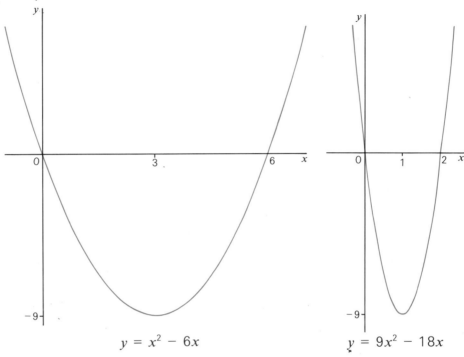

$y = x^2 - 6x$ $\qquad\qquad\qquad$ $y = 9x^2 - 18x$

Exercise 15.2

For each question, sketch the graphs of the two functions, on the same or adjoining sketches, to show the relationship between them.

1. $y = 2x - 5$,
    $y = 2x + 5$.

2. $y = x^2$,
    $y = (x + 2)^2$.

3. $y = x^2 (x - 4)$,
    $y = 2x^2 (x - 4)$.

4. $y = x^2 + 1$,
    $y = 4x^2 + 1$.

5. $y = x^3$,
    $y = (x - 3)^3$.

6. $y = x(x - 2)$,
    $y = 3x(3x - 2)$.

7. $y = x^3$,
    $y = x^3 + 8$.

8. $y = x^2 - 5x$,
    $y = 3x^2 - 15x$.

9. $y = x^2$,
    $y = x^2 - 9$.

10. $y = \frac{1}{2}x + 3$,
    $y = 2x + 3$.

Linear Programming

You have already used inequalities and represented them by regions on graphs. This has a practical use in finding the greatest or least values of a particular function which has to satisfy certain conditions.

Example

The shaded area, including the
boundary lines, is the region

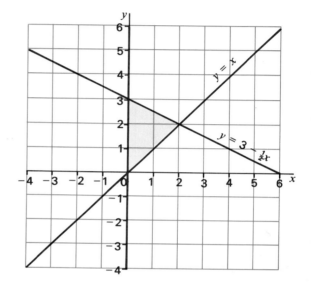

$x \geqslant 0$

$y \geqslant x$

$y \leqslant 3 - \frac{1}{2}x$

Now suppose that we want to
find a point in the region
which gives the greatest
value for $x + y$.
If the greatest value is k,
then $x + y = k$.
This equation is represented by the line $y = k - x$.

On the graph, we could draw the line $y = 6 - x$.
It passes through $(6, 0)$ and $(0, 6)$. You also know that its gradient is -1.
Put your ruler on the graph, passing through these 2 points.
This line does not pass through the region so $k = 6$ is not a solution.
Try $y = 5 - x$, going through $(5, 0)$ and $(0, 5)$.
You will notice that this line is parallel to the 1st one.
But it, too, does not pass through the shaded region.

Keeping your ruler parallel to this line, move it until it just meets the region, which will
be at the point $(2, 2)$.
So $x + y = 2 + 2 = 4$, and this is the greatest value of $x + y$ for a point (x, y) in the
region.

We will show the lines $y = 6 - x$,
$y = 5 - x$ and $y = 4 - x$ on a diagram.
(Normally you would draw lines on the
graph, but do not draw them in the book.)

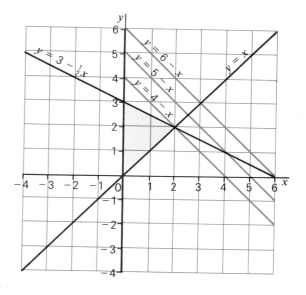

As another example, using the same region, suppose we want to find a point in the
region which gives the greatest value for $2y - x$.
If this greatest value is k, then $2y - x = k$.
This equation is represented by the line $2y = x + k$, i.e. $y = \frac{1}{2}x + \frac{1}{2}k$.
This line has gradient $\frac{1}{2}$.

Possible lines are $y = \frac{1}{2}x$, $y = \frac{1}{2}x + 1$, $y = \frac{1}{2}x + 2$, etc.
Since we want the greatest value of k, we want the highest of these lines which
passes through the region.

The line $y = \frac{1}{2}x$ passes through $(0, 0)$
and $(6, 3)$. Put your ruler on the graph,
passing through these 2 points.
Now keep the ruler parallel to this line
and move it upward until it is as far as it
will go, but still passing through the
shaded region.
This is when it passes through the point
$(0, 3)$.
So the greatest value of $2y - x$ for a
point (x, y) in the region is
$2 \times 3 - 0 = 6$.
The diagram shows the lines $y = \frac{1}{2}x$ and
$y = \frac{1}{2}x + 3$.

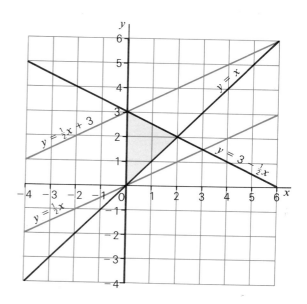

Exercise 15.3

1. The lines in the diagram have
    these equations:

    $AB : 2y = x + 1$
    $BC : 3y = 29 - 4x$
    $AC : y = 6x - 5$

    1 Identify the region of the
    shaded triangle. The
    boundary lines are to be
    included in the region.

    2 Where does the line
    $y = 9 - 3x$ meet the axes ?
    Put your ruler along this
    line and by keeping the
    ruler parallel to this
    line, find the
    greatest value of $y + 3x$ for a
    point (x, y) in the region,
    and state this value.

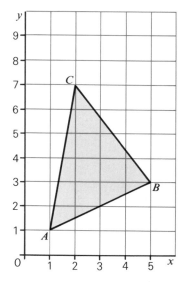

    3 Using the same line, find the least value of $y + 3x$ for a point (x, y) in the
    region, and state this value.

    4 Using another suitable line, find the greatest value of $y - x$ for a point (x, y)
    in the region, and state this value.

2. **1** On graph paper, label the x and y axes from 0 to 16, taking a scale of 1 cm
    to 1 unit on both axes.
    Plot the points A (4, 2), B (10, 4), C (4, 8) and D (0, 6), and join the points
    to enclose the region $ABCD$. The region includes the boundary lines.

    2 Draw the line $y = 16 - x$ and by drawing a line parallel to this line, find the
    greatest value of $x + y$ for a point (x, y) in the region. What is this greatest
    value ?

    3 Draw the line $y = 2 - \frac{1}{2}x$ and by drawing a line parallel to this line, find the
    least value of $x + 2y$ for a point (x, y) in the region. What is this least value ?

    4 Using the line $y = 2 - \frac{1}{2}x$ again, find the greatest value of $x + 2y$ for a point
    (x, y) in the region. What is this greatest value ?

3. **1** On graph paper, label the x-axis from 0 to 16 and the y-axis from -4 to 16, using a scale of 1 cm to 1 unit on both axes.
Draw the lines $x = 8$, $y = x + 3$, $y = x - 3$ and $y = 9 - 2x$, showing as much of the lines as fit on the graph.
Identify the region
$x \leqslant 8$
$y \leqslant x + 3$
$y \geqslant x - 3$
$y \geqslant 9 - 2x$.

2 By drawing a line parallel to the line $y = 9 - 2x$, find the greatest value of $2x + y$ for a point (x, y) in the region.

3 By drawing a suitable line, find the greatest value of $y - 2x$ for a point (x, y) in the region.

Critical Path Diagrams

These are used to help in the planning of a job which consists of a number of operations. They are network diagrams with a beginning and an end. The operations are represented by the lines of the network and the time each operation takes is also shown.
The critical path shows the route through the network from start to end which takes the longest time. The total job cannot be finished in less time than this.
Critical path diagrams can be used in an industrial situation to make the most efficient use of the workforce and machinery, and keep costs to a minimum.

Examples

1 In this diagram, find the critical path. What is the shortest time in which the job can be completed ?

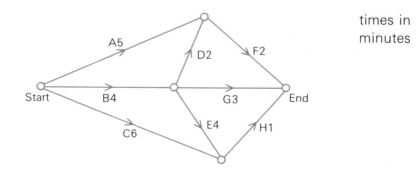

times in minutes

Capital letters have been used to
identify the operations.
The first 3 operations are A, 5 minutes;
B, 4 minutes; and C, 6 minutes.
The other operations are D, E, F, G, H.

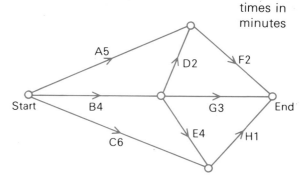

times in
minutes

D and E can only be started after B is finished, that is, after 4 minutes.
Looking at the order shown by the arrows on the diagram, operation F cannot be
started until 6 minutes after the start because it takes 6 minutes to do operations B
and D, and operation F cannot begin until each of these have been completed,
even though A can be done in 5 minutes. Thus, via F, the end can be reached in
8 minutes.
G can be started when operation B is completed, and via G the end can be reached
in 7 minutes.
H cannot be started until 8 minutes after the start, because it takes 8 minutes in
total to do operations B and E, and operation H cannot begin until B and E are
completed, even though C only takes 6 minutes. Thus, via H, the end is reached in
9 minutes.

The critical path is B, E, H, taking 9 minutes.
The job cannot be done in less than 9 minutes.

You may find it helpful to put the earliest starting times near the circles.

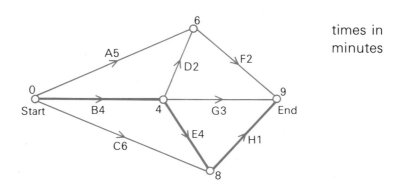

times in
minutes

2   In this diagram, find the critical path. What is the shortest time in which the job can be completed ?

What is the latest time at which operations C and E must be started, if the job is to be finished in the shortest possible time ? The earliest time the job can start is noon.

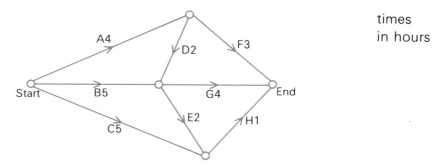

times
in hours

(This network diagram is similar to that of the last example, but the times have been altered. Also in this example, the arrow on operation D is reversed. This means that D cannot be started until operation A is completed, and does not depend on B being completed.)

The first 3 operations are A, B, C.
The other operations are D, E, F, G, H.

D can be started after A is completed, that is, after 4 hours.
Operation E can only be started when all the operations leading to E have been completed. B is completed after 5 hours and operations A and D are completed after 6 hours. So E cannot be started for 6 hours. Similarly, G cannot be started for 6 hours. The end can be reached via G in 10 hours.
F can be started after A is completed, and, via F, the end can be reached in 7 hours.
H can be started after E and C are completed (E 8 hours, C 5 hours), so H cannot be started for 8 hours. Via H the end can be reached in 9 hours.

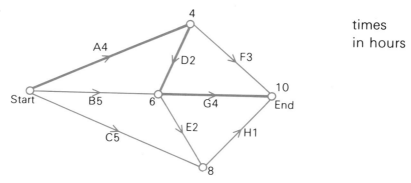

times
in hours

The critical path is ADG, taking 10 hours.
The job cannot be done in less than 10 hours.

Slack time

Since the other routes take less than 10 hours, there is some 'slack time'.
If we let the operations start at noon, the times along the critical path can be noted.

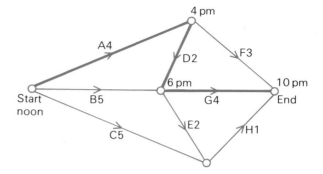

Thus operation B, which takes 5 hours, cannot begin before noon and must finish by 6 pm. Therefore, it could be delayed to start at times up to 1 pm.
The operation F, which takes 3 hours, cannot begin before 4 pm and must finish by 10 pm. Therefore it could be delayed to start at any time up to 7 pm.
The operation H must start at 9 pm at the latest, so the operation E must start at 7 pm at the latest, and operation C must start at 4 pm at the latest.

Exercise 15.4

Copy these diagrams and find the critical path for each diagram. Show it in colour. State the least time needed to complete each job.

1.   times in days

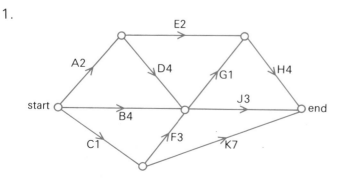

2.

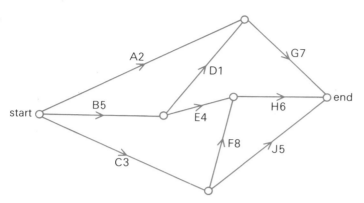

times in hours

3.

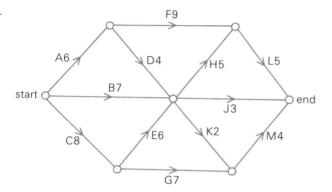

times in minutes

If the job is begun at 1 pm, mark the times of the beginning and ending of each of the operations on the critical path.

What is the latest time that operation J can be started ?
What is the latest time that operation D can be started ?

Exercise 15.5   Applications and Activities

1. **Graphs of $y = x, y = x^2, y = x^3$**

Draw x and y axes labelled from 0 to 1, taking 1 cm to represent 0.1 unit on both axes.
Draw the graphs of the above functions for values of x from 0 to 1.
You could also draw the graphs of $y = \sqrt{x}$ and $y = \sqrt[3]{x}$ as well. What is the relationship between the graphs of $y = x^2$ and $y = \sqrt{x}$, and between $y = x^3$ and $y = \sqrt[3]{x}$?

2. Sketch these graphs, on the same or adjoining sketches, to show the relationship between the 1st graph and each of the others.
$y = x^2$, $y = 3x^2$, $y = x^2 + 3$, $y = (x + 3)^2$

3. On separate sketches, sketch these graphs, showing the relationship between each one and the next.
$y = x^2$, $y = (x - 3)^2$, $y = 2(x - 3)^2$, $y = 2(x - 3)^2 + 4$.

4. An interesting graph to plot is $y^2 = \dfrac{x^2}{x^2 - 1}$.

You can either plot the graph accurately, or you may just draw a sketch graph.

Firstly, make a table of values. These values of x have been chosen so that the values of x^2 are whole numbers.

x	0	1	$\sqrt{2}$	$\sqrt{3}$	$\sqrt{4}$	$\sqrt{5}$	$\sqrt{6}$	$\sqrt{7}$	$\sqrt{8}$	$\sqrt{9}$	$\sqrt{10}$
x^2	0	1	2	3							
$x^2 - 1$	-1	0	1	2							
y^2	0	$-$	2	$\frac{3}{2}$							
y	0	$-$	$\pm\sqrt{2}$	$\pm\sqrt{\frac{3}{2}}$							

Draw the x and y axes from -4 to 4, taking a scale of 2 cm to 1 unit on both axes. Plot the points for positive values of x and y, e.g. $\left(\sqrt{2}, \sqrt{2}\right)$, $\left(\sqrt{3}, \sqrt{\frac{3}{2}}\right)$, etc.

Since the equation can be written as $x^2 = \dfrac{y^2}{y^2 - 1}$, the values of x and y can be interchanged.
So plot $\left(\sqrt{\frac{3}{2}}, \sqrt{3}\right)$, $\left(\sqrt{\frac{4}{3}}, \sqrt{4}\right)$, etc.
Join the points with a smooth curve.
Then reflect the points in both axes and draw 3 other curves, because the graph is symmetrical about both axes. Then there is one more point to plot.
This graph has been called 'Policeman on point-duty'.

5. This network diagram shows the operations involved in repairing a house, and the time taken to complete each operation.

times in days

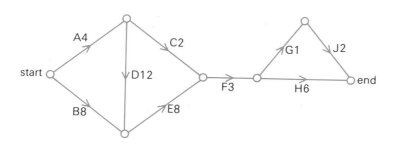

Operations
A   Remove and replace brickwork and flooring where necessary
B   Install new plumbing
C   Fit new windows
D   Re-wire the house
E   Re-plaster where necessary
F   Install fittings
G   Clear the site of building materials
H   Paint and decorate and clean up
J   Lay new paths and tidy the garden

Copy the diagram.
Find the critical path for the operations, and mark it in colour.
State the least time that the job will take.
If the new windows were not available when the repairs to the flooring and brickwork were finished, how many extra days are there for them to be made available if the job is to be finished in the least time ?

6. A coach firm has to carry 450 passengers. Coaches can carry up to 45 passengers and minibuses can carry up to 15 passengers.
If the firm uses x coaches and y minibuses, write down an inequality satisfied by x and y and show that this simplifies to $y \geqslant 30 - 3x$.
If the firm has 20 drivers available, write down another inequality satisfied by x and y.

Draw the x and y axes from 0 to 30 using a scale of 2 cm to 5 units.
Show the inequalities on a graph and identify the region in which $x \geqslant 0$, $y \geqslant 0$ and the 2 other inequalities are satisfied.

To use a coach costs £100 and to use a minibus costs £25.
Write down an expression for the cost of x coaches and y minibuses.
If the total cost is £$25k$, show that the equation to be satisfied is $y = k - 4x$.
Draw the line $y = 20 - 4x$ on the graph. Does this line pass through the region ?
By drawing a line parallel to this line, find the least value of $y + 4x$ satisfied by a point (x, y) in the region.
Hence find the number of coaches and minibuses to be used to make the cost least, and state this cost.

7. A builder has a plot of land available on which he can build houses.
He can either build luxury houses or standard houses.
He decides to build at least 5 luxury and at least 10 standard houses, and he cannot build more than 30 houses altogether.
If he builds x luxury houses and y standard houses, write down 3 inequalities satisfied by x and y.
Draw the x-axis from 0 to 40 and the y-axis from 0 to 50, taking a scale of 2 cm to 5 units on both axes.
Draw the boundary lines of the inequalities on the graph.

The luxury houses require $300 \, \text{m}^2$ of land each, and the standard houses require $150 \, \text{m}^2$ each. The total area of the plot is $6000 \, \text{m}^2$. Write down a 4th inequality, simplify it and draw its boundary line on the graph.
Identify the region in which all 4 inequalities are satisfied.

The builder makes a profit of £6000 on each luxury house and a profit of £4000 on each standard house. Write down an expression for the total profit expected.
If this total profit is £$2000k$, show that the equation to be satisfied is
$2y = k - 3x$.
Draw the line $2y = 90 - 3x$ on the graph.
Does this line pass through the region ?
By drawing a line parallel to this line, find the greatest value of $2y + 3x$ satisfied by a point (x, y) in the region.
Hence find the number of luxury houses and the number of standard houses that the builder should build to make the greatest profit, and say what this profit will be.

PUZZLES

44. Find the missing figures in this
     division sum, in which there is
     no remainder.

```
                              x  5  9
         x  x  7 ) 1  x  8  x  x  x
                   x  x  x  8
                   ─────────
                      x  1  x  x
                      x  x  3  x
                      ─────────
                         x  x  0  x
                         x  x  0  x
                         ═════════
```

45. A caterer bought some eggs from a farmer, paying £5.20. But because the eggs were
     rather small, the farmer added 2 extra eggs to the number.
     How many eggs did the caterer get, if he worked out that the eggs actually cost 2p per
     dozen less than the first asking price ?

46. Arrange 8 coins tails up in a
     circle.
     Starting from any coin, and
     moving clockwise or
     anticlockwise, count one, two,
     three, four and turn over the
     fourth coin so that it is heads
     up.
     Start again from any coin that
     is tails up, and repeat the
     process. Continue until all
     the coins except one are heads up.

47. Using three 3's and any mathematical signs, express the numbers from 1 to 18.

     e.g. $30 = 3^3 + 3$

48. Find the solutions to this multiplication
     question, where every letter stands for a
     different figure.
     There are 3 different solutions, so you
     may like to begin with the one where
     H = 4.

```
        M  A  T  H  S
     ×              9
     ──────────────
     L  O  G  I  C
```

Miscellaneous Section C

Aural Practice

These aural exercises, C1 and C2, should be read to you, probably by your teacher or a friend, and you should write down the answers only, doing any working out in your head. You should do the 15 questions within 10 minutes.

Exercise C1

1.   What is the total cost of 9 articles at 99 pence each ?

2.   If $3x + 4$ is greater than 19, what can you say about x ?

3.   The length of a field is given as 85 m to the nearest metre. What are the lower and upper bounds of the true length of the field ?

4.   What do you get when you take 6 from 90 and divide the result by 7 ?

5.   What is the value of 5^{-2} ?

6.   One angle of a triangle is 40° and the other two angles are equal. What size are they ?

7.   The mean of 5 numbers is 11. The mean of 4 of these numbers is 10. What is the 5th number ?

8.   If £4 was equally divided among 16 children, how much would they each receive ?

9.   What is $2x^2 + 10x$, in factorised form.

10.   If the area of a square is 36 cm^2, what is its perimeter ?

11.   The point (6, 2) is reflected in the x-axis. The image is then reflected in the line $x = 3$. What are the coordinates of the final image point ?

12.   I bought 3 similar cakes and received 43 pence change from £1. How much did each cake cost ?

13.   Give the positive solution of the equation $5x^2 - 2 = 78$.

14. How many pieces of tape of length 0.4 metres can be cut from a piece 4.8 metres long ?

15. If two events A and B are independent events with probabilities of success 0.4 and 0.5 respectively, what is the probability of both events A and B occurring ?

Exercise C2

1. What is the total cost of 200 badges at 13 pence each ?

2. Write $9x^2 - 1$, in factorised form.

3. 8 men can build a wall in 4 days. How long will 4 men take ?

4. What is the smallest number which must be added to 100 in order to make it exactly divisible by 7 ?

5. On a velocity-time graph, what is represented by the gradient of the graph ?

6. What is 0.3×70 ?

7. Laura buys a bicycle for £120 and sells it to gain $33\frac{1}{3}$%. What is the selling price ?

8. If 32 cm was cut from 1 metre of ribbon, how much was left ?

9. There are 3 red counters and 5 blue counters in a bag. Two are picked out at random. What is the probability that they are both red ?

10. A boy was 7 years old in 1992. When will he be 16 years old ?

11. Which of these numbers is not a rational number ?
    3.14, $3\frac{1}{7}$, π, $\left(\sqrt{3}\right)^2$.

12. A water tank is 3 m long, 2 m wide and 1 m deep. How many cubic metres of water does it hold when it is half-full ?

13. What is the name given to a 4-sided figure whose four vertices lie on the circumference of a circle ?

14. What must be added to $\frac{1}{3}$ to make it up to $\frac{1}{2}$?

15. The point (5, 2) is rotated about the origin through 90° in an anticlockwise direction. What are the coordinates of the image point ?

Exercise C3   Revision

1. The table shows the relationship between the times necessary to make a certain journey at various average speeds.

speed v in km/h	30	40	45	60	90	100
time t in hours	6	4.5	4	3	2	1.8

Find the equation connecting t and v.
What would be the time taken for the journey if the average speed was 75 km/h ?

2. **1** Find the ratio of the areas of triangles *ABC* : *ADE* : *AFG*.
    2 Hence find the ratio of the areas of $\triangle ABC$: trapezium *BDEC* : trapezium *DFGE*.

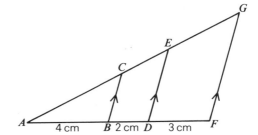

3. Factorise these expressions.
    1 $xy - x - 1 + y$
    2 $x^2 - 2xy + y^2$
    3 $8x^2 - 18y^2$
    4 $3x^2 + xy - 2y^2$

4. Sketch these graphs on the same or adjoining sketches to show the relationship between the first graph and each of the others.
    1 $y = x^3$
    2 $y = x^3 + 1$
    3 $y = (x - 2)^3$

5. A club hires a minibus for a trip. x people agree to go on the trip and share equally the cost of the minibus, which is £90.
    Write down an expression for the amount each person should pay.
    On the day, 5 extra people came, and this reduced the amount to be paid by each person on the trip. Write down an expression for the amount each person now had to pay.
    If this amount was £3 less than the price they originally agreed to pay, write down an equation and solve it to find the value of x.
    How many people actually went on the trip ?

6. This sequence can be used to find an approximate value of the cube root of a number x. The limit of the sequence is $\sqrt[3]{x}$.

$$u_{n+1} = \frac{2}{3} u_n + \frac{x}{3u_n^2}$$

Use this sequence to find the cube root of 40, correct to 3 decimal places, starting with $u_1 = 3$.

7. O is the centre of the circle and PT is a tangent, touching the circle at T.
If $OX = 9$ cm and $PX = 6$ cm, what is the length of PT?

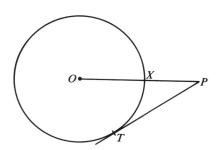

8. The table shows the distribution of personal incomes after tax.
(The figures are for 1985/86, and low earners, who do not pay tax, are not included.)

Income in £1000's	Number of people in 100 000's
2-3	19
3-4	25
4-5	26
5-7	44
7-10	47
10-15	39
15-20	13
20-30	6
30 and over	2

Assume that the last class is 30-50, although a few people had incomes of over £50 000.

Work out the heights of the columns for a histogram.

Draw the histogram.

Comment briefly on its shape.

9. **1** Calculate the length of BC.
    2 Calculate the length of PQ, given that $\cos Q = 0.6$.
    3 Are the triangles congruent ? If so, give the reason for congruence.

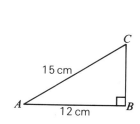

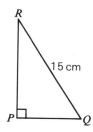

10.   Copy the diagram and find the critical path for the complete job, and mark it on your diagram. State the least time the job will take.
      If the job is started at 9 am, what are the earliest, and latest, times that operation K can be started ?

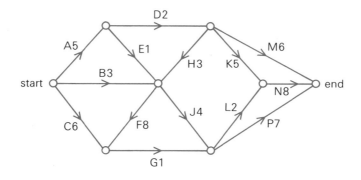

Times in minutes

11.   Solve these quadratic equations.
      1 $x^2 + 3x - 4 = 0$
      2 $(2x + 1)^2 = 25$
      3 $2x^2 + 3x - 4 = 0$, correct to 2 decimal places.

12.   The students in a school club belong to 2 forms, 10A and 10B.
      The table shows the numbers of students in this club.

	10A	10B
girls	10	14
boys	12	16

      If from this club 2 members are chosen at random, what is the probability that
      1   they are both boys,
      2   they are both members of form 10B ?
      3   If one boy and one girl have to be chosen at random, what is the probability that the boy is from form 10A and the girl is from form 10B ?

13.   On graph paper or squared paper, draw x and y axes from -4 to 4, using equal scales on both axes.
      Draw $\triangle ABC$ where $A = (1, 1)$, $B = (4, 1)$, $C = (4, 3)$.
      Transform $\triangle ABC$ into $\triangle A_1 B_1 C_1$ by reflecting it in the y-axis.
      What are the coordinates of the image points A_1, B_1, C_1 ?
      Transform $\triangle A_1 B_1 C_1$ into $\triangle A_2 B_2 C_2$ by reflecting it in the line $y = x$.
      What are the coordinates of the image points A_2, B_2, C_2 ?
      What single transformation would map $\triangle ABC$ into $\triangle A_2 B_2 C_2$?

14. A cylindrical storage tank has base radius 5 m and height 12 m. The external curved surface is to be painted. What is its area ?

15. Draw the graph of $y = 2x^2$, for values of x from -3 to 5, and labelling the y-axis from 0 to 50.

    Using the same axes, draw the line $y = 3x + 20$, and find the values of x at the points where it intersects the curve.

    State the equation for which these values of x are the solutions, and rearrange it into the form $ax^2 + bx + c = 0$.

    Solve the equation by another method, to check your solutions.

16. A large company is planning to move its factory into a rural area, and wants to find out the feelings of the local people about the move. It is decided to send out a questionnaire to a sample of residents.

    Here are some methods suggested for selecting the sample:
    (1) Obtain the electoral roll (the list of voters in the district) and use it to select the sample.
    (2) Stop people in the village street and give them a questionnaire.
    (3) Send questionnaires to every house in the district.

    Say briefly what are the advantages and/or disadvantages of each of these methods.

17. If $x = \sqrt{8}$ and $y = \sqrt{18}$, say whether the numbers given by these expressions are rational or irrational.

    $8x, \quad x^2, \quad x + y, \quad xy, \quad \sqrt{2}y, \quad \pi y^2, \quad \dfrac{y}{x}, \quad x^0, \quad \dfrac{x}{y}, \quad 18x - 8y.$

18. In the diagram, O is the centre of the circle. $\angle ABC = 48°$.

    Calculate
    1 the length of AB,
    2 the size of $\angle BOC$,
    3 the size of $\angle OBC$,
    4 the radius of the circle,
    5 the area of the minor sector BOC of the circle.

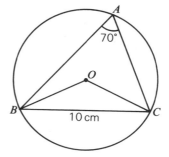

19. A rectangular courtyard has sides of length 24 m and 16 m, correct to the nearest metre.

    Find the least and greatest possible values of its perimeter and its area.

20.   **1**   Copy and complete the table which gives the values of y for values of x
from 1 to 6, for the function $y = \dfrac{12}{x} - 3x$.

x	1	1.5	2	3	4	5	6
$\dfrac{12}{x}$	12	8					
$-3x$	0	-4.5					
y	12	3.5					

2   Draw the graph of $y = \dfrac{12}{x} - 3x$ for values of x from 1 to 6, taking 2 cm to
represent 1 unit on the x-axis, and 2 cm to represent 5 units on the y-axis.

3   From the graph, find a solution of the equation $\dfrac{12}{x} - 3x = 5$.

4   Draw the tangent to the curve at the point where $x = 2$ and estimate the
rate of change of y at the point where $x = 2$.

Exercise C4   Revision

1.   The walls, floor and ceiling of a room, 3.5 m high, are rectangles. A longer side
of the floor is 8 m and a shorter side is 6 m in length.
Find the inclination to the horizontal of a diagonal (from floor to ceiling) of the
room.

2.   On graph paper or squared paper draw axes with x from 0 to 5 and y from -5
to 5, using equal scales on both axes.
Draw the triangle ABC where A is the point $(0, 0)$, B is $(0, 5)$, C is $(3, 4)$.

    1   Mark on the graph the points A', B', C', the images of A, B and C when
$\triangle ABC$ has been rotated about the origin through 90° clockwise. State the
coordinates of A', B', C'.

    2   What is the area of $\triangle ABC$?

    3   What is the area of $\triangle A'B'C'$?

    4   A reflection transforms A into A', B into C' and C into B'. Mark the mirror
line on the diagram and state its equation.

3.   A clock dial is 6.5 m in diameter. Find, to the nearest cm, the distance travelled
along the circumference by the tip of the big hand in 21 minutes.

4. The amount of a quarterly electricity bill when certain units of electricity have been used is shown in this table.

Number of units, n	200	400	600	800	1000	1200
Amount A (£)	25	40	55	70	85	100

Find the equation connecting A and n.
How many units of electricity have been used if the bill is £76 ?

5. *ABCD* is a cyclic quadrilateral with
    $BA = AD$.   *BA* and *CD* are produced to
    meet at *P*. $\angle ABD = 25°$ and $\angle CBD = 55°$.

    Find the angles of $\triangle DAP$ and show that
    $PD = AD$.

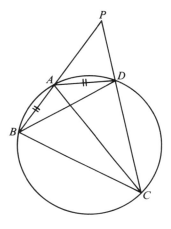

6. In a raffle there are 15 tickets numbered from 1 to 15. Madge has tickets 13, 14 and 15.
    If 2 tickets are drawn for the two prizes, what is the probability that Madge wins at least one prize ?

7. In the diagram *OPQ* represents a
    triangle on horizontal ground
    and *OT* is a vertical tower.
    The point *P* is 70 m due west
    of *O*. The angle of elevation
    of *T* from *P* is 25°.
    1   Find the height of the tower.
    2   A path runs from *P* in the
        direction with bearing 130° for
        50 m to the point *Q*.
        Find the length of *OQ*.
    3   Find the angle of elevation
        of *T* from *Q*.

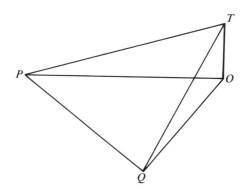

8. The iterative formula $x_{n+1} = \frac{1}{8}(6 - x_n^2)$ is used to generate a sequence of numbers.

    Given that $x_1 = 1$, find x_2, x_3, x_4 and x_5, giving the answers to 3 decimal places.

    Show that the limiting value of the formula will give a root of the equation $x^2 + 8x - 6 = 0$.

    Solve this equation by another method, finding both roots, correct to 3 decimal places.

9. The weights of 10 girls were recorded when they were going horseriding, and were, in kg,

    33   51   49   50   31   44   39   34   41   48

    Find the mean and standard deviation of the weights.

10. An object starting from rest at a point O, moves along a straight line so that its distance, s metres from O after t seconds, is given by the equation $s = t^3 + 2t^2$.

    Copy and complete the table which gives values of s for values of t from 0 to 3.

t	0	$\frac{1}{2}$	1	$1\frac{1}{2}$	2	$2\frac{1}{2}$	3
t^3		$\frac{1}{8}$		$3\frac{3}{8}$		$15\frac{5}{8}$	
$2t^2$		$\frac{1}{2}$		$4\frac{1}{2}$		$12\frac{1}{2}$	
s		$\frac{5}{8}$		$7\frac{7}{8}$		$28\frac{1}{8}$	

    Plot the graph of s against t, taking 2 cm to 0.5 units on the t-axis and 2 cm to 5 units on the s-axis.

    Use the graph to find the velocity of the object after 1 second (i.e. when $t = 1$), and after 2 seconds.

11. Find the values of

    1 $16^{\frac{1}{2}} + 3^{-2}$

    2 $9^{\frac{3}{2}} \div 27^{\frac{1}{3}}$

    3 $5^0 + 25^{-\frac{1}{2}}$

12. OAB is a triangle and O is $(0, 0)$, $\overrightarrow{OA} = \begin{pmatrix} 6 \\ 2 \end{pmatrix}$, $\overrightarrow{OB} = \begin{pmatrix} 2 \\ 4 \end{pmatrix}$.

    P, Q, R are the mid-points of OA, OB and AB respectively.
    By drawing a diagram, or otherwise, find in column form the vectors $\overrightarrow{PA}$, $\overrightarrow{AB}$, $\overrightarrow{PR}$, $\overrightarrow{QA}$.

13. Copy and complete the table of values for the graph of $y = \tan \frac{1}{2}x°$, giving approximate values of y correct to 2 decimal places.

x	0	20	40	60	80	90
$\frac{1}{2}x$	0	10				
$\tan \frac{1}{2}x°$	0	0.18				

Draw the graph of $y = \tan \frac{1}{2}x°$ for x from 0 to 90, and use your graph to find a solution of the equation $\tan \frac{1}{2}x° = \frac{1}{2}$.

14. Solve the equations

1 $\dfrac{x}{6} + \dfrac{3(18 - x)}{4} = \dfrac{2}{3}$

2 $\dfrac{3}{x + 2} = \dfrac{2}{4x + 3}$

15. For a normally distributed population approximately 68% of the population lies within ± 1 standard deviation from the mean,
and approximately 95% of the population lies within ± 2 standard deviations from the mean.

Information obtained from a random sample of workers in a certain industry about their earnings indicates that the mean weekly earnings are £160 with a standard deviation of £20.
Assuming that the earnings are normally distributed, find estimates for the number of workers out of a total of 10 000 who could be expected to earn weekly

1 from £140 to £180,
2 from £160 to £180,
3 from £160 to £200,
4 over £200.

16. The sketch graph shows the functions
$y = x^3$ and $y = 2x + 11$.

1 What equation is solved by finding the value of x at the point of intersection ?

2 Using the graph of $y = x^3$, what other graph should be drawn in order to solve the equation
$x^3 - x^2 + 4 = 0$?

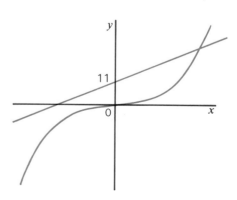

17. A quadrilateral *ABCD* has vertices *A* (0, 1), *B* (3, −1), *C* (0, 6) and *D* (−3, 8). The images of *A*, *B*, *C* and *D* under the transformation represented by the matrix $\begin{pmatrix} 2 & 1 \\ 1 & 1 \end{pmatrix}$ are *A′*, *B′*, *C′* and *D′*.

   1   State the coordinates of *A′*, *B′*, *C′* and *D′*.

   2   Draw the quadrilateral *A′B′C′D′* on squared paper or graph paper, using equal scales on both axes.

   3   Mark on the diagram the lines of symmetry of the quadrilateral *A′B′C′D′*, and state their equations.

18. A check of a large number of pupils' bicycles found that only $\frac{1}{4}$ of them had both brakes in working order.

   If from these bicycles, 3 are chosen at random, what is the probability that

   1   all 3 have both brakes in working order,

   2   at least 2 have both brakes in working order,

   3   only one has both brakes in working order,

   4   none of them have both brakes in working order ?

19. **1**   Factorise $6x^2 - 5x - 6$.

   2   Solve the equation $6x^2 - 5x - 6 = 0$.

20. For a party, Kathleen wants to buy some sweets. She buys *x* packets of fruity sweets and *y* packets of caramels.

   Write down inequalities if she decides to buy at least 3 packets of each kind, but not more than 12 packets of sweets altogether.

   Packets of fruity sweets cost 40p and packets of caramels cost 80p. Kathleen must not spend more than £6.40 altogether. Write down another inequality.

   On graph paper, draw *x* and *y* axes from 0 to 16. Draw lines representing the boundary lines of the inequalities and identify the region which satisfies the inequalities.

   Packets of fruity sweets contain 24 sweets and packets of caramels contain 30 sweets. Write down an equation satisfied if there are 240 sweets altogether in the packets bought, and draw its line on the graph.

   By drawing another line, find the number of packets of each kind of sweet to be bought to give the greatest number of sweets.

Exercise C5   Revision

1.   In the diagram, show that triangles
     ADE and *ACB* are similar.
     If *AD* = 3 cm, *AC* = 9 cm and *DE* = 3.5 cm,
     find the length of *BC*.
     If the area of Δ*ADE* is 4 cm², find
     the area of Δ*ABC*.

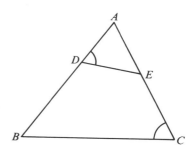

2.   Solve these equations and say whether the solutions are rational or irrational
     numbers.
     1 $13(x + 5) = 6(x - 4)$
     2 $3(x^2 + 2) = x^2 + 9$
     3 $x^3 + 10x = 5(2x + 25)$

3.   The graph shows the speed of a
     train which starts from *A* and
     increases speed steadily until
     it reaches 20 m/s. After
     keeping a steady speed for
     some time it then decreases
     speed steadily until it
     stops at *B*.
     Find the total distance travelled
     between *A* and *B*.

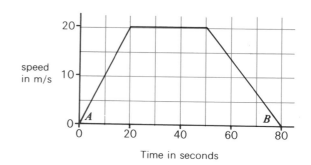

4.   On separate sketches, sketch these graphs, showing the relationship between
     each graph and the next one.
     $y = x^2$, $y = (x + 1)^2$, $y = 3(x + 1)^2$, $y = 3(x + 1)^2 + 5$.

5.   **1**   Factorise $2x^2 - x - 15$

     2   Simplify $\dfrac{2x^2 - x - 15}{2x^2 - 6x}$

6.   A plane flies over a triangular course,
     AB, *BC*, *CA*.
     The direction *AB* is due east.
     1   Find the size of ∠*ABC*
     2   State the bearing on which the
             plane flies on the section *BC*.

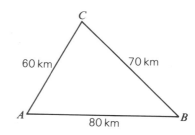

7.   The table shows the distribution of earnings of horticultural workers, in 1989.

Weekly wage in £	% of workers
Less than 100	2.1
100 to <110	6.8
110 to <120	13.7
120 to <130	12.7
130 to <140	13.9
140 to <160	16.0
160 to <180	12.6
180 to <200	7.5
200 and over	14.7

Assume that the first class is 60 to <100 and the last class is 200 to <240.

Work out the heights of the columns for a histogram.

Draw the histogram.

Comment briefly on its shape.

8.   From the top of a tower, 40 m high, which stands on level ground, two objects
      A and B can be seen at ground level. A is due west and B is due south of the
      tower. The angles of depression of A and B are 35° and 20° respectively.
      Find
      1   the distances, to the nearest
              metre, of A and B from the
              foot of the tower,
      2   the distance, to the nearest
              metre, of A from B,
      3   the bearing of B from A.

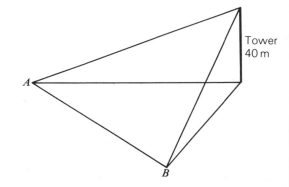

Tower
40 m

9.   In the diagram, AB is the diameter
      of the circle, PT is the tangent
      to the circle at T, and $\angle BAT = 32°$.

      Find the size of $\angle APT$.

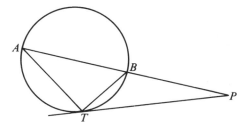

10.   If a projectile is launched into the air with a vertical velocity of 80 m/s, its height
      above ground after t seconds is approximately $(80t - 5t^2)$ metres.
      Find the times at which the height of the projectile above ground is 275 m.
      Hence find the length of time during which the projectile is above this height.

11. A trapezium *ABCD* has vertices *A* (2, 2), *B* (1, 3), *C* (2, 4), *D* (4, 4). The images of *A*, *B*, *C* and *D* under the transformation represented by the matrix $\begin{pmatrix} -2 & 0 \\ 0 & -2 \end{pmatrix}$ are *A'*, *B'*, *C'* and *D'*.

    1   Label axes with *x* and *y* from −8 to 4, and draw *ABCD* and *A'B'C'D'* on the diagram.

    2   Draw the lines *BB'*, *CC'* and *DD'*. What do you notice ?

    3   Find the area of *ABCD*.

    4   Find the area of *A'B'C'D'*.

12. A river flows downstream at 9 km/h and a man can row in still water at 12 km/h. What would be the speed of the boat if the man rowed

    1   downstream,

    2   upstream ?

    3   If he headed the boat to cross the river at right angles to the bank, what would be the size of the resultant velocity of the boat, and at what angle with the bank would it travel ?

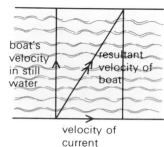

13. The volume of a cuboid is given as 66.5 cm³ and the area of the base is given as 20.4 cm², both values correct to 3 significant figures.
State the lower and upper bounds of these two numbers.
Find the height of the cuboid, giving the usual answer and also the lower and upper bounds of the possible answers, all to 3 significant figures.

14. *ABCD* is a rectangle inscribed in a circle.

    1   Find the radius of the circle.

    2   Find the size of ∠*BDC*.

    3   Find the size of ∠*BOC*.

    4   Find the length of the arc *BC*.

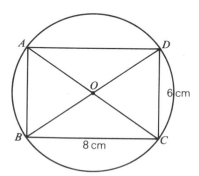

15. A bag contains 9 beads of which 5 are red and 4 are blue. Two beads are drawn together, at random, from the bag.

    1   What is the probability that they are both red ?

    2   What is the probability that they are both the same colour ?

    3   If, instead of drawing two beads together, a bead is drawn and then replaced before the second bead is drawn, find the probability that both beads are the same colour.

16. A liquid is cooling down from 100°C and the temperature is given at various times.

time (min)	0	10	20	30	40	50	60
temperature (°C)	100	81	66	55	46	40	35

Draw the graph of temperature against time, taking 2 cm to represent 10 units on both axes.

By drawing a tangent to the graph, find the rate of cooling 15 minutes after the start.

17. *A* and *B* are two points on the south bank of a river and *B* is 60 m due east of *A*. From *A* the bearing of a point *C* on the opposite bank of the river is 038° and from *B* its bearing is 331°.
Draw a sketch diagram to show this information.
Calculate
1 the distance *AC*,
2 the width of the river, to the nearest m.

18. In the diagram, *O* is the centre of the circle.
Angles *DAB* and *CBA* are equal.
1 Are triangles *ABD* and *BAC*
congruent ? If so, give the reason.

$\angle AOB = 120°$, $\angle ABC = 80°$ and the chord *AB* is 6 cm long.
Find
2 the radius of the circle,
3 the size of $\angle AOC$,
4 the length of *AC*.

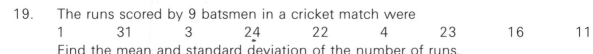

19. The runs scored by 9 batsmen in a cricket match were
    1   31   3   24   22   4   23   16   11
Find the mean and standard deviation of the number of runs.

20. Use this sketch graph of $y = \sin x°$ to make your own separate sketch graphs of
1 $y = -\sin x°$
2 $y = 2 \sin x°$
3 $y = \sin x° + 1$

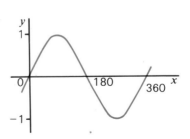

Exercise C6 Activities

1. **Roots of quadratic equations**

A quadratic equation can be written in the form $ax^2 + bx + c = 0$.
e.g. $2x^2 = 5x - 3$ can be written as $2x^2 - 5x + 3 = 0$.
Comparing it with $ax^2 + bx + c = 0$, $a = 2$, $b = -5$ and $c = 3$.

If you work out the value of $b^2 - 4ac$ you can find whether the roots (solutions)
of the equation are rational or irrational, when a, b and c are rational.

If $b^2 - 4ac$ is a perfect square, the roots are rational.
If $b^2 - 4ac$ is positive, but not a perfect square, the roots are irrational.
If $b^2 - 4ac = 0$, there is one repeated root, which is rational.
If $b^2 - 4ac$ is negative, there are no real roots.

In the equation above,
$b^2 - 4ac = (-5)^2 - 4 \times 2 \times 3 = 25 - 24 = 1$
This is an exact square, so the roots are rational. (In fact, they are $x = 1$ or
$x = 1\frac{1}{2}$.)

Find out if there are real roots in these equations, and if so, whether they are
rational or irrational.

1 $x^2 + 2x - 8 = 0$
2 $x^2 + 12 = 6x$
3 $2x^2 + 4x = 3$
4 $4x^2 + 20x + 25 = 0$
5 $10x^2 = 7x + 12$.

The sum and the product of the roots

Solve the following quadratic equations by factorising, giving the exact roots.
Find the sum of the roots and the product of the roots.
Copy and complete this table. The first line has been filled in as an example.
Can you discover anything about the sum of the roots and the product of the
roots compared with the values of a, b and c, if the equation is $ax^2 + bx + c = 0$?

Equation	Roots		Sum of roots	Product of roots
$3x^2 - x - 10 = 0$	$-1\frac{2}{3}$	2	$\frac{1}{3}$	$-\frac{10}{3}$
$x^2 - 11x - 60 = 0$				
$x^2 - 25x + 144 = 0$				
$2x^2 + x - 6 = 0$				
$5x^2 + 14x - 3 = 0$				
$x^2 - 7x - 8 = 0$				
$3x^2 + 10x + 7 = 0$				

2. **'Intersecting chord' properties of a circle**

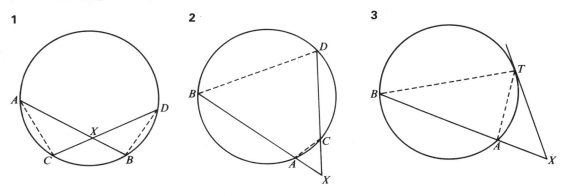

1   **2**   **3**

If 2 chords AB, CD intersect at X as in diagrams **1** or **2**, use angle properties to prove that $\triangle XAC$ is similar to $\triangle XDB$.
Hence show that $XA \times XB = XC \times XD$

In diagram **3**, prove that $\triangle XAT$ is similar to $\triangle XTB$.
Hence show that $XA \times XB = XT^2$.

Use these results to find the stated lengths in these diagrams.

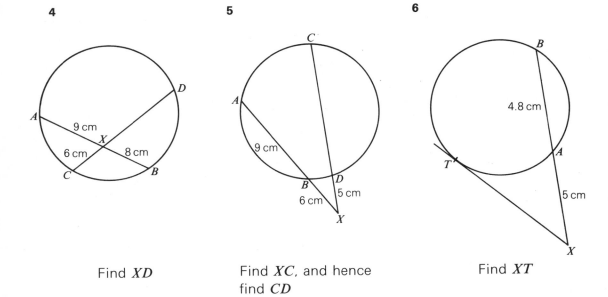

4   **5**   **6**

Find XD Find XC, and hence   Find XT
                         find CD

3. **Areas**

The area under the line $y = x$

Work out the areas under the
line $y = x$ from $x = 0$ to other
lines $x = 1$, $x = 2$, $x = 3$, etc.
Put the results in a table and
see if you can deduce the
general formula for the area
from $x = 0$ to a line $x = a$.

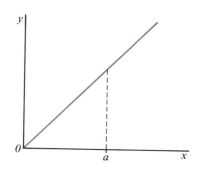

The area under the curve $y = x^2$

It is not so easy to discover the
general formula because it is not
so obvious, and you can only find
approximate areas.
Find the approximate areas from
$x = 0$ to the line $x = 1$, then to
the line $x = 2$, then $x = 3$, etc.

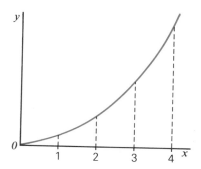

You may be able to discover the formula if you look at 3 × areas.

4. **The birthday problem**

Perhaps there are two people in your class with birthdays on the same day of the
year. You may think that this is a rather unlikely occurrence, considering that
there are only 30 or so of pupils in the class, and 365 days in the year, so it
would be interesting to find the probability of this happening.

Before finding the theoretical probability, find the experimental probability that
out of a group of 30 people, at least 2 have a birthday on the same day.
You will have to get lists of birthdays of groups of 30 people. You may be able to
use the school registers and use the first 30 pupils on each. If there are less than
30 pupils in a class, you can include some dates from another list. If there are
twins born on the same day, only include one of them. (Their birthdays are not
independent.)
If you cannot use class lists, you may be able to use lists of birthdays of famous
people, chosen randomly, from reference books. If that is not possible, you can
program a computer to produce lists of 30 random dates.

Get as many lists as you can, and find the experimental value of the probability.

Now to work out the theoretical probability.

First, find the probability that 30 people all have birthdays on different days. Assume that a year has 365 days. The slight difference of an extra day every 4 years will not affect the result.

Start with one person, who can have a birthday on any one day.
The probability that a second person has a birthday on a different day is $\frac{364}{365}$.
What is the probability that a third person has a birthday on a different day to the first two?
So, what is the probability that 3 people all have different birthdays?
What is the probability that a 4th person has a birthday on a different day to the first 3?
So, what is the probability that 4 people all have different birthdays?

Continue in this way.
You should find that the probability that 30 people all have different birthdays is $\frac{364}{365} \times \frac{363}{365} \times \frac{362}{365} \times \ldots \times \frac{336}{365}$.

Now, you cannot work out all the numerator and then all the denominator on your calculator as the figures will get too big. Instead, divide and multiply alternatively, i.e. $364 \div 365 \times 363 \div 365 \times \ldots \times 336 \div 365$.
If you put 365 into the memory it will save time.
If you have a programmable calculator or a computer, you can work out the expression with a simple program.

Finally, subtract the answer from 1 to find the probability that at least 2 people out of 30 have birthdays on the same day.
Compare the theoretical result with your experimental result.

5.   **Use of trigonometrical tables**

You may need to use trigonometrical formulae at a time when you do not have a scientific calculator available, and instead you have to use trig. tables which were used before calculators were developed.

NATURAL TANGENTS

Degree	0′ 0°.0	6′ 0°.1	12′ 0°.2	18′ 0°.3	24′ 0°.4	30′ 0°.5	36′ 0°.6	42′ 0°.7	48′ 0°.8	54′ 0°.9	1	2	3	4	5
0	·0000	0017	0035	0052	0070	0087	0105	0122	0140	0157	3	6	9	12	15
1	·0175	0192	0209	0227	0244	0262	0279	0297	0314	0332	3	6	9	12	15
2	·0349	0367	0384	0402	0419	0437	0454	0472	0489	0507	3	6	9	12	15
3	·0524	0542	0559	0577	0594	0612	0629	0647	0664	0682	3	6	9	12	15
4	·0699	0717	0734	0752	0769	0787	0805	0822	0840	0857	3	6	9	12	15
5	·0875	0892	0910	0928	0945	0963	0981	0998	1016	1033	3	6	9	12	15
6	·1051	1069	1086	1104	1122	1139	1157	1175	1192	1210	3	6	9	12	15
7	·1228	1246	1263	1281	1299	1317	1334	1352	1370	1388	3	6	9	12	15
8	·1405	1423	1441	1459	1477	1495	1512	1530	1548	1566	3	6	9	12	15
9	·1584	1602	1620	1638	1655	1673	1691	1709	1727	1745	3	6	9	12	15
10	·1763	1781	1799	1817	1835	1853	1871	1890	1908	1926	3	6	9	12	15
11	·1944	1962	1980	1998	2016	2035	2053	2071	2089	2107	3	6	9	12	15
12	·2126	2144	2162	2180	2199	2217	2235	2254	2272	2290	3	6	9	12	15
13	·2309	2327	2345	2364	2382	2401	2419	2438	2456	2475	3	6	9	12	16
14	·2493	2512	2530	2549	2568	2586	2605	2623	2642	2661	3	6	9	12	16
15	·2679	2698	2717	2736	2754	2773	2792	2811	2830	2849	3	6	9	13	16
16	·2867	2886	2905	2924	2943	2962	2981	3000	3019	3038	3	6	9	13	16
17	·3057	3076	3096	3115	3134	3153	3172	3191	3211	3230	3	6	10	13	16
18	·3249	3269	3288	3307	3327	3346	3365	3385	3404	3424	3	6	10	13	16
19	·3443	3463	3482	3502	3522	3541	3561	3581	3600	3620	3	7	10	13	16
20	·3640	3659	3679	3699	3719	3739	3759	3779	3799	3819	3	7	10	13	17
21	·3839	3859	3879	3899	3919	3939	3959	3979	4000	4020	3	7	10	13	17
22	·4040	4061	4081	4101	4122	4142	4163	4183	4204	4224	3	7	10	14	17
23	·4245	4265	4286	4307	4327	4348	4369	4390	4411	4431	3	7	10	14	18
24	·4452	4473	4494	4515	4536	4557	4578	4599	4621	4642	4	7	11	14	18
25	·4663	4684	4706	4727	4748	4770	4791	4813	4834	4856	4	7	11	14	18
26	·4877	4899	4921	4942	4964	4986	5008	5029	5051	5073	4	7	11	15	18
27	·5095	5117	5139	5161	5184	5206	5228	5250	5272	5295	4	7	11	15	18
28	·5317	5340	5362	5384	5407	5430	5452	5475	5498	5520	4	8	11	15	19
29	·5543	5566	5589	5612	5635	5658	5681	5704	5727	5750	4	8	12	15	19

Here is an extract from 3-figure sine tables.

SINES

Degrees	.0	.1	.2	.3	.4	.5	.6	.7	.8	.9
0	0.000	0.002	0.003	0.005	0.007	0.009	0.010	0.012	0.014	0.016
1	0.017	0.019	0.021	0.023	0.024	0.026	0.028	0.030	0.031	0.033
2	0.035	0.037	0.038	0.040	0.042	0.044	0.045	0.047	0.049	0.051
3	0.052	0.054	0.056	0.058	0.059	0.061	0.063	0.065	0.066	0.068
4	0.070	0.071	0.073	0.075	0.077	0.078	0.080	0.082	0.084	0.085
5	0.087	0.089	0.091	0.092	0.094	0.096	0.098	0.099	0.101	0.103
6	0.105	0.106	0.108	0.110	0.111	0.113	0.115	0.117	0.118	0.120
7	0.122	0.124	0.125	0.127	0.129	0.131	0.132	0.134	0.136	0.137
8	0.139	0.141	0.143	0.144	0.146	0.148	0.150	0.151	0.153	0.155
9	0.156	0.158	0.160	0.162	0.163	0.165	0.167	0.168	0.170	0.172
10	0.174	0.175	0.177	0.179	0.181	0.182	0.184	0.186	0.187	0.189
11	0.191	0.193	0.194	0.196	0.198	0.199	0.201	0.203	0.204	0.206
12	0.208	0.210	0.211	0.213	0.215	0.216	0.218	0.220	0.222	0.223
13	0.225	0.227	0.228	0.230	0.232	0.233	0.235	0.237	0.239	0.240
14	0.242	0.244	0.245			0.250	0.252	0.254	0.255	0.257

Use this table to find
1   the 3-figure values for sin 2°, sin 3.5°, sin 9.9°, sin 12°,
2   the angle in degrees, correct to 1 decimal place, whose sine is 0.087, 0.071, 0.189, 0.217.

The tables give values for angles only up to 90°.
For obtuse angles you need to use the formulae $\sin \theta = \sin(180° - \theta)$
$\cos \theta = -\cos(180° - \theta)$
$\tan \theta = -\tan(180° - \theta)$.   You are unlikely to need this one.

e.g. sin 170° = sin (180° − 170°) = sin 10° = 0.174
cos 134° = −cos(180° − 134°) = −cos 46° = −0.695 (from tables)

Using the table above find
3   the values of sin 168°, sin 173.5°, sin 175°, sin 179.3°,
4   the obtuse angle in degrees, correct to 1 decimal place, whose sine is 0.242, 0.144, 0.080, 0.1.

6. **NIM**

This is a very old mathematical game for 2 players.
It is played with a number of counters (or match sticks) which are placed in 3 groups.

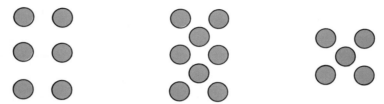

When it is your turn you can remove one or more counters, but they must all be taken from one group only.
You win the game if your opponent takes the last counter.

Play several games, beginning with a number of counters between 12 and 30. It need not be the same number in each game, and the 3 groups can contain unequal numbers of counters at the start of a game.

After playing several games, you may have noticed that if you leave one counter in each of 3 piles then you are bound to win.

You can also win if one pile is empty and there are 2 counters in each of the other two piles.

If you leave 3 counters in one pile, 2 in another and 1 in the third pile, show that whatever your opponent takes away, you can win.

In some cases, this is because you can reduce the position to 1, 1, 1 or 2, 2, 0 and then win, as above.

Find other positions which are such that whatever your opponent moves, you can reduce the counters to 3, 2, 1; 1, 1, 1; 2, 2, 0 or another winning position already discovered.

Make a list of all positions which guarantee you a win if you play carefully.

Now, suppose that 10, 9, 3 is such a position. We now write the numbers as sums of powers of 2, using each power once only. The powers of 2 are 1, 2, 4, 8, 16, . . . (1 is 2^0.) Every number can be written in this way.
$10 = 8 + 2, 9 = 8 + 1, 3 = 2 + 1$.
We can show the three numbers with ticks in columns.

	16	8	4	2	1
10 9 3		✓ ✓		✓ ✓	✓ ✓
		2		2	2

(Total ticks in each column)

Make such a table for all the winning positions you have found. Then make tables for some combinations which are not winning positions.

Apart from the positions 1, 1, 1; and 1, 0, 0; what do you notice about all the winning positions, and what about the losing positions ?

If when it is your turn, there is a losing position, how can you work out what counters to remove to make it into a winning position ?

When you have worked out a winning strategy you can challenge all your friends to try to beat you. You can only lose when it is your first turn and the groups already form a winning combination.

7.   **A perpetual calendar**

You can make this calendar to find the day of the week for any given date.

It is made from cardboard. You need 3 circles, radii 6.5 cm, 5 cm and 4.5 cm. You also need a metal paper-fastener to fasten them through their centres.
Divide all the circles into 7 equal sectors.
Use your protractor to do this.
Draw the lines in red (or another
bright colour). The largest
circle must be marked on both
sides, with the lines matching
on both sides.

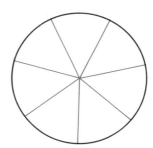

Largest circle:

On one side draw circles of radii 5 cm, 4.3 cm and 3.5 cm.
In each sector, on the outside portion, write the dates of the month, as shown.
Use the 2 inner circles as guidelines to cut out the 7 shaded regions, leaving
about 4 mm on each side of the red lines.
On the other side, draw a circle radius 5.5 cm. In each sector, on the outside
portion, write the years of the century as given. You have to fit 14 or 15 in each
sector so maybe it would be best to write them in pencil first.
One sector is shown here, starting 00, 06, 17, . . .
This one is on the back of the sector with 1, 8, 15, 22, 29 on.
The complete list is given on the next page.

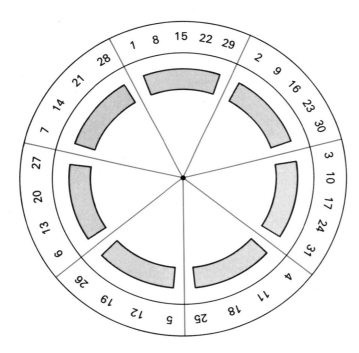

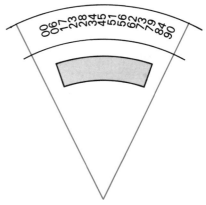

Numbers to go on the back of the sector starting with this number:

1	2	3	4	5	6	7
00	05	04	09	03	02	01
06	11	10	15	08	13	07
17	16	21	20	14	19	12
23	22	27	26	25	24	18
28	33	32	37	31	30	29
34	39	38	43	36	41	35
45	44	49	48	42	47	40
51	50	55	54	53	52	46
56	61	60	65	59	58	57
62	67	66	71	64	69	63
73	72	77	76	70	75	68
79	78	83	82	81	80	74
84	89	88	93	87	86	85
90	95	94	99	92	97	91
				98		96

Middle-sized circle:

Put it in front of the large circle with the centres and the red lines coinciding, then turn both circles over and write the days SUN, MON, . . . , on the smaller circle in the parts seen through the cut-off regions of the large circle. Write them neatly, one in the centre of each space, labelling them clockwise from SUN, MON, onwards.
On the other side, label as shown.
18 is in the sector which has SUN on its back. (19 will be in the sector on the back of FRI.)

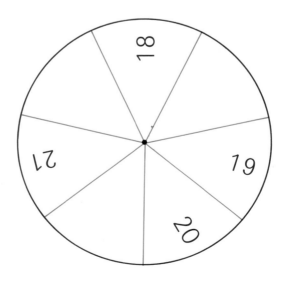

Small circle:

Label each sector as shown.
Cut a small part (shaded) out
of the JUN sector. When you
put the small circle on top
of the large circle with
centres and red lines coinciding,
one of the cut-out holes will
show below this part.

Make a small hole in the centres
for the paper-fastener to go throug|

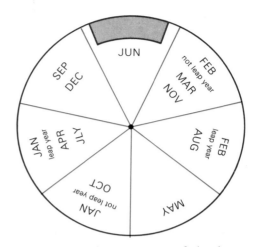

Put the middle-sized circle with the numbers side showing, on top of the large
circle with the small century numbers showing.
Then turn both pieces over together and put the small circle on top of the large
circle, and put the paper-fastener through the centres of all 3 circles.

To find out any day of the week:

e.g. 25th December, 1999.

On the back, turn the medium-sized circle until the red lines coincide, with the
number 19 (for 1900's) in the same sector as the small number 99.
Keeping those 2 circles together, turn over and move the small circle until the red
lines coincide, with DEC in the same sector as number 25.
Through the space, SAT is showing, so Christmas Day in 1999 is on a Saturday.

On what day of the week is your birthday in 1999?
On what day of the week were you born?

If the date you want is in January or February, you use different sectors
depending on whether or not the year is a leap year.
How do you find out if a year is a leap year?
Note that 1800, 1900 were not leap years and 2100 won't be, but 2000 will be a
leap year.

If you want the years starting 22 on your calendar, then find 31 Dec, 2199, and
decide where to put 22 so that 1 Jan, 2200 is on the next day. (The calendar
might have been reformed before that time, though.)
You can also put 17 on your calendar in a similar way, but the calendar is not
accurate before 14 September 1752 when 11 days were left out of September.

8. **Use of the normal distribution for sampling**

When sampling is carried out for testing as part of an industrial or scientific process, the mean of the sample will provide information about the mean of the whole population.

e.g. A random sample of 50 rods is taken from a large batch and measured. The mean size is 21 cm.

Now if you were asked to estimate the mean of the whole batch of rods, then you would probably deduce that it was somewhere near 21 cm.

In fact, the means of all possible samples form a normal distribution, and the population mean is the mean of that distribution.

Using the standard deviation of the sample as well, the manufacturer can use the properties of the normal distribution to fix a range of lengths between which the population mean probably lies.

We will not go into further details here.

If you have a suitable computer program, you can investigate the means of random samples of 20 numbers taken from the set of whole numbers between 0 and 100 inclusive.

When you have 100 sample means, group them in classes 0-<10, 10-<20, etc, to make a grouped frequency distribution. Draw a histogram of the distribution and comment on its shape.

Calculate the mean of the frequency distribution of sample means, and see how close it is to the population mean, which is 50.

If you do not have a computer, then instead, investigate the sample means of a small population of 5 items, which have values 2, 8, 14, 16, 20.

Take all possible samples of 2 numbers, starting with 2 and 8.

There are 10 different possible samples.

Find the mean of each sample and list these means.

Find the mean of all the sample means and compare it with the mean of the population.

PUZZLE

49. In a 2-digit number the units digit is 2 more than the tens digit.
On reversing the digits a number is formed whose square exceeds the square of the original number by 2376.
Find the original number.

Index

Answers

Some answers have been given corrected to reasonable degrees of accuracy, depending on the questions.
There may be variations in answers where questions involve drawings or graphs.
Sometimes it will not be possible to give answers to the same degree of accuracy, depending on the scale used.

Page 3   Exercise 1.1

1. **1** 32 cm
    2 21.3 cm
    3 46.8 cm

2. **1** 30.2 cm
    2 11.0 cm
    3 45.2 cm

3. **1** $\frac{1}{12}$ **4** 135°
    2 $\frac{1}{8}$ **5** 240°
    3 $\frac{2}{5}$

4. **1** 1.78 cm   **4** 12.6 cm
    2 22.7 cm   **5** 4.36 cm
    3 3.77 cm

5. **1** 18.0 cm
    2 27.9 cm
    3 21.1 cm

Page 7   Exercise 1.2

1. **1** 10.6 cm²   **4** 11.1 cm²
    2 10.8 cm²   **5** 22.9 cm²
    3 10.2 cm²

2. **1** $\frac{3}{8}$ **4** 160°
    2 $\frac{1}{5}$ **5** 300°
    3 $\frac{7}{12}$ **6** 108°

3. **1** 19.7 cm²   **4** 5.45 cm²
    2 84.8 cm²   **5** 31.4 cm²
    3 9.37 cm²

Page 9   Exercise 1.3

1. **1** 310 cm²   **3** 736 cm²
    2 336 cm²   **4** 294 cm²

2. **1** 286 cm²   **4** 2430 cm²
    2 75.4 cm²   **5** 339 cm²
    3 104 cm²

Page 11   Exercise 1.4

1. **1** 169 cm³   **3** 600 cm³
    2 800 cm³   **4** 625 m³

2. **1** 539 cm³   **4** 2410 cm³
    2 1360 cm³   **5** 4.19 cm³
    3 3050 cm³

3. 687 cm³

Page 14   Exercise 1.5

1. **1** 64:25   **4** 9:25
    2 16:49   **5** 121:16
    3 1:9   **6** 16:81

2. **1** 4:9, 8:27
    2 49:16, 343:64
    3 1:9, 1:27
    4 25:9, 125:27
    5 1:4, 1:8

3. **1** 22.4 cm²   **4** 12 cm
    2 324 cm²   **5** 15 cm
    3 1350 cm³

Page 16   Exercise 1.6

1. **1** 884 cm²   **2** 1410 cm³

2. 7.0 cm

3. nose: 0.072 m³
    body: 0.543 m³
    tail: 0.029 m³
    total: 0.644 m³ (644 000 cm³)

4. **1** 24 m   **4** 45°
   2 10 m   **5** 20.5 m
   3 22.6°

5. 30.7 cm²

6. **1** ΔXAB, ΔXCD
   2 5 cm
   3 4 : 9

7. **1** 8 : 27
   2 2 : 3
   3 4 : 9

8. **1** 3 cm
   2 8 : 27
   3 8 : 19

9. 22.5 km, 50 km²

10. 40 cm, 1920 cm², 61 440 cm³

11. **1** 700 g   **2** 24 cm

12. 225

13. **1** 96°, 72°, 60°, 132°
    2 £875, £1050, £1925, £2975, £5775
    3 6.3 cm

14. $S = 4\pi r^2$

15. Cone: $S = \pi rl$, 126 cm²

16. 57.3°

Page 28   Exercise 2.1

1. **1** Yes, $\Delta ABC \equiv \Delta DEF$, SSS;
      $\angle A = \angle D$, $\angle B = \angle E$, $\angle C = \angle F$
   2 Yes, $\Delta ABC \equiv \Delta JGH$, AAS; $AC = JH$,
      $BC = GH$, $\angle C = \angle H$
   3 No
   4 Yes, $\Delta ABC \equiv \Delta QRP$, AAS; $AC = QP$,
      $BC = RP$, $\angle B = \angle R$
   5 Yes, $\Delta ABC \equiv \Delta TSU$, RHS; $AC = TU$,
      $\angle B = \angle S$, $\angle C = \angle U$
   6 No
   7 Yes, $\Delta ABC \equiv \Delta GFE$, SAS; $BC = FE$,
      $\angle B = \angle F$, $\angle C = \angle E$
   8 Yes, $\Delta ABC \equiv \Delta JHK$, SSS; $\angle A = \angle J$,
      $\angle B = \angle H$, $\angle C = \angle K$
   9 Yes, $\Delta ABC \equiv \Delta NPM$, RHS;
      $BC = PM$, $\angle A = \angle N$, $\angle B = \angle P$
   10 Yes, $\Delta ABC \equiv \Delta SRQ$, AAS;
       $AB = SR$, $BC = RQ$, $\angle C = \angle Q$

2. (AAS)

3. **1** (SAS)

4. **1** (SAS)
   2 $\angle ODA$
   3 (AAS)
   4 CX

5. **1** (RHS)   **2** (SAS)

6. $\Delta ABD \equiv \Delta CBD$, (RHS)

8. (SSS); $\angle PAB = \angle QAB$,
   $\angle APB = \angle AQB$, $\angle PBA = \angle QBA$

9. $\Delta AMD \equiv \Delta ANE$, (AAS)

10. $\Delta ABP \equiv \Delta CBQ$, (SAS)

Page 35   Exercise 2.2

1. **1** $\overrightarrow{AB} = \begin{pmatrix} 4 \\ 1 \end{pmatrix}$, $\overrightarrow{BC} = \begin{pmatrix} 2 \\ 2 \end{pmatrix}$,

      $\overrightarrow{AB} + \overrightarrow{BC} = \begin{pmatrix} 6 \\ 3 \end{pmatrix}$

   2 $\overrightarrow{AB} = \begin{pmatrix} 2 \\ 3 \end{pmatrix}$, $\overrightarrow{BC} = \begin{pmatrix} 4 \\ -2 \end{pmatrix}$,

      $\overrightarrow{AB} + \overrightarrow{BC} = \begin{pmatrix} 6 \\ 1 \end{pmatrix}$

   3 $\overrightarrow{AB} = \begin{pmatrix} 0 \\ -4 \end{pmatrix}$, $\overrightarrow{BC} = \begin{pmatrix} -4 \\ 1 \end{pmatrix}$,

      $\overrightarrow{AB} + \overrightarrow{BC} = \begin{pmatrix} -4 \\ -3 \end{pmatrix}$

   4 $\overrightarrow{AB} = \begin{pmatrix} 6 \\ 1 \end{pmatrix}$, $\overrightarrow{BC} = \begin{pmatrix} -3 \\ 2 \end{pmatrix}$,

      $\overrightarrow{AB} + \overrightarrow{BC} = \begin{pmatrix} 3 \\ 3 \end{pmatrix}$

2. **1** $\overrightarrow{AB} = \begin{pmatrix} 4 \\ 0 \end{pmatrix}$, $\overrightarrow{AD} = \begin{pmatrix} 1 \\ 3 \end{pmatrix}$,

      $\overrightarrow{AB} + \overrightarrow{AD} = \begin{pmatrix} 5 \\ 3 \end{pmatrix}$

   2 $\overrightarrow{AB} = \begin{pmatrix} -1 \\ -4 \end{pmatrix}$, $\overrightarrow{AD} = \begin{pmatrix} 3 \\ -3 \end{pmatrix}$,

      $\overrightarrow{AB} + \overrightarrow{AD} = \begin{pmatrix} 2 \\ -7 \end{pmatrix}$

3 $\overrightarrow{AB} = \begin{pmatrix} -2 \\ 2 \end{pmatrix}$, $\overrightarrow{AD} = \begin{pmatrix} 4 \\ -1 \end{pmatrix}$,

$\overrightarrow{AB} + \overrightarrow{AD} = \begin{pmatrix} 2 \\ 1 \end{pmatrix}$

4 $\overrightarrow{AB} = \begin{pmatrix} 0 \\ -3 \end{pmatrix}$, $\overrightarrow{AD} = \begin{pmatrix} 5 \\ 0 \end{pmatrix}$,

$\overrightarrow{AB} + \overrightarrow{AD} = \begin{pmatrix} 5 \\ -3 \end{pmatrix}$

3.
1 $\begin{pmatrix} 2 \\ -1 \end{pmatrix}$ 3 $\begin{pmatrix} 4 \\ -5 \end{pmatrix}$

2 $\begin{pmatrix} -2 \\ 5 \end{pmatrix}$ 4 $\begin{pmatrix} 9 \\ -1 \end{pmatrix}$

4.
1 $\begin{pmatrix} 3 \\ -3 \end{pmatrix}$ 3 $\begin{pmatrix} -6 \\ 3 \end{pmatrix}$

2 $\begin{pmatrix} -4 \\ -1 \end{pmatrix}$ 4 $\begin{pmatrix} -5 \\ -3 \end{pmatrix}$

6.
1 $\overrightarrow{AC}$ 3 $\overrightarrow{AC}$ 5 $\overrightarrow{BG}$
2 $\overrightarrow{DB}$ 4 $\overrightarrow{AD}$

7.
1 $\overrightarrow{OA} = \begin{pmatrix} 3 \\ 3 \end{pmatrix}$, $\overrightarrow{OC} = \begin{pmatrix} 5 \\ 1 \end{pmatrix}$

2 $\overrightarrow{OC}$
3 $\overrightarrow{OB}$
4 $\overrightarrow{OC}$
5 E (10, 2)
6 F (−8, −4)

8.
3 X (8, 8)

4 $\overrightarrow{AX} = \begin{pmatrix} 7 \\ 6 \end{pmatrix}$, $\overrightarrow{XC} = \begin{pmatrix} 7 \\ 6 \end{pmatrix}$

5 10 units

9. $\begin{pmatrix} 5 \\ 14 \end{pmatrix}$

10. $a = 1, b = -1$

11. $\begin{pmatrix} 2 \\ -59 \end{pmatrix}$, pentagram

12. Q (5, 7), R (11, 3); $\overrightarrow{OG} = \begin{pmatrix} 7 \\ 4 \end{pmatrix}$

Page 39   Exercise 2.3

1. 1 $\frac{1}{2}(\mathbf{b} + \mathbf{d})$ 2 $\mathbf{d} - \mathbf{b}$ 3 $\frac{1}{2}\mathbf{d} - \mathbf{b}$
2. $\overrightarrow{AB} = \overrightarrow{AC} + \overrightarrow{CB}$, $\overrightarrow{ED} = 2\overrightarrow{CB} + 2\overrightarrow{AC}$
5. 1 $\mathbf{b}$ 3 $\mathbf{a} - \mathbf{b}$
   2 $-\mathbf{a}$ 4 $\frac{1}{2}\mathbf{a} + \frac{1}{2}\mathbf{b}$
7. 2 $2\overrightarrow{CM}$ 3 $2\overrightarrow{NM}$

Page 41   Exercise 2.4

9. 2.1 km, 050°

10. 1 26 km/h, 23°
    2 19 km/h, 24°
    3 33 km/h, 10°
    4 62°, 15 km/h, $\frac{1}{2}$ minute
    5 206 km/h, 076°

11. 1 9.2 N, 14°
    2 11.5 N, 42°
    3 6.1 N, 32°
    4 T_1 = 20 N, T_2 = 34.6 N

Page 66   Exercise 4.1

1. 1 AC = 20 cm, AG = 20.6 cm
   2 17.4°
   3 14.0°

2. 1 25 cm
   2 24.5 cm
   3 73.7°
   4 78.3°

3. 1 10 cm 4 63.4°
   2 8.7 cm 5 60°
   3 17.3 cm

4. 1 6.9 cm
   2 17 cm
   3 24.1°

5. 1 8.1 cm
   2 60.3°
   3 9 cm
   4 51.1°

6. 1 8.7 cm
   2 11.2 cm
   3 50.8°

Page 68   Exercise 4.2

1. **1** 65 m
   2 6.8 m
   3 6°

2. $DB = 110$ m, $DC = 72$ m, distance 132 m

3. **1** 3.6 m
   2 5.6 m
   3 40°

4. $AD = 670$ m, $DC = 1490$ m; C to A, 1630 m, 336°

5. **1** C, G
   2 $AB = 10$ cm, $EF = 5$ cm, $FG = 13$ cm
   3 37°

6. **1** 4.24 m
   2 6.56 m
   3 54°
   4 50°

7. 22°

8. Direct, 8.77 m; via P, 10.82 m; via BF, 11.70 m; via EH, 11.18 m; least via P

9. 7.9 m

10. **1** 8.57 km
    2 10.46 km
    3 4.00 km
    4 21°

Page 75
Example 1 $x = 1.6$ or 6.4

Page 76
Example 2 $x = -3.9$ or 0.7 or 3.2

Page 78   Exercise 5.1

1. **1** $(-1, 1), (0, -2), (1, 1),$ $(2, 10), (3, 25)$
   2 $(-1, \frac{1}{4}), (0, \frac{1}{5}), (1, \frac{1}{6}), (2, \frac{1}{7}), (3, \frac{1}{8})$
   3 $(-1, 0), (0, 0), (1, -4), (2, -6),$ $(3, 0)$

2. $f(0) = 0, f(10) = 70, f(-2) = 10,$ $f(3x) = 9x^2 - 9x,$ $f(x + 1) = x^2 - x - 2$

3. **1** $\dfrac{1}{x} = 5 - 2x \quad (2x^2 - 5x + 1 = 0)$
   2 $x^3 = 2x^2 + 1 \quad (x^3 - 2x^2 - 1 = 0)$
   3 $y = x - 2$
   4 $y = x^3 - 1$

4. **1** $x = -1.73$ or 1.73
   2 $x = -2.82$ or 1.07; $4x^2 + 7x - 12 = 0$
   3 $x = -0.73$ or 2.73

5. **1** $x = 5.24$
   2 $x = 2.62$; $x^2 + 5x - 20 = 0$
   3 $x = -1.31$ or 3.81

6. **1** $x = 3.68$
   2 $x = -3.16, 0$ or 3.16; $x^3 - 10x = 0$
   3 $x = -2.35$

7. **2** $x = -3.81$ or 2.67; $x^3 + 10x^2 - 90 = 0$; other root negative

8. **2** $x = 1.39$ or 8.61; $x^2 - 10x + 12 = 0$

9. **1** $x = -0.79$ or 3.79
   2 $x = -1.45$ or 3.45

Page 85   Exercise 5.2

1. **2** $x = 35$ or 325
   3 $x = 37$ or 323
   4 $x = 75$ or 265

3. **3** $x = 72$
   4 $x = 252$

4. $x = 120$ or 240

5. $x = 12$ or 48

Page 86   Exercise 5.3

1. $x = -3.8, 0.7$ or 3.1; $x = 0.69$

2. $x^2 - 6x + 6 = 0$; 1.27 m and 4.73 m

3. 2.52

4. $10t - 5t^2 = -10$ (or $t^2 - 2t - 2 = 0$); 2.7 s after it is thrown

5. 38.2°

6. 4 m

7. semicircle centre (2, 0), radius 6 units; 5.7 units

8. maximum $y = 2.24$ when $x = 63.4$; $x = 15.6$

Page 90   Exercise A1

1. 96

2. 4

3. £3.14

4. $\frac{1}{2}$

5. $\frac{3}{4}$ hour

6. 20%

7. $4\,cm^2$

8. 75

9. 9 cm

10. $x^3 = 2x + 10$

11. **1** Yes   **2** No

12. £3.25

13. 48

14. 23, 29

15. $40\,cm^3$

Page 91   Exercise A2

1. 50

2. 45°

3. 41

4. $\begin{pmatrix} -4 \\ 10 \end{pmatrix}$

5. 3^n

6. 60°

7. £2.70

8. 13 cm

9. 0.054

10. 90

11. 8 cm

12. 1st Dec

13. $\frac{1}{4}$

14. $11\frac{1}{2}$ kg

15. 5 cm

Page 92   Exercise A3

1. 25ℓ

2. $AB = 12.1$ cm, $BC = 8.8$ cm

3. **1** $\frac{1}{4}$ **2** $\frac{5}{16}$ **3** $\frac{1}{4}$

4. 54°

5. $-6, 0, 0, 0, 6$

7. $v = \sqrt{\dfrac{2E}{m}}$

8. 28

10. **1** $4x^2 + 4x - 3$
    2 $4x^2 - 11x - 3$
    3 $4x^2 - 12x + 9$
    4 $4x^2 - 1$

11. $1 : 250\,000$

12. 40

13. 450

14. $B\,(3, 0)$, $C\,(6, 10)$; B, E, F lie on a straight line and $BE = 2EF$

15. $BC = 4.5$ cm

16. $\frac{3}{5}$

17. **1** 36.9°   **3** 17 cm
    2 15 cm   **4** 32.0°

18. **1** $x > 7\frac{1}{2}$ **2** $-5 \leqslant x \leqslant 5$

19. **1** 5   **2** -4

20. $x = 30, x = 90$

Page 95   Exercise A4

1. **1** 8890 km
    2 5000 km
    3 3340 km
    4 1930 km

2. area of $OABC = 22$ unit^2

7. **1** $22.5\,cm^2$ **4** $36.9\,cm^2$
    2 $45.1\,cm^2$ **5** $11.1\,cm^2$
    3 $6.80\,cm^2$

Page 110   Exercise 6.1

1. **1** $\frac{1}{32}$ **2** $\frac{13}{32}$

2. **1** $\frac{5}{28}$ **2** $\frac{1}{56}$ **3** $\frac{45}{56}$

3. **1** $\frac{12}{145}$ **2** $\frac{14}{29}$ **3** $\frac{63}{145}$

4. **1** $\frac{1}{6}$ **3** $\frac{3}{10}$
    2 $\frac{1}{2}$ **4** $\frac{1}{30}$

5. **1** $\frac{5}{42}$ **2** $\frac{1}{21}$

6. $\frac{1}{6}$

7. **1** 0.857   **2** 0.143

8. **1** 28   **3** $\frac{1}{4}$
   2 $\frac{1}{4}$ **4** $\frac{3}{7}$

9. **1** $\frac{27}{70}$ **2** $\frac{43}{70}$

10. **1** 0.16   **2** 0.3

11. $\frac{1}{5}, \frac{1}{2}$

12. **1** $\frac{1}{16}$ **2** $\frac{25}{412}$

13. **1** $\frac{1}{200}$ **2** $\frac{7}{50}$ **3** $\frac{171}{200}$

14. **1** $\frac{2}{5}$ **2** $\frac{7}{10}$ **3** $\frac{1}{2}$

15. **1** $\frac{4}{5}$ **2** $\frac{4}{25}$

Page 114   Exercise 6.2

1. **1** 0.735   **2** 0.265   **3** 0.0025

2. **1** $\frac{1}{6}$ **3** $\frac{2}{3}$

   2 $\frac{4}{15}$ **4** $\frac{5}{12}$

3. **1** $\frac{9}{50}$ **2** $\frac{37}{100}$

4. $\frac{15}{16}$

5. **1** $\frac{17}{24}$ **3** $\frac{1}{10}$

   2 $\frac{23}{120}$ **4** $\frac{11}{40}$

Page 123   Exercise 7.1

1. $y = 5x - 3$ 6. $y = 3^x$

2. $y = x^3$ 7. $y = x^2 + 2x$

3. $y = 10^x$ 8. $y = \dfrac{1}{x + 3}$

4. $y = \dfrac{36}{x}$ 9. $y = x^2 - 4$

5. $y = 10 - 4x$ 10. $y = x^3 + x$

Page 125   Exercise 7.2

1. **1** $\frac{1}{64}$ **5** 2   **8** 4
   2 1   **6** $\frac{1}{3}$ **9** 2
   3 $\frac{1}{27}$ **7** 27   **10** $\frac{1}{1\,000\,000}$
   4 5

2. **1** 1   **4** d
   2 b **5** $e^{-\frac{3}{5}}$
   3 c^3

3. **1** 5   **5** 0
   2 4   **6** $-\frac{1}{2}$
   3 -2 **7** $\frac{3}{4}$
   4 $\frac{1}{3}$ **8** 2

4. **1** 10^7 **4** 10^2
   2 10^{-2} **5** $10^{1\frac{1}{2}}$
   3 10^{10} **6** 10^2

Page 131   Exercise 7.3

1. **1** $a(a - 4)$
   2 $3(4b^2 + 1)$
   3 $2c(1 + 3c)$
   4 $d(d - 2e + 1)$
   5 $g^2(f - g)$
   6 $7h(3 + j^2)$
   7 $6k(5 - 2m + 4n)$
   8 $5pq(pq + r)$
   9 $2t(3s - t)$
   10 $u(1 - 2u + 3u^2)$

2. **1** $(a + 2)(a - 2)$
   2 $(9 + b)(9 - b)$
   3 $(2c + 1)(2c - 1)$
   4 $(d + 8)(d - 8)$
   5 $(1 + e)(1 - e)$
   6 $(3f + g)(3f - g)$
   7 $(4h + 5)(4h - 5)$
   8 $(7 + 2j)(7 - 2j)$
   9 $(k + 1)(k - 1)$
   10 $3(m + 1)(m - 1)$
   11 $(9n + 1)(9n - 1)$
   12 $(pq + 3)(pq - 3)$
   13 $5(1 + 2r)(1 - 2r)$
   14 $2(5s + t)(5s - t)$
   15 $4(3 + u)(3 - u)$

3. **1** $(a - p)(b + 2r)$
    2 $(c + d)(3 + c)$
    3 $(e - f)(p - 3q)$
    4 $(h - 5)(g + 1)$
    5 $(3 - 2k)(4 + 5m)$
    6 $(p - q)(3 - a)$
    7 $(7s + 4)(3r - 4)$
    8 $(t - 3)(t - 2u)$
    9 $(x + 1)(x^2 + 1)$
    10 $(y - 1)(x + 1)$

4. **1** $(a + 5)(a + 4)$
    2 $(b - 3)(b - 2)$
    3 $(c + 20)(c - 4)$
    4 $(d + 2)(d - 6)$
    5 $(e + 5)(e - 2)$
    6 $(f + 4)(f - 5)$
    7 $(g - 8h)(g - 4h)$
    8 $(h + 2)^2$
    9 $(j + 7)(j - 3)$
    10 $(k - 16)(k - 9)$
    11 $(m + 8)(m - 6)$
    12 $(n + 7p)^2$
    13 $(p - 10)(p - 6)$
    14 $(q + 12)(q + 7)$
    15 $(r + 2s)(r - 10s)$
    16 $(s - 15)(s - 1)$
    17 $(t + 4u)(t - 3u)$
    18 $(v + 5)(v - 8)$
    19 $(x + 15)(x + 3)$
    20 $(y + 2z)(y - 4z)$

5. **1** $(3x + 2)(x + 1)$
    2 $(2x - y)(x - 6y)$
    3 $2(x + 5)(x - 3)$
    4 $(2x + 5y)(x - 2y)$
    5 $(3x + 4)(x - 5)$
    6 $3(x + 3)(x + 1)$
    7 $(5x - 4)(x + 2)$
    8 $(3x - 1)(x - 7)$
    9 $(3x + 4)(x - 3)$
    10 $2(x + 7)(x - 1)$
    11 $(2x - 1)(x + 6)$
    12 $(3x - 16y)(x + 2y)$
    13 $(2x + 3)(x + 2)$
    14 $(2x - 3)(x - 5)$
    15 $3(x + 2)(x - 7)$
    16 $(3x - 2y)(x + y)$
    17 $(5x + 6)(x + 2)$

    18 $4(x - y)^2$
    19 $2(x + 3)^2$
    20 $(3x + 2)(x - 3)$

6. **1** $3a^2(3a - 8)$
    2 $(3b + 1)(b - 4)$
    3 $(c - d)(p + 2q)$
    4 $2(e + 6)(e - 3)$
    5 $5(f + 2g)(f - 2g)$
    6 $h(h - 9)$
    7 $(1 + k)(1 - 4k)$
    8 $(2m - n)(m + 4n)$
    9 $(3p + 2)(p - 1)$
    10 $(3s + 2t)(5s - 1)$
    11 $2(x + 2)(x - 2)$
    12 $(3x + 2)(2x + 1)$
    13 $x(x^2 + 16)$
    14 $(x - 2)(2y + 1)$
    15 $(3x - 4y)(x + 2y)$
    16 $2(3x + 2y)(3x - 2y)$
    17 $4(3 + x^2)$
    18 $(2x + y)(x - 3y)$
    19 $2(x + 9y)(x - y)$
    20 $(4x - 1)(x + 3)$

Page 133   Exercise 7.4

1. $81, (x + 9)^2$ 4. $\frac{1}{4}, (x - \frac{1}{2})^2$

2. $9, (x - 3)^2$ 5. $20\frac{1}{4}, (x + 4\frac{1}{2})^2$

3. $6\frac{1}{4}, (x + 2\frac{1}{2})^2$

Page 135   Exercise 7.5

1. **1** $\dfrac{11}{6x}$ **4** $2x$

    2 $\dfrac{7 - 3x}{6y}$ **5** $\dfrac{1}{x - 3}$

    3 $\dfrac{x + 4}{(2x - 1)(x + 1)}$

2. **1** $\dfrac{x - 2}{x}$ **4** $\dfrac{4y + 3x}{6}$

    2 $-\frac{1}{3}$

    3 $\dfrac{2x - 1}{x + 3}$ **5** $\dfrac{4(x - 4)}{x - 3}$

3. **1** $x = -4$　　　　**4** $x = 2$
　　2 $x = 3$　　　　　**5** $x = 5$
　　3 $x = -3\frac{1}{2}$

Page 136　　Exercise 7.6

1. 30, 35　　　　　　　6. 125, 625

2. $-16, -20$　　　　　7. $10\frac{2}{3}, 7\frac{1}{9}$

3. 0.125, 0.0625　　　8. $-128, 256$

4. 96, 192　　　　　　9. $2 - \frac{1}{64}, 2 + \frac{1}{128}$

5. 0.00002, 0.000002　10. $\frac{8}{6}, \frac{9}{7}$

Page 139　　Exercise 7.7

1. **1** 22, 27; divergent
　2 $3 - \frac{2}{81}, 3 - \frac{2}{243}$; convergent to 3
　3 $25 + 1, 36 + 1$; divergent
　4 $\frac{1}{4}, -\frac{1}{8}$; convergent to 0
　5 $10 + 0.0001, 10 - 0.00001$;
　　　convergent to 10
　6 720, 5040; divergent
　7 $\frac{60}{5}, \frac{60}{6}$; convergent to 0
　8 $\frac{35}{36}, \frac{48}{49}$; convergent to 1
　9 16, 22; divergent
　10 $\frac{19}{6}, \frac{22}{7}$; convergent to 3

2. **1** 10th term, 488 282; divergent
　2 convergent to 4
　3 convergent to 2.41
　4 convergent to 1.19
　5 10th term, 59 060; divergent
　6 convergent to 0
　7 10th term, 515; divergent
　8 convergent to 1.66 (1.67)

Page 143　　Exercise 7.8

1. **1** $\sqrt[3]{1000}$　$(=10)$
　2 $-4, 0, \sqrt[3]{1000}$
　3 $2\frac{9}{11}, 3.72, -3\frac{1}{2}, 2.\dot{2}0\dot{1}$
　4 $\sqrt{20}, 3\pi, \sqrt[3]{7}$
　5 all of them

2. **1** $(x = 7\frac{1}{2})$, rational not integer
　2 $(x = -4)$, integer
　3 $(x = \pm\sqrt{3})$, irrational

3. **1** $0.\dot{6}, 0.667$　　　**4** 0.096
　2 0.875　　　　　　**5** $0.\dot{4}5\dot{0}, 0.450$
　3 $0.\dot{4}\dot{5}, 0.455$　　**6** $0.\dot{3}0769\dot{2}, 0.308$

4. **1** $\frac{4}{5}$　　　　　　**4** 6
　2 $1\frac{3}{4}$　　　　　**5** 3
　3 $3\sqrt{2}$　　　　　**6** 5

5. **1** 1.414, irrational
　2 9.870, irrational
　3 0.707, irrational
　4 1, rational
　5 $\frac{5}{9}$ (or 0.556), rational
　6 3.162, irrational
　7 0.1, rational
　8 4.414, irrational
　9 6, rational
　10 3, rational

Page 144　　Exercise 7.9

1. **1** $v = 9.8t$　　　**4** $t = 10 - 0.006h$
　2 $W = 15r^2$　　**5** $W = 0.8h^3$
　3 $W = \dfrac{32}{d}$

2. **1** $n = 3, y = 1.25, x = 1.2$
　2 $n = \frac{1}{2}, y = 18, x = 0.25$

3. **1** 16　　　**5** $\frac{3}{8}$　　　**8** 6.01
　2 $2\frac{2}{3}$　　**6** 9　　　**9** $\frac{1}{9}$
　3 127　　**7** 8　　　**10** $2\frac{1}{3}$
　4 $\frac{1}{5}$

4. $(2a - 1)^2$; $(2a - 1 + b)(2a - 1 - b)$

5. volume $= \pi ht(2r + t)$; $880\,\text{cm}^3$

6. $(3x + 2)(2x + 1)$

7. **1** 7 cm　　　**4** 8 cm
　2 11 cm　　**5** 2 cm
　3 12 cm

8. 20

9. 15, 20

10. 15 km/h

11. 13th

12. $\sqrt{70} = 8.3666, \sqrt[3]{100} = 4.6416$

13. $\sin 30° = \cos 60° = \frac{1}{2}(=0.5)$, rational

$\cos 30° = \sin 60° = \frac{\sqrt{3}}{2}\ (=0.8660)$

$\tan 30° = \frac{1}{\sqrt{3}}\ (=0.5774)$

$\tan 60° = \sqrt{3}\ (=0.7321)$

Page 152   Exercise 8.1

Frequency densities, in order:

1. 18, 24, 20.5, 16, 14.5, 11, 10, 4.33

2. 2.75, 11, 19, 15, 9, 3.75

3. 3.6, 3.3, 5.0, 3.6, 1.6

Page 157   Exercise 8.2

1. $\bar{x} = 49$, $s = 2.79$

2. $\bar{x} = 16°$, $s = 2.14$ deg

3. $\bar{x} = 40.4$ min, $s = 9.60$ min

4. $\bar{x} = 28$ years, $s = 4.05$ years

5. $\bar{x} = 1.58$ m, $s = 8.87$ cm

6. $\bar{x} = £107.50$, $s = £16.47$

7. $\bar{x} = 504$ g, $s = 3.46$ g

8. $\bar{x} = 25.8$, $s = 1.72$

9. $\bar{x} = 29.5$ cm, $s = 2.22$ cm

10. $\bar{x} = 69.8$, $s = 12.42$

Page 162   Exercise 8.3

10. **1** 50%
    2 68%
    3 95%
    4 4.3 lb to 10.9 lb

11. **1** 68%   **4** $13\frac{1}{2}$%
    2 16%   **5** $2\frac{1}{2}$%
    3 95%

Page 165   Exercise 8.4

1. frequency densities, in order:
    males: 3.9, 3.72, 3.48, 4.18, 4.7, 3.9, 3.69, 3.0, 2.76, 1.6, 0.41
    females: 3.72, 3.54, 3.3, 3.98, 4.57, 3.87, 3.68, 3.06, 3.11, 2.33, 0.97

2. **1** 1360   **4** 2
    2 950   **5** 50
    3 998

3. Boys: $\bar{x} = 158.0$ cm, $s = 7.29$ cm
    Girls: $\bar{x} = 158.0$ cm, $s = 5.26$ cm

4. mean 3, proportion 0.3, median 3, mode 3

5. **1** $\bar{x} = 38.0$p, $s = 5.96$p
    2 $\bar{x} = 76.0$p, $s = 11.92$p
    3 $\bar{x} = 42.0$p, $s = 5.96$p

Page 172   Exercise 9.1

1. **1** 2.3   **5** 0.072   **8** 300
    2 10.9   **6** 12   **9** 4200
    3 9.72   **7** 140   **10** 0.808
    4 0.42

2. **1** 4.205, 4.215   **6** 115, 125
    2 0.685, 0.695   **7** 21.95, 22.05
    3 3.2585, 3.2595   **8** 3350, 3450
    4 14.5, 15.5   **9** 91.995, 92.005
    5 7.825, 7.835   **10** 2095, 2105

3. Possible answers:
    1 1.61 m, nearest cm; 1.605 m, 1.615 m
    2 $3\frac{3}{4}$ h, nearest $\frac{1}{4}$ h; $3\frac{5}{8}$ h, $3\frac{7}{8}$ h
    3 7600, nearest 100; 7550, 7650
    4 93 000 000 miles, nearest million miles; 92 500 000 miles, 93 500 000 miles
    5 40 ℓ, nearest 5 ℓ; 37.5 ℓ, 42.5 ℓ
    6 2000 m^2, nearest 100 m^2; 1950 m^2, 2050 m^2
    7 121 kg, nearest kg; 120.5 kg, 121.5 kg
    8 80p, nearest 10p; 75p, 85p
    9 10 y 9 m, nearest month; 10 y $8\frac{1}{2}$ m, 10 y $9\frac{1}{2}$ m

3. **10** 12 000 tonnes, nearest 1000 tonnes;
           11 500 tonnes, 12 500 tonnes
    11 29 000, nearest 1000; 28 500,
           29 500
    12 8.05 km, nearest 10 m; 8.045 km,
           8.055 km

Page 176   Exercise 9.2

1. **1** 7.65; 7.64, 7.66
    2 4.19; 4.18, 4.20
    3 74.17; 74.07, 74.26
    4 276.63; 276.41, 276.85
    5 75.17; 75.08, 75.26

2. **1** 75; 74, 76
    2 30; 29, 31
    3 84; 75, 94
    4 0.27; 0.26, 0.28
    5 4.4; 4.2, 4.7

3. **1** 15.5; 15.4, 15.6
    2 18.3; 18.2, 18.4
    3 271; 269, 273
    4 1.84; 1.82, 1.87
    5 2.25; 2.24, 2.27

4. **1** 85.9; 85.8, 86.0
    2 0.430; 0.428, 0.432
    3 6.06; 6.05, 6.07
    4 0.370; 0.369, 0.371
    5 9450; 9440, 9460

Page 177   Exercise 9.3

Possible answers:

1. **1** 27.6 cm, 28.0 cm
    2 44.5 cm^2, 45.9 cm^2

2. 65.3 cm, 65.5 cm

3. 527.5 g, 532.5 g

4. **1** 2480.5 g, 2485.5 g
    2 496.1 g, 497.1 g

5. **1** 138 m, 142 m
    2 1190 m^2, 1260 m^2

6. 3.10, 3.19

7. 219 000, 225 000

8. 29.8 g, 30.2 g

9. 542 g, 544 g

10. 11.25 cm, 11.55 cm

11. 20.0 m, 21.4 m; 20 m

12. 24 mph; 22.1 mph, 26.1 mph

14. **1** 0.05 cm, 2.3%
    2 0.005 kg, 0.4%
    3 £5, 0.9%
    4 0.5 month, 5.6%
    5 2.3%
    6 0.4%
    7 0.05%
    8 0.3%
    9 0.05 g, 2.2%; 115 g, 2.5 g, 2.2%
    10 5 m, 2.1%; 12 m, 0.25 m, 2.1%

Page 190   Exercise 10.1

1. **1** 2.89   **4** −2.43
    2 0.36   **5** 0.29
    3 −0.97

2. **1** 1.44   **2** −1.75

3. 3.33

4. gradients in order: 4, 8, 12; at (0, 0), 0

5. gradients in order: −48, −12, −3,
    −1.33

Page 195   Exercise 10.2

1. **1** 3 s
    2 40 m/s, −20 m/s; 20 m/s, −40 m/s

2. **1** 10 cm/s^2, 14 cm/s^2, 18 cm/s^2

3. **1** 4 s   **3** 2 s
    2 20 m/s^2 **4** −10 m/s^2

4. 13.8 bacteria per hour

5. 4.3 deg per minute

Page 203   Exercise 10.3

1. **1** 28 unit^2
    2 700 unit^2
    3 122$\frac{1}{2}$ unit^2

2. 21 unit^2

3. 68 unit^2

4. **1** 112.5 m   **2** 37.5 m

5. 181.5 cm

6. **1** 27 s   **2** 450 m

7. velocities, in cm/s: 6.5, 18, 34.5, 56, 82.5. distance 41.8 cm

Page 204   Exercise 10.4

1. **1** 16 cm   **4** 2 cm/s
   2 8 s   **5** −4 cm/s
   3 4 s

2. **1** 15 m/s   **4** 70 m
   2 5 m/s   **5** 1 m/s^2
   3 7 s   **6** 9 m/s

3. **2** 2 m/s^2, $1\frac{1}{3}$ m/s^2 **3** 270 m

4. **2** 12 s   **4** 22.5 m
   3 0.33 m/s^2

5. **1** 144 m^3 **4** 32 m^3/min

6. volume 1600 cm^3; $\frac{3}{4}$

7. area 57.0

8. gradients in order:
   3.03, 2.72, 2.22, 1.57, 0.81; 0

9. area 37.2; approximate area of ellipse 148.8

10. rates of decrease: 7.3, 6.2, 5.2, 4.3 (% per day)

Page 208   Exercise B1

1. 44   9. 4 kg

2. rhombus   10. velocity

3. 16   11. £24

4. $\frac{2}{3}$ 12. 54 cm^2

5. $\sqrt{81}$ 13. 0.9

6. £13.20   14. 120

7. 3400   15. 1.2 units

8. $(x + 9)(x + 1)$

Page 209   Exercise B2

1. 16 (hours)   9. 49

2. 6   10. 7

3. 18 (deg)   11. 0.778

4. 81 cm^2 12. £27

5. 12 650, 12 750   13. $\frac{1}{18}$

6. 27   14. 10

7. $\frac{1}{20}$ 15. 9.3×10^7

8. distance

Page 210   Exercise B3

1. **1** (SSS)   **2** $\angle DAE$

2. rational: 3.142, $\sqrt[3]{8}$, $\sqrt{1\frac{7}{9}}$, 0.$\dot{7}$1428$\dot{5}$, $\frac{3}{4} + \frac{1}{12}$, $6^0 \times 6^{-2}$; irrational: $\sqrt{5}$, $\pi + 5$, $3^{\frac{1}{3}}$, π^2

3. 10 : 16 : 9

4. $A = 1.08P$

5. **1** 0.8 m/s^2 **2** 420 m   **3** 570 m

6. **1** 0.28   **2** 0.18   **3** 0.54

7. **1** $u_1 = 0.1$, $u_2 = 0.3$, $u_3 = 0.9$, $u_4 = 2.7$, $u_5 = 5.4$, $u_6 = 13.5$, divergent
   2 $u_1 = 0.1$, $u_2 = 0.2326$, $u_3 = 0.2129$, $u_4 = 0.2156$, $u_5 = 0.2152$, $u_6 = 0.2153$, convergent to 0.215

8. **1** 2**b** + 2**d**   **5** 2**b** + **d**
   2 **b** + **d**   **6** **b** + 2**d**
   3 2**d** − 2**b**   **7** **d** − **b**
   4 **d** − **b**

9. **1** a **2** b^4 **3** c^2

10. **1** 42.4 cm
    2 34.9°
    3 64.9°
    4 45.3 cm

11. frequency densities: 0.55, 1.8, 3.8, 5.2, 4.2, 1.3

12. $x = -2.40$ or -0.44 or 2.84; $x^3 = 7x + 3$

14. 4.55 cm, 4.65 cm; 368 m, 364 m, 372 m

15. **1** $x(x-9)$
     2 $(x+3)(x-3)$
     3 $(x-7)(x-2)$
     4 $(x+5)(x-14)$

16. 66.0 cm^2

17. **3** 53   **4** 307

18. mean 62.0, standard deviation 10.79

19. **1** $\frac{5}{18}$ **2** $\frac{8}{27}$

20. 80 unit^2

Page 214   Exercise B4

1. **3** area $= \dfrac{b^2}{2}(\pi - \sqrt{3})$

2. **1** minimum, -7 **4** maximum, $4\frac{1}{4}$
    2 minimum, $-60\frac{1}{4}$ **5** minimum, -31
    3 maximum, 54

4. **1** $\bar{x} = 1.9$, $s = 1.35$
    2 $\bar{x} = 11.5$ hours, $s = 1.51$ hours
    3 $\bar{x} = 5.0$, $s = 1.58$
    4 $\bar{x} = 699.8$ mm, $s = 1.31$ mm
    5 $\bar{x} = 14\,600$ km, $s = 2650$ km
    6 $\bar{x} = 32$ mm, $s = 5.01$ mm

5. **1** $\begin{pmatrix} 2 \\ 5 \end{pmatrix}$ **2** $\begin{pmatrix} 2 \\ 8 \end{pmatrix}$

    3 $\begin{pmatrix} -6 \\ 12 \end{pmatrix}$ **4** $\begin{pmatrix} 2 \\ -2 \end{pmatrix}$

    5 $\begin{pmatrix} -4 \\ 4 \end{pmatrix}$ **6** $\begin{pmatrix} 9 & 2 \\ 16 & 8 \end{pmatrix}$

    7 $\begin{pmatrix} 23 & -1 \\ 72 & -8 \end{pmatrix}$ **8** $\begin{pmatrix} 36 & 22 \\ 3 & 3 \end{pmatrix}$

    9 $\begin{pmatrix} -3 & 3 \\ 24 & -4 \end{pmatrix}$ **10** $\begin{pmatrix} 4 & 2 \\ -3 & 1 \end{pmatrix}$

    11 $\begin{pmatrix} 4 & 2 \\ -3 & 1 \end{pmatrix}$ **12** $\begin{pmatrix} 1 & 0 \\ 0 & 1 \end{pmatrix}$

13 $\begin{pmatrix} 1 & 0 \\ 0 & 1 \end{pmatrix}$ **14** $\begin{pmatrix} 1 & 0 \\ 0 & 1 \end{pmatrix}$

15 $\begin{pmatrix} 1 & 0 \\ 0 & 1 \end{pmatrix}$ **16** $\begin{pmatrix} 3 & -4 \\ -2 & 3 \end{pmatrix}$

17 $\dfrac{1}{4}\begin{pmatrix} -1 & -3 \\ 2 & 2 \end{pmatrix} = \begin{pmatrix} -\frac{1}{4} & -\frac{3}{4} \\ \frac{1}{2} & \frac{1}{2} \end{pmatrix}$

18 $\begin{pmatrix} 0 & -1 \\ 1 & 2 \end{pmatrix}$

19 $\dfrac{1}{5}\begin{pmatrix} 2 & 5 \\ 3 & 10 \end{pmatrix} = \begin{pmatrix} 0.4 & 1 \\ 0.6 & 2 \end{pmatrix}$

20 $\dfrac{1}{10}\begin{pmatrix} 3 & -8 \\ -1 & 6 \end{pmatrix} = \begin{pmatrix} 0.3 & -0.8 \\ -0.1 & 0.6 \end{pmatrix}$

21 $\begin{pmatrix} -5 \\ -10 \end{pmatrix}$ **22** $\begin{pmatrix} 5 \\ -18 \end{pmatrix}$

23 $\begin{pmatrix} -3 \\ -8 \end{pmatrix}$ **24** $\begin{pmatrix} -5 \\ 2 \end{pmatrix}$

25 $\begin{pmatrix} -6 \\ 2 \end{pmatrix}$

6. **1** $P(0) = P(4) = \frac{1}{16}$, $P(1) = P(3) = \frac{1}{4}$,
       $P(2) = \frac{3}{8}$
    2 $P(0) = 0.064$, $P(1) = 0.288$,
       $P(2) = 0.432$, $P(3) = 0.216$
    3 $P(0) = \frac{9}{16}$, $P(1) = \frac{3}{8}$, $P(2) = \frac{1}{16}$
    4 $P(0) = \frac{64}{125}$, $P(1) = \frac{48}{125}$, $P(2) = \frac{12}{125}$,
       $P(3) = \frac{1}{125}$; $P(\text{at least } 2) = \frac{13}{125}$
    5 (a) 0.656   (b) 0.948

Page 231   Exercise 11.1

1. **1** $x = 5$ or 3 **4** $x = -1$ or -9
    2 $x = \frac{1}{2}$ or -4 **5** $x = 0$ or $1\frac{1}{3}$
    3 $x = -1\frac{1}{2}$ or $\frac{2}{3}$ **6** $x = \frac{1}{4}$ or $1\frac{3}{4}$

2. **1** $x = -2$ or 5 **6** $x = -6$ or 1
    2 $x = -3$ or -2 **7** $x = 0$ or 4
    3 $x = -10$ or -1 **8** $x = -4$ or 15
    4 $x = -8$ or 2 **9** $x = -1$ or 4
    5 $x = -4$ or -3 **10** $x = -12$ or -2

3.   **1** $x = -2\frac{1}{2}$ or -2 **6** $x = -3$ or $\frac{1}{5}$
    2 $x = 2\frac{1}{2}$ or 3 **7** $x = 0$ or $\frac{2}{3}$
    3 $x = -\frac{1}{2}$ or 0 **8** $x = -1$ or $1\frac{1}{2}$
    4 $x = -4$ or $-\frac{1}{3}$ **9** $x = -1$ or $\frac{2}{3}$
    5 $x = -3$ or $\frac{1}{2}$ **10** $x = -2\frac{1}{2}$ or $\frac{1}{2}$

4.   **1** $x = -3$ or 20 **4** $x = 9$ or 16
    2 $x = 4$ or 12 **5** $x = -\frac{1}{2}$ or 3
    3 $x = 2$ or 4 **6** $x = -6$ or $\frac{2}{3}$

Page 234   Exercise 11.2

1.   **1** $x = -11$ or 11
    2 $x = -3\frac{1}{2}$ or $3\frac{1}{2}$
    3 $x = -2.92$ or 2.92
    4 $x = -0.55$ or 0.55
    5 $x = -6$ or 12
    6 $x = -8.41$ or -5.59

2.   **1** $x = -\frac{2}{5}$ or $1\frac{1}{2}$
    2 $x = -1$ or $-\frac{3}{4}$
    3 $x = -1\frac{1}{2}$ or $\frac{1}{3}$
    4 $x = 1\frac{3}{4}$ or $5\frac{1}{2}$
    5 $x = -2\frac{2}{3}$ or 9
    6 $x = -2$ or $\frac{5}{6}$

3.   **1** $x = -2.30$ or 1.30
    2 $x = -1.72$ or 0.39
    3 $x = 0.72$ or 2.78
    4 $x = -0.37$ or 2.17
    5 $x = 0.36$ or 4.14
    6 $x = -0.64$ or 1.24
    7 $x = -0.41$ or 2.41
    8 $x = -3.44$ or 0.44
    9 $x = -11.59$ or 2.59
    10 $x = -0.84$ or 0.59

4.   **1** $x = -11$ or 9
    2 $x = 1\frac{1}{2}$ or 8
    3 $x = -1$ or 12

Page 235   Exercise 11.3

1. 12
2. 3 m
3. 6
4. 1.6 m and 7.4 m

5. $\left(\dfrac{75}{x} + \dfrac{100}{x-15}\right)$ hours, $x = 45$

6. $AB = 21$ cm, $BC = 20$ cm, $AC = 29$ cm

7. 9.1 cm

8. $AP^2 = (16 + x^2)$ cm^2,
$BP^2 = (x^2 - 20x + 116)$ cm^2;
$AP^2 = 4BP^2$, $x = 8$

9.   **1** $x = -0.57$ or 10.57
    2 $x = -3.24$ or 1.24
    3 $x = 0.90$ or 11.10

10. **1** -1.24 **4** 0.39
    2 -1.36 **5** -0.63
    3 0.29

Page 249   Exercise 12.1

1. 5 cm
2. 36°
3. 15 cm
4. 18.5 cm

5.   **1** $a = 130°$
    2 $b = 72°$, $c = 18°$
    3 $d = 124°$, $e = 62°$
    4 $f = 95°$, $g = 102°$
    5 $h = 31°$
    6 $j = 90°$, $k = 56°$, $m = 124°$
    7 $n = 35°$, $p = 90°$, $q = 55°$, $r = 55°$
    8 $s = 90°$, $t = 90°$, $u = 138°$, $v = 69°$
    9 $w = 31°$, $x = 53°$
    10 $y = 70°$, $z = 35°$

6.   **1** $a = 44°$, $b = 68°$
    2 $c = 37°$, $d = 37°$
    3 $e = 90°$, $f = 65°$, $g = 115°$, $h = 32\frac{1}{2}°$
    4 $g = 64°$, $h = 128°$
    5 $j = 62°$, $k = 62°$, $m = 52°$
    6 $n = 15°$, $p = 15°$, $q = 40°$, $r = 55°$
    7 $s = 87°$, $t = 48°$, $u = 39°$
    8 $v = 44°$, $w = 90°$, $x = 46°$
    9 $y = 41°$, $z = 41°$
    10 $a = 162°$, $b = 9°$

Page 252   Exercise 12.2

1. **1** $x + y = 90$ **4** $x + y = 180$
    2 $x = y$ **5** $x + y = 180$
    3 $x + \frac{1}{2}y = 180$ **6** $x = y$

3. 52°

4. 7 cm

5. a circle on *AB* as diameter

8. $\angle DAC = 40°$

9. $61\frac{1}{2}°$

10. 112°

12. **1** 17.3 cm
    2 120°
    3 41.9 cm
    4 76.5 cm

13. 15 cm

Page 264   Exercise 13.1

1. 5.57 cm
2. 6.31 cm
3. 7.94 cm
4. 4.89 cm
5. 9.36 cm
6. 15.2 cm
7. 9.82 cm
8. 10.5 cm
9. 7.61 cm
10. $AB = 5.76$ cm, $BC = 10.0$ cm

Page 266   Exercise 13.2

1. 50.6°
2. 19.5°
3. 43.4°
4. 40.1°
5. 42.5°
6. 21.2°
7. 23.6°
8. 28.0°
9. $\angle A = 55.7°$, $\angle C = 59.3°$
10. $\angle B = 58.5°$, $\angle C = 37.5°$

Page 268   Exercise 13.3

1. 4.6 cm   5. 7.2 cm   8. 2.9 cm
2. 13.2 cm   6. 6.2 cm   9. 9.1 cm
3. 6.3 cm   7. 2.1 cm   10. 5.8 cm
4. 5.9 cm

Page 269   Exercise 13.4

1. 71.8°   5. 39.4°   8. 28.1°
2. 124.1°   6. 101.5°   9. 50.8°
3. 56.3°   7. 22.0°   10. 83.7°
4. 100.3°

Page 270   Exercise 13.5

1. 8.25 cm
2. 9.06 cm
3. 3.76 cm
4. 9.32 cm
5. 15.7 cm
6. 121.9°
7. 19.5°
8. $\angle B = 17.4°$, $\angle C = 77.6°$
9. 75.0°
10. $\angle A = 75.5°$, $\angle B = 57.9°$, $\angle C = 46.6°$

Page 271   Exercise 13.6

1. 19.1 cm
2. **1** 421 m   **2** 281 m
3. **1** 50.5°   **2** 62 m
4. 10.6 km
5. $\angle BAC = 38.6°$, bearing 219°
6. **1** 141 m   **2** 89 m
7. **1** 51 m   **2** 69 m   **3** 49 m
8. $XT = 50$ km, $XS = 28$ km;
    height 5000 m, angle 5.8°
11. 62.7° or 117.3°

Page 283   Exercise 14.1

2. **1** reflection in the *y*-axis
    2 rotation through 90° anticlockwise
          about the origin
    3 translation -6 units in the
          x-direction and -5 units in the
          y-direction

4 rotation through 180° about the origin

5 translation 2 units in the x-direction and -8 units in the y-direction

6 reflection in the line $y = 2$

7 reflection in the line $y = x$

8 rotation through 180° about the point (0, 2)

9 reflection in the x-axis

10 translation 8 units in the x-direction and -3 units in the y-direction

3. reflection in the line $y = -x$

4. **1** (4, 5) **2** (0, 5)

5. A_1 (3, -2), B_1 (6, 0), C_1 (5, 3);
A_2 (-3, 0), B_2 (0, 2), C_2 (-1, 5);
translation -4 units in the x-direction and -1 unit in the y-direction

6. A_1 (1, 1), B_1 (4, -1), C_1 (3, -4);
A_2 (1, 1), B_2 (-1, 4), C_2 (-4, 3);
rotation through 90° anticlockwise about A.

7. A_1 (1, -1), B_1 (4, -3), C_1 (3, -6);
A_2 (-1, 1), B_2 (-4, 3), C_2 (-3, 6);
reflection in the y-axis

8. A_1 (-1, 1), B_1 (-3, 4), C_1 (-6, 3);
A_2 (-1, -1), B_2 (-3, -4), C_2 (-6, -3);
reflection in the line $y = -x$

9. **1** reflection in the y-axis
2 rotation through 90° anticlockwise about the origin
3 translation 2 units in the x-direction and 3 units in the y-direction

Page 287   Exercise 14.2

1. A' (3, 3), B' (6, 3), C' (3, 9); ratio 3 : 1

2. scale factor $1\frac{1}{2}$, B_1 (5, 6), ratio 3 : 2

3. 4 : 1, 16 : 1, $\frac{1}{4}$

4. scale factor 3, E (0, 3)

5. 5

Page 288   Exercise 14.3

1. **1** $\begin{pmatrix} 1 & 0 \\ 0 & -1 \end{pmatrix}$ **2** $\begin{pmatrix} 0 & -1 \\ 1 & 0 \end{pmatrix}$ **3** $\begin{pmatrix} 2 & 0 \\ 0 & 2 \end{pmatrix}$

4 $\begin{pmatrix} 0 & 1 \\ 1 & 0 \end{pmatrix}$ **5** $\begin{pmatrix} -4 \\ 3 \end{pmatrix}$ **6** $\begin{pmatrix} -1 & 0 \\ 0 & -1 \end{pmatrix}$

7 P' (3, 5), Q' (2, -6), R' (-1, -4)
8 P' (5, -3), Q' (-6, -2), R' (-4, 1)
9 P' (-5, -3), Q' (6, -2), R' (4, 1)
10 P' (-3, 5), Q' (-2, -6), R' (1, -4)
11 P' (15, -25), Q' (10, 30), R' (-5, 20)
12 P' (-9, 15), Q' (-6, -18), R' (3, -12)

2. **1** reflection in the line $y = x$
2 reflection in the line $y = -x$
3 rotation about the origin through 90° clockwise
4 rotation about the origin through 180° (enlargement with origin as centre and scale factor -1)

3. enlargement with origin as centre and scale factor 3

4. **1** parallelogram with vertices (0, 0), (3, 2), (10, 7), (7, 5); area 1 unit²
2 parallelogram with vertices (0, 0), (11, 7), (15, 10), (4, 3); area 5 unit²
3 parallelogram with vertices (0, 0), (2, 3), (0, 2), (-2, -1); area 4 unit²

5. **1** P' (7, 9), Q' (-1, -1);
$A^{-1} = \begin{pmatrix} 3 & -2 \\ -7 & 5 \end{pmatrix}$

2 P' (-7, -18), Q' (5, 10);
$A^{-1} = \begin{pmatrix} 0.6 & -0.4 \\ -0.2 & 0.3 \end{pmatrix}$

3 $A^{-1} = \begin{pmatrix} 0.3 & -0.4 \\ 0.1 & 0.2 \end{pmatrix}$

4 $C = \begin{pmatrix} 9 & 7 \\ -22 & -16 \end{pmatrix}$

$C^{-1} = \begin{pmatrix} -1.6 & -0.7 \\ 2.2 & 0.9 \end{pmatrix}$

Page 302   Exercise 15.1

4.   **1**   minimum point
     2 $(-3, 0)$, $(4, 0)$
     3 $(0, -24)$

5.   **1**   maximum point
     2 $(-\frac{1}{2}, 0)$, $(4, 0)$
     3 $(0, 4)$

Page 312   Exercise 15.3

1.   **1** $2y \geqslant x + 1$
              $3y \leqslant 29 - 4x$
              $y \leqslant 6x - 5$
     2 $(3, 0)$, $(0, 9)$, greatest value 18
     3   4
     4   5

2.   **2**   14   **3**   8   **4**   20

3.   **2**   27   **3**   1

Page 316   Exercise 15.4

1.   A, D, G, H; 11 days

2.   C, F, H; 17 hours

3.   C, E, H, L; 24 minutes;
     J 1.21 pm, D 1.10 pm

Page 317   Exercise 15.5

5.   A, D, E, F, H; 33 days, 18 days

6.   5 coaches, 15 minibuses, cost £875

7.   10 luxury, 20 standard houses, profit
     £140 000

Page 322   Exercise C1

1.   £8.91   9. $2x(x + 5)$

2. $x > 5$ 10.   24 cm

3.   84.5 m, 85.5 m   11. $(0, -2)$

4.   12   12.   19p

5. $\frac{1}{25}$ 13. $x = 4$

6.   70°   14.   12

7.   15   15.   0.2

8.   25p

Page 323   Exercise C2

1.   £26

2. $(3x + 1)(3x - 1)$

3.   8 days

4.   5

5.   acceleration

6.   21

7.   £160

8.   68 cm

9. $\frac{3}{28}$

10. 2001

11. π

12. $3(m^3)$

13. cyclic quadrilateral

14. $\frac{1}{6}$

15. $(-2, 5)$

Page 324   Exercise C3

1. $t = \dfrac{180}{v}$, 2.4 hours

2.   **1** $16:36:81$
     2 $16:20:45$

3.   **1** $(x + 1)(y - 1)$
     2 $(x - y)^2$
     3 $2(2x + 3y)(2x - 3y)$
     4 $(3x - 2y)(x + y)$

5.   £$\dfrac{90}{x}$, £$\dfrac{90}{x + 5}$; $x = 10$; 15 members

6.   3.420

7.   12 cm

8.   frequency densities:
     19, 25, 26, 22, 15.7, 7.8, 2.6, 0.6, 0.1

9.   **1**   9 cm
     2   9 cm
     3   yes, RHS (or other reasons)

10. A, D, H, F, G, L, N; 29 min; 9.07 am, 9.16 am

11. **1** $x = -4$ or 1
    2 $x = -3$ or 2
    3 $x = -2.35$ or 0.85

12. **1** $\frac{63}{221}$ **2** $\frac{145}{442}$ **3** $\frac{1}{4}$

13. A_1 $(-1, 1)$, B_1 $(-4, 1)$, C_1 $(-4, 3)$; A_2 $(1, -1)$, B_2 $(1, -4)$, C_2 $(3, -4)$; rotation about the origin through 90° clockwise

14. 377 m^2

15. $x = -2.5$ or 4.0; $2x^2 - 3x - 20 = 0$

17. rational: x^2, xy, $\sqrt{2}y$, $\frac{y}{x}$, x^0, $\frac{x}{y}$

    irrational: $8x$, $x + y$, πy^2, $18x - 8y$

18. **1** 9.4 cm   **4** 5.3 cm
    2 140°   **5** 34.6 cm^2
    3 20°

19. perimeter 78 m, 82 m; area 364 m^2, 404 m^2

20. **3** $x = 1.33$
    4 -6 units of y/unit of x

Page 328   Exercise C4

1. 19.3°

2. **1** A' $(0, 0)$, B' $(5, 0)$, C' $(4, -3)$
   2 $7\frac{1}{2} \text{ unit}^2$
   3 $7\frac{1}{2} \text{ unit}^2$
   4 $y = \frac{1}{2}x$

3. 7.15 m

4. $A = 10 + 0.075n$; 880 units

5. $\angle DAP = \angle DPA = 50°$, $\angle PDA = 80°$

6. $\frac{13}{35}$

7. **1** 32.6 m
   2 45.1 m
   3 36°

8. $x_2 = 0.625$, $x_3 = 0.701$, $x_4 = 0.689$, $x_5 = 0.691$; $x = -8.690$ or 0.690

9. $\bar{x} = 42.0 \text{ kg}$, $s = 7.14 \text{ kg}$

10. 7 m/s, 20 m/s

11. **1** $4\frac{1}{9}$ **2** 9   **3** $1\frac{1}{5}$

12. $\overrightarrow{PA} = \begin{pmatrix} 3 \\ 1 \end{pmatrix}$, $\overrightarrow{AB} = \begin{pmatrix} -4 \\ 2 \end{pmatrix}$, $\overrightarrow{PR} = \begin{pmatrix} 1 \\ 2 \end{pmatrix}$,

    $\overrightarrow{QA} = \begin{pmatrix} 5 \\ 0 \end{pmatrix}$

13. $x = 53°$

14. **1** $x = 22$ **2** $x = -\frac{1}{2}$

15. **1** 6800
    2 3400
    3 4750
    4 250

16. **1** $x^3 = 2x + 11$
    2 $y = x^2 - 4$

17. **1** A' $(1, 1)$, B' $(5, 2)$, C' $(6, 6)$, D' $(2, 5)$
    3 $y = x$, $y = 7 - x$

18. **1** $\frac{1}{64}$ **2** $\frac{5}{32}$ **3** $\frac{27}{64}$ **4** $\frac{27}{64}$

19. **1** $(3x + 2)(2x - 3)$
    2 $x = -\frac{2}{3}$ or $1\frac{1}{2}$

20. $x \geqslant 3$, $y \geqslant 3$, $x + y \leqslant 12$, $x + 2y \leqslant 16$; if 240 sweets, $4x + 5y = 40$; 8 packets of fruity sweets, 4 packets of caramels

Page 333   Exercise C5

1. $BC = 10.5 \text{ cm}$, area $= 36 \text{ cm}^2$

2. **1** $x = -12\frac{5}{7}$, rational
   2 $x = \pm\sqrt{1.5}$ $(= \pm 1.22)$, irrational
   3 $x = 5$, rational

3. 1.1 km

5. **1** $(2x + 5)(x - 3)$
   2 $\dfrac{2x + 5}{2x}$

6. **1** 46.6°   **2** 317°

7. frequency densities:
    0.0525, 0.68, 1.37, 1.27, 1.39, 0.8, 0.63,
    0.375, 0.3675

8. **1** A, 57 m; B, 110 m
    2 124 m
    3 153°

9. 26°

10. 5 s, 11 s; for 6 s

11. **1** 3 unit^2 **4** 12 unit^2

12. **1** 21 km/h
    2 3 km/h
    3 15 km/h, 53°

13. volume, 66.45 cm^3, 66.55 cm^3;
    area, 20.35 cm^2, 20.45 cm^2;
    height, 3.26 cm, 3.25 cm, 3.27 cm

14. **1** 5 cm   **3** 106.2°
    2 53.1°   **4** 9.3 cm

15. **1** $\frac{5}{18}$ **2** $\frac{4}{9}$ **3** $\frac{41}{81}$

16. 1.44 deg per minute

17. **1** 57.0 m   **2** 44.9 m

18. **1** yes, AAS
    2 3.5 cm
    3 160°
    4 6.8 cm

19. $\bar{x} = 15.0$, $s = 10.15$

Page 337   Exercise C6

1. **1** real, rational
    2 no real roots
    3 real, irrational
    4 real (one repeated), rational
    5 real, rational

2. **4** 12 cm
    5 $XC = 18$ cm, $CD = 13$ cm
    6 7 cm

5. **1** 0.035, 0.061, 0.172, 0.208
    2 5.0°, 4.1°, 10.9°, 12.5° or 12.6°
    3 0.208, 0.113, 0.087, 0.012
    4 166.0°, 171.7°, 175.4°, 174.2° or 174.3°